CW00606807

Linguistic Ecology and Language Contact

Contributions from an international team of experts revisit and update the concept of linguistic ecology in order to critically examine current theoretical approaches to language contact. Language is understood as a part of complex socio-historical–cultural systems, and interaction between the different dimensions and levels of these systems is considered to be essential for specific language forms. This book presents a uniform, abstract model of linguistic ecology based on, among others, two concepts of Edmund Husserl's philosophy (parts and wholes, and foundation). It considers the individual speaker in the specific communication situation to be the essential heuristic basis of linguistic analysis. The chapters present and employ a new, transparent, and accessible contact linguistic vocabulary to aid reader comprehension, and explore a wide range of language contact situations in Europe, Africa, the Middle East, Latin America, Asia, and the Pacific. Fascinating reading for students and researchers across contact linguistics and cultural studies.

RALPH LUDWIG is Professor of Romance Linguistics at Martin-Luther-University Halle-Wittenberg.

PETER MÜHLHÄUSLER is the Emeritus Foundation Professor of Linguistics at the University of Adelaide and Supernumerary Fellow of Linacre College, Oxford.

STEVE PAGEL is Assistant Professor of Romance Linguistics at Martin-Luther-University Halle-Wittenberg.

Cambridge Approaches to Language Contact

Founding Editor

Salikoko S. Mufwene, University of Chicago

Co-Editor

Ana Deumert, University of Cape Town

Editorial Board

Robert Chaudenson, *Université d'Aix-en-Provence*
Braj Kachru, *University of Illinois at Urbana*
Raj Mesthrie, *University of Cape Town*
Lesley Milroy, *University of Michigan*
Shana Poplack, *University of Ottawa*
Michael Silverstein, *University of Chicago*

Cambridge Approaches to Language Contact is an interdisciplinary series bringing together work on language contact from a diverse range of research areas. The series focuses on key topics in the study of contact between languages or dialects, including the development of pidgins and creoles, language evolution and change, world Englishes, code-switching and code-mixing, bilingualism and second language acquisition, borrowing, interference, and convergence phenomena.

Published titles

Salikoko S. Mufwene, *The Ecology of Language Evolution*
Michael Clyne, *Dynamics of Language Contact*
Bernd Heine and Tania Kuteva, *Language Contact and Grammatical Change*
Edgar W. Schneider, *Postcolonial English: Varieties around the World*
Virginia Yip and Stephen Matthews, *The Bilingual Child: Early Development and Language Contact*
Bernd Heine and Derek Nurse (eds), *A Linguistic Geography of Africa*
J. Clancy Clements, *The Linguistic Legacy of Spanish and Portuguese: Colonial Expansion and Language Change*
Umberto Ansaldo, *Contact Languages: Ecology and Evolution in Asia*
Jan Blommaert, *The Sociolinguistics of Globalization*

Carmen Silva-Corvalán, *Bilingual Language Acquisition: Spanish and English in the First Six Years*

Lotfi Sayahi, *Diglossia and Language Contact: Language Variation and Change in North Africa*

Emanuel J. Drechsel, *Language Contact in the Early Colonial Pacific: Maritime Polynesian Pidgin before Pidgin English*

Enoch Oladé Aboh, *The Emergence of Hybrid Grammars: Language Contact and Change*

Zhiming Bao, *The Making of Vernacular Singapore English: System, Transfer, and Filter*

Braj B. Kachru, *World Englishes and Culture Wars*

Bridget Drinka, *Language Contact in Europe: The Periphrastic Perfect through History*

Salikoko S. Mufwene, Christophe Coupé, and François Pellegrino (eds.), *Complexity in Language: Developmental and Evolutionary Perspectives*

Ralph Ludwig, Peter Mühlhäusler and Steve Pagel (eds), *Linguistic Ecology and Language Contact*

Further titles planned for the series

Rakesh Bhatt, *Language Contact and Diaspora*

Gregory D.S. Anderson *Language Extinction*

Ellen Hurst and Rajend Mesthrie (eds.), *Youth Language Varieties in Africa*

Cecile Vigouroux, *Migration, Economy, and Language Practice*

Sandro Sessarego, *Language Contact and the Making of an Afro-Hispanic Vernacular*

Linguistic Ecology and Language Contact

Edited by

Ralph Ludwig, Peter Mühlhäusler, and Steve Pagel

CAMBRIDGE
UNIVERSITY PRESS

CAMBRIDGE
UNIVERSITY PRESS

University Printing House, Cambridge CB2 8BS, United Kingdom

One Liberty Plaza, 20th Floor, New York, NY 10006, USA

477 Williamstown Road, Port Melbourne, VIC 3207, Australia

314–321, 3rd Floor, Plot 3, Splendor Forum, Jasola District Centre,
New Delhi – 110025, India

79 Anson Road, #06–04/06, Singapore 079906

Cambridge University Press is part of the University of Cambridge.

It furthers the University's mission by disseminating knowledge in the pursuit of
education, learning, and research at the highest international levels of excellence.

www.cambridge.org
Information on this title: www.cambridge.org/9781107041356
DOI: 10.1017/9781139649568

First published 2019

Printed in the United Kingdom by TJ International Ltd. Padstow Cornwall

A catalogue record for this publication is available from the British Library.

ISBN 978-1-107-04135-6 Hardback

Contents

Figures

Tables

Contributors

CYRIL ASLANOV, Aix-Marseille Université

CYNTHIA DERMARKAR, Albert-Ludwigs-Universität Freiburg

FRANÇOISE GADET, Université Paris Ouest

JUAN CARLOS GODENZZI, Université de Montréal

SILKE JANSEN, Friedrich-Alexander Universität Erlangen-Nürnberg

SIBYLLE KRIEGEL, Aix-Marseille Université

RALPH LUDWIG, Martin-Luther-Universität Halle-Wittenberg

LORENZA MONDADA, Universität Basel

PETER MÜHLHÄUSLER, The University of Adelaide

STEVE PAGEL, Martin-Luther-Universität Halle-Wittenberg

STEFAN PFÄNDER, Albert-Ludwigs-Universität Freiburg

PHILIP W. RUDD, Pittsburgh State University

TABEA SALZMANN, Universität Bremen

ANNE SCHRÖDER, Universität Bielefeld

Series Editor's Foreword

The series *Cambridge Approaches to Language Contact* (CALC) was set up to publish outstanding monographs on language contact, especially by authors who approach their specific subject matter from a diachronic or developmental perspective. Our goal is to integrate the ever-growing scholarship on language diversification (including the development of creoles, pidgins, and indigenized varieties of colonial European languages), bilingual language development, code-switching, and language endangerment. We hope to provide a select forum to scholars who contribute insightfully to understanding language evolution from an interdisciplinary perspective. We favor approaches that highlight the role of ecology and draw inspiration both from the authors' own fields of specialization and from related research areas in linguistics or other disciplines. Eclecticism is one of our mottoes, as we endeavor to comprehend the complexity of evolutionary processes associated with contact.

Exceptionally we publish anthologies that display a strong thematic unity, as in the case of the present volume: *Linguistic Ecology and Language Contact*, whose specific focus is ecological aspects of language contact. Its editors start it with an informative history of 'ecolinguistics' and 'ecology-of-language' approaches to various aspects of particular languages since the mid-twentieth century. Because the term *ecology* was borrowed directly from biology, where it has been in usage since the mid-nineteenth century, as the editors make so clear, they treat its application to linguistics as metaphorical. Thus they invite the reader, perhaps unwittingly but quite appropriately, to think over whether invocations of notion of *ecology* to account for linguistic behaviour should not be interpreted literally, in reference to the relevant environmental factors. Must the 'environment', the explanation typically associated with *ecology* (note its application in the word *environmentalist*!), be understood strictly in the sense of climate, vegetation, topography and other relevant geographic notions that bear on biological evolution? What then prompted linguist pioneers of the extrapolation of this notion, viz., Erving Goffman, Charles F. Voegelin, Florence M. Voegelin, Noel W. Schutz, and Einar I. Haugen, to consider applying it in linguistics? Aren't there any ways in which usage of *ecology* in linguistics can inform its application in biology? I favor a broad interpretation of *ecology*, whose nature varies according to what it is invoked to explain, consistent with the interdisciplinary nature that the editors themselves advocate for ecological approaches to language (see below). But the reader will be the ultimate judge.

The different contributors to this volume articulate in their respective chapters various ecological factors that rolled the dice one way or another on the evolution of the structures of some languages they have investigated, the emergence of contact-induced ethnolinguistic practices in some colonial populations, or the unfolding of a conversation. In the latter case, attention is drawn to a fundamental aspect of contact: that which applies in our daily interactions with each other, even in a monolingual population. From the point of view of discourse, the exchange of ideas and points of views certainly involves contact, notwithstanding that of idiolects. And there is certainly an ecology that constrains how the conversation develops. The editors characterize the approach as 'ecological discourse analysis and interpretation'.

The reader is implicitly invited to think beyond traditional 'sociolinguistic' and/or 'ethnographic' factors in thinking 'ecological'. I have often underscored the impact of economic factors on linguistic practices and language vitality, which are part of the 'indirect external ecology', simply because their effects are mediated by the individuals that evolve in the relevant population or socioeconomic structures and react to them directly. However, is the term *ecology* simply an alternative that brings more breadth to non-structural factors that bear on the practice and evolution of languages but does not displace *sociolinguistics* and *ethnography*? I think so, but it's up to the reader to assess whether this volume leads to a different answer. One of the rather novel elements contributed by the editors is certainly the Husserlian part–whole and foundation perspective.

From the beginning, the reader is also invited to reflect on what practitioners of 'ecolinguistics' do that those of the 'ecology-of-language' approach do not, and vice versa, whether they all (can) claim the legacy of the practice of ecology in biology, and what has led them to diverge intellectually. Do 'ecolinguists' articulate the connection between language and the world, apparently that in which the social ecology is embedded, more adequately than those who practice the 'ecology of language'? Can one always tell the difference between these ecological paradigms in linguistics, or does the difference lie in what particular scholars are specifically interested in and focus on? The chapters in this book reveal that there is often a disconnect between the labels that individual scholars claim for their particular practices and the substance of what they do, showing that the difference may lie more in whether, for instance, one capitalizes on the moral consequences of the impact of particular ecological dynamics on the relevant languages, or on explaining how those particular dynamics work. The contributions to this volume show the various ways in which the notion of LANGUAGE/LINGUISTIC ECOLOGY helps us better understand the manifold aspects of language contact, from the Levant to India, to Latin America, and to Black Africa, and from both diachronic and synchronic perspectives. Ecologically, or ecolinguistically, one can focus on synchronic or diachronic dynamics, on how various factors external to language influence the behaviours of speakers and what effects these adaptations of speakers exert on the structures, uses, and vitality of the relevant languages.

Then also arises the issue of the connection between the Sapir–Whorf hypothesis and ecolinguistics. This book includes two chapters by Peter Mühlhäusler, the promoter of the connection, on this topic. The reader may also want to follow the exchange between him and myself in the pages of the *Journal of Pidgin and Creole Languages* 30 (2015), if they are interested in my reservations about this aspect of ecolinguistics. At issue is, first, whether languages are tools for thought and influence the way that their speakers manage their geographic ecologies and, second, whether an ecolinguistic approach sheds (better) light on linguistic diversity and how. Can linguistic diversity hold a key to addressing, if not solving, some of the environmental problems the world faces today? The reader would be remiss to omit Mühl-häusler's chapters in the present book.

Though it is debatable whether all the contributions to this volume can be lumped in one category which the editors claim to be *ecological linguistics*, the latter are certainly correct in arguing that matters of the ecology of language cannot be reduced to 'socio-political, environmental and linguistic minority issues'. According to them, *ecological linguistics* also subsumes 'explicitly cognitive parameters such as speaker competence, language acquisition, and universal aspects of grammaticization'. They argue that 'corpora are considered to be the point of departure of any ecological linguistic analysis'. The question is whether corpora are all it takes to understand how languages behave and evolve; and these are considerations that should weigh heavily on the reader's mind if they want to make 'ecolinguistics', or 'the ecology of language', or 'ecological linguistics' more informative about various aspects of language. They must bear in mind that it is not so much the label that explains how things work as the substance of the explanations provided by the relevant scholars. And that is certainly not lacking from the present book.

However, one must also distinguish between the inaccurate explanations provided by individual analysts and the potential that a particular approach holds for providing adequate explanations, for instance, because it makes it possible for the practitioners to ask the right questions and suggests adequate research avenues for answering them. Thus one must consider more carefully the implications of the editors' claim that they 'consider language, primarily language usage, as *part of a whole* (*Teilganzes*, according to Husserl) in a complex socio-historical–cultural system, which additionally is dependent on cognitive-neural cross-linking'. According to them, this volume offers a third, holistic kind of ecological approach to language (contact), which must be interdisciplinary and pluralistic, because no discipline alone can explain everything about it. Undoubtedly, ECOLOGY cannot subsume all explanations about every aspect of language; the message I got is that it enables linguists to address the actuation question in perhaps a more satisfactory way. The causation of change can be indirect, lying for instance in colonization, which imposes a new socio-economic structure, which in turn affects various ethnographic conditions that influence speakers' behaviours. The approach also makes it possible to deal with the non-structural aspect of complexity regarding the cultural embeddedness of language, which guides human behaviour. The editors submit that ECOLOGY must also be understood as complex and structured in a hierarchical fashion, within which history plays a very critical role, as its effects filter through several layers of ecological conditioning to the interacting individuals. These assertions contain a novel element on which the reader is well invited ponder against the backdrop the body of empirical data that the book provides.

The editors and other contributors to the book militate for giving up some old terminology they consider 'misleading', proposing terms such as *linguistic ecology* instead of *language ecology*, *copying* instead of *borrowing*, *code alternation* instead of *code-mixing/switching*, and *covert copy* instead of *calque*. Along with this preoccupation arises the question of what is a 'natural phenomenon' in linguistics and how does one capture it in their investigation. Is there such as thing as 'ecological data'? The reader is invited to assess this. Some chapters focus on the urban environment as a contact ecology, where individuals from different parts of a country bring different rural traditions that face the competition of others. They are modified by the emergent urban cultures, which they also help reshape, though the claim of an urban culture itself can be questioned, because of its peculiar population structure, which may prevent the emergence of homogeneous language practices shared by all. Population structure also accounts for the conditions under which a language of an elite minority can survive in an exogenous territory, such as French in the Levant, and for how long. It likewise accounts for how the Spaniards' naming practices of the seventeenth century spread, albeit with modification, in their insular colonies of the Caribbean and undoubtedly their other colonies. The dynamics of cultural competition are particularly noteworthy, as they are influenced by colonial politics. This is a thought-provoking collection of essays that we the editors of CALC are happy to share with our readers.

Salikoko S. Mufwene, *University of Chicago*

Acknowledgements

The impetus for this book dates back a few years already. As our contact person at Cambridge University Press, Helen Barton, recently put it, in polite but nevertheless growing impatience: 'This book has a long history'. It goes back to discussions on linguistic ecology and language contact between Ralph Ludwig, Steve Pagel, and Peter Mühlhäusler in 2009, when the latter visited Halle again, and a few other guests were invited.

The book concept originated in a rather complex environment, in which the binational (DFG and ANR) research project 'CIEL-F' (Corpus International Écologique de la Langue Française) also played a firm role. The road was long enough to present and discuss our ideas on various occasions. Without naming all of them, we thank our many discussion partners for their attention and suggestions.

Our manuscript quickly took shape, and from the first moment on we had found a discussion partner who showed us that amity and relentless criticism are not mutually exclusive: Salikoko S. Mufwene. Sali's impact on us and our book is perhaps comparable to that of the thinker-printer-publishers of the French sixteenth century, such as Geoffroy Tory or Robert and Henri Estienne. We owe him constancy, tenacity, tireless questioning, and concurrent support.

Commitment on the part of the editors for such a long period of time must be endured. Without substantive support from our wives, our undertaking would have been impossible to realize. We are indebted to Florence Bruneau-Ludwig, Jacky Mühlhäusler, and Franziska Schramm.

This book would also not have been completed without continuous support in the editing process, which came in particular from Susanne Vollmer.

Perhaps because we are forgetful, or because they are simply too many, we have named only a few friends and colleagues here. For this we want to apologize.

Part I

Introduction and Theoretical Frame

1   Linguistic Ecology and Language Contact: Conceptual Evolution, Interrelatedness, and Parameters

Ralph Ludwig, Peter Mühlhäusler, and Steve Pagel

1.1   Linguistic Ecology: an Outline

1.1.1   From οἶκος to Ecology

As is the case with most abstract concepts, the concept of *ecology* is essentially rooted in a metaphor, linking the respective referent to a concrete and, in this case, rather modern object. The word *ecology* is a composition of the Greek lexemes *οἶκος* 'house', 'household', or 'home', and *λόγος*, which covers a series of meanings, the most common ones being 'word', 'speech', 'discourse', 'reason', and 'principle of order'. The suffixed form of the latter, *-λογία*, is best translated as 'the study of'. Literally, therefore, *ecology* is 'the study of (the governing principles of) the household'. We note the shared morpheme *eco-* in both *economy* and *ecology* as well as the ongoing debate on whether these are opposing principles (as argued by Weinrich 1990) or whether both areas of study are concerned with the optimal use of limited means. The far greater number of parameters introduced by ecological studies distinguishes them from an economic interpretation.

The ecology metaphor, as we will see, was first used in biology in order to describe a radically new way of understanding nature, where organisms interact with one another and their environment. When it was adapted to the concept of *language*, it was seemingly just another metaphor that linguistics had copied from the natural sciences in order to find a fitting approach to its exceptionally abstract subject. And, just like other metaphorical concepts, the ecology metaphor (in which languages are interconnected with all kinds of production of meaning) will have to prove its value in the course of time. Still, other metaphorical concepts are in use and are, in part, expedient conceptions, such as the organism metaphor (languages are living things which come to life, compete, age, and die), the instrument metaphor (languages are instruments, tools, means of communication), or the system metaphor (languages are more or less closed bodies of interconnected and interdependent data, each constituting a system of its own). As the

3

ecological approach in linguistics allows a considerably larger range of parameters underlying language structure and use, it is potentially more powerful than system-oriented approaches, which are poorer in parameters – assuming it is possible to make the numerous additional parameters do explanatory work.

Metaphors, as well as metonyms, are vital for all living languages because, to begin with, they provide a linguistic solution to the problem of communicating about immaterial and imagined referents and about processes occurring beyond the immediate experiences of the speaker. Metaphors also privilege certain perceptions and actions and, when employed heuristically, enable their users to overcome cognitive constraints. These insights range among the most important ones the study of language has achieved in the last century (e. g. Ortony 1979; Lakoff and Johnson 1980; Rorty 1989; Goatly 1996/2001) and they can certainly be called ecological, as they are based on the assumption that there are far-reaching interconnections between a language, the society that speaks it, and the physical environment in which this society evolves. Furthermore, the theoretical implications are enormous: in different languages metaphors may be rooted in different concepts (Mühlhäusler 1995b), thought by the speaking community to be the best fitting, and different languages may thus provide their speakers with different approaches to the world, which, in turn, may result in different ways of dealing with this world. Conversely, languages that spread to remote parts of the world, particularly during colonial expansions, may contain metaphors that are, at first, inappropriate for managing their new ecologies[1] and must adapt to them.

Metaphors do not only determine and constrain human perceptions; they can also be employed heuristically to explore the unknown. In the absence of immaculate perception, any research that extends the boundaries of necessary knowledge relies on metaphors (Harré 1961; Paprotte and Dirven 1985). In the history of linguistics there have been numerous heuristic metaphors, including the family tree of language genetic relationships, the conduit metaphor of communication (Reddy 1979), the stratum metaphor of language mixing, linguistic drift, and the pervasive reification/objectification metaphor, which converts dynamic processes into a static object called *language*. It has been said that metaphors never reveal the full truth but selectively highlight small aspects of it. At times they may conceal key

---

[1] We use the term *ecology* in two different meanings. The first is in accordance with the etymology of Greek *logos/-logia*, as the 'study of' or a certain perspective of research (e.g. *the ecological parameters*). The second designates the object (ecology) that can be grasped through the ecological perspective (e.g. *the Levant ecology*). Mufwene and Vigouroux (2012) use *ecology* in a similar fashion. See also Lechevrel (2010: 46ff.) who identifies and discusses five different ways of designating ecological approaches in linguistics.

properties of the subject matter, such as when the reification metaphor of language conceals the dynamic, open-ended nature of human communication. It becomes clear that metaphors have their serious pitfalls, and linguists cannot be too cautious when dealing with them. The ecology metaphor, we would like to argue, is by contrast capable of highlighting the dynamics, interrelatedness, and situatedness of human communication and therefore promises to capture its essential properties.

In order to achieve an accurate understanding of the ecology metaphor, it is, therefore, helpful to have a closer look at the semantics of the Greek word *oίκος* and especially the aspects that distinguish it from that of modern houses and households. The latter can be described as corresponding (concretely) to the concepts of *nuclear family, couple* or even the *individual*, i.e. private spheres of the rather unmarked social entities of modern western civilization, settled in an otherwise (e.g. socially, economically and politically) heavily interconnected and interdependent society. Modern houses and households are by no means self-sufficient. On a social level they depend on family (nuclear as well as extended) and circles of friends. Economically they are highly dependent on production facilities, markets, and money, and politically they are bound to external decisions such as laws and taxes. The *oίκος* of ancient Greece, in contrast, was not only a key social entity but also a key economic and, to a more limited extent, a key political entity. It comprised the extended family, all kinds of property including land, livestock, and personnel; and life in it was ruled, for the most part, by decisions made and supervised by the host. Socially and politically, but especially economically speaking, the *oίκος* was thus largely self-sufficient. In order to be so, the individuals living in it were tightly interconnected in terms of social rank and profession and highly interdependent in both a social and economic way. We must grasp this dimension when aiming for a thorough understanding of the origin and meaning of the ecology metaphor and its application to other fields such as linguistics.

The first ecological approaches to nature date back at least to scientists of the eighteenth and nineteenth centuries, such as Carl von Linné, the founder of modern botanical and zoological taxonomy, Alexander von Humboldt, and of course Charles Darwin. The term *ecology*, however, was first used and defined in 1866 by the German zoologist Ernst Haeckel, himself a great admirer of Darwin's theory (Stauffer 1957). Haeckel places the Darwinian key concepts *economy of nature* and *struggle for life* in a new science called *Oecologie* (Birch and Cobb 1981: 29):

Unter Oecologie verstehen wir die gesamte Wissenschaft von den Beziehungen des Organismus zur umgebenden Außenwelt, wohin wir im weiteren Sinne alle 'Existenz-Bedingungen' rechnen können. Diese sind teils organischer, teils anorganischer

Natur; sowohl diese als jene sind … von der grössten Bedeutung für die Form der Organismen, weil sie dieselbe zwingen, sich ihnen anzupassen.[2] Zu den anorganischen Existenz-Bedingungen, welchen sich jeder Organismus anpassen muss, gehören zunächst die physikalischen und chemischen Eigenschaften seines Wohnortes, das Klima (Licht, Wärme, Feuchtigkeits- und Electricitäts-Verhältnisse der Atmosphäre), die anorganischen Nahrungsmittel, Beschaffenheit des Wassers und des Bodens etc.

Als organische Existenz-Bedingungen betrachten wir die sämmtlichen Verhältnisse des Organismus zu allen übrigen Organismen, mit denen er in Berührung kommt, und von denen die meisten entweder zu seinem Nutzen oder zu seinem Schaden beitragen. Jeder Organismus hat unter den übrigen Freunde und Feinde, solche, welche seine Existenz begünstigen und solche, welche sie beeinträchtigen. (Haeckel 1866: 236)

[By ecology, we mean the whole science of the relations of the organism to the environment including, in the broad sense, all the 'conditions of existence'. These are partly organic, partly inorganic in nature; both … are of the greatest significance for the form of organisms, for they force them to become adapted. Among the inorganic conditions of existence to which every organism must adapt itself belong, first of all, the physical and chemical properties of its habitat, the climate (light, warmth, atmospheric conditions of humidity and electricity), the inorganic nutrients, nature of the water and of the soil, etc.

As organic conditions of existence we consider the entire relations of the organism to all other organisms with which it comes into contact, and of which most contribute either to its advantage or its harm. Each organism has among the other organisms its friends and its enemies, those which favor its existence and those which harm it. (translation by Stauffer 1957: 140–141)]

Ecology in the modern sense of the word developed as a natural science in its own right in the first half of the twentieth century. One of the typical modern definitions is essentially similar to Haeckel's one and a half century ago:

Ecology is the scientific study of the distribution and abundance of organisms and the interactions that determine distribution and abundance. (Begon, Townsend and Harper 2006: xi)

The first application of the ecology metaphor in a theoretical linguistic context is usually attributed to Haugen and his 1972 paper 'The ecology of language'. Prior uses of the term *ecology* by Goffman (1964) and Voegelin, Voegelin and Schutz (1967) didn't refer to the same general level but focused on immediate communicational encounters in the first and, as Haugen himself recognizes (1972: 327ff.), on bi- and multilingual societies in the latter case. Haugen defines the ecology of language as 'the study of interactions between any given language and its environment' (1972: 325). In contrast to other authors before (and after) him dealing with ecological linguistic features, such as the relationship between language, thought and reality, his definition of *environment* does not cover 'the referential world to which

---

[2] The adaptation of languages to wider ecological conditions has become a recurring theme in present-day ecological linguistics (see Mühlhäusler 1996b, 2003).

language provides an index' (1972: 325). In fact, Haugen considers the 'true environment of a language' primarily as the society using the language, although he also contemplates a series of multilingual, social and psychological societal facets.[3] At the end of his paper, Haugen provides a preliminary list of ten questions which, in his opinion, could shed light on the ecology of a given language. They regard, for instance, the typological classification of a language, the nature of its users, the latter's attitudes towards the language, concurrent languages, internal variation, domains of use, and written traditions. These questions have not lost any of their relevance, especially when it comes to the study of language contact phenomena, which is why they will, in part, play a role in the contributions to this volume too. For the most part, these questions touch issues we could also call sociolinguistic – and most of them probably are. But the sociolinguistic question, as will be pointed out later, is just one element among others in an ecological linguistic approach. In Haugen's concept of the study of a language's ecology, the scope of these questions already goes well beyond sociolinguistics. This is the case, for example, for the notion that phenomena such as language contact and bilingualism appear to be natural elements of most (if not all) linguistic ecologies, and not exceptional matters, as they had been treated by mainstream linguistics of the time. When Haugen himself addresses some of these contact-related processes in his paper (such as diglossia, bilingualism, creolization, and borrowing), he does not give an entirely new or coherent perspective but opens fascinating paths to an integral conception of language(s) and speaker(s).

1.1.2 Streams of Development

Following Haugen, in the 1980s and 1990s a group of linguists from rather different fields developed and refined what we would today call *ecolinguistics*. Fill (1998/2001: 43) distinguishes two – ultimately complementary – directions of this discipline that emerged from the primarily sociolinguistic impetus of Haugen.[4] A first approach interprets Haugen in a closer sense: *ecology* is primarily understood as a metaphor and is transferred to languages and their speaking communities, since it does more justice to the complexity of the

---

[3] It should be noted that Haugen, while proposing a dynamic metaphor of language ecology nevertheless subscribes to the static reification metaphor of a *given language*. He also supports the idea of the separation of languages and their environment rather than exploring the notion that the boundary between language and non-language is ultimately arbitrary. As an attempt to do justice to the latter notion, ecolinguists such as, e.g., Trampe (1990, 1991) and Fill, Penz and Trampe (2002) speak of the *Mitwelt* ('world with') of language rather than of its *Umwelt* ('world around').

[4] A clear-cut summary of the development of ecological approaches in linguistics is given in Mufwene and Vigouroux (2012). For a detailed and critical survey of ecological approaches in the social sciences and particularly linguistics, see Lechevrel (2010).

situation than other metaphors do (e.g. the computing or the organism metaphor). The notion of *ecology* has a rather methodological meaning here and lacks the evolutionary correlation it has in biology. In a second approach, ecology is interpreted as including the referential world in a more biological (and thus evolutionary) sense. This approach points out that language is inescapably linked with and part of the world. It explores the role of language in environmental and social problems such as climate change, the extinction of species (and here one can include the linguistic variety: languages/language diversity), classism and sexism, and furthermore reflects on possibilities of (linguistic) intervention.

This is a useful, but of course also a simplifying distinction. Some more complex models include aspects of both currents, such as the one proposed by Salikoko Mufwene (2001, 2008), discussed below. All ecological linguistic approaches also owe a considerable portion of their insights to scientific roots other than Haugen, especially the so-called *linguistic relativism/constructivism* or *Sapir–Whorf theory complex*, which comprises two logically independent hypotheses:

- languages encode different cultural and cognitive categories and can vary in an indefinite number of ways; and
- languages shape their speakers' world-view and other non-linguistic behaviour.[5]

Both hypotheses can be called ecological as they regard languages, their speakers' environment, and their speakers' world-view as being substantially interconnected. This conception of language is strongly tied to the names of Franz Boas, Edward Sapir, and Benjamin Lee Whorf who, at the beginning of the twentieth century and by studying Native American languages and comparing them to what Whorf called SAE (Standard Average European) languages, arrived at conclusions such as the following:

Human beings do not live in the objective world alone, nor alone in the world of social activity as ordinarily understood, but are very much at the mercy of the particular language which has become the medium of expression for their society. It is quite an illusion to imagine that one adjusts to reality essentially without the use of language and that language is merely an incidental means of solving specific problems of communication or reflection. The fact of the matter is that the 'real world' is to a large extent

---

[5] It is useful to distinguish between a stronger and a weaker form of this hypothesis. The stronger version claims that language determines thought and behaviour, and is rejected by most linguists today. A weaker version assumes that language exerts some influence on cognitive and other non-linguistic behaviour, and is widely, though not universally, accepted. In recent years, the Amazonian language Pirahã has become a challenging case with regard to this hypothesis (for a discussion see Everett 2005, 2008, 2009; Frank, Everett, Fedorenko and Gibson 2008; Nevins, Pesetsky and Rodrigues 2009a, 2009b).

unconsciously built up on the language habits of the group ... We see and hear and otherwise experience very largely as we do because the language habits of our community predispose certain choices of interpretation. (Sapir 1929: 209ff.)

We dissect nature along lines laid down by our native languages. The categories and types that we isolate from the world of phenomena we do not find there because they stare every observer in the face; on the contrary, the world is presented in a kaleidoscopic flux of impressions which has to be organized by our minds – and this means largely by the linguistic systems in our minds. (Whorf 1940/1956: 213)

We are thus introduced to a new principle of relativity, which holds that all observers are not led by the same physical evidence to the same picture of the universe, unless their linguistic backgrounds are similar, or can in some way be calibrated ... The relativity of all conceptual systems, ours included, and their dependence upon language stand revealed. (Whorf 1940/1956: 214)

Some ecolinguists, especially those engaged in a critique of Western languages and in ecocritical discourse analysis do indeed make reference to Sapir and Whorf (e.g. Chawla 2001). However, as Mühlhäusler (2000a: 90) points out, these names are often introduced as a means of demonstrating the legitimate roots of ecolinguistics rather than as a serious effort to develop the theories of linguistic relativity and determinism.

It is also necessary to point to the fact that Sapir and Whorf have important precursors in Wilhelm von Humboldt and especially in Johann Gottfried Herder.[6] In his 'Fragments on recent German literature' (1767), Herder considers language not only a tool or instrument for human beings to express their thoughts, but also the content and even the form of human cognition (Herder 2005: 102) – an idea of far-reaching consequences:

If it is true that we cannot think without thoughts, and learn to think through words, then language sets limits and outline for the whole of human cognition.
　We think in language, whether we are explaining what is present or seeking what is not yet present. In the first case we transform perceptible sounds into intelligible words and intelligible words into clear concepts. Hence a matter can be dissected for as long as there are words for its component concepts, and an idea can be explained for as long as new connections of words set it in a clearer light. (Herder 2002: 49)

---

[6] It is important to note, however, that these ideas have a long history in Western philosophy. It spans, to name only a few examples, from Plato's 'Allegory of the cave' in the *Politeia* to the epistemological investigations of George Berkeley ('A treatise concerning the principles of human knowledge', where the essence of ideas is said to be their being perceived [§3] and the nature of human knowledge is reduced to ideas and spirits, but not matter [§86]) to the structuralism of Ferdinand de Saussure (according to whom linguistic signs constitute an autonomous system in which the relation between these signs determines their meaning; therefore: 'La langue est un système dont tous les termes sont solidaires et où la valeur de l'un ne résulte que de la présence simultanée des autres,' Saussure 1915/1986: 159). See also Toulmin (1972) who gives a functional interpretation of the dichotomy *relativism* vs. *universalism/absolutism* in Western thought (see section 1.2.2).

Proceeding from the general to the more particular, Herder asks: What does it mean for the 'nature' of a 'national language' (*Nationalsprache*) if it is a tool of the organs of its people, a content of their 'world of thoughts' (*Gedankenwelt*), and a form of their kind (2002: 102–103)? The answer is clear for Herder and fits in with a central thought expressed in his treatise 'The origin of language' (1772), according to which human language has no divine origin:[7]

[E]ach nation speaks in accordance with its thought and thinks in accordance with its speech. However different was the viewpoint from which the nation took cognizance of a matter, the nation named the matter. And since this was never the viewpoint of the Creator ... but was instead an external, one-sided viewpoint, this viewpoint got imported into the language at the same time too. (2002: 50)

For Herder, language is a 'huge area' (*Umfang*) of thoughts that have become visible, a limitless land of terms, coined by the centuries (2005: 94). Although the intimate relation between language and nation stated by Herder – and later Humboldt – was a prominent topic in the German national movement, their notion of *nation* should not be interpreted too narrowly here. It was a rather cosmopolitan conception, emphasizing the diversity of human history, thoughts, and speech, but by no means favouring one nation or language in principle over another. Its meaning is probably closer to that of the modern term *society* than that of the modern *nation*. Furthermore, Herder's conception of *language* was all but static: he speaks of a 'language becoming' (*werdende Sprache*) that varies through all the educational levels of its speakers and changes through all its days of being created (2005: 103).

It was for Wilhelm von Humboldt to take up and cultivate many of Herder's ideas. For Humboldt, language constitutes an 'organic whole' (*organisches Ganzes*) and is not as much a 'product' (*Werk*, Greek εργον) as it is a 'practice' or an 'action' (*Tätigkeit*, Greek ενέργεια, cf. Herder's *werdende Sprache*). Expanding Herder's thoughts concerning the heterogeneity of languages among nations and classes, Humboldt points to the relation between language and the individuals speaking it:[8]

---

[7] It may be of some interest here that Edward Sapir (1907) wrote an essay on Herder's treatise.

[8] In his essay 'On the different methods of translating' (1813), Friedrich Schleiermacher ties in with both Herder's and Humboldt's ideas: 'Every human being is, on the one hand, in the power of the language he speaks; he and his whole thinking are a product of it. He cannot, with complete certainty, think anything that lies outside the limits of language. The form of his concepts, the way and means of connecting them, is outlined for him through the language in which he is born and educated; intellect and imagination are bound by it. On the other hand, however, every freethinking and intellectually spontaneous human being also forms the language himself. For how else, but through these influences, would it have come to be and to grow from its first raw state to its more perfect formation in scholarship and art?' (Schleiermacher 1813/ 1992: 38).

Nicht bloß, daß die Sprache selbst ein organisches Ganzes ist, so hängt sie auch mit der Individualität derer, die sie sprechen, so genau zusammen, daß dieser Zusammenhang schlechterdings nicht vernachlässigt werden darf. (Humboldt 1795/1830: 201)

[Not only that language is itself an organic whole, [but] this way it is connected with the individuality of those speaking it so closely, that this relation must not, by all means, be neglected. (our translation)]

In our own conception of linguistic ecology, which will be laid out in the next part of this chapter, we speak of several reference levels of ecology (e.g. speaker, speaker group, and speech community) and tie in with these ideas of Herder and Humboldt.

   In an often-quoted passage from his essay 'On the comparative study of language and its relation to the different periods of language development' (1820), Humboldt underlines what Herder had stated before him: 'The differences between [languages] are not those of sounds and signs but ultimately of interpretations of the world' (1820/1997: 18). Moreover, '[i]t is here that the reason for, and the ultimate purpose of all investigations into language are to be found' (ibid.). For our conception of ecology we consider another passage of some importance, because it contains a clearer methodological formulation. In his introduction to 'On the Kavi language in the island of Java' (1836), Humboldt shows that the mutual interdependence of thought and language is more than just a metaphor for him: one element should be perfectly deducible from the other:

The *mental individuality* of a people and the *shape of its language* are so intimately fused with one another, that if one were given, the other would have to be completely derivable from it. For *intellectuality* and *language* allow and further only forms that are mutually congenial to one another. Language is, as it were, the outer appearance of the spirit of a people; the language is their spirit and the spirit their language; we can never think of them sufficiently as identical. (1836/1999: 46)

As Pagel (2018) shows in an extensive historical and scientific-theoretical work on the roots of contact linguistics, the scientific study of language contact phenomena begins in the last third of the nineteenth century. Here, an early offshoot of 'ecological' ideas can be found in William Whitney's essay 'On mixture in language' (1881). Whitney is concerned with the question of whether 'true' language mixture – defined as grammatical mixture on more or less equal grounds – is theoretically possible. He also provides a simple but effective systematization of phenomena of contact-induced language change (see Pagel 2015) and emphasizes that contact-induced change is rather unpredictable because the parameters influencing it are manifold:

[W]herever two tongues come in contact, each is liable to borrow something from the other; and more or less, according to wholly indeterminable circumstances: the measure and nature of the intercourse, the resources of the respective tongues, their degree of facilitating kinship or structural accordance, and so forth. (Whitney 1881: 10)

The first detailed examinations of language contact phenomena explicitly under the ecological perspective were conducted in William Mackey's papers 'Towards an ecology of language contact' and 'The ecology of language-shift', dating from 1979 and 1980, respectively. In the latter, Mackey begins with a tempting comparison to evolution-based ecologies in biology, which, however, has its pitfalls:

Languages too must exist in environments and these can be friendly, hostile or indifferent to the life of each of the languages. A language may expand, as more and more people use it, or it may die for lack of speakers. Just as competition for limited bio-resources creates conflict in nature, so also with languages. If a smaller fish gets in contact with a big fish, it is the smaller which is more likely to disappear. (Mackey 1980/2001: 35)

However, as Mackey continues to explain, this sort of reasoning

places us in danger of falling into the fallacy akin to that of the nineteenth century comparatists who began regarding and dealing with language as if it were an organism, after having promulgated, on the model of the physical sciences, language laws, some of which admitted of no exceptions. Language is not an organism. Nor is it a thing. It does not obey the laws of physics or those of biology. It's rather a form of behavior – not animal, but human, traditional behavior – not racial but cultural, in that it has to be learned as a trait or skill identified with a group of people. It's not what the people are but what they do. (ibid.)

The analogies between linguistic and natural ecologies are without doubt limited. Nevertheless, the idea of parallels between nature and culture in this respect has fascinated both linguists and natural scientists, particularly in the wake of Darwin's evolutionary theory at the end of the nineteenth century (for details, see Pagel 2018). Darwin himself dedicated an impressive section of his book *The descent of man* (1871) to language. Here, he points to a number of similarities between linguistic and biological evolution:

The formation of different languages and of distinct species, and the proofs that both have been developed through a gradual process, are curiously parallel. But we can trace the formation of many words further back than that of species, for we can perceive how they actually arose from the imitation of various sounds. We find in distinct languages striking homologies due to community of descent, and analogies due to a similar process of formation. The manner in which certain letters or sounds change when others change is very like correlated growth. We have in both cases the reduplication of parts, the effects of long-continued use, and so forth. The frequent presence of rudiments, both in languages and in species, is still more remarkable. The letter *m* in the word *am*, means *I*; so that in the expression *I am*, a superfluous and useless rudiment has been retained. In the spelling also of words, letters often remain as the rudiments of ancient forms of pronunciation. Languages, like organic beings, can be classed in groups under groups; and they can be classed either naturally according to descent, or artificially by other characters. Dominant languages and dialects spread widely, and lead to the gradual extinction of other tongues. A language, like a species, when once extinct, never... reappears. The same language never has two birth-places. Distinct languages may be crossed or blended together. We see variability in every tongue, and new words are continually cropping up; but as there is a limit to the powers of the memory, single words, like whole languages, gradually become extinct ... The survival or preservation of certain favoured words in the struggle for existence is natural selection. (Darwin 1901: 137–139)

Labov (2001: 6–10) deals with these considerations of Darwin and provides examples for each of the similarities stated. The whole parallelism, however, seems to depend on the argument of natural selection Darwin refers to in the last sentences. Yet

the general consensus of 20th-century linguists gives no support to this contention, and finds no evidence for natural selection or progress in linguistic evolution. (Labov 2001: 9)[9]

The same analogy is found in a number of ecolinguistic publications of the 1990s, that draw attention to the increasing loss of linguistic diversity, which in turn is considered just as harmful to the human environment as the loss of biodiversity (e.g. Mühlhäusler 1996a). The chain of argumentation here is as follows: (1) the development of either diversity, biological or linguistic, takes time; (2) over the course of time, information about the environment of a biological or linguistic entity is being encoded in its inherited domains (genes, structure); (3) every chunk of information was selected from a number of competing alternatives because it fitted best to the respective environment; (4) therefore the totality of these entities represents invaluable knowledge about human environment; and (5) each entity lost is a derogation of this knowledge. In other words, linguistic diversity, too, 'reflects thousands of years of human accommodation to complex environmental conditions' (Mühlhäusler 1996a: 270). As we have seen, this sort of reasoning goes back at least to the mentioned writings of Herder – lacking there, of course, an ecological terminology.[10]

---

[9] Mufwene (p.c., November 2013) disagrees with Labov on this matter, arguing that Labov probably misunderstands what *selection* means and how it works: there's great evidence for *selection* in linguistic behaviour, starting with accommodations speakers make to each other. See the discussion in Mufwene (2008, especially chs. 6 and 7).

[10] E.g. Herder (2005: 95, our translation): 'Every nation has a peculiar storehouse of these thoughts that have become signs, this is their national language. A stock, to which they have added for centuries'.
    A late twentieth-century equivalent can be found e.g. in Dixon (1999: 144): 'Each language encapsulates the world-view of its speakers – how they think, what they value, what they believe in, how they classify the world around them, how they order their lives. Once a language dies, a part of human culture is lost forever.'

An important implication of such reasoning is that language diversity could be the key to understanding and solving the environmental problems humans face today, just as biodiversity is thought to be the key to biological ecosystems and their being well. The analogy could even be extended to a proper interdependence between biodiversity and linguistic diversity, as has been argued in a number of studies on biocultural diversity (e.g. Mühlhäusler 1995a; Maffi 2001). Human knowledge about the different human environments disappears along with linguistic diversity, which causes the very biodiversity of these environments to be in danger of disappearing too. This can already be illustrated on the level of vocabulary: if an autochthonous language has a word for a particular element of its environment, and this word disappears as a result of the dominance of another imported language, which has no word for this element, then the speakers will not and cannot recognize the relevance of the element for their environment, and the element will probably not be treated with the necessary care or consequence.[11] Particular forms of language contact that involve the expansion of the language of a powerful and/or highly prestigious speaker group create this kind of situation all the time. If a globally expanding language like English, which classifies a great deal of flora under hyperonyms such as *grass* or *weed* (see also the German *Unkraut*), drives smaller local languages to extinction, the local flora will be classified essentially in the English fashion, regardless of the *local* significance of its elements. By doing so, it could be argued, these elements might be driven to extinction, too.

The metaphorical and the biological meaning of the term *ecology* merge in the work of Peter Mühlhäusler and other linguists who draw attention to the importance of linguistic diversity. This merger also reveals a highly practical aspect of ecolinguistics: it can constitute a call for and an attempt to sustain smaller linguistic ecologies ('mobile' or 'static') which are in danger of being driven out or absorbed by the ecologies of so-called world, national, or regional languages. This call seems to be readily accepted by most ecolinguists studying the facets of linguistic diversity.

In the early 1990s, another branch of ecolinguistics came into being. It is often attributed to Michael Halliday who, building on the works of his teacher John R. Firth, developed systemic functional linguistics. In this approach, language is considered a system of interrelated networks of choices – choices that speakers have to make when communicating. The specific structure of

---

[11] Of course, the reverse is also true: the new speakers of the imported language will introduce concepts and words to this language that are specific to its new ecology and haven't existed in this language prior to the contact. This process is part of the so-called *indigenization* of an imported language.

these networks is thought to reflect the functions the language and its particular systems have to serve. In other words, these networks of choices

are presumed to have taken the form they have, in all languages, in order that speakers and hearers can make use of their language to meet their requirements as determined by the general human situation and by their own particular culture. (Robins 1997: 245)

In a paper, which became seminal for the language-critical branch of ecolinguistics, Halliday (1990/2001) points to the relation between language(s) and environmental problems. He chooses the most widespread of the so-called SAE languages, English, as his object of study and shows (following the Sapir–Whorfian paradigm) how English grammar provides the very conditions of westerners' destructive behaviour towards nature. His examples comprise the encoding of natural resources such as *water, air*, and *oil* as mass nouns, which suggests the inexhaustibility of these resources, and the strict separation of non-human life forms from human life forms, for instance, in the pronoun system (*he/she* vs. *it*), reflecting and at the same time sustaining the western claim for human dominance over other life forms.

This 'ecocriticism' (of language system and discourse) has received many interesting contributions in the 1990s, such as that of Andrew Goatly. Goatly (1996/2001) illustrates how SAE language structure lags behind the modern western scientific understanding of the ecological conditions of the world we live in. One argument in point is the division in language between an 'agent', an 'experiencer', and a 'recipient' – according to Goatly, this fragmentation of the universe reflects the view of traditional Newtonian science and contradicts the insights of, for example, the quantum theory.[12]

The practical aspect of these findings – the fact that speakers and/or linguists must change language in order to change the destructive western approach to nature, and by doing so solve modern environmental and social problems, seems to be obvious. Nevertheless, it has not been expressed very often. Most ecolinguists deny the idea (or even the possibility) of manipulating language and creating a more functional *newspeak*, to use a term from George Orwell's negative utopia *Nineteen Eighty-Four*. This is especially true for those ecolinguists who are concerned with the deep structure of language. Goatly (1996/2001), for one, seems convinced that SAE languages will adapt to the insights of modern science by themselves (i.e. by their speakers) in the course of time. Others, however, who criticize the rather superficial linguistic

---

[12] Here, one could raise the objection that, unlike the Newtonian world, the quantum world is not part of the reality humans perceive. It is therefore unlikely that this physical reality, which is observable only at the smallest scales, will be or has to be reflected in human language. In a way, this view is expressed in a famous statement of the physicist Richard Feynman, according to whom 'nobody understands quantum mechanics' (1967: 129).

revelations of anthropocentrism or sexism (i.e. revelations in the vocabulary or more peripheral structural categories), more often tend to express a prescriptive attitude (e.g. Berman 1994/2001).

It was, among other things, this 'eco-purist' attitude that earned ecolinguistics some criticism in the late 1990s and beyond, criticism that was surely justified for certain contributions, but not for the approach as a whole. Christopher Hutton and Douglas Kibbee, however, expressed rather substantial criticism of this approach. Hutton (2001) understands linguistics as ideology and the notion of *world-view* as a matter of policy. He investigates the theoretical tensions between *cultural relativism* and *universalism*, the first (underlying e.g. the ecological approach to language and language rights advocacy) often being understood as 'politically liberal' and 'progressive' and the second as 'scientifically sanctioned' and 'objective'. The description and preservation of different linguistic world-views, Hutton argues, requires the existence of an objective meta-language. The same is true for discourse–critical linguistics:

[D]istortion and manipulation can only be identified by reference to some form of objectivity. But distortion and manipulation are also pejorative terms for 'world view'. (2001: 277)

The important question asked by Hutton is this: 'How do we distinguish legitimate differences in world-view between cultures from pathological or manipulative forms of discourse?' (ibid.). The distinction proves to be difficult, as both cultural relativism and universalism are Western ideologies:

Linguistic theories that claim to represent the relativity of world views and to draw political conclusions from that claim can at best be described as pseudo-relativistic, caught in the paradox of an attempt to represent and defend cultural difference through the universalistic meta-language of linguistics. But what of linguistics as a universal objective descriptive meta-language, a claim implicit in the term 'General Linguistics'? Attempts to ground political and moral analyses of metaphor in the objectivity (however defined) of cognitive linguistics are vulnerable to the criticism that the objectivity appealed to is a convenient construct and that the ideological conclusions are under-determined by the linguistic analysis. (2001: 294–295)

With regard to the preservation of a 'natural' linguistic diversity, the matter appears to be particularly paradox,

[f]or the process of labeling alone brings artificial distinctions to that natural continuum. Yet, without that labeling one cannot speak of saving 'languages', since the concept of discrete language is an artificial product of modernity. (2001: 294)

But apart from the fact that all science must deal with this paradox (as science itself is an artificial product), one could argue in this case that speaking of *languages* is not the same as speaking of *discrete languages*. Speakers, too, label their languages, notwithstanding that others (including linguists) may label the same language differently (see Mühlhäusler Chapter 12 in this volume). We can, if not avoid this paradox, certainly ease it by accepting a more open and dynamic conception of *language* and *language system*, as will be done in our framework (see section 1.2).

Kibbee (2003) also compares two competing ideologies concerning language, called here the 'free-market approach' and the 'ecolinguistic approach'. He argues that both are ultimately based on the deterministic version of the Sapir–Whorf theory and as such are both biased, if in opposite directions. The agents of the 'free-market' ideology emphasize the superiority of standard national and the so-called 'world languages' as, for instance, bearers of democratic ideals, while those of the 'ecolinguistic approach' stress the inferiority of these national or global languages as expressions of capitalism, imperialism, homogenization of cultures, and so on. Kibbee resolutely rejects far-reaching analogies between linguistic and biological ecologies, particularly

the equivalence of language to species, and the notion that the loss of a language is equivalent to the loss of a natural species ... A language is a behavior, not a physical characteristic. If two languages are in contact, then they influence each other. If a dog lives in the same house as a bird it does not grow wings, nor does the bird sprout paws. If two languages are in contact, they create a new language. Thus, the genealogical tree produced to illustrate the descent of the human species works very poorly to illustrate the relationships between languages. A very grave danger on the part of geostrategists from both camps – the free-market language capitalists and the ecolinguists – is that they perceive influences between languages as a degradation of those languages. (Kibbee 2003: 51)

Referring to language contact, Kibbee repeats in part what Mackey already stated in 1980. However, his argument goes deeper and addresses questions that have not been posed sufficiently: Where do analogies between a linguistic and a biological species, between linguistic diversity and biodiversity end? If the two are equated, would we not have to interpret any language contact as an interruption of a vital and grown linguistic ecology? What does it mean for a linguistic ecology to 'grow'? Does contact-induced change involve a degradation of the language or variety in which it occurs? How does such a perception influence our understanding of the evolution of languages and linguistic diversity? What consequences does it have for the fundamental tools of linguistics, such as the family tree model of genetic relationship? On what grounds could we manipulate or prevent further linguistic evolution, knowing there has always been evolution?

Salikoko Mufwene addresses some of these questions, for example in his books of 2001 and 2008. Departing from a creolist's perspective, he outlines a general theory of language evolution and, thus, language change. By analogy,

Mufwene compares language with species, not with organisms (as has been done already in the 19th century by Whitney, see Pagel 2018: 329), and particularly with parasitic species, more specifically viruses, in biology. Further analogies are drawn between idiolects and individuals, and between structural features and genes. He argues that competition and selection are also decisive mechanisms in language evolution, while it is ecology that 'rolls the dice' and determines which species, idiolect, or structural feature, in their respective contexts, is 'more fit than others' (2001: 21). Mufwene also resorts to biology to adopt the distinction between internal and external ecology (2001: 22, ch. 6): while internal ecology concerns, above all, structural features and cognitive parameters (e.g. the coexistence of variants and the influence of systemic economy on feature selection), external ecology refers to the sociolinguistic framing and includes contact between different linguistic systems (which may have structural consequences but needs sociolinguistic explanation). Mufwene's contribution to the ecological approach to the study of language is significant but not shared by all ecological linguists (see Mühlhäusler's 2005 review of Mufwene 2001). His position is best described as an intermediate between the two currents in the approach to linguistic ecology we have outlined in this section. On the one hand, his careful analysis of language-internal and -external parameters, his focus on their interrelation, and the search for an adequate metaphorical picture of the evolution of languages situates him close to the first, i.e. the primarily metaphorical, methodologically motivated interpretation of ecology in language, which we also favour. On the other hand, the question as to the precise relation between biological and linguistic species and their evolution, between genes and structural features, or in short: the scope of metaphors copied from biology is crucial in his writings, so that his position also touches the second current, in which ecology is interpreted as including the referential world in a more biological, evolutionary sense.[13]

It becomes clear that, despite critics, ecological approaches to language have not been abandoned. Numerous anthologies, textbooks, and articles on the subject were published in the first decade and a half of the third millennium (e.g. Fill 2000; Fill, Penz, and Trampe 2002; Mühlhäusler 2003; Garner 2004; Fill and Penz 2007; Lechevrel 2010; Vandenbussche, Jahr, and Trudgill 2013; Eliasson 2015). In contact linguistics, too, there has been an increasing interest in an ecological paradigm, as is illustrated not only in the cited works of Mufwene but also in, e.g., Calvet (2006), Ansaldo (2009), Clements (2009), Pagel (2010, 2015, 2018), and Vandenbussche, Jahr, and Trudgill (2013). In fact, ecological approaches to language appear to be on their way to a

---

[13] See e.g. Mufwene (2014: 13), where human languages are said to have 'emerged as communicative technologies responding to various ecological pressures experienced by the hominine species during its protracted evolution'. Similar thoughts have been expressed, again, already by Whitney in the late 19th century (Pagel 2018: 340–41).

scientific comeback, and it is apparently the metaphorical – or Haugenian – interpretation of ecology that is again becoming the centre of attention. The parameters of the linguistic ecology paradigm will have to be thought through again and some will have to be reinterpreted and reassembled. The next section and the other contributions in this volume are a first attempt in this direction.

The current interest in ecological approaches also indicates, however, that the distinction between two currents in ecological linguistics made by Fill (1998/ 2001: 43) falls short if applied to the present. We can distinguish at least two influential contemporary applications of the ecology metaphor to linguistics, associated with the names of Salikoko Mufwene on the one hand, and the term *ecolinguistics* on the other, leading to two different historical sources. Mufwene's interest lies mainly in the evolution of language and language change vis-à-vis the evolution of man. He understands the ecology of language as showing analogies to the ecology of biological species, and language evolution and change as crucial elements in the evolution of a particular species: humankind. Thus, for Mufwene ecology serves as a model to capture and explain *historical* processes. Linguists working under the theoretical framework often called *ecolinguistics* such as Peter Mühlhäusler, on the other hand, focus on the interdependence between linguistic and environmental (i.e. social, cultural, biological, and other) ecosystems. Here, the non-linguistic world is integrated in *synchronic* linguistic questions (such as the question of why and how preserve languages with few speakers) and the *social responsibility* of the linguist is being emphasized. While Mufwene's approach is essentially theoretical, ecolinguistics can be understood, in principle, as an applied science (but see Mühlhäusler Chapter 12 in this volume). Historically, the first approach echoes many facets of Whitney's language theory (e.g. 1867, 1875), and the second seems to be rather in a Herderian tradition (see Pagel 2018 for details).

In this volume we wish to develop a third way that differs from the two mentioned. In our theoretical consolidation of the linguistic ecology paradigm we take a primarily *synchronic* perspective, but suggest that historical links and integrations (or *foundations*, as we say), among other dimensions, must be included in the analysis of linguistic data. At the heart of our approach is a model of linguistic ecology in which we combine Haugen's initial thoughts with two key concepts of the philosophy of Edmund Husserl. This model is construed in the most abstract and open fashion and allows for an ecological epistemology with respect to a maximum of linguistic questions and problems. Our model leads to certain postulates in which we call, for example, for data selection in terms of 'natural' empirical data, for a focus on language contact as contact between speakers, for interdisciplinary analysis, and for methodological flexibility. The strong discourse–corpus orientation of our framework can be deduced directly from our synchronic perspective and includes also a call for the reconsideration of the instruments of ecological discourse analysis and interpretation.

1.2   Linguistic Ecology and Language Contact: a Theoretical Consolidation

1.2.1   *Linguistic Ecology as a Multidimensional System of Foundations*

After this outline of the bifurcated evolution of and currents and positions in the ecological linguistic debate, we shall try to summarize the ideas of our own approach.

We prefer the term *ecological linguistics* over *ecolinguistics*. The latter term has been applied to a group of scientific studies particularly from the 1980s and 1990s, many (but not all) of which were motivated primarily by political, environmental, and social, but not always properly linguistic questions.[14] Although we do not (and cannot) exclude questions of this kind, we want to stress that the ecology paradigm is not restricted to socio-political, environmental, and linguistic minority issues. The core of our framework will hence be linguistic in a narrow sense, and corpora are considered to be the point of departure of any ecological linguistic analysis. The pretension of our framework in turn is holistic, as it covers the dimensions of *speakers, space, time*, and *language systems*. These dimensions again are carefully linked to societal contexts such as the speech situation, attitudes, and competences among others.

As the title of this volume indicates, we prefer *linguistic ecology* over *language ecology* because we take into account all linguistic phenomena from macroscopic linguistic areas like the Francophony to the individual speaker and speech situation, including a level like *individual language*, but not being restricted to it – which a term like *language ecology* could suggest. Our notion of *linguistic ecology* encompasses the whole perceptible spectrum of animate and inanimate aspects around speaker and speech, the entire scale from rule-governed actions and their being perceived by the society to the concrete material contexts that provide potential to action. In a sense we tie in with the distinction made in biology and ecology of interactions between different animate and inanimate spheres (e.g. organisms with themselves, other organisms, and their inanimate environment).[15] Thereby we do not, however, imply an analogy between languages and biological species or organisms. We also do not support premises of the kind 'linguistic evolution equals biological evolution' (or that of mathematical or logical systems). Our framework is construed in the most abstract fashion in order to allow for different readings. We focus on the interactions between

---

[14] See the discussion on the distinction of these two terms and the respective approaches in Mufwene and Vigouroux (2012: 112ff.).

[15] Human cultural history shows, however, that a clear distinction of the entities of reality into animate and inanimate can be problematic and ultimately depends on philosophical dispositions.

different ecological levels, but leave open (and must leave open, for reasons that will be explained below) how these are defined in a specific case.

Our interpretation of *ecology* is in the tradition of the metaphorical understanding of this term and is, thus, connected with many of Haugen's original ideas. Haugen's (1972) main concern was to perceive language as interactive language usage in its various functional connections. From the very start, he considered multilingualism and language contact to be among the psychological and social realities of this interaction:

Language exists only in the minds of its users, and it only functions in relating these users to one another and to nature, i.e. their social and natural environment. Part of its ecology is therefore psychological: its interaction with other languages in the minds of bi- and multilingual speakers. Another part of its ecology is sociological: its interaction with the society in which it functions as a medium of communication. (Haugen 1972: 325)

Haugen names several factors here. By 'social environment' we can most likely understand the partners of communication in a particular situation; and 'interaction with the society' refers to the relevant social group or the general social context – a superordinate, abstract dimension. The 'natural environment' is the concrete, special context of the speech situation. Furthermore, the competence of each speaker and the processing of language in the speech situation is a psychological dimension. Finally, individual languages (or rather varieties) are entities that interact and come into contact with other languages (varieties). In this way, Haugen enumerates various parameters on different levels of abstraction, showing certain degrees of dependence.

One important consequence of this conception of multiple parameters is that linguistics has to proceed in a multidisciplinary way:

Language ecology would be a natural extension of this kind of study and has long been pursued under such names as psycholinguistics, ethnolinguistics, linguistic anthropology, sociolinguistics, and the sociology of language. (Haugen 1972: 327)

The theoretical elements hinted at in Haugen's interpretation – multiple parameters, different levels of abstraction of the parameters and modes of mutual dependence of language and these parameters – are crucial for the following theoretical suggestions.

Mackey (1980/2001), too, emphasizes that taking an ecological position on language means above all examining interdependencies: 'Ecology is essentially the study of interdependence within a system' (ibid.: 67). We will take up this last aspect and generalize it, resorting to Husserl's concepts of *foundation* (*Fundierung*) and of *wholes and parts* (*Ganze und Teile*). Both concepts, the most important aspects of which will be resumed below, already had an important impact in the early phase of structuralism in modern linguistics, specifically in the opus of Roman Jakobson. The latter uses the concept of *foundation* in 'Child language, aphasia and phonological universals' (first published in 1944 in German) to define the rules of sound acquisition and pathological sound reduction in an accurate implicational pattern, an insight that was subsequently adopted by creolists and variation sociolinguists.[16] The acquisition of the fricatives (*Engelaute*), for instance, is therefore always preceded by – and hence *founded in* – the acquisition of the plosives (*Verschlusslaute*, Jakobson 1944/1962: 59ff.). In a later study, Jakobson insists that Husserl's concept of *wholes and parts* is associated with the different types of foundation in language. The distinction between different levels of parts constituting wholes on higher levels allows for the conception of multiple embedding of a linguistic message and its elements (Jakobson 1963/1971).[17]

Contributions from the cognitive sciences, such as Smith (1994) or Bundgaard (2010), demonstrate that although the study of language proper is not a quantitatively essential part of Husserl's oeuvre, his reflections on language have much to offer for contemporary linguistic theory. Bundgaard reveals that Husserl's considerations on language in the 'Logical investigations' reflect the fundamental division in linguistics, as well as the philosophy of language, between 'formal grammars ... and functional/pragmatic or cognitive grammars' (2010: 371). While in the 'First logical investigation' language is defined 'within a mainly communicative context', suggesting a pragmatic interpretation, the 'Fourth logical investigation' defines the same subject 'as an autonomous formal symbolic system', laying the groundwork for structuralist, Chomskyan, and post-Chomskyan grammars (Bundgaard 2010: 372). This divergent, or rather parallel, approach suggests that one should deal cautiously with Husserl's thoughts on language within an ecological linguistic framework, though it is fruitful.

In our framework we will refer exclusively to the notion of *foundation* (*Fundierung*) and to his reflections on *wholes and parts* (*Ganze und Teile*) according to the 'Third logical investigation'. Husserl's thoughts regarding these terms provide us with the most explicit and differentiated model for the description of dependency and interdependency relationships (one sided and mutual foundation, immediate and mediate foundation, etc.) to date. We do not take a general phenomenological position, nor do we subscribe to all of Husserl's reflections on language in the 'Fourth logical investigation'. Rather, we have tried to find a model that would be differentiating enough to cope with

---

[16] A brief overview of implicational scaling in linguistic analysis can be found in Mühlhäusler (1996c: 7–11).

[17] 'A systematic consideration of multiform whole–part relations broadly extends the scope of our science; it allows a systemic analysis of verbal messages with respect both to the code and to the context; it uncovers the complex interaction of the various levels of language, from the largest to the smallest units, and the constant interplay of diverse verbal functions. It introduces time and space factors into descriptive linguistics' (Jakobson 1963/1971: 284).

the systematic horizontal and vertical relationships which, as we believe, structure the ecology of languages. We think that the aforementioned concepts introduced by Husserl present a good starting basis for the formulation of types of relatedness in the ecology of languages, and we additionally consider it fruitful to position our thoughts in a scientific-historic background.

Our considerations and their consequences can be summarized in the following postulates.

Postulate 1

Linguistic ecology can be seen as an essential general attitude to language and language analysis. We consider language, primarily language usage, as *part of a whole* (*Teilganzes*, according to Husserl) in a complex socio-historical–cultural system, which additionally is dependent on cognitive-neural cross-linking.

We see a step in this direction in Thomason and Kaufman's (1988: 60) statement: 'we consider a language as a complex whole – a system of systems, of interrelated lexical, phonological, morphosyntactic, and semantic structures'. Our conception of linguistic ecology, however, considers this whole being also a part of larger wholes. It also goes deeper in applying new metaphors for the build-up of this whole, comprising different sets of parameters.

For our considerations we use two essential ideas from Husserl's 'Third Logical investigation' that concern the constitution of wholes. They relate to the complexity of wholes, their constitution in parts, and the nature of the relation between those parts.

Husserl assumes that objects are either simple or complex; in the latter case they are made up of parts:

Objects can be related to one another as Wholes to Parts, they can also be related to one another as coordinated parts of a whole ... Every object is either actually or possibly a part, i.e. there are actual or possible wholes that include it. (Husserl 2001: 4)

[Gegenstände können zueinander in dem Verhältnis von Ganzen und Teilen, oder auch in dem Verhältnis von koordinierten Teilen eines Ganzen stehen ... Jeder Gegenstand ist wirklicher oder möglicher Teil, d.h. es gibt wirkliche oder mögliche Ganze, die ihn einschließen. (Husserl 1913: 226)]

Parts can again be made up of parts. Taking into consideration the potential multiplicity of parts on only one level gives us a horizontal perspective. The idea of wholes, each of which is constituted of parts, combined into complexes leads to a vertical (hierarchical) perspective. Husserl expresses the hierarchical scaling of complex structures of parts and wholes with the distinction of mediate and immediate parts. Wholes, on the highest hierarchical level, are constituted directly by the elements on the next lower level. These elements are therefore called *immediate parts* of the whole. Immediate parts can be constituted by other elements on the next lower hierarchical level. These elements then constitute the whole in an indirect manner and are therefore called *mediate parts* of the whole. A melody is made up of individual tones, immediate parts, which themselves are constituted by parameters such as intensity and quality.[18] Intensity and quality are thus mediate parts of the melody.

The second idea concerns the different types of relation between the parts and the whole, and between the parts themselves. Wholes, as well as parts, are either autonomous or dependent. A colour, such as red, cannot exist without the reference to an object. Hence, the quality 'red' is dependent, because it needs a complement by quantity: 'extension' (Husserl 1913: 232ff., 2001: 7ff.). The types of (in)dependence can be explained more precisely with the notion of *foundation*. If a part *a* needs a complement *b*, then, according to Husserl, *a* is founded in *b*. Depending on whether both or only one of the parts are dependent, the foundations can be either reciprocal or one-sided. Interpreting Husserl's melody example further, a melody (the whole) is constituted by individual tones (immediate parts), but the foundation relation between these two levels is only one-sided, since the melody depends on the tones for its existence, whereas the tones do not depend on the melody or their coexistence with one another for theirs. Hence, vertically, the melody is founded in its sequence of tones but the individual tones are not founded in the melody. Likewise, horizontally, the individual tones can exist independently from one another and are therefore not founded in each other. On the next lower level, the constituents of the tones, such as intensity and quality (mediate parts of the melody), are mutually interdependent because the intensity of a musical tone cannot exist without a quality (i.e. a certain frequency) and vice versa. Hence, in Husserl's example from music, intensity and quality are reciprocally founded.

From our point of view, Husserl's concepts of *wholes and parts* and *foundation* provide the most abstract and differentiated instrument for characterizing *ecology* as a complex open system of relations and dependencies. It may also prove useful in dealing with the seemingly paradoxical situation of holistic or ecological approaches in science: an ecological perspective must constantly emphasize the inseparability of the organic whole and (quasi-natural) continua and equilibriums; the principal scientific method, however,

---

[18] For the horizontal and at the same time vertical orientation of Husserl's concept, see for example his explanations on 'association' (*Verknüpfung*) and 'concatenation' (*Verkettung*); (Husserl 2001: 32–34, 1913: 272–275), as well as his definition of 'pieces' (*Stücke*): "'Pieces' are essentially mediate or remote parts of a whole whose "pieces" they are, if combinatory forms unite them with other "pieces" into wholes which in their turn constitute wholes of higher order by way of novel forms' (ibid.: 40). "Stücke" sind wesentlich mittelbare oder fernere Teile des Ganzen, dessen Stücke sie sind, wenn sie mit anderen Stücken durch verbindende Formen zu Ganzen geeinigt sind, die selbst wieder durch neuartige Formen Ganze höherer Ordnung konstituieren' (Husserl 1913: 286). (See Raible 1980: 43.).

is analysis which in turn requires the dissection of that whole into artificial parts and labels (see the discussion of Hutton's critique above). That is to say, whenever linguists conduct research on a specific linguistic variety, they reify the activity 'speaking' into an object and label and define their object of study as a *language*, a *dialect*, or a *variety* and dissect that object into further parts. This procedure inevitably violates the holistic or ecological conception of language. But by resorting to Husserl's ideas we believe that our approach to linguistic ecology provides the means to keep the multiple relations between parts and wholes in focus.[19]

1.2.2   Dynamic and Open Systems

If we assume that languages constitute multidimensional foundation relations and are themselves part of these, it follows that foundation relations compete, change, transform themselves, etc. This leads us to two further central hypotheses that tie in with arguments already expressed by Haugen.

> **Postulate 2**
> Language-systems are dynamic; therefore, the science of language must develop the epistemological consequences of this dynamic character.

This statement immediately emanates Haugen's reflections, according to which '[e]cology suggests a dynamic rather than a static science' and '[t]he concept of a language as a rigid, monolithic structure is false, even if it has proved to be a useful fiction in the development of linguistics' (Haugen 1972: 329, 335).[20] We will name only some more related aspects:

Language systems can have internal (cognitive and universal) dynamics that interact with external communicative-functional factors (e.g., interests and functions of the speaker-hearer; and situational and social frameworks). Furthermore, systems emerge from the communicative activities of speakers in speaking situations, and these systems are thus permanently transformed by the speaking activity. Any particular study in the science of language can therefore rely not (just) on one universal method or a fixed set of parameters,

---

[19] This may call to mind a frequent criticism made of Gestalt psychology. As Wolfgang Köhler (1947: 168–169) wrote, '[s]ome critics maintain that Gestalt Psychologists repeat the word 'whole' continually, that they are neglecting the existence of parts of wholes, and that they show no respect for the most useful tool of scientific procedure, which is *analysis*. No statement could be more misleading. Throughout our discussion of organization we have found it necessary to refer to segregation as well as to unification.'

[20] While in Haugen's day the grammatical description of language was still very structurally orientated and focused on searching for closed systems, in a spatial and temporal space invariant, nowadays a change of paradigms becomes apparent, as argued lately by Gadet et al. (2009). In this respect, the fact that Haugen emphasizes the vitality, openness, and interaction of systems acquires new relevance.

nor can it alone as one of the disciplines concerned with language capture the entire ecology of the object of its investigation. Ecological linguistics must proceed interdisciplinarily and flexibly with regard to the methods and the parameters in focus.[21]

In the philosophy of science, at least two theories regarding conceptual change respond to these needs. On the one hand, Paul Feyerabend (1993) argues for a methodological and theoretical pluralism and against what he calls 'law-and-order science':

A complex medium containing surprising and unforeseen developments demands complex procedures and defies analysis on the basis of rules which have been set up in advance and without regard to the ever-changing conditions of history. (Feyerabend 1993: 10–11)

By means of historical and abstract theoretical analysis Feyerabend shows that 'the only principle that can be defended under *all* circumstances and in all stages of human development … is the principle: *anything goes*' (1993: 18–19, italics original).

Stephen Toulmin's (1972) theory of conceptual change, on the other hand, is more elaborated and makes explicit use of the ecology metaphor. Toulmin deduces from the historical and cultural diversity of human ideas the need for an impartial standpoint of rational judgment, which in Western philosophy has been sought, primarily, in abstract logical terms. The failure of these terms when (re-) applied to the historically and culturally diverse ideas led to an escape from this 'absolutism' (i.e., rationality can be defined in absolute and universal terms) to 'relativism' (rationality can only be defined relative to time and cultural space). Toulmin rejects an evaluation of conceptual change both on absolutistic and relativistic grounds and opposes them with an evolutionary model of conceptual change:

We must begin … by recognizing that rationality is an attribute, not of logical or conceptual systems as such, but of the human activities or enterprises of which particular sets of concepts are the temporary cross-sections. (Toulmin 1972: 133)

In analogy to the organic ecology in biological evolutionary theory, Toulmin speaks of *intellectual ecology*, meaning the organization of concepts in more or less distinct and defined disciplines. The contents, methods and aims of

---

[21] Thomason and Kaufman (1988) seem to have something similar in mind when saying that 'In our view, an explanation [for a given linguistic change] should be as complete as possible' (1988: 58); and 'The appropriate methodology [for explaining linguistic changes], then, requires examination of a contact situation as a forest rather than as a collection of isolated trees. In order to support a claim that feature x arose in language A under the influence of language B, we need to show that features a, b, c, y, z – at least some of which belong to a subsystem different from the one x belongs to – also arose in A under the influence of B' (ibid.: 61).

each discipline underlie both continuity and change, this being a result of the double process of innovation and selection. Innovation is understood here as the creation of conceptual variation by professionals of the discipline as a reaction to existing problems, selection as the assertion and perpetuation of a concept against competing ones. For Toulmin, the validity of a concept can thus be defined as its explanatory power with respect to the goals and problems of a discipline at a given time and in a given context (1978: 168–170).

Resorting to the ideas of Herder, Humboldt, Whitney, and others, and applying Toulmin's theory to our framework, we argue that linguistic entities and processes are manifestations of human concepts and that therefore in linguistics, too, the 'impartial standpoint of rational judgment' (Toulmin) must not be sought in abstract logical, universal terms. The rationality in linguistic continuity and change cannot be attached to logical or other conceptual systems as such, but are attributes of speaker activities and enterprises of which particular sets of concepts are the temporary cross-sections. Universal criteria of distinction (such as e.g. 'the distinct language X' or 'the ideal speaker-hearer' in Universal Grammar) should be avoided, as should be any a priori criteria of judgment (see Toulmin 1978: 560–561). A similar view is also expressed by Richard Rorty (1989):

To see the history of language, and thus of the arts, the sciences, and the moral sense, as the history of metaphor is to drop the picture of the human mind, or human languages, becoming better and better suited to the purposes for which God or Nature designed them, for example, able to express more and more meanings or to represent more and more facts. The idea that language has a purpose goes once the idea of language as medium goes. (Rorty 1989: 16)

The rise and fall of metaphors are at the heart of Rorty's essentially ecological interpretation of the evolution of language:

Old metaphors are constantly dying off into literalness, and then serving as a platform and foil for new metaphors. This analogy lets us think of 'our language' – that is, of the science and culture of twentieth-century Europe – as something that took shape as a result of a great number of sheer contingencies. Our language and our culture are as much a contingency, as much a result of thousands of small mutations finding niches (and millions of others finding no niches), as are the orchids and the anthropoids. (ibid.)

This takes us to our next postulate:

Postulate 3
Communication and language-systems are open. Languages are open to language contact and hybridization.

Usage of language is usually hybrid; pure languages are societal constructions, as aptly expressed already in the late nineteenth century, for instance by Hugo

Schuchardt (1884: 5): '[Die Sprachmischung] ist nicht sowohl Ausnahme als Regel. Mit mehr Recht als Max Müller gesagt hat: "es gibt keine Mischsprache", werden wir sagen können: "es gibt keine völlig ungemischte Sprache"'.[22] It is important to stress (and has been neglected so far) that the 'conflict' sketched here by Schuchardt results from a misinterpretation of Müller's view, perhaps a deliberate one: Müller, in the work quoted by Schuchardt, explicitly rejects the idea of a fully unmixed language, too: 'There is hardly a language which in one sense may not be called a mixed language' (Müller 1862: 63 [82]).[23] In its most general form, a view like the one expressed in our postulate 3 must hence be considered neither novel nor exceptional. Nevertheless, it has not yet met with general acceptance.[24]

We presume that the primary locus of any language contact is the specific communication situation, therefore linguistic analysis must preferably begin there. As a methodological consequence of our postulate 3, hybrid texts must not be omitted when establishing corpora for linguistic analysis. Hybridity also encompasses the contact of various language varieties and registers.

A theory of the hybridization processes in language contact that meets with these findings has been developed in Johanson (e.g. 2002a), Kriegel, Ludwig, and Henri (2009), Kriegel, Ludwig and Salzmann (this volume) and Pagel (2015). It is based on the key terms *code copying* and *code alternation* which replace the traditional contact linguistic terms *borrowing, code-mixing, code-switching, transfer, calque*, and the like. These terms are being rejected for two related reasons: First, they are metaphorically misleading, as has been stressed amply and from the earliest days of contact linguistics on (especially with regard to *borrowing* and *mixing*), e.g. by Schuchardt (1914: 390), Haugen (1969: 362–63), Van Coetsem (2000), and Johanson (2002a). In the words of the latter, and regarding borrowing:

Nothing is borrowed in language contact: the 'donor language' is not deprived of anything; and – more importantly – the 'recipient language' does not take over anything identical with anything in the 'donor language'. Terms such as 'transfer' pose the same problem, since they also suggest identicality of originals and copies. (Johanson 2002a: 288)

---

[22] '[Linguistic mixing] is not so much exception as rule. With greater right than Max Müller has said, "There is no mixed language", shall we be able to say, "There is no fully unmixed language"' (translation taken from Bailey 1979: 144).

[23] For a discussion see Pagel (2015, 2018) and Whitney (1881).

[24] See also the more recent expression by Mufwene, developed in relation to his hypothesis that idiolects are mutually accommodating, with different speakers continually borrowing from each other through selections from their common, generally hybrid feature pool: 'Thus . . . the history of modern mankind shows that every language spoken today has either been influenced by others or emerged from the contact of other languages spoken before it' (Mufwene 2008: 132).

The second reason for a rejection of these terms is that the concepts they describe derive from different sources and ultimately lead to a heterogeneous and incoherent model of the processes in language contact. Our own model can be sketched as follows (for more details see Kriegel, Ludwig and Henri 2009; Kriegel, Ludwig and Salzmann, this volume; Pagel 2015): Following Johanson, we distinguish between *code alternation* and *code copying*. *Code alternation* 'means shifting from one code to another, juxtaposing elements belonging to different systems. Many cases of so-called 'code-switching' imply alternate choices of codes' (Johanson 2002a: 287). The notion of *code copying*, in turn, 'is construed in a rather wide scope. It includes various phenomena such as borrowing and calquing and deals with them as similar types of interaction within one and the same paradigm' (ibid.: 286). Therefore, we consider *copying* to be effective in what is diachronically perceived as code maintenance, code shift and code creation alike. Copies of linguistic material are always spontaneous and interactional at first but can be conventionalized, through the process of 'propagation' (Croft 2000), and become more systematic. One way to visualize the full range of copying processes in language contact is through a continuum spanning from *interactional copies* to highly *conventionalized* (or *nativized*) copies (see Chapter 7, this volume).

Further distinctions with relevance to this volume are between *overt* and *covert copies*, and between *exoteric* and *esoteric/hermetic languages*. By *overt copy* we mean a linguistic element that has been copied more or less in its entirety from the model code (i.e. with its phonetic encoding and its meaning in a broad sense, that is to say lexical–semantic and/or structural–grammatical components). In a *covert copy*, in turn, only the lexical–semantic and/or structural–grammatical information has been copied and is supplemented by encoding material from the copying code (e.g. German *Wolkenkratzer* 'skyscraper').

Mühlhäusler (1996a), following Thurston (1987: 96–97), distinguishes between *exoteric* and *esoteric languages*, the former being freely available for intergroup communication, while the latter are restricted to a well-defined social group that often contributes to its exclusiveness by deliberately making the language difficult for outsiders to learn. In the Pacific area, for example, there are languages such as Yeletnye or some Reef Santa Cruz languages whose grammars are highly complex, which makes transfers from and to other languages virtually impossible, owing to social barriers, as explained by Whinnom (1971: 93–96). The wider implications of the notion of *esotericity* for an understanding of language evolution have recently been discussed by, e.g. Wray and Grace (2007) and Operstein (2015). More generally, one can say that languages or linguistic ecologies are characterized by different degrees of contact receptiveness, ranging from *esotericity* (or hermeticism) to *exotericity* (or openness). Differing attitudes with regard to contact receptiveness emerge historically and change in the course of social and cultural history,[25] and their imprint in the respective language's structure can be enormous. Generally, the conception of grammar as an a priori independent system has proven to be a hindrance to an understanding of the diversity of human languages and of language contact. Grammar, as any other part of human language, is shaped considerably by social and cultural factors. In a particularly clear illustration of this point, Daniel Everett (2005, 2008) has attributed the many peculiarities found in the Amazonian language Pirahã (such as the lack of recursion, of numbers and colour terms) to a cultural principle of this people he calls 'the immediacy of experience principle'. Everett considers the notion of esoteric communication as a key to the understanding of these peculiarities:[26]

Esoteric communication could very well contribute to our explanation of some of the more controversial aspects of Pirahã grammar.

   The usefulness of the concept of esoteric communication for understanding Pirahã is demonstrated in part by current research by the psychologists Thomas Roeper of Massachusetts and Bart Hollebrands of the University of Groningen. This research suggests that recursion might be a device that is useful for packing sentences with more information in societies with a higher degree of exoteric communication where more complex information is the rule, such as modern industrialized societies. But in a society like the Pirahãs', the esoteric nature of their communication renders recursion less useful, while the immediacy of experience principle is incompatible with it. (Everett 2008: 241)

Moderate forms of esotericity/hermeticity (which according to the previous quote could be called 'pre-modern') are for instance the different sorts of purism in the history of several European societies (see Ludwig 2003).

   In a larger perspective, a language can be said to have a multilayered time dimension that ranges from the sequentiality of individual speech acts in the situation of communication to the change of entire language systems and the historic constitution of linguistic macro-ecologies (see below). The idea of multidimensional foundation also leads us to the following interpretation of language change:

> **Postulate 4**
> A monocausal explanation of language change begs the question why other diachronic factors are discarded; diachronic change appears to be multicausal a priori.

---

[25] Aslanov's contribution (Chapter 5, this volume) in particular shows the importance of this scale.

[26] Esotericity combined with the Pirahã's feeling of superiority is used by Everett to explain another interesting detail concerning that language: despite long-term asymmetric contact with Brazilian Portuguese, Pirahã displays virtually no signs of contact-induced language change, neither in the form of copying, nor in an increasing bilingualism, nor in language shift (Everett 2008).

In fact, the only possible result of the basic ecological assumption of the multiple foundation of language and language usage is to suppose that language change is conditioned multicausally. The simultaneous relevance of several different parameters in a diachronic perspective is usually denominated *convergence* or *multiple birth*.[27]

1.2.3   From Linguistic Interaction to Historically Constituted Macro-ecology: a Hierarchical Model

In accordance with the notion of *natural data* discussed by Gadet and Pagel (Chapter 2, this volume), all linguistic relations of foundation, or all relations of foundation in which language is, have one primary place of manifestation, practice, and development: the speech situation.

Postulate 5
> The speech situation, or the speakers' situated talk, must play a key role in linguistic analysis. Empirical data collecting and corpus analysis are the preferred methods of operation in ecological linguistics.

Speech situation, in our terminology, is roughly equivalent to Hymes's 'speech event' and Goffman's communicative 'encounter'. As part of his descriptive theory of language use (and in the broader context of an 'ethnography of communication'), Hymes (1972/1986) identifies a set of three types: *speech situation, speech event*, and *speech act*. While *speech situation*, in his terminology, designates 'situations associated with (or marked by the absence of) speech', often described as, for instance, 'ceremonies, fights, hunts, meals, lovemaking, and the like' (ibid.: 56), and *speech act* is the 'minimal term of the set', it is the intermediate term *speech event* that comes closest to our understanding of *speech situation*: 'The term speech event will be restricted to activities, or aspects of activities, that are directly governed by rules or norms for the use of speech' (ibid.).

As explained by Mondada (Chapter 3, this volume), Erving Goffman (1964: 135) talked of an 'ecological huddle' even before Haugen's first and programmatic application of the ecology metaphor to linguistics. He employed this expression for the reciprocal mechanisms of orientation, used by those who are part of a communicative encounter. He also characterized such an encounter as a 'micro-ecological orbit' (1964: 133; also Goffman 1961, 1981a, and particularly 1981b).

We will adapt the speech situation as the micro-ecological level of our model in this framework. Mufwene highlights the importance of macro-ecology for the concept of the ecology of language (e.g. Mufwene and

---

[27] See, for example, Aitchison (1995), Bollée (1982), Thomason (2001a, especially p. 262), and Zuckermann (2009).

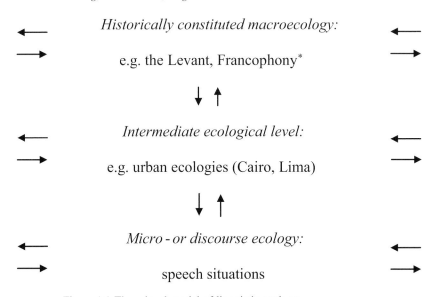

Figure 1.1 Three-level model of linguistic ecology
* The examples/situations given in this figure (Levant, Francophony, etc.) will be dealt with in this volume. That is, they have been chosen here for reasons of coherence and not of prototypicality.

Vigouroux 2012). Complementing these observations with an intermediate step, we propose the three-layer, hierarchically structured model of ecological levels, as depicted in Figure1.1.

Even if our position towards a simplifying parallelization of biological and linguistic ecology is a sceptical one, the fact that biological ecology uses a similar three-level, hierarchical model deserves to be noted and mentioned here:[28]

The living world can be viewed as a biological hierarchy that starts with subcellular particles, and continues up through cells, tissues and organs. Ecology deals with the next three levels: the individual *organism*, the *population* (consisting of individuals of the same species) and the *community* (consisting of greater or lesser number of species populations). (Begon, Townsend, and Harper 2006: xi)

The micro- or discourse ecology is governed by its local specifications: 'embodied participation' (Chapter 1, this volume), medial conditions (spoken and/or written language, aspects influencing the perception of language such as noise, etc.), positioning within space, sequentiality of actions and turns, sequential ties to earlier or future interactions, etc. Although not being a mere 'reverberation' of the higher ecological levels, the discourse ecology is the

---

[28] A distinction between the macro and micro level has also been made in sociolinguistics, e.g. by Auer, Hinskens and Kerswill (2005), but in a theoretically less explicit way.

place of the manifestation, staging, or reproduction of these levels, which naturally only express themselves through individual perspectives and evaluations. We can tie in with Schegloff here, who recurrently uses the metaphor of the interaction as the 'natural home' or 'habitat' of a language (e.g. Schegloff 1996). The higher ecological levels represent complex socio-cultural–historical facilities with an existence beyond the individual speech situation, for instance in narratives (in the broadest sense of this term), cognition, or also reifications of juridical or administrative kind (e.g. blacks and whites during the South African apartheid).[29]

This model is an application of Husserl's conception of vertical and horizontal relations of foundation. Foundation relations are depicted as arrows. They can be vertical as well as horizontal, and can at least potentially work in both directions at each level. The consideration of these foundation relations essentially helps to understand hybridization processes in language contact. Any individual speech situation is founded in (and refers to) at least one intermediate ecology (e.g. the urban speech of Paris), which in turn is founded in (and refers to) at least one macro-ecology (e.g. the Francophony). The speech situation recruits its options and constraints from these higher-level ecologies, and the higher-level ecologies, in turn, are being constituted and changed by the individual speech situations that are constructed, more or less, within their frames. Speakers can refer to several intermediate ecologies and macro-ecologies at the same time and thereby create both the possibility and the necessity for linguistic hybridization. Horizontal connections can exist at all three levels: an individual speech situation is probably always connected to other speech situations within the same intermediate and macro-ecological settings. Important (and often dichotomous) connections on the intermediate level are, for instance, urban vs. rural or resident vs. migrant. On the highest level, macro-ecologies can be connected, for example, in immigrant or colonial settings, such as the Malayo-Polynesian macro-ecology and the Hispanophony in the case of Chamorro (see Pagel, Chapter 10, this volume).

1.3   Concluding Step: a Larger Picture

In a last step, our three-level model (Figure1.1) can be enlarged to four major dimensions that provide us with an organized view of important parameters in linguistic ecology. The four dimensions are derived from the Bühlerian

---

[29] At this point, considerations on language systems can be followed up. Language systems are also higher cognitive-cultural constructs that are realized and changed on the level of discourse. Questions concerning for example macro systems of each language in e.g. Anglo-, Franco- and Hispanophony are part of the level of macro-ecology. These questions have lately gained importance in research, as for example the search for *Angloversals* (Szmrecsanyi and Kortmann 2009).

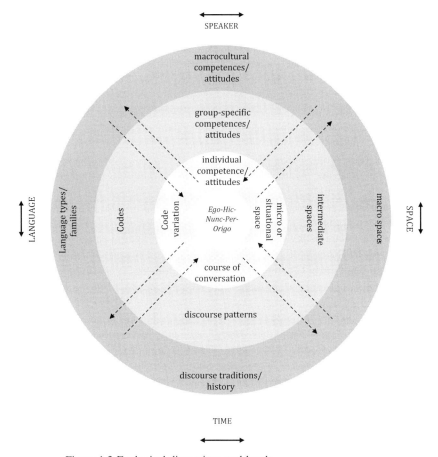

Figure 1.2 Ecological dimensions and levels

Ego-Hic-Nunc Origo,[30] completed by a fourth element covering the medium or media of communication (labelled with the Latin instrumental preposition *per*). Since communication and language systems are considered to be dynamic and open in our framework, phenomena such as language variation, choice, and hybridization are not confined to the study of language contact but are deemed to be crucial to any language's ecology. The *Ego-Hic-Nunc-Per Origo* provides a useful point of orientation throughout the complex structure of language ecologies: it is the speaker's point of departure in any utterance and thus embodies the fundamental structure of linguistic ecology. Ecological

[30] *Origo* is the reference point on which deictic relationships are based. In deictic systems, the origo typically coincides with the current speaker.

linguistic research can locate the principal subject of its studies and correlate it to various levels, from the micro to the macro perspective, along the four basic dimensions of language ecologies: *Speaker* (in accord with the *Ego*-part of the Origo), *Space* (*Hic*), *Time* (*Nunc*), and *Language* (*Per*).[31]

Note that both the three major levels and the horizontal and vertical foundations from the three-level model in Schema 1 are maintained. The apparently discrete borders between the three levels should be understood as a graphical tool that is supposed to help comprehend a complex, four-dimensional universe reduced to a flat, two-dimensional model. In general, one must think of the space between the levels and dimensions as one of transitions. The arrows in Schema 2 indicate again relations of foundation. These are considered to be potentially bidirectional, although they must not necessarily be realized in both, or in either of the two directions. For example, discourse patterns (as a category) are typically founded on the micro-level, i.e. in concrete verbal interactions, manifesting themselves in the *Time*-dimension as courses of conversation. The sum of all courses of conversation continuously constitutes discourse patterns and, potentially in the long run, discourse traditions. As will be shown in several contributions of this volume, many societies in contact constellations develop hybrid communication strategies as new discourse patterns.

We can therefore say that a single course of conversation *can* be founded in the category of discourse patterns as it depends on a discourse pattern for its existence (and vice versa). However, not every course of conversation *necessarily* represents or constitutes discourse patterns. It is also conceivable that a particular course of conversation reveals no foundation in any established discourse pattern and will also not constitute a new one, given that it is only ephemeral. Its sole raison d'être could be to solve an immediate communicational problem, as in multilingual contact situations or in unstable pidgin situations.[32] In more general words: the arrows in schema 2 can be understood as questions for possible relations of foundation.

According to this model, various ecological parameters are situated on three different levels and in four different dimensions.[33] Before going into the details of these dimensions, a general epistemological aspect of this model can be emphasized: it allows the localization and integration of different linguistic disciplines within an ecological framework, and is in so far the direct continuation of Haugen's call for a multidisciplinary approach to language

[31] Cf. the composite ecological factor *timespace* in Mufwene and Vigouroux (2012).
[32] For different degrees of foundation of the three main levels, see the comparison of 'teaching discourses' in Mauritius and New Delhi in Kriegel, Ludwig, and Salzmann (Chapter 7, this volume).
[33] An interesting list of contact parameters is provided by Hinskens, Auer, and Kerswill (2005); it could be easily related to Figure 1.2.

(i.e., the perspectives of structural–empirical linguistics, sociolinguistics and sociology, historical linguistics and historic-cultural investigations through to several cognitive disciplines can be combined).

SPEAKER *(*Ego*)*: *Language* is first and foremost the speaking and processing of language and the linguistic action of a speaker in a particular situation, in which his specific competences, attitudes/values, and intentions are involved.[34] On the next level, linguistic choices also depend on the speaker's association with (or dissociation from) social groups and, in turn, can contribute to the constitution of groups. The individuals' as well as the groups' (self-) perception and identitary projection can function by mobilizing and combining certain specific parameters. Groups, from smaller social groups to complete societies, are often characterized by the sharing of specific language competences. Such linguistic competences can allow access to macrocultures or constitute them, for example the *Francophony*.

TIME *(*Nunc*)*: This dimension encompasses first and foremost the emerging time of the utterance (see Hopper 1988) and the temporal–deictic orientation of the speaker on this occasion. It is in reference to the higher levels that the so-called calendar time becomes important. In more or less short periods of time, copies can become conventionalized, types of interaction, discourse traditions, etc. can become stable (Wilhelm 2001; Gadet, Ludwig, and Pfänder 2009). A macro-timespan can be constituted through historical patterns of events, such as *la Francophonie* in the course of the colonial expansion of France between the seventeenth and twentieth centuries.

SPACE *(*Hic*)*: Consistent with Haugen's account, the elementary meaning of *space* in our model refers to the physical space surrounding the given speech situation. On the next level (e.g. in the urban space of Cairo) speakers oscillate between different social groups (French-speaking bourgeoisie, Arabic-speaking workers) and interactional types (private informal talks, working coordination), as articulated by Mondada (2009). On the macro level one can find large interactive spaces (intra- and intercontinental) linked by parameters like common history, language, mobility, or migration.

LANGUAGE *(*Per*)*: Instead of *language*, we speak of *code* on the two lower levels in order to leave open the questions of whether and on what grounds the division of linguistic expression into discrete dialects, languages, and the like is possible and to include hybrid communication in linguistic analyses. On the highest level, and in correspondence with the parameter *history* in the *Time*-dimension, we accept the postulation of historically stabilized individual languages without, however, excluding hybrid communication within and across these languages.

[34] For the importance of linguistic attitudes in contact situations, see for example, Díaz, Ludwig, and Pfänder (2002).

By definition, a model can never cover *all* parameters at work in the processes or entities it is supposed to illustrate. We assembled in our model what we consider to be *significant parameters* at each level for each dimension. In accordance with our postulates above (especially postulate 2) we cannot offer a fixed set of parameters and no universal method for an ecological investigation of language and language contact. We assume that from a theoretically indefinitely large number of parametes only some become active, and of these only some become dominant in a specific contact situation at a given time. It is conceivable that some parameters are active in many or even all contact situations at any time (like, for example, the sociocultural pressure exerted by one group on the other), but still their level of dominance will vary. It will vary according to many different factors, if nothing else depending on the phenomena studied by the linguist (in one and the same contact situation, for instance, sociocultural pressure could be a less important parameter if the object of investigation is code alternation and not code shift). Therefore, individual ecological linguistic studies will emphasize varying selections of particularly relevant parameters, in accordance with the studied ecosystem and the specific perspective of investigation.[35]

1.4   The Present Volume

In this introductory chapter we have surveyed the history and main streams of ecological approaches to language and language contact in order to provide, in a second step, the theoretical groundwork for the volume. We have proposed a reformulation of the linguistic ecology paradigm that is based on two key concepts of Edmund Husserl's philosophy, represented by the terms *wholes–parts* and *foundation*. These concepts offer the most abstract and open possibility for an understanding of linguistic ecology as a multilevel system of reciprocal dependencies. A model of linguistic ecology was introduced that builds on these concepts and connects individual communicative situations with abstract socio-historical, cultural, cognitive, and structural linguistic frames. The contributions following this chapter for the most part apply this theoretical framework to specific objects of linguistic investigation, and/or deepen certain aspects of the framework. This volume's part-titles (see the Contents pages) in part refer to the dimensions laid out in the last paragraph. They indicate primarily thematic priorities and orientations and are not supposed to make a strict separation.

---

[35] To give a simple example: the parameter *discourse traditions* can be extended without difficulty to other types of actions, whose procedures are rooted in cultural or societal conventions and traditions, e.g. the 'types d'activités interactionnelles' described in Gadet, Ludwig, and Pfänder (2009).

In the second contribution to this volume, Françoise Gadet and Steve Pagel widen the theoretical reflections to a discussion of the notion of *natural* in linguistics. Departing from the observation that this notion has played a key role in Western linguistic thought from the very beginning, they address the metaphorical weight of the term *natural* when it is applied to linguistics, as well as some philosophical foundations of such applications. Central in this chapter is a discussion of the two most important interpretations of this term: in the first, *natural* refers to a condition of linguistic data that is considered to be 'ideal' for linguistic analysis. The authors show that views concerning this condition have varied in the history of linguistics and from one field of research to another. In the second interpretation, *natural* refers to linguistic features, processes, and trends found in and across languages. *Natural* in this interpretation has been an essential notion for example in research on language change, language contact, vernacular universals, markedness, natural morphology, and optimality theory. Gadet and Pagel search for and discuss the precise meaning of *natural* in these fields of research and provide suggestions concerning the semantics and use of this notion in ecological linguistics.

Part II of the book is concerned with the ecology of the dimensions *Speaker* and *Space*. These contributions focus on the situational and the intermediate space, as well as the relation between these two levels, considering also the possible mutual foundations in the parameters *code* and *competence*.

The first contribution, by Lorenza Mondada, offers a conceptualization and empirical demonstration of what an ecological and 'naturalistic' approach can mean when dealing with social interaction. One central question she investigates is how the embodied and material space of an interaction and the way in which it is made relevant by the actions of the participants can structure that interaction and bear on future interactions of the participants. The emphasis on the ecology of interaction (as a micro-level space) is reflected in a methodology that aims at collecting and studying *ecological data*. Her empirical data thus covers both audio and video recordings as well as texts, all collected during a brainstorming session of a participatory democracy project in France. Mondada regards the turns in the talk she recorded at that meeting not just as forms, which can be subjected to a grammatical analysis, but as actions (proposals) that were produced and addressed in a situated way by referring to the relevant features of the local ecology: the institutional context, the spatial and material environment, and the participation framework, which shape not only their adequacy and their reception in this setting but the very way in which they are assembled.

In Chapter 4, Juan Carlos Godenzzi shifts the focus towards the intermediate level of the model proposed in this introductory chapter by dealing with what we have called here an intermediate ecology. He demonstrates how linguistic spaces, seen not only as physical space but also as relationship networks, are created in the urban ecology of the Peruvian capital Lima. One important insight is that higher levels of space are not only constituted physically but are also founded in sociocultural concepts or entities. Godenzzi identifies specific language properties (mixing, variation, and stability) and urbanity properties (density, diversity, and mobility) and takes into account the Spanish spoken by three people living in three different areas of Lima. He argues that a description of the relations between these properties will allow us to understand the ways in which the systemic composition of a language is arranged and the ways in which language takes part in urban dynamics.

Part III of the book focuses on the ecology of the dimensions *Space* and *Time* up to the macro-level, and thus pursues what is traditionally called a historical or diachronic perspective. It is argued here that personal interactions can be founded in macro-ecologies, which are the result of long-term historical traditions.

In Chapter 5, Cyril Aslanov shows how contemporary interactional strategies can be fully understood against the background of a macro-ecological, historical description. He opens a wide and enlightening perspective on the constitution, adaptation, and maintenance of the Francophone element in the Levantine macro-ecology from the twelfth to the twenty-first century, providing numerous examples from Arabic, Greek, and Armenian-speaking areas. In the course of these reflections, Aslanov also considers the contact between French and other Romance languages (such as Italo-Romance and Judeo-Spanish) in the Levant, to make an interesting claim: the languages in contact in a macro-system are not necessarily endogenous languages. They may have been transplanted to that ecology, like Western languages were transplanted to the Levant. In the latter case, the linguistic ecosystem of the Eastern Mediterranean functioned as a meeting point between languages that would not have come into contact with each other in their Western Mediterranean homeland. Next to the mutual interaction between Western languages transplanted to the Levant, each of them underwent a process of Levantinization due to the intensive contact with local languages (Arabic, Greek, and Turkish to mention the most commonly spoken).

In Chapter 6, Silke Jansen revisits the complex changes caused by the introduction of Spanish to the Caribbean macro-ecology, focusing especially on changes of naming systems on Hispaniola, Cuba, and Puerto Rico. She starts with the observation that the early Spanish settlements in the Greater Antilles had a dramatic impact not only on the habitat and social structure of the indigenous people, but also on the way of life of the Spanish settlers. Both parties had to adapt to changing environmental conditions, which lead to the emergence of new forms of social organization, and of linguistic behaviour. Regarding anthroponomy, personal names of Antillean natives did not only stand for individual human beings but also related these human beings to ecologically meaningful entities such as other individuals, functions within the social group, and their locations. Jansen argues, on an empirical basis, that in the Spanish-speaking Caribbean, geographic displacement and language contact have led to the emergence of a new naming system which particularly reflected the social ecology of the *encomienda* system.

The focus of Part IV is the ecology of *Language* from the perspective of how a language is appropriated by new speakers in a novel space. A crucial topic of this part of the book is the *hybridization* of code and discourse. The term *hybridization* is used here in a generic sense, covering all kinds of structural contact phenomena.

In Chapter 7, Sibylle Kriegel, Ralph Ludwig, and Tabea Salzmann argue that a scalar approach to phenomena of contact-induced language change has many advantages over approaches based on binary terms. In their analysis of language contact phenomena in two traditionally multilingual regions – Mauritius and Northern India – they use an elaborate model of *code-copying* rather than the traditional categories *code-mixing* and *code-switching*. From a corpus covering authentic oral conversation from both regions they extract different types of *code alternation* and *code copying*. Kriegel, Ludwig, and Salzmann highlight the role of hybridization as a communicative resource with identity-marking, text-structuring, and other functions. Within this theoretical and empirical frame, they underscore the importance of scalar terms such as *conventionalization* and *structural integration*.

In Chapter 8, Anne Schröder and Philip W. Rudd illustrate the correlations between language contact, variation, and urban ecology. The authors discuss the structures and sociolinguistic environments of two hybrid codes spoken in the urban centres of Cameroon and Kenya, respectively: Camfranglais and Sheng. The linguistic origins of both hybrid codes can be traced genetically to different language (sub)families and different macro-ecologies. Schröder and Rudd argue that, on a scale from situational copying to conventionalized copies (see Chapter 7, this volume), these codes have proceeded far towards the latter pole. Camfranglais and Sheng are interpreted as results of linguistic choices that are governed by specific social and discourse–pragmatic parameters within complex ecologies. In these ecologies, they fill ecological niches.

Chapter 9, by Cynthia Dermarkar, Françoise Gadet, Ralph Ludwig, and Stefan Pfänder describes the French of Cairo as part of a Levantine tradition and macro-ecology. The authors discuss macro-ecological aspects such as historically developed social identities and linguistic attitudes down to specific phenomena of discourse such as pronunciation, and thereby emphasize the permanent interrelation of macro- and micro-ecological levels. Their analysis of present-day conversations involving French in Cairo reveals that the changing political and social conditions in a globalizing world have also caused the traditional ecology to change: while traditional conversations held in French often tend to orient themselves towards a 'pure' usage of the language, types of hybridization and their productive multifunctionality now become manifest.

In the last contribution of Part IV, Steve Pagel deals with some theoretical problems of contact linguistics and their impact on studies of the historical contact situation between Spanish and the Austronesian language Chamorro on the Mariana Islands. After examining the theoretical foundations of the *new/ mixed language* type and its difficult relation to the family tree model of genetic relationship, Pagel compiles heterogeneous contact-typological evaluations of Modern Chamorro, in which classifications in and beyond several categories of this type (e.g. pidgin, creole, mixed language) have been proposed. He analyses the underlying methods as well as individual problems of these evaluations and demonstrates how non-ecological analysis and the use of 'non-natural' data (in the sense of Gadet and Pagel, Chapter 2) have led to very questionable judgments. An alternative classification of Modern Chamorro is proposed that is guided by an ecology-sensitive analysis of the Spanish–Chamorro contact situation and based on 'natural' data. Tying in with the ideas expressed in Kriegel, Ludwig, and Salzmann (Chapter 7), this classification is made within an essentially continuous model of contact-induced change (as laid out in Pagel 2015).

The book closes with Part V, titled 'The multiplicity of ecological parameters: echoing the theoretical frame and going beyond'. It links a large number of ecological parameters from structural language phenomena to environmental and societal conditions and, in so doing, also addresses methodological aspects of the question of how the complexity of ecologies can be dealt with in practical ecological linguistic work. It completes the present volume with discussions of issues arising from this introductory, theoretical chapter, fathoming the relation between theory and practice, and assessing the approaches and solutions proposed, including his own.

In the first of his two contributions, Peter Mühlhäusler emphasizes that the way linguists conceive of languages, language contact, and typology is shaped fundamentally by non-structural aspects such as professional traditions, practices, and shared metaphors. He argues that linguistics does not meet the requirements to be a science in the strict sense since even its most basic concepts and terms are often not reliable, statements often not falsifiable, and linguists themselves play a major role in 'making' the entities studied by them (i.e., languages). This is illustrated in an examination of three typological properties (pronouns, spatial orientation grammar, and categorical multifunctionality) as they appear in two contact languages (Tok Pisin and Pitkern-Norf'k) and in the grammars of the languages that were involved in their formation. Major insights gained from this examination are that generalizations across grammars are not warranted, that observationally adequate description requires many years of observation, and that the shape of contact languages is determined more by the cultural and natural ecology in which they are spoken than by the grammars of the languages involved in their formation.

Mühlhäusler's second contribution is dedicated to the theory and practice of language planning, which enables him to bridge ecological linguistic theory and possible practices. The question he asks is: under what circumstances can policies become part of the ecological support system that strengthens endangered languages? Mühlhäusler gives a number of positive examples from his own work and questions some important notions that underlie most other language-planning programs, such as the most basic notion of *a language* as something independent from other representations of social and cultural semiotics that could be reduced non-arbitrarily to a closed system. After giving an outline of the main discourses on language planning (the scientific, economic, moral and aesthetic discourse), the remainder of the chapter addresses the question of how one can actually go about developing ecological language planning. The proposed strategy is one that aims at the maintenance of linguistic diversity, the restoration of functional links between different languages and the embedding of languages in a meaningful cultural, economic, and ecological context. It is one that focuses on practical work and requires long-term commitment.

2　On the Notion of *Natural* in Ecological Linguistics

Françoise Gadet and Steve Pagel

> The notion of 'naturalness' is widely found in linguistic writings, although it is often used in an ill-defined way.
>
> (Mühlhäusler 1986: 60)

2.1　Introduction

A revision of the notions *ecology* and *environment* in linguistics also brings to our view a conception that, although it has been used since the very beginning of Western linguistics thought, deserves special attention in an ecological linguistics framework: the conception of *natural* or *naturalness* (from Latin *natura*; see also Greek *physis*). Thus, the question discussed in Plato's dialogue *Cratylus*, one of the earliest testimonies of linguistics thought in the Western hemisphere, is precisely whether objects get their names by '(inner) nature' (Gr. *physis*) or 'convention' (*nomos* or *thesis*). From the formal-logical treatment of language by Aristotle, through the speculative grammars of Medieval Europe, the Cartesian linguistics of the Port Royal school, the natural-scientific approaches of historical linguistics and Neogrammarians, to the universalistic approaches of Noam Chomsky and Joseph Greenberg – the search for the *nature* of language, for its undistorted essence has always been a primary concern of linguistics. Although non-universalistic approaches to language such as sociolinguistics, ethnolinguistics, or ecolinguistics often (and sometimes instinctively) deny the importance or even existence of *natural* features of languages in the sense laid out by the approaches mentioned, they cannot avoid their own usage of the term in contexts like *natural data* or the *natural environment* of a language.[1] Since the ecological linguistic framework

---

[1] The distinction between *universalistic* and *non-universalistic approaches* made here should be understood as a tool for broad classification, not as a strict theoretical distinction. While the universalistic approaches mentioned are interested primarily in universal tendencies in language structures and for that matter neglect variation and variability, non-universalistic approaches focus precisely on this variation and variability. However, the ultimate goal of the latter is also to reveal the 'universal' trends behind or in this variability.

proposed in this volume highlights awareness to the metaphors and analogies linguistic theory and description build on, it is obvious that the notion of *natural* must be addressed here in a chapter of its own.

A first important observation in this respect is that the notion of *natural* in linguistics lacks the self-understanding it has in the physical sciences. This is because linguistics is not a physical science (as to whether it is a true science at all, see Mühlhäusler in Chapter 11) since its objects of investigation do not, as such, inhabit the physical world. *Languages, dialects, sentences, words, language contact, linguistic attitudes*, etc. are human conceptions, constructs, abstractions, or implications of facts observed in everyday life. This, of course, holds in principle for all elements of human knowledge, including physical elements such as *molecules, atoms, electrons, planets*, or *continents*. In fact, as Alfred Schütz summarizes the view of many thinkers in the tradition he subscribes to:

> All our knowledge of the world, in common-sense as well as in scientific thinking, involves constructs, namely, a set of abstractions, generalizations, formalizations, idealizations specific to the respective level of thought organization. Strictly speaking, there are no such things as facts, pure and simple. All facts are from the outset facts selected from a universal context by the activities of our mind. (1953: 2)

But a major difference between the natural and the social sciences is revealed when we look at the structure of the fields they observe and investigate:

> It is up to the natural scientist to determine which sector of the universe of nature, which facts and events therein, and which aspects of such facts and events are topically and interpretationally relevant to their specific purposes. These facts and events are neither preselected nor preinterpreted; they do not reveal intrinsic relevance structures. Relevance is not inherent in nature as such; it is the result of the selective and interpretative activity of man within nature or observing nature. The facts, data, and events with which the natural scientist has to deal are just facts, data, and events within this observational field but this field does not 'mean' anything to the molecules, atoms, and electrons therein. (ibid.: 3)

The social scientist, on the other hand, has before him an observational field that is neither principally unstructured nor meaningless to the facts observed in that field:

> It has a particular meaning and relevance structure for the human beings living, thinking, and acting therein. They have preselected and preinterpreted this world by a series of common-sense constructs of the reality of daily life and it is these thought objects which determine their behaviour, define the goal of their action, the means available for attaining them – in brief, which help them to find their bearing within their natural and socio-cultural environment and to come to terms with it. (ibid.)

Unlike the natural world, the social world is characterized by inherent *relevance structures*. Whether the facts observed in the natural world are called this or that, or are investigated one way or another, is irrelevant for these facts. But whether certain linguistic facts as part of the social world are analysed as belonging, for example, to a *language* or a *dialect* is of relevance for the social beings dealing with these facts and therefore affects the facts themselves. In short, the social scientists' decisions, their constructs, or thought objects always interact with and exert influence on the observation field (which is a thought object itself), while the natural scientists' do not.

Furthermore, facts from the social world never *immediately* affect the physical world, while the latter provides the ultimate basis of the first and therefore always affects it immediately. This may be illustrated by relating ecological perspectives in the physical sciences and in linguistics to one another: in the physical world any given set-up of facts can be said to belong to a specific ecosystem so that any minor change in this set-up will provoke changes in the ecosystem. These changes may also trigger other changes in human social and cultural ecosystems (see e.g. the so-called Sapir–Whorf hypothesis). The ecological linguistic perspective assumes a similar connection between changes of set-ups and changes of linguistic ecologies, which is settled in larger sociocultural ecologies. But none of the two assumes that the change of any linguistic set-up, at least not from the phonetic level up, will *immediately* affect the non-human physical environment. Obviously, human attitude and behaviour towards the physical environment can affect the way humans treat that environment (a basic assumption of what in Chapter 1 of this volume is presented as *ecolinguistics*); but it will never immediately affect that environment if, for example, people speak Spanish or French, if they speak either of the two 'correctly' or not, if they copy into Spanish from English or Quechua or not at all, if the code used is predominantly agglutinating or inflectional, or if its basic word order is SVO or VSO. Linguistics, thus, concerns the social, not the physical sciences.[2]

The notion of *natural* in linguistic contexts therefore involves the application of a metaphor. This metaphor suggests that linguistic facts, events, or structures can be more or less similar to facts, events, and structures observed by natural scientists in the physical world. It is part of a larger set of metaphors and analogies used in linguistics which we could call, following Lakoff and Johnson (1980), a *conceptual metaphor*, according to which 'linguistic entities are physical entities'. Like all social sciences, linguistics depends heavily on metaphors and analogies in order to visualize the facts and events in its observational field. Furthermore, the metaphors and analogies used in linguistics are heavily reliant on historical traditions: the life metaphor at the heart

[2] A noteworthy exception is phonetics in a narrow sense: sounds, intonation, and the like are thought objects in the natural world. Whether linguistics can be a mathematical science, as is proposed e.g. by generative grammarians, is a different issue.

of the genetic classification of languages, for one, is a direct heritage of historical–comparative linguistics in the nineteenth century.[3] But as in all social sciences, and as explained above, the observational field itself and the facts and events therein are affected by the structure these metaphors and analogies imply. Although this can hardly ever be prevented, it is imperative for linguists to uphold a reflective attitude with regard to the metaphors and analogies used. It is often forgotten that metaphors and analogies are not evidence for anything, but that they are just that: metaphors and analogies, and their function is merely to visualize.

After this brief discussion of the metaphorical significance of the term *natural* in linguistics, we will discuss two of the most important interpretations of this term in this science. The first regards the quality of data, it is most relevant in the non-universalistic approaches to language such as conversation analysis, sociolinguistics, and ecological linguistics. The second interpretation regards features and trends that are assumed to be natural in a broad sense (distinguished from non-natural) in and across languages. This interpretation is more popular in the universalistic approaches, but it is not restricted to these. We will discuss the sources, developments, and applications of the two major interpretations of *natural* in linguistics and make some suggestions regarding the semantics and use of the notion of *natural* in an ecological linguistic framework.

2.2   'Natural' Data

It seems obvious that 'language simply does not exist but as part of the human condition, hence we cannot even begin to study it without referring to a human being' (Coulmas 1981: 2). Obvious as it may be, not all approaches to language have been interested in its human aspects. Outside of the more universalistic approaches, the term *natural* is encountered, above all, in conversation analysis, sociolinguistics, and ecological linguistics, where it refers to a specific type of data and data analysis.[4] Here, the property of *naturalness* is typically assigned to data that is considered to be representative for unmonitored interactions, therefore relevant for linguistics analysis, and to those techniques of analysis that give most justification to the naturalness of the data obtained.[5] Data of this kind are often labelled 'natural speech', 'naturally

---

[3] See Pagel (2018) on how the application of this metaphor contributed significantly to the emergence of the contact linguistic paradigm in the late 19th century.

[4] Ethnomethodology and conversation analysis probably influenced sociolinguistics on this point. Interestingly, none of the dictionaries of sociolinguistics consulted (Moreau 1997; Duranti 2001; Chambers, Trudgill and Schilling-Estes 2002) contain specific entries on data (except for methodological considerations on field techniques) or the basic criteria that corpora are required to meet.

[5] Other applications of *natural* include e.g. language learning.

occurring interactions', 'natural communication settings', or 'naturalistically observed' and may even include interviews in which an attempt is made to make the interviewee feel comfortable (sometimes called 'sociolinguistic interviews';[6] see Sankoff and Sankoff 1973 for the first survey concerning Montreal French). What precisely is meant by *natural*, then, varies from one research area to another and across authors. Referring to the conversation analysis approach to data collection, Mondada (2013c) provides a more narrow localization and useful delimitation (see also Chapter 3, this volume):

CA [Conversation Analysis] insists on the study of *naturally occurring activities* as they ordinarily unfold in social settings, and, consequently, on the necessity of recordings of actual situated activities for a detailed analysis and their relevant endogenous order. This analytic stance contrasts with other ways of collecting data in the social and cognitive sciences. (33, italics original)

These other ways include, for example, introspection (where the researcher's own competence is the main source of data), field notes gained from participant observation, interviews, and experiments (ibid.).

Thus, CA aims to discover the natural living order of social activities as they are endogenously organized in ordinary life, without the exogenous intervention of researchers imposing topics and tasks or displacing the context of action. (ibid.: 34)

Important conceptual roots of this naturalistic perspective can be seen in Edmund Husserl's phenomenology and Alfred Schütz's sociology of everyday life.[7] In 'The crisis of European sciences and transcendental philosophy' (first published in German in 1954), Husserl develops the concept of the *life-world* (*Lebenswelt*) as the unreflected, pre-theoretical, and pre-scientific world of everyday experience and action. It is the lived world, the taken-for-granted, pre-given world of experience, both subjective and intersubjective, the background, constantly in motion, on which all things appear as being and meaningful. It is in this context, before this background and on this ground that science, theoretical and philosophical practice developed, that is presupposed by these practices, and to which these practices cannot but refer:

[T]he everyday surrounding world of life is presupposed as existing – the surrounding world in which all of us (even I who am now philosophizing) consciously have our existence; here are also the sciences, as cultural facts in this world, with their scientists and theories. In this world we are objects among objects in the sense of the life-world, namely, as being here and there, in the plain certainty of experience, before anything

---

[6] This is, to our knowledge, the only occasion in social sciences where data are characterized according to the scientific objectives of the researchers.

[7] This is also pointed out by Mondada (2013c: 34): 'the term [natural] is not used in order to oppose "social" vs. "natural" conduct, but rather refers to what Schütz (1962) and phenomenology call the *natural attitude*: a pre-reflexive posture that characterizes ordinary life as it is seen by people in a fluent, spontaneous way, without calculations or reflexive deliberations. Thus, "natural" refers to the practices themselves prior to the collecting of data.'

that is established scientifically, whether in physiology, psychology, or sociology. On the other hand, we are subjects for this world, namely, as the ego-subjects experiencing it, contemplating it, valuing it, related to it purposefully; for us this surrounding world has only the ontic meaning given to it by our experiencings, our thoughts, our valuations, etc.; and it has the modes of validity (certainty of being, possibility, perhaps illusion, etc.) which we, as the subjects of validity, at the same time bring about or also possess from earlier on as habitual acquisitions and bear within us as validities of such and such a content which we can reactualize at will. To be sure, all this undergoes manifold alterations, whereas 'the' world, as existing in a unified way, persists throughout, being corrected only in its content. (Husserl 1970: 104–105)[8]

The *life-world* can be made thematic in two fundamental ways, the first being the naive and natural straightforward attitude (*naiv-natürliche Gemeinhinein-stellung*), and the second a consistently reflective, or phenomenological attitude:

The *natural attitude* is the focus we have when we are involved in our original, world-directed stance, when we intend things, situations, facts, and any other kinds of objects. The natural attitude is, we might say, the default perspective, the one we start off from, the one we are in originally. We do not move into it from anything more basic. The *phenomenological attitude*, on the other hand, is the focus we have when we reflect upon the natural attitude and all the intentionalities that occur within it. It is within the phenomenological attitude that we carry our philosophical analyses. (Sokolowski 2000: 42)

Alfred Schütz takes over these concepts of Husserl and develops a philosophy of the social sciences in which the natural attitude, or – in his terms – the 'common sense' that implies such an attitude, takes a central role. Husserl's conception of *foundation*, which is given a prominent position in the theoretical framework of the present volume, is also applied by Schütz in explaining the relation between common sense and scientific thinking:

The thought objects constructed by the social scientists refer to and are founded upon the thought objects constructed by the common-sense thought of man living his everyday life among his fellowmen. Thus, the constructs used by the social sciences are, so to speak, constructs of the second degree, namely constructs of the constructs made by the actors on the social scene whose behavior the scientist observes and tries to explain in accordance with the procedural rules of his science. (Schütz 1953: 3)

The social scientist's task is, thus, to focus in his/her analysis on everyday life, on common-sense experience and subjective interpretation. His/her role is that

---

[8] See also Husserl (1970: 130–131): 'The knowledge of the objective-scientific world is "grounded" in the self-evidence of the life-world. The latter is pregiven to the scientific worker, or the working community, as ground; yet, as they build upon this, what is built is something new, something different. If we cease being immersed in our scientific thinking, we become aware that we scientists are, after all, human beings and as such are among the components of the life-world which always exists for us, ever pregiven; and thus all of science is pulled, along with us, into the – merely "subjective-relative" – life-world.'

of a 'disinterested observer' of the social world, in which s/he is, during his/her analysis, not involved and within which s/he does not act:

[W]e take the position that the social sciences have to deal with human conduct and its common-sense interpretation in the social reality, involving the analysis of the whole system of projects and motives, or relevances and constructs ... Such an analysis refers by necessity to the subjective point of view, namely, to the interpretation of the action and its settings in terms of the actor. Since this postulate of the subjective interpretation is ... a general principle of constructing course-of-action types in common-sense experience, any social science aspiring to grasp 'social reality' has to adopt this principle, also. (ibid.: 27)

Schütz's distinction between natural and social sciences is abstract and rather one of prototypes, and can therefore be problematic in actual cases. To which realm, for example, would psychology or neurobiology belong? Nevertheless, the distinction is legitimate because it proved to be fruitful in terms of a prototypical/scalar heuristics. Schütz's philosophy, building on Husserl's thoughts, has inspired to a large extent ethnomethodology and conversation analysis, not least in the conception of *natural* that is under scrutiny in this section.

Various other terms have been used as alternatives to or near-equivalents of *natural* in the approaches mentioned and in sociolinguistics. These include *real*, as in 'real-world data' or 'real-life interaction' (see, e.g., the title of Milroy and Milroy 1993); *authentic* (Coupland 2003, 2007, 2010), in opposition to *commodified*; *direct, unmediated, unplanned* (see Ochs 1979), or *attested*. Other adjectives to be found, that add social values, are *mundane, casual, ordinary*, and *spontaneous*. These terms are seldom defined or even explicitly considered to be objects of discussion, with some exceptions such as Miller and Weinert (1998), or a special issue of the French journal *Revue française de linguistique appliquée*, entitled 'L'oral spontané' (Bilger 1999). In this respect, it is informative to visit Forlot and Eloy (2010), and Miller and Weinert (1998: 22), who define *spontaneous* with five properties: (1) real time, impromptu, with no opportunity for editing; (2) limitations of short-term memory; (3) face-to-face interaction in particular contexts; (4) involvement of pitch, amplitude, rhythm, and voice quality; and (5) accompaniment of gestures, eye-gaze, facial expressions, and body postures. One could add to this list other adjectives that are rarely attested in the linguistic literature, such as *true, pure, faithful, accurate*, and *genuine*, as well as other terms copied from social sciences, such as *contextualized* or *situated*.

These different terms point to different descriptive or cognitive approaches, whose links can be established by investigating the context of their emergence in the respective disciplines. In the following, we will focus on some important assignments of meaning to the terms *natural, authentic*, and *ordinary* (used as synonyms for that purpose) in sociolinguistics and other disciplines.

2.2.1   *Everyday Life and Relevant Data*

In order to become fruitful for linguistics, the philosophical preliminaries laid out in the previous section must be followed by methodological and practical considerations. These concern the selection of speakers, media, registers, and other aspects, according to their being perceived. This selection has varied in the history of linguistics and across disciplines.

Linguistic data vary in a number of dimensions, of which for instance space, social attributes, and register/style are covered in the so-called diasystem of language (as diatopic, diastratic, and diaphasic variation). To these we can add media, age, speech situation, and many others. A trivial, though important observation is that not all available data of a language or code (or members of a speech community in the Labovian sense) can be considered in linguistic analysis. Therefore, the linguist must decide which data to favour. These decisions are always made on the basis of theoretical presuppositions, a phenomenon described in the philosophy of science as the *theory-ladenness of observation*. This means that there is no 'pure', objective observation that could serve as the initial step of theory formation; instead all observation is inherently selective and theory-laden (see e.g. Popper 1935; Kuhn 1970; Feyerabend 1993). The theoretical presuppositions, in turn, reflect at least in part the temporary relevance structure of the social world (of which language is a part), and, together with the linguists' decisions, at the same time act on this structure.

From the very beginning and for most of its history, Western linguistics has preferred data with attributes like [+written], [+formal register], [+central], [+standard], [+elite] over those with negative values or unmarked in these dimensions. The interest of linguists in spoken, informal, peripheral, non-standard, and non-elite language is relatively recent and refers to both intra- and extra-linguistic or sociocultural questions. Primarily intra-linguistic questions concern e.g. the role of vernaculars in language change and the way they reflect fundamental orientations towards social life (as shown e.g. in Labov's 1972 study of Martha's Vineyard, where different orientations to life on the island are reflected in the degree of centralization of two diphthongs). We will deal with some of these questions in section 2.3. Primarily sociocultural questions lie at the heart of sociolinguistics and other non-universalistic approaches to language such as ecolinguistics (i.e., ecological linguistics as it was practised mainly in the 1980s/1990s).[9]

Several factors played a role in this discovery of everyday life as a relevant database for linguistic analysis. New technologies are one, as recording data with the attributes mentioned was difficult or even impossible

---

[9] For the relation between sociolinguistics and ecological linguistics see Gadet et al. (2009).

before the 1950s. But technological progress is rather a minor factor here, as can be seen from the fact that 'ordinary' written vernacular data were also discovered quite recently as a relevant source, although they have been there all the time.[10] New philosophical and sociological perspectives, such as Husserl's and Schütz's laid out above, were most decisive in this process and influenced many different disciplines in the humanities. We can actually speak of the social sciences' 'discovery' of the agency of 'ordinary' social agents, taking place around the mid-twentieth century. This 'discovery' is well known for sociology and ethnomethodology (exemplarily Garfinkel 1967, a student of Schütz's), but probably less so for other disciplines such as history. Instructive in the latter observation is, for instance, the title selected by the historian Michel de Certeau (1980) 'L'invention du quotidian'. An example from the history of language is Lodge (2004, 2010), who shows the role of everyday life in the history of French: Lodge contrasts a traditional language historiography built on the data produced by the written, literary language of 'authorities' with what can be reconstructed of the way 'ordinary' language used to be spoken by 'ordinary' people in 'ordinary' settings.

The shift of relevance with regard to the medium (from written to spoken) requires new strategies of data collection. Focusing on written language, collection consists primarily of consulting archives and libraries. In this case, data selection has been made by chroniclers and other writers and requires little, if any, agency by the researching linguist (who, in most cases, will be happy if there are documents at all or not all documents are lost). Focusing on spoken language, in turn, requires immersion in a community and the conscious selection of informants, places, speech situations, registers, etc. – all decisions being made by the investigator, who for this matter relies on recognized methods of data collection (most of which have been copied from disciplines such as anthropology and ethnography). In this case, speakers are considered as more than data suppliers: the linguist tries to understand his/her ways of thinking and strategies in discourse production.[11] Before discussing

---

[10] Similar processes can be stated for the 'discovery' of code-switching in the 1960s. As Myers-Scotton (1993: 48) puts it, a discipline can 'discover', name, and study phenomena although they have been frequently heard and even considered obvious before. This has to do with the ideological processes Irvine and Gal (2000) call 'erasure', when some linguistic differences are considered salient, while others are cognitively ironed out to the point where the representation of the language is drastically simplified by homogenization. One effect of these processes is the production of 'imagined communities' in the sense of Anderson (1983), as social constructions.

[11] See the role of an *insider* understanding (often referred to as *emic* – opposed to the *etic* view of the researcher), in 'being a member' (in ethnomethodology), or acting as a 'participant-observer' (in ethnography, and specifically for language in the ethnography of communication).

some of the methodological considerations made with respect to data collection, concerning the dimensions of *Speaker, Language*, and *Space* as laid out in Chapter 1 (this volume), let us note that the search for 'natural' data requires that linguists carefully examine all data available to them, and measure the impact of every choice made by them as investigators and by the scientific community.

2.2.2   *Whose Ways of Speaking?*

In the social world, pre-structured with regard to relevance, some speakers' data are considered more authentic than other speakers' data. Thus, the history of sociolinguistics is marked by frequent methodological discussions regarding who counts as a 'good informant'. A first relevance distinction is typically made between *non-native* and *native speakers* of a language (see Coulmas 1981 and Berruto 2003 on the difficult definition of the term, as well as that of *mother tongue*; and see Chapter 12 in this volume), the latter being considered more authentic than the first. Linguists seek to capture linguistic data and knowledge about languages from the more relevant level of native speakers.

Labov (1972) revisited the question of informant selection as it used to be practised in dialectology, where it was articulated qualitatively in terms of the extent to which selected informants may be considered representative of their communities. Some speakers were considered bearers of a 'naturally ideal' way of speaking, needing minimal or no reflexivity and social supervision. Criticizing this naturalistic approach on the basis of the so-called observer's paradox, and reflecting on how to bypass it in linguistic analysis, Labov (1972: 209) shifts the focus from speakers to situations of data collection. Traditionally, the representative speaker in dialectology was typically a NORM (Non-mobile Older Rural Male, see e.g. Meyerhoff 2006: 18),[12] but from Labov on, sociolinguistics has favoured the quest for vernacular data, or 'ordinarily' contextualized uses of language by 'ordinary' speakers in 'ordinary' settings (with the meaning of *ordinary* becoming almost equivalent to that of *natural* here). Authenticity has thus shifted from speakers and their social and local attributes to contexts of use, interaction, and linguistic resources.

---

[12] Coupland (2010) underscores the evolution from traditional dialectology with mainly folk values to urban sociolinguistics tied to linguistic change and modernity, if not always late modernity in a globalized world. The idea, shared by folklorists and ethnologists of everyday life, is that authenticity is protected in isolationism and minimal access to modernity (in particular users with no education, no mobility and thus the least possible contact). But see also Britain (2009) for a criticism of the opposition between rural and urban, as well as a review of the variationist approaches to space.

2.2.3   Which Ways of Speaking?

In addition to selecting informants as carriers of authentic or representative data, discussions around the term *vernacular* give an indication of what the main source or cause of differentiation in linguistic production could be. Calvet (1997) identifies two different applications of this term:[13]

> Si l'on s'en tient aux dictionnaires d'usage courant, une langue vernaculaire est tantôt une langue «domestique», tantôt une langue «indigène». Toutefois, ces deux adjectifs n'ont pas tout à fait le même sens. Si nous considérons que *vernaculaire* signifie «domestique», le terme s'oppose alors à véhiculaire, mais si vernaculaire signifie «indigène», alors vernaculaire s'oppose à étranger. (291–292)

> [If we stick to commonly used dictionaries, a vernacular language is sometimes described as a 'domestic' language, and sometimes as an 'indigenous' language. However, these two adjectives do not mean quite the same thing. If we consider that *vernacular* means 'domestic', the term is then opposed to vehicular, but if vernacular means 'indigenous', then vernacular is opposed to foreign. (our translation)]

The two meanings mentioned can overlap and are, without doubt, semantically related. In fact, the semantic scope of the term is even larger and stretches from the basic distinction mentioned by Calvet in at least five dimensions. Referring primarily to the semantic field of 'indigenous', *vernacular* contrasts with (a) an introduced contact variety, (b) a supraregional lingua franca, and (c) a supraregional standard variety. Focusing on the semantic field of 'domestic' or 'intimate', *vernacular* contrasts with (d) the formal registers of a variety and (e) the high variety in diglossic situations. *Vernacular data* according to the first semantic field, then, refers primarily to diatopic (from a certain location) and the second primarily to diaphasic dimensions (from 'ordinary' speakers in face-to-face interaction in 'ordinary' situations). Uses of the term corresponding to (a)–(e) are therefore distributed in a non-arbitrary fashion among different linguistic disciplines: *vernacular* with the semantic content of 'indigenous' (a–c) is preferred in general linguistics, contact linguistics, and dialectology while it is *vernacular* with the content of 'domestic' or 'intimate' (d–e) that is typically referred to by sociolinguists.

   In order to dispel the perceived imprecision of the concept, Calvet proposes to reserve the notion of *vernacular* to the second, that is

> à une langue utilisée dans le cadre des échanges informels entre proches du même groupe, comme par exemple dans le cadre familial, quelle que soit sa diffusion à l'extérieur de ce cadre (qu'elle soit ou non véhiculaire). (ibid.: 292)

---

[13]   See also Forlot and Eloy (2010) for *spontaneous*.

[a language used in the context of informal exchanges between relatives of the same group, such as among family members, whatever its distribution outside this framework may be (vehicular language or not). (our translation)]

Vernacular in this sense is too narrow a term to explain the notion of *natural data* in the ecological approach proposed in this volume. This notion includes data obtained from informal interactions among strongly connected speakers, as these must indeed be considered close to the 'nature' of the social world observed, but it cannot be restricted to it. Many speakers spend a significant amount of time in their lives in situations with a higher degree of formality, among other speakers they are not necessarily strongly connected with, and exposed to other regional varieties, standard varieties, or even different standards. Examples include working situations, school lessons, sports clubs, holidays, etc. The notion of *natural* in ecological linguistics must therefore also subsume dimensions like *regional/supraregional, standard/nonstandard*, and also different types of (inter)actions.

2.2.4   *Speakers and Space*

Questions concerning the relation between *speakers* and *space*, as in the diatopic characterization of *vernacular* discussed above, were largely inherited in sociolinguistics from dialectology. In early variationism a key role was ascribed to the *community* as a spatially anchored entity. Studies such as Johnstone (2004), Eckert (2004), and Britain (2009), however, have shown that variationism did not problematize *space* any more profoundly than dialectology had done before: *space* is considered a static physical–geographical entity, a natural foundation of the social world studied. Speakers are thought of as having no agency on and therefore no participation in the shaping of the place they consider 'theirs'. In such a reified conception, then, *space* is considered to be one of the major causes of linguistic variation, or in other words: 'natural' linguistic variation is spatial variation. Criticism of the alleged spatial givenness, stability, and homogeneity of linguistic communities led to alternative conceptions, such as that of the *communities of practice*, according to which highly local networks imply a mutual engagement, the sharing by members of some jointly negotiated enterprise, and a shared repertoire (Eckert 2004; Meyerhoff 2002 and 2006: 189). These alternatives can be considered another aspect of the mentioned shift of focus in sociolinguistics away from individual speakers and their social attributes to linguistic practices.

As shown for example by Blommaert (2010) in his *Sociolinguistics of globalization*, these linguistic practices are constantly changing in a globalizing world. A linguistic conception focusing 'on static variation, on local distribution of varieties, on stratified language contact and so on' (Blommaert 2010: 1), one in which *local* implies 'traditional' and 'static', is no longer tenable. In times of increasing globalization and increasing mobility of speakers and linguistic resources, linguistic varieties/dialects reflect less and less local attributes, except through stereotypes.

In other words, the conception of *space* in sociolinguistics gained in symbolic and abstract meaning at the expense of the physical and concrete interpretation in the last decades. As a result, *linguistic spaces* or *territories* are no longer considered to correspond to physical–geographical spaces and territories, as in dialectology, but align themselves along the boundaries constructed by agents or in which agents perform.[14]

The notion of *type of talk* or *type of interaction* in conversation analysis is important in this respect, because it covers essential aspects of this *speaker–space* performance. One function of this notion is to answer a question like: what is/are the most 'natural' situation/s of talk? While in foundation works of conversation analysis (Schegloff 1968; Sacks, Schegloff and Jefferson 1974; Sacks 1992) the focus was on talk in informal conversation (for instance, Sacks' study of telephone conversations on a suicide hotline), it has been extended in the last decades to other types of talk such as lessons (see Chapter 3, this volume), medical interaction, or news interviews (Mazeland 2006: 153). This extension can be explained by the reasoning that, if informal conversations were the only 'natural' or authentic type of talk, then most people would spend most of their lives in non-authentic situations of talk. Like sociolinguistics, conversation analysis has moved away from fixed parameters of *space* and *speaker* in the definition of *natural talk*. The major insight was that different types of interactions can be distinguished, all of which are potential sources of 'natural' or authentic data.

The framework proposed in the present volume takes up this insight, but makes an important restriction which is explained by the structure of linguistic ecologies as proposed in Chapter 1. As *natural data* we consider all data from characteristic types of interaction that are important for a major portion of the respective society and that are embedded in a three-level structure (micro- vs. meso- vs. macro-level) as described in Chapter 1. This includes, at least for the Western Hemisphere, telephone talks and classroom sessions, as almost all speakers in Western societies perform for some time in their lives in these situations. The concrete situations of these types are located on the micro-ecological level, and are embedded in meso-ecological (e.g., school, university, specific educational systems, etc.) and macro-ecological levels (cultural, historical, linguistic areas). But it excludes highly specialized types of talk such as interactions between medical doctors, linguists, or philatelists, as these are, strictly speaking, irrelevant to most speakers of a society and, in a

[14] In this context, see the notion of *timespace* in Mufwene and Vigouroux (2012).

prototypical form, are located on only one macro-ecological level (that of medicine, linguistics, and philately).

2.2.5   A First Conclusion

To sum up so far, we can say that the demand for 'natural' data in non-universalistic approaches to language such as sociolinguistics and ecological linguistics has its conceptual roots in phenomenology and phenomenological sociology. Linguists collect and select data according to what they consider to be relevant to the questions they address. For the questions asked in the disciplines mentioned here, the conception of *natural data* constitutes an epistemological and methodological ideal, which has been characterized by Mondada as the intention to 'discover the natural living order of social activities as they are endogenously organized in ordinary life, without the exogenous intervention of researchers imposing topics and tasks or displacing the context of action' (Mondada 2013c: 34). The quest for 'natural' data involves active and conscious choices on the part of linguists with respect to the speakers, varieties/registers/styles, situations and places, and media considered in their analysis. Historically, this quest involves a shift in linguistic relevance principles from attributes like [+written], [+formal register], [+central], [+standard], [+elite] to either the negative or their unmarked specifications. It is preferably, but not exclusively, the latter that are also the values attributed to the notion of *natural data* in the ecological linguistic framework proposed in this volume. From another perspective, this shift in relevance – and thus in the focus of linguistic observation – has been from physical units like speaker and space to linguistic practices. In one aspect of this perspective, the framework proposed here localizes *natural data* in most types of interactions except for highly specialized ones. Seen from the point of view of the history of science, both the ideal of *natural data* and the precise content of this ideal must be considered contextual and temporary.

As has become clear at some points of this discussion, definitions of what is 'natural' in linguistics cannot always avoid being circular. They also depend enormously on what is assumed to be the *ideal state of the social world*: in a sense, the written, formal language of elite speakers in earlier linguistic research, or in contemporary purist approaches, were or are considered to be 'natural' data, too. Both observations can be explained by the metaphorical application of an attribute of the physical to the social world.

2.3   Natural Trends and Features in and across Languages

'Naturally' occurring data can be collected for conversation–analytic or ethnographic purposes, and they can be used to help build hypotheses on variation and change in language. This brings us to a second meaning of *natural*, logically related to the first although seldom considered by sociolinguists but rather by scholars from other disciplines. In this meaning, natural data are considered to bear witness to *natural states, trends*, and *processes* in the languages themselves. Reflections on large linguistic corpora, especially of spoken data collected in unmonitored conditions, bridge these two meanings of *natural*.

Regarding the focus of this chapter, *natural* thus refers to the identification and explanation of principles in the evolution of languages in general, and of principles concerning a specific language. 'Naturalness' *across languages* is a subject of investigation for example in research on language change, language contact, and vernacular universals, as well as in markedness and naturalness theory. A popular synonym for natural features and trends across languages is 'universal'. The 'naturalness' of certain features and trends *in specific languages*, in contrast, is investigated for example in the framework of optimality theory. In the remainder of this section we focus on the notion of *natural* in the above-mentioned research areas. Despite this separation, it must be kept in mind that the notions of *natural* in all but the last (optimality theory) are intrinsically related; that is, the cognitive processes underlying the presence of or tendency towards certain 'natural' features across languages are often similar or even identical.

2.3.1   Language Change

One of the aims of historical linguistics has been to show that diachronic language change does not proceed randomly but follows certain more or less general principles. In analogy to what Adam Smith stated for economy, Rudi Keller (1990) describes language change as guided by an invisible hand: individual speakers select linguistic forms or speech acts according to specific goals and conditions, but the frequent use of some forms and speech acts produced by these individual selections is governed by super-ordinate ('natural') processes, with no underlying goals or intentions.[15] Language, then, is a phenomenon of the third order, which can be distinguished from natural phenomena (in the literal meaning of the term) on the one hand and intentionally produced artefacts on the other.

Historical linguists consider all language change to be caused by either *language drift* (following structural tendencies inherent in languages, independent from outside influence), *dialect borrowing/interference*, or *language interference* (see e.g. Thomason 2009: 349). Given the lack of a neutral definition of both *language* and *dialect*, the ultimate indistinctiveness of language-internal and external motivations, and other factors, this division is arguably of heuristic rather than of practical value. Outside of historical linguistics, this is also a critical distinction theoretically because a static

---

[15] This idea, too, has been expressed already by William Whitney in the late 19th century (see Pagel 2018: 316).

conception of *language* and a visualization of the contact between languages as one between quasi-monolithic entities or organisms are involved. Drawing on Haugen's (1972) thoughts, the ecological framework laid out in this volume argues for a replacement of this static conception by a more dynamic one (denying, in contrast to Haugen, even the very notion of 'a given language'), in which language contact is thought of primarily as contact between speakers. It follows from this argumentation that language change always involves some form of language contact – a conception which, although dating back to at least the 19th century with, e.g., Whitney and Schuchardt (see Pagel 2018), is gaining more and more acceptance. It also allows us to consider languages not as bundles of distinct varieties, all of which are assumed to be describable through a list of phenomena, but as pools of coexistent and sometimes competing features that are accessible to speakers (Mufwene 2001, 2008).

Resorting, however, to the heuristic value of the distinction between internal and external motivations of language change, this section will be concerned primarily with language change caused by drift while the next will deal with contact-induced change.[16]

As regards drift, we can speak of 'natural' principles of language change if similar processes of change are found among varieties that are not connected historically or geographically (and thus genetically) and if contact with other varieties is not the obvious cause (although it probably can never be ruled out entirely). The most prominent of such principles are sound laws, grammaticalization, analogy, and reanalysis. We will restrict ourselves in this section to the first two.

Sound laws (*Lautgesetze*) were established by comparative linguists and so-called Neogrammarians, concerned with the historical relations between European and Indian languages, in the second half of the nineteenth century. Sound laws make statements in two directions: they describe and explain the diffusion (or drift) of languages, and at the same time serve as evidence for the genetic relations between those languages. For example, the First Germanic Sound Shift (also called 'Grimm's law') defines the drift of the Germanic language group away from the other Indo-European languages, and at the same time demonstrates the historical coherence among the Germanic and between the Germanic and the Indo-European languages, that is: their genetic relation. While diffusion or drift in terms of change according to sound laws is a 'natural' principle of language evolution, specific sound laws are valid for individual languages or language groups.

---

[16] To maintain this distinction in empirical work requires precise argumentation. See e.g. Mougeon et al. (2005), who provide evidence to show that several Canadian French innovations are due to contact with English, whereas others are better understood as indigenous to French. Pfänder (2010) does the same for Spanish and its primary contact language Quechua in the Spanish of Cochabamba, Bolivia. And Pagel (2010), too, separates innovations in several Malayo-Polynesian contact languages of Spanish from those copied from Spanish.

Grammaticalization describes the acquisition or increase of grammatical meaning of a linguistic entity at the expense of its lexical meaning. Typical examples, found in many unrelated languages, include the grammaticalization of full verbs to auxiliary verbs (such as English *have* or Latin *habēre* to markers of perfect) or, as an even more specific path in this category, the grammaticalization of verbs of motion (such as English *go*, French *aller*, or Spanish *ir*) to future auxiliaries. The 'naturalness' in these grammaticalization processes is explained by the semantic and cognitive proximity of the source and target notions, and by similar metaphoric and metonymic processes performed by the speakers. For example, motion verbs are considered to be cognitively close to the category *future tense* because any motion in space involves also a motion forward in time.

A theoretical challenge for the division between internal and external motivations of language change, and an exciting transition to the next chapter, is Heine and Kuteva's (2003, 2005) conception of *contact-induced grammaticalization*. Their proposal is that some patterns of grammaticalization found in languages in contact situations are not the result either of internal grammaticalization or of polysemy copying (i.e., an element is copied in both the source meaning and the target meaning/function reached via grammaticalization, such as French *aller* as motion verb and marker for future tense) but of language contact: speakers draw on a pattern attested in a language in contact with theirs to create one in their language (by resorting to universal strategies of grammaticalization) or simply replicate it.

2.3.2   Contact-Induced Language Change

The notion of *naturalness* becomes particularly important in linguistic changes that involve language contact because it is here that the traditional understanding of *a language* as a static, systematic entity is hardest to maintain.

According to an overview provided by Winford (2003: 23–24), three major outcomes of language contact can be distinguished: *language maintenance, language shift*, and *language creation. Language maintenance* is said to be accompanied by processes of either *borrowing* or *convergence, language shift* by *interference*, all conceptualized in a more or less scalar fashion. In *language creation*, three types of seemingly unrelated contact languages are opposed to each other: *bilingual mixed languages, pidgins*, and *creoles*. While the processes that lead to the creation of *bilingual mixed languages* are said to be '[a] kin to cases of maintenance', *pidgins* are characterized as '[h]ighly reduced lingua francas', and the process involved in the formation of *creoles* as '[a]kin to both maintenance and shift' (Winford 2003: 24).

As Pagel (2015) shows, a conception of contact-induced change as depicted (rather exemplarily) by Winford is non-continuous and based on rigid categories and types with no or only vague relations to each other. Both the history of research on language contact (see Pagel 2018) and empirical data from different contact situations demonstrate, however, that continuous conceptions of contact-induced language change have many advances over non-continuous ones. Pagel therefore proposes a new, continuous model of contact-induced change. Its main idea is to bring together and arrange *all* processes and outcomes of language contact in a single space, to conceptualize them not as separate categories and types but as essentially continuous phenomena, and to allow, therefore, for *any point* in the space of contact-induced language change to be occupied by a specific contact situation at a specific time (see Pagel 2015 and Chapter 10, this volume, for details).

Models of processes and outcomes of contact-induced change like Winford's and Pagel's do not involve *explicit relevance structures* in the sense of Schütz discussed above. That is, with regard to the notion of *naturalness*, all processes and outcomes included in these models are considered equally 'natural' instances of language change, regardless of statistical (or other) notions. But relevance structures are inherent to the social world, Schütz reminds us, and therefore are likely to play a role in contact linguistic discourses too. The most obvious example concerns the notion of *languages* as historical phenomena, which is deeply embedded in the family tree model of genetic relatedness developed by philologists in the nineteenth century. This model is based on the interpretation of *languages* as unitary organisms which reproduce through parthenogenesis (i.e. asexually, through split); the comparative method serves as the main tool for uncovering inherited features and thus the 'family relations' between these organisms. As a result of this interpretation, a language is thought to have one – and only one – direct ancestor, and its genetic relationship can be illustrated in the form of a family tree.[17] The most important implication with regard to language contact is that languages with double parentage are an impossibility, therefore the existence of thoroughly mixed languages must be denied (as has been done consistently in the form of an 'axiom' by Müller 1862). Conversely, this means that codes exhibiting thorough linguistic mixture must be excluded from the realm of *languages*. This model of genetic relationship seems to reflect and at the same time strengthen a relevance structure of the (Western) social world in which historically continuous phenomena are ranked higher than historically non-continuous ones. One expression of this hierarchy in linguistics is the distinction between *languages* (and perhaps *dialects*) on the one hand, and *jargon*s, *pidgins, vernaculars, bastard tongues, gibberish,* etc. on the

---

[17] See Noonan (2010) for a concise overview of the conception of genetic relatedness in linguistics and its relevance for the study of language contact.

other,[18] or put more generally: between *languages* and *non-languages*. Already in the second half of the nineteenth century, however, philologists such as Clough (1876), Lepsius (1880), and Schuchardt (1884) have argued against a denial of mixed languages, bringing to the attention of their colleagues not only heavily mixed jargons, creoles and other outcomes of intensive contact situations, but also the mixed nature of many (historically continuous) European languages such as English or the Romance languages – then all anomalies to the family tree model (see again Pagel 2018 for details). The question whether creoles and other contact languages represent special kinds of mixture and should therefore be distinguished from 'normal' languages continues to be a theoretical problem to the present. Although alternative models of genetic relatedness have been proposed (e.g. by Croft 2000 and Mufwene 2001, 2008), the unitary organism and the family tree model remain the most influential scientific tools. This is not least the merit of Thomason and Kaufman (1988), who acknowledged the empirical evidence of mixed languages and conceded that these simply mark the epistemological limits of the family tree model. The fact that most languages appear to be not mixed, however, and the scientific value the model has proven to possess so far provide good arguments for its maintenance:

there are indeed mixed languages, and they include pidgins and creoles but are not confined to them; **mixed languages** do not fit within the genetic model and therefore **cannot be classified genetically at all; but most languages are not mixed**, and the traditional family tree model of diversification and genetic relationship remains the main reference point of comparative-historical linguistics. (1988: 3, emphasis original)

The relevance structure (mentioned above), however, is being maintained: languages that can be genetically classified (because they are not mixed) obviously seem more 'natural' than those that cannot be genetically classified (because they are mixed), especially if combined with the observation that most languages are not mixed. Compared with 'genetic' languages, then, 'non-genetic' languages have a stigma, they are marked languages, 'non-natural' languages. This interpretation is also behind many of the objections to Thomason and Kaufman's proposal. Thus, if the standard model of genetic relationship is being maintained, it is important to keep in mind its *purely technical* nature, as is emphasized by Thomason (1997) too:

[Thomason and Kaufman's] claim is rejected by some creolists, who have objected that pidgins and creoles must surely be considered to be related to their source languages – at least to the lexifier language, and (in most specialists' opinion) to the substrate

---

[18] The title of McWhorter (2008) *Our magnificent bastard tongue: The untold history of English*, for instance, alludes to this distinction and hierarchy.

languages as well. This objection arises, I believe, from a misunderstanding of the technical nature of the historical linguist's notion of genetic relationship: the assumptions listed above are indeed quite standard in historical linguistics, and a language that is not a changed later form of a single language spoken at some earlier time cannot be genetically related in the technical sense to any other language(s). Of course this does not mean that the lexicon and grammar of a pidgin or creole have no historical antecedents; the claim is merely that the language's component systems cannot all be traced back to *the same* source language. The standard notion has proved so fruitful as an organizing principle for unraveling the histories of languages that it would probably be unwise to try to change its meaning in order to include mixed languages. (74)

The same relevance structure is reflected in the contact linguistics distinction between languages that show 'ordinary' contact-induced change (or variation) and *mixed* or *contact languages*, that is, outcomes of language contact that are interpreted as genetically 'new' languages. Among the latter, pidgin and creole varieties have been the subject of the biggest controversies. It is undisputed today that these varieties belong to the realm of 'natural' (as opposed to artificial) languages, though, as Mühlhäusler (1986: 61) reports, this has not always been so. They have been considered as lacking a fully-fledged linguistic structure of their own, their linguistic systems described as highly reduced, deficient versions of the systems of the codes involved in the contact from which they emerged. An interpretation of this deficiency as a marker of 'unnaturalness' suggests itself, and joins in easily with the 'genetic'–'non-genetic' languages distinction. But, as Mühlhäusler points out, the opposite interpretation has also been made: 'applying roughly the same meaning of naturalness, pidgin languages have been characterized as maximally natural' (ibid.) – for they are, at least in their very early period of formation and development, undisturbed by cultural forces. At this stage, 'natural categories' evolve and 'natural rules/solutions' are preferred over 'non-natural' ones. The meaning of *natural* Mühlhäusler has in mind here is the one found in *natural morphology* (see section 2.3.5) – that is, rules or solutions that are easier to process for the human brain. In this meaning, it is characteristic of language-internal 'natural' rules that they are

more resistant to change; more frequent (token frequency); more frequent cross-linguistically; more likely to be the basis of neutralization; and more likely to be the model in analogical change than an abnatural category. (Mühlhäusler 1986: 61–62)

Since it is typically the more 'natural' alternative in grammatical categories that is chosen in pidgins (*natural* being explicitly synonymous with *unmarked*), these are 'maximally natural languages' (ibid.: 62) also from a structural point of view. The initial 'natural' state, however, achieved through rather unconscious development in a situation of great communicative need is altered as soon as the code is used for social purposes (such as group identification, styles, etc.) and hence is being changed consciously. 'Naturalness' decreases as the pressure of social and cultural forces increases, which is a path followed by all languages. In Mühlhäusler's words, 'languages seem gradually to move from their natural basis and become cultural artefacts' (ibid.).

Exploring the structural fundamentals of creoles, represented by the *creole prototype*, McWhorter (2011) interestingly choses an opposite position with regard to the notion of *naturalness*. Contrary to Mühlhäusler, McWhorter claims 'that the natural state of human language is the extensive marking of fine shades of semantic and syntactic distinctions, plus rampant allomorphy and irregularity' (ibid.: 1). McWhorter's argumentation is not so unlike Mühlhäusler's: because of the circumstances that lead to the emergence of creoles and their young age as compared to other languages, creole structures reflect human language in its primordial functional and least complex form. McWhorter's claim is that 'The world's simplest grammars are creole grammars' (the title of McWhorter 2001), his interpretation of simplicity and complexity, however, and his understanding of the 'nature' of language structure turn Mühlhäusler's upside down. An explanation can be found in the differing ideologies of the two authors: Mühlhäusler argues for a constantly dynamic (in later works: ecological) view of language and language change, emphasizing the importance of socio-historical context and the selectiveness of the comparative method appealed to in establishing language families and types. McWhorter's aim, on the other hand, is to define a *creole prototype* on purely synchronic grounds (i.e. by means of structural criteria, without reference to socio-historical data; see McWhorter 2005) in order to typologically distinguish creole from noncreole (or 'normal') languages (see the basic assumptions 1–3 in McWhorter 2011: 1–4). Contra McWhorter, other scholars like Mufwene (2000, 2009) and DeGraff (2003, 2005) maintain that creolization is overall a social and not a structural process, thereby rejecting the possibility to theoretically define and empirically recognize creoles on purely structural grounds.[19] Closing the circle to what has been called above a relevance structure in theoretical assessments of contact-induced change (that between 'normal'/'genetic' languages and contact/'non-genetic' languages), Mufwene (2009), as did many before him, argues for an interpretation of creoles as dialects of their lexifier languages.

Other relevance structures in contact linguistics concern for example the categorial derivatives of creoles, such as semi-creoles, anti-creoles, or mixed creoles. While creoles (and other types of contact languages) stand out from 'normal' languages in historical–genetic linguistics, the derived categories mentioned stand out from prototypical creoles in contact linguistics (see Chapter 10, this volume).

---

[19] See also Mühlhäusler (1986: 61): 'it is generally admitted that without a knowledge of the history of a language one cannot determine whether one is dealing with a creole'.

Relevance structures such as the ones mentioned in this paragraph are based on degrees of deviation from categories, types, and prototypes that have been established in historical–genetic linguistics and contact linguistics, but often lack a solid theoretical (and sometimes also an empirical) basis. In the framework proposed in this volume it is assumed that a theoretically infinite number of ecological parameters influences the linguistic choices of speakers in speech situations. It follows from this assumption that the outcomes of language contact must be conceptualized not in the form of categories and types, but as a continuous space spanning between the involved speakers' codes and potential linguistic creations resulting from the contact of these codes, as has been done in early contact linguistic theory in the 19th century, and recently in the model proposed by Pagel (2015, see also Chapter 10, this volume, and Pagel 2018). Within this space, anything goes. In a theoretical consolidation of the nature of contact-induced language change, then, established categories, types and prototypes should recede into the background where they can be useful landmarks.

2.3.3   Vernacular Universals

Many of the 'natural' features or tendencies found in pidgins, creoles, and other contact varieties are also attested in language acquisition and in vernaculars (Chaudenson, Mougeon, and Beniak 1993; Chambers 2004: 128–129). In fact, these three fields appear to be related with regard to *naturalness*, which is associated with different notions such as *simplification*,[20] *neutralization*, *(un)markedness, orality*, and the *absence of codified standard varieties*. Before dealing with orality and markedness in the next paragraphs, we will briefly discuss the notion of *vernacular universals* in this section.

Research on vernacular universals was pioneered by Jack Chambers (2001, 2003, 2004, 2009) and has focused mainly on varieties of English. However, the claims appear to be valid cross-linguistically. The notion of *vernacular* here covers both the diatopic and the diaphasic dimension of the term as explained by Calvet (1997; and see section 2.2.3) and is opposed to that of *standard variety*. A simple definition of *vernaculars* as 'regional and social non-standard varieties' is given by Kortmann (2004b: 1). *Vernacular universals*, then, 'are meant to denote . . . features that are found (more or less

---

[20] The terms *simple, simplicity*, and *simplification* are too often taken for granted in research on language change and variation. Ferguson and DeBose (1977) take *simplification* as a technical term, comprising an increase in morphophonemic *regularity* (produced by regularization or analogy) and in *transparency* (i.e., regular correspondence between content and form). These two phenomena 'make utterances easier to perceive, understand or produce [and so] may be regarded as simplifying processes if they omit material, reduce irregularity, or make sound-meaning correspondences more transparent' (ibid.: 105).

universally) across all kinds of (nonstandard) varieties of different languages'
(Filppula, Klemola, and Paulasto 2009b: 2). One particular aim of anglophone
research on vernacular universals was 'to find a typological distinction
between types of English' (Trudgill 2009: 304).

The basic idea behind the concept is that *vernaculars* 'represent more
"natural" developments than (more or less strictly) codified standard varieties'
(Filppula, Klemola, and Paulasto 2009b: 3). Since these 'natural' developments typically work towards more regularity and transparency, it can be
said that increasing regularity and transparency (subsumed under the notion
of *simplification* by Ferguson and DeBose 1977; see n. 20) are very basic
vernacular universals (Winford 2009). The forces counterbalancing these
developments are fewer and less powerful in vernacular than in standard
varieties, and linguistic awareness, metalinguistic reflexivity, and sensitivity
to (overt) norms are considered to be smaller here (Gadet 2011: 109).[21] Similar
ideas have been expressed before in different fields of research, for example by
Kroch (1978), who considers standard dialects as differing from nonstandard
ones by resisting certain 'natural' tendencies, and notices that the roots of this
difference are ideological and not linguistic. From the perspective of pidgins
and creoles, Mühlhäusler (1986) also observes that 'naturalness' in language
structure decreases with the increasing use of that language for certain social
purposes, in which we can include standardization:

> Human beings seem to be prepared to accept a considerable cost in linguistic simplicity
> and communicative efficiency in order that their languages should promote their social
> standing. In sum, maximally natural solutions tend to be sensitive to external social
> pressure. (Mühlhäusler 1986: 63)

Frequently cited examples of vernacular universals comprise the phonetic and
the grammatical level and include, for example, morpheme final consonant
cluster reduction, final obstruent devoicing, conjugation regularization and
multiple negation (e.g. Chambers 2004; Kortmann et al. 2004; Schneider
et al. 2004). Filppula, Klemola, and Paulasto (2009a) summon contributions
discussing the issue of vernacular universals from different perspectives
(sociolinguistics, typology, contact, and variational linguistics) and for different linguistic levels. In one of the most interesting contributions to that
volume, Trudgill (2009) recognizes the importance of the impetus given by
Chambers, but suggests that the

> attempt to establish a typological distinction between vernacular and nonvernacular
> varieties, by showing that vernacular varieties have a number of features in common
> which are absent from nonvernaculars, has ultimately been in vain. (304–305)

---

[21] In this regard Chaudenson (1992, see also Chaudenson, Mougeon, and Beniak 1993) speaks of
'auto-regulation' processes, which can be observed as soon as the normative pressure is relaxed.

Trudgill explains that the proposed 'universals' are neither universally spread among vernaculars nor have they been entirely absent in Standard English. He turns the perspective around, saying that it is the peculiarities of Standard English that stand out as remarkable, not the features many vernaculars have in common. These peculiarities are precisely the result of standardization, the function of which is to inhibit or retard structural change. The kind of change Trudgill has in mind is simplification, comprising, in his definition, regularization and loss of redundancy (ibid.: 314). Simplification processes are abundant in both standard and nonstandard varieties of English, and, more importantly, they are in both cases at least in part the consequence of language contact. Thus, in the case of many vernacular universals, we are actually dealing with 'dialect contact-induced simplification' (ibid.), processes that occur only at a slower pace in Standard English. There is no vernacular universals *versus* language contact, Trudgill argues, in unison with Sarah Thomason (2009) in the same volume. There is, nevertheless, a true typological split between the varieties of English, according to Trudgill. This split is not between standard and nonstandard varieties, but between the high-contact (comprising the mainstream vernaculars and Standard English) and the low-contact varieties ('traditional dialects'). It is in the latter, and in the relative absence of contact, where reverse processes become active, that is, complexification in terms of the development of irregularity and redundancy (Trudgill 2009: 316).

2.3.4   Some Words on the Role of Orality

Even if the claim for vernacular universals seems too strong, the similarity of ecological conditions in the discursive uses of vernaculars (in local proximity, between strongly linked users, most of the time in face-to-face interaction, with low degree of formality) is likely to produce common linguistic trends. An important dimension in this respect is *orality*. The use of language in 'ordinary' *spoken* conditions implies specific constraints as opposed to *written* language. These constraints are both material (see Chafe 1985 for the consequences of linearity in time) and cognitive in the different modes of structural elaboration within short-term memory (Miller and Weinert 1998; Blanche-Benveniste 2010). The effects of these constraints can be observed at different levels, and their impact on syntax and discourse, in particular, is often underestimated. Drescher and Neumann-Holzschuh (2010), for example, discuss the impact of properties such as implicitness, polyfunctionality and transparency on the interactional chain of discourse, as well as modes of expression such as decompacting processes, and aggregated and temporary constructions. Other characteristics of oral language include high indexicality, elaborated deictic systems, and heavy usage of deictic reference. Oral language is closely tied to situations (concrete spatiotemporal events) and displays intensive cooperation on the levels of discourse (e.g. turn-taking) and meaning (presupposition of common knowledge).

It is obvious that oral language is anthropologically primary and written language secondary. The first is elementary, and the second depends on it for its existence. This is where *naturalness*, the topic of this chapter, is concerned: from an anthropological perspective, oral language can be considered the 'natural' state of language. Many languages are still unwritten or are used predominantly in oral situations, which is why they have often elaborated many of the characteristics discussed above in their grammars. Nonetheless, cultural processes can heavily influence this relationship. The development of a written standard, its wide circulation and acceptance, for example, can not only lead to expanding cognitive abilities (such as reading and writing) but also change the perception of the relation between oral and written.[22] According to Trudgill it is the aim of standardization to inhibit or prevent all structural change, this being 'especially true for written standards, so that a growing gap between written and spoken language is a well-known phenomenon' (2009: 309).

Against the shared background of the notion of *naturalness*, features of oral language correlate in many ways with those found in vernacular languages, in pidgins and creoles, and in language acquisition. And they correlate with observations that have been made with regard to the concept of *(un)markedness*, which is the topic of the next and final section.

2.3.5   *Markedness, Naturalness Theory, and Optimality Theory*

Another notion that is often found in relation to the 'naturalness' of features and trends in and across structures of languages (and other sociocultural institutions) is *markedness*. Filppula, Klemola, and Paulasto (2009b: 5), for instance, note that many of the contributors to their volume on vernacular universals approach the topic from the perspective of markedness, although they use the term in quite different senses. In the most neutral working definition (insufficient, as we will see) we could say that *markedness* denotes an opposition relation (preferably gradual or relative) between elements of a given linguistic structure. In this structure as frame of reference, one element is said to be more marked than another. Unmarked elements are easier to produce

---

[22] In this context, see Tomasello's (1999) idea of the cultural origins of human cognition. Ludwig (2014) shows that languages comprise classifications/categorizations of reality that are passed on as 'made' knowledge, as cognitive interpretational accomplishments. This understanding of cultural progress can be found already in Condillac, and was extended by Tomasello.

and perceive for language users, which is why they are preferred cross-linguistically, while marked ones are generally avoided.[23]

Ludwig (2001) and Haspelmath (2006) provide elaborated overviews of the notoriously heterogeneous applications of the term. Ludwig's focus is on the history and development of the *markedness* concept from its origin in works of Nikolai Trubetzkoy and Roman Jakobson through applications in Chomskyan generative linguistics, Greenbergian research on language universals, natural morphology, contact linguistics, and creolistics to, then relatively recent, Givónian functional linguistics, and optimality theory. In the attempt to bring together the major theoretical approaches to the markedness concept in one scheme, Ludwig makes a distinction between vertical and horizontal levels of markedness (*Markiertheitsebenen*; see table in Ludwig 2001: 409). Vertically (and hierarchically from the top to the bottom) markedness can be described in universal categories, typological categories, individual language categories, and individual language forms. Main parameters of evidence for markedness, such as ontogenetically early acquisition, iconicity/transparency, and frequency are listed and ascribed to these levels by Ludwig. In the horizontal dimension, these levels are then related to three linguistic functions: the referential, the textual, and the interpersonal function.

Refreshingly polemical in a paper called (perhaps in reminiscence of Paul Feyerabend's 'Against method') 'Against markedness', Haspelmath (2006) contrasts twelve different senses of markedness to be found in the linguistic literature and argues for the 'downright elimination of "markedness" from linguists' theoretical arsenal' (ibid.: 27). This strong claim derives from his conviction that 'some of the concepts that [the term markedness] denotes are not helpful, and others are better expressed by more straightforward, less ambiguous terms' (ibid.: 25), for instance, *frequency of use* (ibid.: 43ff.). We will outline Haspelmath's paper in some detail because it contains both the clearest representation of and the most critical position on the issue.

The twelve distinct senses of markedness are grouped by Haspelmath into four classes: markedness as (1) complexity, (2) difficulty, (3) abnormality, and (4) a multidimensional correlation. Among the senses in group (1) we find, for example, *semantic* and *formal markedness*. *Semantic markedness* can be explained with a pair like *dog/bitch* where the first is said to be the unmarked term because it can describe both male dogs (as opposed to bitches) and dogs in general, including the then marked term *bitches*. The marked term is therefore semantically more specific or 'complex'. Haspelmath suggests that language learners must deal with many such specific properties of words, and a variety of factors (among them frequency of use and conventionalization) is

---

[23] See Kager (1999: 2–3) for a similar, general definition.

responsible for semantic distributions, so that a bifurcated notion like *markedness* has little to contribute to their understanding (ibid.: 53). *Formal markedness* means nothing more but that one term is overtly coded as opposed to the other (s), like the plural form in *dog/dogs* that is 'marked' by the suffix *-s*. Haspelmath suggests speaking of 'overtly coded' or 'phonetically longer' in order to avoid misunderstandings (ibid.: 30).

Perhaps the most important senses of markedness with respect to the topic of this chapter are found in Haspelmath's group (2) and read as 'markedness as phonetic difficulty' and 'markedness as morphological difficulty (dispreference/unnaturalness)' (ibid.: 31). These uses of the term are found in what is known as *naturalness theory/natural phonology/natural morphology* (e.g. Mayerthaler 1981; Dressler 1984; Wurzel 1984; Dressler et al. 1987; Boretzky et al. 1995). The basic claim of this theory is that linguistic forms are more or less easy/difficult for the human brain to process; of these the first are considered to be more 'natural' than the latter (*natural* being explicitly synonymous with *unmarked*) and are therefore preferred by language users. In natural morphology, for example, users are said to prefer structures that show (i) constructional iconicity (a combination of semantic and formal markedness as laid out above; e.g. the singular/plural pair *dog/dogs* is iconic while *sheep/sheep* is not), (2) uniformity (invariant shapes; e.g. *dog/dogs* is less marked than *goose/geese*, because the plural form in the latter is different from the more frequent one in the first), and (3) transparency (one form = one function; e.g. English verb inflection is more marked in the plural than in the singular, because in the plural one form covers all persons while in the singular at least the third person is distinguished formally from the first and second). Haspelmath summarizes a number of reflections of unmarked structures in various domains:[24]

Unmarked morphological structures are claimed to (i) be widely found cross-linguistically, (ii) be acquired early, (iii) be processed more easily, (iv) be affected less by language disorders, (v) used more frequently, and (vi) be more resistant to language change. (2006: 32)

As for the notion of *markedness* in naturalness theory, Haspelmath concludes, and provides evidence, that 'unnatural' phenomena 'can all be explained with reference to concrete substantive factors like token frequency, type frequency, and regularities of language change' (ibid.).

The notion of *markedness* in Haspelmath's group (3) is best translated as 'abnormal' in the sense of 'unexpected'. It includes markedness as sheer rarity (or low frequency) in texts, typological markedness (unmarked features are

---

[24] Not surprisingly, they coincide largely with what Mühlhäusler (1986: 61–62) states with regard to pidgins as 'maximally natural languages' (see section 2.3.2).

more frequent cross-linguistically than marked ones, and the presence of marked features implies that of unmarked features in the same frame of reference), and markedness as deviation from default parameter setting in Chomsky's Universal Grammar. The latter sense is considered to be different from all others because 'its domain is not linguistic categories but cognitive states'; it should therefore be understood as 'a metaphor derived from other senses of "markedness"' (ibid.: 37).

Group (4), finally, covers combinations of two or more of the senses of *markedness* listed in the other groups. The view of markedness as a multidimensional correlation is found especially in Greenberg's (1966) and Croft's (1990, 2003) work on language typology and universals. The major discovery here is

that universally, comparable linguistic structures exhibit the same markedness values for the different markedness dimensions (or 'criteria'). Thus, some categories (such as the plural or the future tense) are semantically complex, overtly coded, rare in texts, found only in some languages, and restricted in their distribution (i.e. marked in all these respects), whereas other categories (e.g. the singular or the present tense) are semantically simple, not overtly coded, frequent in texts, found in all or most languages, and unrestricted in their distribution. (Haspelmath 2006: 38)

Haspelmath follows Greenberg and Croft in concluding that the markedness correlations can actually be reduced to frequency of use, as it explains all the other correlates (ibid.: 40).

For some reason not included in the twelve senses of *markedness* (and hence the four groups), but addressed in a chapter of its own, is the notion of *markedness* in optimality theory. This development of generative grammar, invoked by Prince and Smolensky (1993), is based upon the idea that grammars are systems of conflicting constraints. A constraint is a statement about which characteristics must be avoided in a linguistic form – if a form shows these characteristics, the constraint is said to be violated. The most innovative element of optimality theory is that it allows all constraints to be violated, that

[v]iolation of a constraint is not a direct cause of ungrammaticality, nor is absolute satisfaction of all constraints essential to the grammar's outputs. Instead what determines the best output of a grammar is the least costly violation of the constraints. (Kager 1999: 3)

While constraints are generally universal, the hierarchical ranking of constraints is what distinguishes (and thereby defines) individual languages/grammars. Of all candidate forms available, the one that violates a given constraint ranking less or the least (i.e. has the fewest high-ranking constraints) in an individual grammar is considered the best or 'optimal' output.

Two types of constraints are distinguished in optimality theory:

> The first is MARKEDNESS, which we use here as a general denominator for the grammatical factors that exert pressure toward *unmarked types of structure*. This force is counterbalanced by FAITHFULNESS, understood here as the combined grammatical factors *preserving lexical contrasts*. (ibid.: 4–5, emphasis original)

Haspelmath has studied the markedness constraints proposed in optimality theory and concludes that the respective notions mostly correspond to others in his list, especially to markedness as difficulty, complexity, and multidimensional correlation in the Greenbergian sense (2006: 41). While Ludwig (2001: 416) finishes his paper with an optimistic outlook on the future role of *markedness*, because with optimality theory this term – again – becomes a central tool in linguistics, Haspelmath maintains his general criticism as to the usefulness of the concept. Markedness constraints in optimality theory, he argues, contribute little to the understanding of markedness itself. The nature of these constraints is to be explained by the same factors underlying earlier markedness notions, especially ease/difficulty of perception and production and frequency of use (2006: 41). As a final conclusion of his critical assessment, Haspelmath attests the general (or 'intuitive') sense of marked/unmarked in linguistics to be

> not distinguishable from the sense of everyday words like *uncommon/common, abnormal/normal, unusual/usual, unexpected/expected*. Apart from the larger class of markedness as abnormality . . ., we also find markedness as complexity . . . and as difficulty . . ., but since complexity and difficulty typically lead to lower frequency, abnormality is in effect what all markedness senses share. But we do not need a technical linguistic term for abnormality/uncommonness/unusualness/unexpectedness. Simple everyday concepts should be expressed by simple everyday words. (2006: 63)

As plausible as this assessment may seem at first glance, it is not unproblematic, especially not from an ecological linguistic point of view. The observation that markedness aspects interpreted in terms of complexity and difficulty *typically* lead to lower frequency in language use does not provide evidence for the general unusefulness of the term *markedness*. *Typical* does not mean *always*, and there are numerous examples, some of them touched in this chapter too, for increasing complexity and difficulty in languages (for example in isolated or low-contact societies or through the development of writing and standardization, see Trudgill 2009) that does not correlate with low but with *increasing* frequency. There is, without doubt, a strong relation between complexity/difficulty/salience on the one hand, and low frequency on the other, but a generalization of this relation is oversimplifying the matter and may prevent us from dealing with cases where this relation is impeded or overruled by other factors. It may keep us from asking important questions such as: what is the nature of this relation, and why is it overruled in some cases? The overviewing and structuring work done in Haspelmath's article is highly important – nevertheless, it fails to recognize the main value of the term *markedness* behind the conceptual ambiguity discussed: beyond the notions of *markedness* collected by Haspelmath, this term indicates the complex linkage of several related phenomena, and thus may enable us – like no other term – to investigate and understand precisely these interrelations. *Markedness* in linguistics is not generally synonymous with *abnormality/uncommonness/unusualness/unexpectedness*, and it must not be substituted by these terms, if only because these imply an objective, universal perspective that is quite impossible to adopt, especially in a social science ('abnormal' with regard to what? 'Uncommon'/'unusual' with respect to which language(s) and/or varieties? 'Unexpected' for whom?). Haspelmath's perspective, echoing those of Greenberg and Croft before him (see above), may be useful, and perhaps even methodologically necessary in their fields of investigation, that is: linguistic typology and universals, the distribution of structural features among the world's languages. In order to perform such macroscopic studies, researchers must aim for terminological unambiguity and make generalizations on many different levels (e.g. to choose one variety as representative for each language, typically the variety presented in standard grammars and dictionaries). This can be interpreted as consistent with the ecological linguistic framework laid out in the previous chapter of this volume, according to which researchers *must* select, from a theoretically infinite number, those parameters they consider the most relevant in their field of research and with respect to the goal to be achieved by it. But according to the same framework the usefulness of one generalization or parameter set-up in one field does not guarantee its usefulness in another; nor does it suggest its applicability to linguistics as a whole. Overgeneralizations would be fatal for other, less macroscopic studies, and particularly for ecological linguistic investigation, because many important distinctions and perspectives on interrelations would be lost.

2.4   Conclusion

It was the aim of this contribution to gather and discuss the most important semantic and functional aspects of the term *natural* as it is used in different linguistic disciplines and with different theoretical backgrounds in order to determine a role for this term and its underlying conceptions in ecological linguistics. It has become clear in the course of this chapter that the metaphoricity of the term *natural* allows manifold interpretations of its meaning, and that explanations of its meaning often involve some circularity.

The term *natural* has two main fields of application in linguistics that were discussed in this chapter, the first being *natural data* and the second *natural trends or features in and across languages.* With regard to the first, a major result of our discussion was that, for the theoretical reasons laid out in Chapter 1 (this volume) and the present contribution, the notion of *natural data* in ecological linguistics is not identical with traditional uses of this notion. It includes a variety of dimensions, such as the formality/informality of the speech situation, oral/written, regional/supraregional, and standard/non-standard varieties, as well as different types of (inter)action. The notion of *natural data* suggested here covers many possible values and combinations of values in these dimensions. For example, we would argue that the data obtained in an 'ordinary' working situation with a set-up such as [+formal, written, standard] is as 'natural' as that found in an 'ordinary' talk between family members with a set-up containing opposite values in these dimensions [+informal, oral, nonstandard]. In general words, then, our notion of *natural* with regard to linguistic data is wider and more flexible than similar notions in other disciplines and approaches.

Regarding the 'naturalness' of trends and features in and across languages, we take an equally wide and flexible stance in general. Language change, including contact-induced change, is universal to all human languages spoken, because it is found in all languages and can obviously not be completely prevented by human actions (but see below). In this sense, language change and contact-induced language change are 'natural' to human language, and all instances and processes of language change (including the perhaps rarer, allegedly 'exotic' results of contact-induced change such as pidgins and creoles) must be considered equally 'natural' in this respect. In all other applications to language structure (comprising here, for reasons of convenience, phonological and lexical resources), *natural* is an essentially relative notion, indicating complex interrelationships on multiple levels that must be investigated individually. Many applications of *natural/unnatural* to language structure involve dimensions that are discussed in this chapter under the notion of *markedness* (section 2.3.5), and *frequency of use* appears to be a decisive factor (but not the only one) in linguists' decisions to regard a specific trend or feature in language structure as 'natural' or not (an observation that allows us to refer back to the Husserlian notion of *life-world* and the grounding of science therein).

An interesting matter, however, remains the application of *natural* to a (primordial) structural state of languages, and the idea that this state is altered by (succeeding) cultural and social developments. Alteration is not only brought about by obvious cultural elaborations such as the development of writing and standard varieties, but also through languages being used for purposes of social and other identitary distinction. Languages *are* not, but *become* cultural artefacts, according to Mühlhäusler (1986: 62) because 'maximally natural solutions tend to be sensitive to external social pressure' (ibid.: 63). Trudgill's (2009) observation that it is in the closely tied speaker communities of low-contact varieties that structural complexification can develop, seems to go in the same direction. However, if these tendencies observed by Mühlhäusler and Trudgill are 'universal' in the sense that they are valid for all living human languages at all times, if they are, in other words, 'natural' tendencies, then the term *natural* is also not helpful in distinguishing between those features from the primordial, 'natural' state and the subsequent socioculturally motivated (and in this sense 'unnatural') alterations. It leads us to questions regarding the evolution of language as a feature that distinguishes homo sapiens from other hominids (and in fact from all other species). Perhaps the most important of these (then inconvenient) questions is: where does biological evolution end and cultural elaboration start?

These problems of definition and demarcation can ultimately be traced back to the metaphoricity of the term *natural* when it is used in linguistics. Language is, if not entirely, but overwhelmingly a sociocultural matter. Consequently, there is hardly any 'natural' behaviour in language in the literal meaning of the term, and it is probably confined to the most general observations.

Part II

On the Ecology of *Speaker* and *Space*:
from Situational to Intermediate Ecology

3 An Interactionist Perspective on the Ecology of Linguistic Practices: the Situated and Embodied Production of Talk*

Lorenza Mondada

3.1 Introduction

The terms *ecology of language, ecological data*, and *ecological validity* have been used with very different meanings in the last decades and have opened an emergent field wherein different linguistic projects have been developed. They manifest an increasing concern for the diversity of languages and linguistic practices as they are observable in a variety of ordinary settings. They also manifest a growing interest in linguistic data, corpora, and materials which are not orchestrated by research protocols but which document linguistic forms and conduct as they emerge, develop, and change, evolving into specific language games and forms of life.

Within linguistics, the emerging paradigm of linguistic ecology has focused on the ecology of minority and endangered languages (Mühlhäusler 1996a) as well as on the ecology of language evolution (Mufwene 2001), while the ecological linguistic perspective approaches language in various contexts, recognizing its embeddedness within the natural ecosystems that sustain life, and addressing environmental issues (Fill and Mühlhäusler 2001). These research trends refer to Haugen (1972) as the founding father of the 'ecology of language'.

Interestingly, a few years before the publication of Haugen's work, Goffman (1964) wrote a plea for the 'neglected situation', in which he defines the encounter in terms of 'an ecological huddle wherein participants orient to one another and away from those who are present in the situation but not officially in the encounter' (1964: 135). In the same text, he also speaks of 'micro-ecological orbit' (1964: 133). He had actually already used this notion

* This chapter originates in the framework of a Franco-German project funded by the ANR and the DFG, 2009–2012, and in CIEL-F (Corpus International Écologique de la Langue Française), in which we have been collecting an international ecological corpus of French varieties.

Acknowledgements: this study has been made possible thanks to long-term fieldwork and continuous collaboration with the urban services of the Grand Lyon and with the local population. I am grateful to both, as well as to my team, for helping me while video recording in the field: Vassiliki Markaki, Sara Merlino, Florence Oloff, Emilie Jouin, Justine Lascar, and Leila Bensadoun.

three years earlier (1961: 17–18). He was himself inspired by the urban ecology developed by the Chicago School from the 1920s onwards, where he studied in the 1940s.

This chapter shows, within an interactionist perspective developed by Erving Goffman and then elaborated recently by conversation analysts and interactional linguists, how it is possible to retrace an interactionist perspective on the ecology of situated language. In this framework, ecology refers to the embeddedness of language practices in interaction within their local environment – both the social context and the material space. Thus, the focus is on what Ludwig, Mühlhäusler, and Pagel (Chapter 1, this volume) refer to as the immediate relationships of dependency and foundation upon the micro-ecological level. Within the field of interactional linguistics and conversation analysis, this chapter aims to make explicit: (a) how the term *ecology* has been and can be used in a Goffmanian sense for the study of language in social interaction; and (b) how the idea of *ecological data* makes sense within a naturalistic approach to language as situated within a range of social contexts. Both aspects rely on a project that aims at studying talk and social practices as they are 'naturally' occurring and within a conception of language that understands it as fundamentally situated in social settings and material environments.

3.1.1   The Ecology of the Interaction: from Goffman's 'Ecological Huddle' to Contemporary Studies

Goffman's notion of the 'ecological huddle' contributes to a wider discussion about the context of social interaction. In his 1964 paper, he critically opposes the 'microecological orbit' defined by the co-participants' bodies to be a mere correlationist vision of contextual parameters. From then on, the definition of *context* has been extensively discussed (Duranti and Goodwin 1992; see Mondada 2006b).

Within the interactionist tradition, and especially that of ethnomethodology and conversation analysis, the 'situated' nature of social interaction has always been the focus. For instance, Garfinkel's programme (1967) focuses both on *indexicality* and *reflexivity*. In his own words:

I use the term 'ethnomethodology' to refer to the investigation of the rational properties of indexical expressions and other practical actions as contingent ongoing accomplishments of organized artful practices of everyday life. (1967: 11)

Members' accounts . . . are constituent features of the settings they make observable. Members know, require, count on, and make use of this reflexivity to produce, accomplish, recognize, or demonstrate rational-adequacy-for-all-practical purposes of their procedures and findings. (1967: 8, see also Garfinkel and Sacks 1970)

Reflexivity has been further developed by showing the double character, both *context-shaped* and *context-renewing*, of turns at talking. Actions are produced by adjusting to the context, but in doing so they orient to and make relevant some of its features, which renew, maintain, or alter it (Heritage 1984: 242). Within conversation analysis, the situatedness of talk in interaction is shaped by the participants' orientation to matters of contextual relevance. This orientation reveals those aspects of context that matter to the participants, are procedurally consequential for the organization of the details of their speech and conduct, and, in turn, reflexively produce the social structure (Schegloff 1991: 51, 1992: 111). This means that speakers' identities, social ties, institutional constraints, linguistic choices, and adjustments are made intelligible by the participants who embody the relevance of interaction, in a mutually observable way, in the manner in which they arrange linguistic resources while formatting their turns and organizing their ongoing action.

While, in this tradition, context has been first treated in terms of institutional and social structures (namely, by showing how the organization of speech in a variety of institutional contexts adjusts and reproduces them within a diversity of specialized sequential formats, see Drew and Heritage 1992), more recently it has also been treated in terms of material and spatial environments. It is in this context that Goffman's 'ecological huddle' has been revisited. Scholars have taken into account the details of the embodied talk and action and the way in which orientation towards the relevant features of the local setting are manifested by the arrangement of multimodal resources, such as gesture, gaze, body position, and movement. This new focus on the ecology of the activity has been made possible, on the one hand, by studies of video recordings, which document not only the linguistic but also the multimodal sequential organization of talk and other conducts (Goodwin 1981, 2000). On the other hand, this has been favoured by an analytical interest within professional interactions in complex workplace settings characterized by fragmented spaces, technologies, and artefacts (Heath and Luff 2000; Luff, Hindmarsh, and Heath 2000).

These more recent advances have re-elaborated Goffman's 'ecological huddle' in terms of an *ecology of conversation*, taking into account the detailed sequential organization of interaction in two dimensions: the *temporal* dimension – as it unfolds moment by moment, as it is incrementally formatted within turns at talking (Schegloff 1996; Auer, Couper-Kuhlen, and Müller 1999) – and the *spatial* dimension, as it is embodied in the dynamic establishment of mutual attention, in the emergence and dissolution of participation frameworks, in the achievement of the interactional space, and in the manipulation and distribution of artefacts in the local ecology.

Goffman's 'ecological huddle' highlights the importance of mutual attention and of the visual accessibility characteristic of face-to-face encounters, which maximizes reciprocal monitoring (1961: 17–18, 1964: 135). Goffman draws on Simmel's idea that

> of the special sense-organs, the eye has a uniquely sociological function. The union and interaction of individuals is based on mutual glances ... This mutual glance between persons, in distinction from the simple sight or observation of the other, signifies a wholly new and unique union between them ... What occurs in this direct mutual glance represents the most perfect reciprocity in the entire field of human relationships. (1908/1969: 148)

Consequently, Goffman too emphasizes the importance of direct eye contact for establishing social relations in what he calls 'focused interaction' (1963: 92), as opposed to 'unfocused interaction' characterized by 'civil inattention'. Later on, Charles Goodwin (1981) demonstrates that the absence of mutual glancing is made relevant by organizing restarts in an individual's turn to speak, showing that restarts are a technique both for delaying the beginning of a turn until mutual gaze is achieved and for attracting the other's gaze. In this sense, Goodwin shows that the syntactic format of the turn not only is interactively constructed but also relies heavily on the ecology of the conversation. More recently, these findings were summarized by Erickson's (2004: 4) idea of an ecology of speaking and listening, according to which 'speaking and listening are reflexively related in an ecology of mutual influence'.

Charles Goodwin and Candy Goodwin's work broadens Goffman's concerns by investigating the embodied and spatial dimensions of another one of his key notions: the 'participation framework'. Goodwin and Goodwin (2004) criticize Goffman's static and asymmetric typology (1981b), which uses very different categories to decompose the layered roles of the speaker as animator, author, principal, figure, etc., as well as the status of the hearer as ratified vs. non-ratified and addressed vs. non-addressed. Displacing the focus from a typology of speakers to the activities enabling participation, Goodwin and Goodwin argue that participation is a highly dynamic configuration, as it changes moment by moment within the incremental emergence of turns-at-talk, within the transformation of its recipient-designed features, and occasions a shift in the use of diverse linguistic resources. According to them, participation is enacted and organized through the bodies of the speaker and the co-participants. 'Embodied participation' concerns both the way in which the relevant participants are identified, ratified, and addressed, and the way in which polyphonic voices are expressed and animated in the laminated structure of utterances, for example when quoting others' speech. Goodwin (2007b) calls these phenomena 'interactive footing'.

Moreover, a focus on embodied participation entails an interest in how participation is embedded in the local ecology. This concerns not only mutual attention within the ecological huddle but also, and more generally, the dynamic disposition of the bodies within the local environment. Noting that 'there is a systematic relationship between spatial arrangement and mode of interaction', Kendon (1990: 251) invokes Goffman's description of focused interactions (1963) and on Scheflen's context analysis (1972) to support his notion of 'K-Formation'. This refers to the arrangement of the interacting bodies in different configurations, such as face to face or side by side, which defines a territory delimited by the common focus of attention relevant to the ongoing activity. I became interested in the way in which this common space is created in openings between interactions (Mondada 2009) and is plastically adjusted and recomposed by the use of deictic terms and by turns at talk (Mondada 2005a). I then proposed an analysis of the way in which the participants' bodies and gestures, the focus of their attention, and the artefacts they manipulate configure an *interactional space* which is constantly monitored, configured, and relevantly orientated on a moment-by-moment basis within the sequentially unfolding action (Mondada 2013a).

Although Goffman (1964) had already noted that it seems impossible to analyse gestures without taking into account the material surroundings in which they are achieved, the embeddedness of gesture in the environment, and thus the physical, social, and cultural properties of this environment (LeBaron and Streeck 1997; Heath and Hindmarsh 2000; Haviland 2005; Mondada 2005a, 2007, 2009) have seldom been taken into consideration. The concept of *symbiotic gesture* (Goodwin 2003) is a reminder of this. Symbiotic gestures are built through the articulation of speech, gesture, and the material and graphic structure of the environment (Goodwin 2007a; note also his use of the notion of 'environmentally coupled gesture'). A speaker's gesture does not make sense if it is separated from the body and the space occupied by the speaker, as well as from the participation framework. Still, little attention has been paid to the ways in which the structure of the environment contributes to organizing gesture. With even more focus on the crucial importance of the artefacts in interaction, Goodwin (2000: 1490) shows with his notion of 'contextual configuration' the mutually determining relationships that emerge between gesture, speech, features of the environment, semiotic inscriptions, tools, and other objects, as they are mobilized within the activity.

This research tradition shows that the local ecology is actively constituted and constantly maintained or transformed by actions which make possible the spatial configuration of the ongoing interaction in its situated organization.[1]

---

[1] This sketch of an emerging domain could be further expanded by noting the convergence between the interactionist tradition initiated by Goffman and similar developments within the study of situated and distributed cognition. Hutchins (2010) describes the field of 'cognitive ecology' by referring to Bateson's (1972) 'ecology of mind', Gibson's (1979) 'ecological psychology', as well as activity theory. He also advocates micro-ethnographic methods as a way of developing this approach. All show the importance of the spatial/environmental

In return, the local ecology reflexively constrains and shapes the format of the utterances that are produced within it.

3.1.2   *Ecological Data as Records of Naturally Occurring Activities*

The emphasis on the ecology of the interaction is consequently implemented in a methodology which aims at collecting and studying 'ecological' or 'naturalistic' data, i.e. in building corpora-documenting activities as they naturally occur in their ordinary environment (see Mondada 2013c; Chapter 2, this volume, for a detailed discussion).

The use of audio and video recordings of everyday linguistic practices and social actions as they happen ordinarily is a direct consequence of conversation analysts' interest in the endogenous and situated organization of social activities. According to this perspective, interaction is the most 'natural habitat' of language (Schegloff 1996); this situated dimension has been described as 'the fundamental natural environment or ecological niche of language' (Schegloff 1998: 535; cf. Schegloff 2006b). Consequently, this approach focuses on social interaction as it is organized collectively by the co-participants, in a locally situated way. The organization is achieved incrementally through its temporal and sequential unfolding by the mobilization of a large range of vocal, verbal, visual, and embodied resources, which are publicly displayed and monitored *in situ*. This conception of language in action, insisting on its indexical, contingent, emergent accomplishment, produces specific demands on the way in which fieldwork, data collection, and the quality of audio-visual materials are achieved. A naturalistic approach derives from these presumptions: on the one hand, it insists on the study of *naturally occurring activities* as they unfold in their ordinary social settings; on the other hand, recordings of actual situated activities are necessary for a detailed analysis of their relevant endogenous order (Mondada 2006a).

This analytical stance contrasts with other ways of collecting data, as often practised in other related fields of the social and cognitive sciences. It is different from *introspection*, practised in formal linguistics, where the researcher, who is a native or fluent speaker, commonly imagines the sentences to be analysed. As Sacks (1992: 1, 419–420) reminds us, the objects of study in the naturalistic approach are situated actions (and not isolated sentences), which constitute phenomena that can only be 'discoverable', but not

---

dimension of context and all stress the importance of *not* separating cognitive processes from the body and from the environment in which the embodied action and interaction are embedded. Another domain pursuing a similar line is the study of 'situated action' (Suchman 1987) which has produced, within ergonomics and workplace studies, a range of analyses inspired both by Goffman and by Gibson that show the complexities of work ecology (Luff et al. 2003) and the affordances of the work place (Kirsh 1995; cf. de Fornel and Quéré 1999).

'imaginable'. It also contrasts with *field notes* gathered by *participant obser-vation*, practised in classical anthropology and recommended in variationist sociolinguistics. Whereas field notes document the unique labile experience and post-hoc recollection of the observer (and are thus subject to memory limitations, to situated selectivity, and to locally occasioned interpretation and intuition), recordings allow for the repeated viewing of a unique event (Sacks 1992: 1, 622) and therefore for the study of temporal and embodied details that are impossible to capture immediately. (See Schegloff 2002: 322 on 'the decisive and "surprising" relevance of "detail" discoverable from recorded data but inaccessible to once-in-real-time observation or occasioned and "interested" recollection'.) Recordings of actual activities also contrast with *interviews*, largely practised within the social sciences and sociolinguistics, which offer post-hoc declarative reconstructions of actions in narratives or in responses to questions within a constrained and limited interactional format (Button 1987; Suchman and Jordan 1990).

Whereas interviews produce participants' interpretations and descriptions in speaking *about* action, but not the action itself, audio and video recordings document the action as it happens in its situated orderliness. Likewise, whereas interviews produce social interaction characterized by a specific turn-taking organization, the records of naturally occurring interactions document a variety of organizations, adequate for the activities at hand. Finally, recordings of naturally occurring interactions contrast with *experiments*, an approach favoured in the cognitive sciences, which aim at controlling a range of parameters and at constraining the performances of the subjects in order to test pre-established hypotheses. On the contrary, video recordings of talking and action in their local ecology aim at discovering the way in which social actions are naturally and relevantly organized by participants in the context of their situation, taking into consideration the fact that their organization is locally and indexically adjusted and must therefore be observed in the very settings in which it ordinarily happens. (See, for example, Schegloff 2006a: 142 on the problematic character of Levelt's study of self-repair in experi-ments.) Thus, instead of trying to control the subjects' performance, the researcher adapts to the specific action of the participants.

Although these alternative methodologies have been largely reformed in recent years, by adopting more 'ecological' formats (such as 'semi-directed' interviews or focus groups instead of survey interviews or role-playing; or 'ecological' tasks instead of highly abstract experimental procedures), these contrasts still hold in principle. Experimental approaches have increasingly been concerned with the *ecological validity* of their methods, materials, and setting, thus trying to approximate the behaviours as they actually happen in real-life situations. Audio and video recordings in conversation analysis relate to a different perspective: they aim at discovering the natural living order of social activities as they are endogenously organized in ordinary life, without the exogenous intervention of researchers imposing topics or tasks and displacing the ecology of the action.

This *naturalistic* perspective has been largely discussed within the literature (see Speer 2002 and the responses to her paper by Lynch 2002, ten Have 2002, and Potter 2002), often at a methodological level, concerning the notion of *naturally occurring data* rather than the conceptual notion of *naturally occurring activities*. At the methodological level, the most common arguments have been versions of the Labovian 'observer's paradox' (Labov 1972), according to which *naturally occurring data* do not exist, because the very fact of recording an activity disrupts and transforms it. Responses to this problem concern both the refinement of the way in which recordings of naturally occurring actions are accomplished (not only as far as their technological, but also ethnographical and ethical adequacies are concerned), and the identification of observable moments in which participants orient to the recording devices. Contrary to what is often said, the camera, although permanently present, is not always relevant for the participants; moments at which they orient to the camera can be identified and studied. Moreover, these occasions often reveal issues, problems, conflicts, and delicacies that are relevant to understanding the ongoing action. (See Heath 1986: 176; Laurier and Philo 2006; Speer and Hutchby 2003, for analyses of such situations.) At the conceptual level, the notion of *natural* is deeply rooted in Sacks's references to early natural sciences and to the possibility of natural observations and natural descriptions of social life (Lynch and Bogen 1994). As noted by Lynch (2002), the term is not used in order to oppose *social vs. natural* conducts; rather, it refers to what Schütz and phenomenology call the 'natural attitude' (Schütz 1962), i.e. a pre-reflexive posture that characterizes ordinary life (see also Chapter 2, this volume).

Thus prior to the collected data, *natural* refers to the practices themselves (Garfinkel 1967): '"naturally organized", in this context means an ordering of activity that is spontaneous, local, autochthonous, temporal, embodied, endogenously produced and performed as a matter of course' (Lynch 2002, 534). This naturalistic perspective is very much in agreement with the Goffmanian stress on the importance of local ecology for the study of situated activities and situated language practices.

3.2   Taking into Account the Ecology of the Activity: the Situated and Embodied Production of Proposals during a Meeting

In order to show how the ecology of the activity matters for the way in which a variety of linguistic and multimodal resources are situatedly arranged within interaction, I now turn to a particular phenomenon, which can reveal both the methodological potentialities of an ecological corpus and the analytical contributions of a description of the ecological production of language in interaction.

The phenomenon studied here concerns the situated production of proposals during a meeting. During extended fieldwork on a participatory democracy project, I video-recorded a brainstorming session in which citizens were invited to propose ideas for the transformation of military barracks into a public park. Their proposals were formatted as self-standing noun phrases (NP), such as *un parc de quartier* ('a neighbourhood park'), *des modes de déplacement aménagés* ('adapted modes of transportation'), *flânerie, valorisation patrimoniale et historique* ('flânerie, promotion of heritage and history'), but also as utterances such as *je ne veux pas qu'il y ait un skate parc* ('I don't want a skate park'), *il faut valoriser le bâtiment militaire* ('we have to make the military building attractive'), *qu'y ait des voies vertes aux accès du parc* ('that there will be green paths to access the park'). These utterances are not just forms which can be subjected to a grammatical analysis, they are also actions (or proposals) produced and addressed in a situated way by orienting to the relevant features of the local ecology: the institutional context, the spatial and material environment and the participation framework, which shape not only their adequacy and their uptake in this setting but also the very way in which they are assembled. My aim was to show that the ecology of the activity matters deeply for the way in which these forms are actually produced and treated; their analysis, in turn, shows what relevant features of the ecology shape their production and reception.

In order to demonstrate the systematic character of these orientations towards the local ecology, I analysed a collection of proposals by taking into account the larger sequence in which they were produced. The sequence begins with the chairman (CHA) selecting the next speaker, here TUR, who utters a proposal about a specific feature of the future park (line 3) (dialogues are transcribed according to Jefferson's conventions):

(1) (fermé la nuit)

```
1   CHA:    y avait autre cho:se?
            was there anything else?
2           (0.6)
3   TUR:    donc euh: ferm- fermé la nui[:t, (et)
            so ehm: clos- closed at night, (and)
4   CHA:                                [fermé la nuit, h
                                        [closed at night, h
5   ?:      °oui .hh°
            yes .hh
6   ?:      °non°
            no
```

```
7  ROS?:    °non on [n'est pas d'accord, [nous°
            no we [don't agree, [we
8  MAU:            [°non°              [°non°
                   [no                 [no
9  CHA:     Ah, pas d'accord ici,
            Oh, not agreeing here,
```

The Chairman selects the next speaker in a way that projects the next action and situates this as a continuation of the previous one, thus indicating that the expected contribution is one among several in a series. This constrains the type of contribution to be made and shapes the type of action to come, as well as its format. Also, TUR's proposal, beginning with *donc* ('so'), exhibits her action as the continuation of some action already initiated. Her proposal, after some hesitation and a self-repair, takes the form of *fermé la nuit* ('closed at night'). It is also formatted as projecting that there is more to come, as shown by its continuative intonation and by the production of (*et* 'and') following the phrase (3). It is however overlapped by the Chairman (4) who repeats it, orienting to the completion of the expected action and even curtailing any further development. After its repetition, members of the audience respond to the proposal with some agreeing (5), others disagreeing (6–8), and the Chairman notices that some disagreement is in the air (9). The episode continues (not shown here!) with a long discussion about advantages and disadvantages of closing or opening the park at night and finally, three minutes later, the Chairman inscribes *fermé ou non? la nuit* ('closed or not? at night') on the whiteboard, in a specific position where controversial proposals are registered. The entire episode will not be analysed here (but see Mondada 2011), and I will focus only on the beginning.

This sequence shows that the proposal is an interactional action (see Goodwin 1979 on the interactive construction of an utterance), achieved in a multi-party interaction building a complex participation framework: the proposal is solicited by the Chairman, addressed to him, then voiced by him to the other participants who can either agree or disagree with it. Its production orients to the local setting in which it is occasioned and received: it treats the subject or topic as commonly known, thus as taken for granted; it is not even mentioned. The format of the proposal orients to the fact that it will be written on a whiteboard, where other proposals have already been written, and that it is exposed to public scrutiny, where other participants have the right to accept, criticize, modify, or reject it. As shown below, it is oriented towards a spoken *vs.* written ecology, towards a multi-party ecology, and towards a polyphonic ecology. The timed production of the proposal, the sequential slot in which it is uttered, its form, the way it is addressed, all orient to the specific ecology of the activity.

This ecology can be reconstructed in various ways depending on one's methodological, technological, and analytical choices. It can be ethnographically reconstructed on the basis of the observer's field notes. In this case, a narrative of the

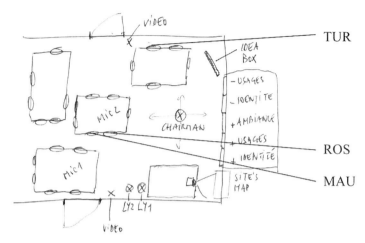

Figure 3.1 A sketched map of the meeting room
("video" indicates the position of the two cameras, "mic" of the microphones
on the tables)

urban project, as well as notes and sketches taken during that session, can be useful
in reconstructing the local ecology of TUR's proposal (Figure 3.1). The participants are seated at four tables scattered around the room; TUR is not sitting at the
same table as ROS and MAU (see Figure 3.1), who are part of another group.

Moreover, the Chairman moves between the space of the room and the wall,
where a large whiteboard has been installed, consisting of different sheets,
organized in different thematic sections. These help to differentiate between,
on the one hand positive uses, ambiances, and identities, and, on the other,
negative uses, ambiances, and identities of the park, plus an 'idea box', in
which controversial topics are written down (see Figure 3.3). Alternatively
turning to the room or to the wall, moving back and forth between these two
places, the Chairman mediates the transformation of spoken proposals into
written ones once the audience has ratified their content and their formulation.
Thus, the spatial ecology of his embodied action echoes the spoken and written
ecologies of the activity.

The ecology of the activity can also be reconstructed through videography,
thanks to the availability of audio and video recorded data. In this study, the session
was recorded using two video cameras (Figures 3.2(a)–(b)) and by two independent
audio recorders placed on two tables (indicated as 'video' and 'mic' in Figure 3.1).

Video recordings allow us to both document the unfolding of the session
from the opening to the closing (and even the series of sessions constituting
the project, which were entirely videotaped) and to reconstruct the material
environment and its local relevance, built within the temporal and praxeo-
logical way in which multiple and changeable participation frameworks,

(a)   (b)

Figure 3.2(a)–(b) Partial views of the room as produced by the two cameras

Figure 3.3 View of the wall with various 'inscription spaces'

Figure 3.4 Focus on a thematic sheet ('positive usages')

the groups constituting the audience, the participants' bodies distributed within the room, and how the written materials emerged, changed, and evolved during the session. The actions of the participants within the room build the *interactional space* organized by the multi-party interaction during the discussion, whereas the action of writing on the board builds an *inscriptional space*, organized through the spatialized manner in which the Chairman inscribes the proposals. Both contribute to building the ecology of the debate.

Whereas maps drawn of the field and texts collected at the end of the session offer a static representation subsequent to the action, recordings document the temporal unfolding of the circumstances and the transforming ecology in which proposals are produced and received. In other words, whereas final texts produced by the participants archive the result of the action, video recordings preserve the dynamic emergence of ideas, proposals, and acts of writing making their embodied dimension observable and analysable as they are shaped by gesture, body positions, facial expressions, and mutual orientations which give sense and accountability to the ongoing action as they are embedded in the local ecology.

3.3 Exploring the Various Steps of the Ecologically Embedded Production of an Utterance

The following analysis shows how the ecology of interaction, as documented by video recordings, configures the proposals, and how it is possible to describe the latter as achievements situated in time and space. The analysis follows the sequential emergence of the proposal step by step, beginning with the selection of the proposer, the production of the proposal, its repetition or reformulation by the Chairman, and his subsequent orientation towards the audience's response. Each of these sequential moments is analysed on the basis of a small collection of cases (Schegloff 1996; Mondada 2005c) which shows the systematicity of the multimodal, material, and spatial details constituting proposals as situated, embodied, and occasional actions.

3.3.1 Selecting the Proposer

The selection of the person who is about to deliver the proposal is systematically undertaken by the Chairman (Mondada 2013b). This Other-selection occurs when the Chairman has completed or is about to complete the writing of the previous proposal on the whiteboard (embodied conduct is transcribed according to Mondada's conventions – see end of this chapter for glossary):

(2) (fermé la nuit; MED1 34.45, PUB1 40.57, T1_2.02, T2_40.34)

```
1   CHA:    #*y avait   #    *aut'    cho:#*se?
            was there         anything else?
            *turns to room*points to TUR*walks twd audience-->
    fig     #fig.3.5      #fig.3.6        #fig.3.7
2           (0.4) * (0.2) #
               --->*positions in front of the audience, but looks at TUR --
    fig                   #fig.3.8
```

The Chairman finishes writing on the whiteboard (Figure 3.5), turns back at the beginning of his turn to speak (Figure 3.6), and points when he says *aut' cho:se* ('something else') (Figure 3.7), before walking back to the front of the audience (Figure 3.8). In this way he achieves both his transition from the previous episode (completed with the inscription of the previous proposal) to the next, and his transition from the wall (the inscriptional space) and the room (the interactional space).

A glance at other occurrences shows very similar features:

Figure 3.5 The chairman begins to turn to the room

Figure 3.6 The chairman turns to the room, beginning to point at TUR

Figure 3.7 The chairman points at TUR

Figure 3.8 The chairman walks towards the audience

(3) (voies d'accès vertes – med1_38.34; pub1_44.45)

```
1   CHA:    est-ce* qu'y avait# d'autre cho:*se, dans vos propositions?#
            was there          something else,  in your propositions?
            -->*points at TUR's table---*looks at it-->
    fig                        #fig.3.9                      fig.3.10#
```

Figure 3.9 The chairman points at TUR's table

Figure 3.10 The chairman looks at TUR

(4) (parking – med1_1.05.02)

```
1   CHA:    *d'aut` # cho*se pour vot` groupe?#
            something else for your group?
    fig             #fig.3.11                #fig.3.12
            *points group*looks at the group-->
```

Figure 3.11 The chairman points at the group

Figure 3.12 The chairman looks at the group

The Chairman selects the next speaker by pointing at him or her. Afterwards, he adopts a receptive body posture by looking at the party selected without any more gesturing. The pointing gesture is performed in a visible and publicly displayed way: thus, it not only imparts to the selected party the right and obligation to speak but also exhibits for the other parties that somebody has been selected and will speak. These gestures show the importance of the spatialization of turn-taking in such a context.

The selected speaker is identified both by the pointing gesture, locating him or her in the room, and by the Chairman's turn. The latter projects the proposal to come in a specific way:

(5)

```
CHA:    y avait aut' cho:se?
        was there something else?
```

(6)

```
CHA:    est-ce qu'y avait d'autre cho:se, dans vos propositions?
        was there something else, in your propositions?
```

(7)

```
CHA:    d'aut` chose pour vot` groupe?
        something else for your group?
```

On the one hand, *autre chose* ('something else') alludes to the fact that this is not the first proposal but a subsequent one, indicating that this episode is a continuation, or a new round, of the previous one. Moreover, the reference with *dans vos propositions* ('in your proposals') (extract 6) treats the party as having a set of proposals to offer: it alludes to the fact that the group worked on it at the beginning of the session, at which point it was instructed as follows: *ce que je vous demande par table, c'est d'essayer de vous mettre d'accord sur l'idée qu'est-ce que vous ne voulez pas qu'il soit (1.0) et puis qu'est-ce que vous voulez qu'il soit. (.) on s'donne quinze minutes* ('what I ask of each table, is to try to reach an agreement about an idea of what you don't want it to be (1.0) and then what you want it to be. (.) we will take fifteen minutes'), where *il* ('it') refers to the park.

On the other hand, the Chairman refers not to a particular person but to a group, using the second person plural pronoun. Although the same form is used for polite and formal address, here a collective person is clearly referred to (cf. *vot' groupe* 'your group' 7). Thus, the person selected is not an individual speaking for him or herself but a spokesperson speaking on behalf of his or her group. Moreover, the pointing gesture locates the spokesperson as well as the group seated around the table: the table/group is both a spatial unit and a participation unit. The table has explicitly been identified as an interactional party in the instructions given at the beginning of the meeting (such as: *chaque table (.) y réfléchit et puis propose une: (0.3) répon:se* 'each table (.) thinks about and then proposes a: (0.3) respon:se'). Thus, the 'author' of a proposal is a composite figure that is both linguistically and gesturally defined, and which is crucially embedded in the local ecology.

So, the pointing gesture and the turn selecting the next speaker, in a very economic way, embody a series of expectations and a normative principle of organization which have shaped previous contributions and which are reflexively reproduced by and project the imminent contribution conforming to them. This is done in a publicly accountable way which shows that the next action concerns not only one table, but all of the participants.

3.3.2   *Formulating the Proposal*

Once a proposer has been selected, (s)he offers a proposal, addressed to the Chairman who stays immobile, without gesturing, gazing at the speaker.

```
(8)
TUR:     ferm- fermé la nui:[t, (et)#
         clo- closed at nigh:[t, (and)
fig                             #fig.3.13
(9)
TUR:     les voies d'accès au parc qu'elles soient vertes, et qu'il ait
         the access paths to the park, they have to be green and there has
         qu'il ait une amélioration des: pistes cyclables
         to be an improvement of the cycle lanes
(10)
COL:     nous on a beaucoup parlé des bancs et des tables,
         we we have talked a lot about benches and tables,
(11)
BLF:     la la val- la val- la va- enfin on a parlé aussi la
         the the pro- the pro- the pro- well we spoke as well about the
         vala- val:orisation, patrimoniale et histori:que,
         promo- promotion, of the heritage and the history,
(12)
ROS:     [euh oui o- on avait dit qu'on voulait pas de par[ki:ng,
         [ehm yes w- we said that we didn't want any parkin[g lots,
```

These proposals are often introduced by a *verbum dicendi* in the past tense (*on a parlé* 'we talked', *on avait dit* 'we said'), or even simply by the complementizer *que* 'that' (9). They refer to previous discussions; moreover, they report collective voices (*nous on, on* 'we'). These formulations contribute to the presentation of the speaker as belonging to the category of *spokesperson*, with the proposer not expressing his or her individual opinion but that previously negotiated collectively by the group. Some of these proposals are voiced with consulting notes taken during these preceding discussions (Figure 3.13).

Figure 3.13 TUR holds her notes while uttering her proposal

Unfortunately, we did not collect all of the notes from all of the participants and we missed the details of TUR's notes. However, we have recorded
the notes COL took during the previous discussion (see his proposal in
excerpt 10). They reveal that his proposal voices what has been inscribed
by him as a note-taker for the group and restates past fragments of their
discussion:

(13) (bancs; beginning of the meeting, 26.15)

```
1   COL:    ( ) j'arrive jamais à m'asseoir
            ( ) I never get a seat
2   ROU:    mais ça,
            but this,
3   COL:    dimanche dimanche les bancs sont tous [pris
            on sunday on sunday all benches are ta[ken
4   BLF:                                          [bien sûr
                                                  [of course
5   BLF:    [mais le dimanche, même en ville
            [but on sunday, even downtown
6   ROU:    [ouais. mais alors, des bancs avec accoudoirs
            [yeah. but then, benches with armrests
7   JEA:    avec des tables, (.) y en avait [d'ailleurs
            with tables, (.) there were tables [by the way
8   COL:                                      [avec des tables
                                              [with tables
9   COL:    ((writes# 'bancs + tables'))
    fig               #fig.3.14A and fig.3.14B
```

COL's notes show that his actual proposal (excerpt 10) is in fact the
sedimentation of various versions assembled in past discussions, and previously inscribed by him. Figure 3.14(a) shows that, during the previous group
discussion, COL held his notes in the middle of the table in such a way that
they were visible to all of the participants, thus accountably distinguishing
between the collective status of his note taking and the individual status of
others' note taking thus establishing his notes as representative of the
collective view.

(a)

Figure 3.14(a) COL writing notes and acting as collective note taker for his group

(b)

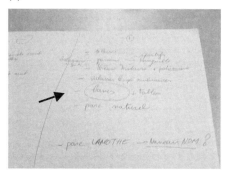 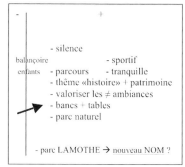

Figure 3.14(b) COL's notes and their transcription

Proposals are not only shaped by past discussions; they are also shaped by their future inscription by the Chairman on the whiteboard. The space allowed for inscription constrains the proposals in advance, through the embodied orientations towards it during the discussion (see below), through explicit references to its thematic rubriques, and by the fact that other proposals have already been discussed and inscribed on the whiteboard, working as models for future proposals. The space for inscription (Mondada 2005b, 2011) configures the proposals in at least two ways. On the one hand, it constrains the format of the spoken turn, imposing a concise written formulation, such as free-standing NPs, nominalizations, etc. On the other hand, it foreshadows a categorization of the proposal as belonging to one of the thematic sections (positive *vs.* negative proposals, concerning uses, ambiances, identities of the park). These constraints are particularly visible in those cases in which the format of the proposals is amended, for example:

(14) (continuation of 10)

```
1   COL:    nous on a beaucoup parlé des bancs et des tables,
            we we spoke a lot about benches and tables,
```

```
2   JEA?:    °hi H hh°
3   COL:     donc euh:: (.) -fin des usages de réunion d'fami:lle,
             so ehm:: (.) well uses of family meetings,
4            de groupes d'ami:s, [de-
             of groups of friends, [of-
5   CHA:                          [alors comment j'peux l'for- c'est
                                  [so how can I for- that's
6            intéressant, comment j'peux le formuler en termes d'usa:ges.
             Interesting, how can I formulate it in terms of use.
```

COL formats his proposal in a first turn-constructional unit (TCU) (1), which the Chairman does not respond to but which occasions a light laughter from JEA sitting at the same table. Orienting to the absence of a response, COL amends his proposal (3), transforming it in an expression which explicitly uses one of the thematic categories inscribed on the whiteboard ('usage') in a clumsy formulation (*usage de réunion de famille, de groupes d'amis* 3–4). This formulation is interesting: it shows how COL plastically articulates two structuring constraints, beginning with the written mould and ending with an expression closer to the initial informal discussion. Paradoxically, although this second formulation radically alters the first, abandoning its practical and concrete character in order to abstract it and include the word *usage*, the Chairman does not ratify it, but instead, after a positive assessment, produces a request for reformulating it *en termes d'usa:ges*. In different ways, both the proposer and the Chairman explicitly orient to the normative constraints of the future written formulation.

Thus, the formulation of the proposal is shaped both *retrospectively* by past discussions, past instructions and other inscriptions, and *prospectively* by its future inscription in a constrained semiotic space. These future constraints are further embodied by the way in which the proposal is received and revoiced by the Chairman.

3.3.3   Repeating and Reformulating the Proposal

Once formulated by the spokesperson, the proposal is further elaborated by the Chairman who either accepts it, by repeating or reformulating it, or asks for further elaboration. Some proposals are repeated by the Chairman, such as the first one:

(15) (fermé la nuit)

```
1   TUR:     donc euh: #ferm- fermé la nui:t,* (.) *[(et)   *
             so ehm: clo- closed at night,      (.) [(and)
2   CHA:                                            [fermé la nuit,# h*
                                                    [closed at night, h
             >>looks at TUR---------------*.....*looks at aud------*
    fig            #fig.3.15                         fig.3.16#
```

Figure 3.15 CHA   Figure 3.16 CHA looks at the audience
looks at TUR

Describing the Chairman's turn (line 2) as a mere repetition does not yet account for the action he is achieving by repeating the proposal. If we observe the body posture of the Chairman, we can describe what he does as 'revoicing' the proposal. During TUR's utterance the Chairman looks at her; but as soon as he begins to repeat it, he turns to the audience. This change of orientation achieves a 'redirection' of the proposal, which was first addressed to him and now is readdressed to the audience as a whole. This revoicing is embedded in the local ecology, since he rearranges the interactional space from a focus of attention on the source of the proposal (Figure 3.15) to a focus of attention on its recipient (Figure 3.16), which is visible in the change in position of the Chairman's head. The local surroundings are successively oriented to in different ways and by different postures, making relevant different portions of the room, within changing interactional spaces.

Likewise, TUR's other proposal is reformulated by the Chairman turning towards the audience:

(16) (voies d'accès vertes)

```
1    TUR:    les voies d'accès au parc, qu'elles soient vertes et qu'il ait qu'il
             the access paths to the park, they have to be green and there has to
2            ait une amélioration des: pistes cyclables
             be an improvement of the cycle lanes
3    CHA:    d'ac*cord. *voie d'accès# vertes et pistes cycla:bles, (0.3) donc* (.) ça,*#
             okay.        green access paths    and cycle lines,      (0.3) so (.) that,
             ->*,,......*turns to audience, approaches----------------------*,,,,,,,,*
     fig                            #fig.3.17                            fig.3.18#
4            *(.) [ça nous met on est un peu# déjà dans le dé*tail
             (.) [that goes a bit already into details
             *turns to TUR's table-------------------------*turns to audience-->
     fig                            #fig.3.19
```

Figure 3.17 The chairman turns and moves closer to the audience

Figure 3.18 The chairman oriented towards the audience turns his head towards TUR's table

Figure 3.19 The chairman turns completely towards TUR

In Figures 3.17–3.19 black arrows show the orientation of the upper body, white arrows of the lower body. In Figure 3.18, the upper body is oriented towards TUR (circled) whereas the lower part is oriented to the audience.

When the Chairman repeats TUR's proposal (3), he turns to the audience (Figure 3.18) but he looks back at TUR when he adds a new, parenthetical, TCU (4) which assesses the receivability of her argument. Thus, we notice that the Chairman's turn is finely recipient-designed, successively addressed to two parties by embodying different recipient orientations in the positions of his body and the directions of his gaze. The Chairman can be completely turned to the proposer's group (Figure 3.19) or to the audience (Figure 3.17); alternatively, his lower body can be oriented to the audience while his head and gaze are directed at the group (Figure 3.18) in a body-torque position (Schegloff 1998). These positions are finely organized, taking into account not only recipient-design, but also the ongoing action, the transitions from one TCU to the next and from one action to another, as well as the internal structure of the TCUs.

The next excerpt shows the production of another proposal. The proposer, BLF, is sitting at the first table on the left-hand side of the room, in front of the Chairman, who is quite close to her:

(17) (valorisation du patrimoine, med1_40.02=pub146.17=T17.36)

```
1   BLF:  *la la la val- va- va- enfin on a parlé *aussi la va*la- va*la-
           the the the pro- pro- pro- well we spoke too (about) promo- promotion,
     cha   *looks at BLF------------------------*looks&points to BLF*looks
                                                                    at BLF-->
2          val:orisation, patrimoniale et histori:que,# (.) °°du:°°
           of the heritage and the history, (.) of:
     fig                                              #fig3.20
3          (0.5)*
     cha   -->*
4   CHA:  *donc *c'est# un lieu, * qui donne à voir l'patrimoine?#
           so that's a place, which shows the heritage?
           *.....*looks at aud--*looks at BLF--------->
     fig            #fig3.21                          #fig3.22
```

Figure 3.20 The chairman looks at BLF

Figure 3.21 The chairman looks at the audience

Figure 3.22 The chairman looks at BLF again

The Chairman waits for BLF's turn completion by looking at her (Figure 3.20). After a pause, he reformulates the proposal, gazing first at the audience (Figure 3.21) and then back at BLF at the end of his interrogative turn (4, Figure 3.22). This action of looking back at her offers her a new possibility to repair or to complete her contribution (see below).

As noted above, the Chairman manages in his repeats and reformulations to maintain a double orientation, towards both the source of the proposal and the addressed audience. This double orientation is performed bodily by various body-torque positions (Schegloff 1998), as in the following extended fragment, in which TUR's proposal is reformulated twice:

(18) (modes de déplacement divers)

```
1  CHA:    j'ai entendu:, (.) un parc dans lequel:, (0.3) on peut:, (.)
            I've heard:,   (.) a park in which,    (0.3) one can, (.)
            >>still writing the previous agreed upon item on the board-->
2           se *enfin, on #se détpla:#ce, (0.4) tavect des
            well one moves around,   (0.4) with various
            ->*turns to the audience-->
                                tlooks at TUR---t,,,,t
     fig                    #fig.3.23 #fig.3.24
3           modes tde tdé#placemetnt ditve:rs,
            means of transportation,
                    t...tpoints TURt,,,,tlook L->
     fig                    #fig.3.25
4 ((15 omitted lines: inserted sequence going back to the previous proposal))
```

Figure 3.23 The chairman turns to and looks at the audience

Figure 3.24 The chairman turned to the audience looks at TUR

Figure 3.25 The chairman turned to the audience points at TUR

```
20 CHA:    mais *j'ai en*tendu que dans la propo#sition qui
           but I have heard that in the proposal which
           >>aud*.......*points to TUR's table------>
    fig                                              #fig.3.26
21         nous est faite [i#ci:,*
           is done for us [here,
22 BLF?:                  [°oui:°
                          [°yes:°
    cha                          ->*
    fig                    #fig.3.27
```

Figure 3.26 The chairman turns to and points at TUR

Figure 3.27 The chairman looks at the audience and points at TUR

Figure 3.28 The chairman points laterally at TUR

```
23         (0.5)
24 CHA:    y a du déplacement piéton mais y a aussi du *déplacement #vélo,*
           there is pedonal transportation but also bike transportation,
                                                    *points laterally-*
    fig                                             fig.3.28#
25         donc c'est *†des déplacements qu'vous appelez† doux, hh*
           so it's a transportation      that you call soft, hh
                          *large circle with both arms---------------*
                          †looks from left to right-------†circul. look aud->>
```

The Chairman is still writing the previous proposal on the whiteboard when he begins his reformulation (1), explicitly attributed to a voice that has been heard. On line 2, he moves from the board to the room, facing the audience (Figure 3.23) and immediately orients to TUR, turning his head towards her (Figure 3.24) or pointing at her (Figure 3.25), although maintaining his body orientation to the overall audience (white arrow). After an inserted sequence, the Chairman reformulates the same proposal again either turning totally towards TUR (Figure 3.26) or readopting a body-torque position (Figures 3.27 and 3.28).

The reformulation of the proposal is deeply embedded in the ecology of the activity. Due to the body torque, the Chairman maintains a double orientation, that is, to the source of the proposal and to the recipients. Both are located within the interactional space and contribute to its structure.

Moreover, the way in which the Chairman repeats or reformulates the proposal, orients to its imminent inscription: whereas *fermé la nuit* ('closed at night' excerpt 15) is displayed by its repetition as adequately formed for a possible inscription, the reformulation of other proposals (such as *voie d'accès vertes et pistes cyclables* 'green access paths and cycle lines' excerpt 16) transforms them progressively into a format more compatible with the future inscription than the original. In the latter cases, the gaze and head orientations towards the proposer continue to recognize his authorship, even if the proposal is transformed, thus achieving equivalence between the various versions for all practical purposes.

3.3.4   Monitoring Reception: Looking for Consensus and Spotting Disagreement

In the previous section, I demonstrated that the reformulation of the proposal orients towards two parties: the source and the audience. As soon as the reformulation is achieved, the Chairman engages in another embodied relationship with the audience, scrutinizing it for possible responses, closely monitoring the reception of the proposal.

(19) (fermé la nuit)

```
1    CHA:                                          *[fermé la nuit, h*
                                                    [closed at night, h
                  >>looks at TUR-----------------*.....*looks at aud------*
2    ? :         *°oui .hh°
                  °yes .hh°
     cha         *circular glance: on his L, then on his R----->
3    ?:           °non°
                  °no°
4    ROS?:        °non on [n'est pas d'accord, [nous°*
                  °no we are not agreeing, [as far as we are concerned
5    MAU:              [°non°                  [°non°*
                       [°no°                   [°no°
     cha                                            --->*
6    CHA:        *ah, pas d'accord ic#i,=
                  ah, not agreeing here,=
                 *points to ROS's table-->
     fig                       #fig.3.29
```

Figure 3.29 The chairman points at ROS's table

Immediately after repeating the proposal, the Chairman glances at the audience, first to his left, then to his right, with a circular gaze scrutinizing the various responses. Here, the Chairman is no longer oriented towards the source of the proposal, but to its recipients. Moreover, the Chairman does not gaze at the audience the same way he did during the repetition, during which he was looking in front of him at the entire audience; now, the audience is progressively inspected, table by table, by a dynamic monitoring gaze.

For a short moment, the Chairman silently observes the responses; then he moves again, identifying a place (*ici* 'here' 6) characterized by dissension and pointing to it (Figure 3.29). This way, the Chairman constantly organizes the audience spatially first by identifying a possible speaker, then by addressing both authors and recipients, and finally by spotting emergent zones of disagreement and clustering groups characterized by either consensus or dissension.

In some cases, the audience remains silent and the Chairman's gaze 'fishes' for a response:

(20) (ouverture aux écoles)

```
 1  CHA:    monsieur
            sir
 2  LUN:    oui parce qu'on en a pas du tout parlé, (0.2) on l'a pas évoqué (0.3)
            yes cause we had'nt at all talked about, (0.2) we haven't evoked it (0.3)
 3          mais y a euh douze écoles (0.6) euh primaires tout autour, i` y a (0.4)
            but the're ehm twelve schools (0.6) eh primary all around, the're (0.4)
 4          cinq milles collégiens lycéens (0.4) il faut quand même savoir si:, (0.5)
            five thousand high school students (0.4) one has to know if:, (0.5)
 5          *on: * (0.6) *ce parc, (0.9)  on (.) l'autori:*se disons, (0.5) à-
            if: (0.6) this park, (0.9) we (.) open it lets say, (0.5) to-
    cha     *nods*         *points rep to LY and looks at LY*looks LUN--------->
 6          l'OU:V*RE, (0.4) à aux écoles (0.4)* pour pou*voir veni*r[:
            OPEN, (0.4) to the schools (0.4) to let them come[:
    cha     -->*looks on his right---------*nods----*palm obliq*palm vert twd aud*
 7  CHA:                                             [alors, (0.2) CA, (.)*
                                                     [well, (0.2) THIS, (.)
 8          *c'est une vraie question,* j`voudrais qu`vous vous pronon*ciez là-d`ssus,
            is a true question, I would like that you take position about that,
            *palm circ towards the right*bis-------------------------*
 9          (0.3)
10  CHA:    *ou*ve:rt, à l'environ*nement* et en particulier, (0.2) l'environnement
                                                                            scolai*re
            ope:n, to the environment and in particular, (0.2) to the school environment
            *RL*circle L->R-------*,,,,,,*points w palm obliq to LUN----------------*,,
11  AUD:    <(( h#ubbub# ))  # (1.9)>
    cha     ,,,points to the audience w 2 hands and looks circularly-->>
    fig        #fig.3.30#fig.3.31#fig.3.32
```

Figure 3.30 The chairman double points in front of him

Figure 3.31 The chairman double points at the audience

Figure 3.32 The chairman double points looking at the audience

LUN's proposal is presented as an individual contribution, not emanating from a group: he is selected individually (*monsieur* 'sir' 1) and he explicitly says that the topic he proposes has not been discussed (2). Moreover, he asks a question, rather than stating a proposal. The Chairman's reception is different from the previous cases, since he displays interest and support during LUN's turn (5, 6), pointing to him and alternatively looking at LY, who is a member of the City Hall staff who organized the debate and now participates more as an observer than as a citizen. After LUN completes his turn, the Chairman offers a positive assessment and immediately turns to the audience with both a circular gaze and a circular gesture, inviting them both verbally and gesturally to respond (8). As they are not responding yet (9), the Chairman reformulates a more compact version of the proposal, while scrutinizing the public and looking at LUN, acknowledging him as the source. The audience responds in a hubbub, and the Chairman monitors this, pointing with both arms, searching for possible participants to select next to either agree or disagree (Figures 3.30–3.32).

The same gestures are produced by the Chairman when searching for a consensus about the formulation of the proposal concerning the benches:

(21) (bancs)

```
1   CHA:    usages de convivialité,
            uses of conviviality,
2   BLO:    oui.
            yes.
3   ROU:    *oui,
            yes,
    cha     *looks at the audience -->>
4   COL?:   par exemple
            for example
5   CHA:    c'*est #ça,*
            that's it,
            ->*points--*
    fig           #fig.3.33
6   BLO?:   des rencontres, (.) des aires de rencontre
            meetings, (.) places to meet
7   ROU:    faire des *bancs,* (.)# [des bancs entourés de] verdu*re#
            install benches, (.) [benches surrounded by greenery
8   BLF?:                        [lieux de convivialité]
                                 [places of conviviality]
    cha     -->*......*2 palms vert---------------*p w 2 h->>

    fig                    #fig.3.34                    fig.3.35#
9   HAB?:   lieu de rencontre,
            meeting places,
10  ?:      °rencon:tre, [échan:ge,°
            °meeting, [exchange,°
11  BLO?:              [un lieu d'rencon:tre
                       [a place for meeting
```

Figure 3.33 The chairman points at BLF's table

Figure 3.34 The chairman raises the two hands palm vertical up

Figure 3.35 The chairman does a double pointing

Although the Chairman's reformulation (1) receives positive responses from three participants (2–4), he produces a new confirmation question (5). The respondents search for alternative formulations (6–11) and are monitored by the Chairman, who is not only gazing at the audience but also moderating the various self-selected speakers with both hands extended forward and palms open vertically (Figure 3.34), then with two hands pointing in a very similar way as in the previous excerpt (Figure 3.35).

In this case, we observe an early orientation to potential recipients of the proposal, including some observers: the bodily postures of the Chairman make relevant different portions of the room, which are occupied by different types of participants.

The Chairman's orientation towards the source of the proposal and the audience's consensus or dissension can alternate. This is the case when the repetition of a proposal is not treated as being obviously equivalent to the previous version, but is produced interrogatively as needing a confirmation, as in the following case:

(22) (valorisation du patrimoine) (continuation of exc. 17)

```
4  CHA:     donc *c'est un lieu,* qui donne à voir l'patrimoine?#
            so that's a place,   which shows the heritage?
            -->*looks at aud--*looks at BLF--------->
   fig                                                          #fig.3.36
5  BLF:     qui donne à [voir, *à:# à:# (0,9)** #euh* un patrimoine# &
            which shows to: to: (0.9) ehm a heritage
   cha                  -->*pointing to aud----*points to BLF------->
                                     **looks at BLF------------->
   fig                  fig.3.37#   #fig.3.38 #fig.3.39  fig.3.40#
6  ?:       [°oui,°
            [°yes,°
```

Figure 3.36 The chairman looks at BLF

Figure 3.37 The chairman points at the audience

Figure 3.38 The chairman looks at the audience

Figure 3.39 The chairman
looks at BLF

Figure 3.40 The chairman looks
and points at BLF

```
 7  BLF:    &qu'on expli**:que, qu'on::**
            &that we explain    that we::
     cha        -->**nods-----------**
 8  COL:    en mettant en avant dans [l'ambiance, le: l'histoi:re, le patrim-
            by foregrounding in the atmosphere, the: the history, the herit-
 9  CHA:                             [d'ac*cord, est-ce que vous êtes d'accord? en termes de:*
                                     [okay,       are you agreeing?           in terms of:
                                     -->*turns to audience, holding the pointing------------*
10          (.) *l'idée c'est-à-dire que c'est un lieu:, [*alors j'sais pas si c'est
            (.) the idea is to say that it is a place:, [then I don't know if it is
                *gesticulates towards the audience -------*turns, pt to whiteboard->
11  BLF:                                                      [°qui a une histoi:re,°
                                                             [°which has a histo:ry°,
12          d'ailleurs un usage, ou une* ambiance,
            by the way a use, or an atmosphere,
                                      -->*
13  ?:      [°les [deux°
            [°both°
14  COL:    [°hum°
15  NIC:        [°c'est une ambi[ance.°
                [°that's an atmosphere.
16  BLF:                        [°c'est une ambiance,°
                                [°that's an atmosphere°,
17  CHA:    mais m-* ce groupe nous pro*po[se, un lieu: (.) où on en profi]te pour&
            but m- this group proposes a place where we take advantage in order to&
                  *points to BLF's group*gesticulates with 2 hands twd aud-->>
18  BLO?:                                  [c'est une ambiance, (.) c'est une ambiance,]
                                          [it's an ambiance, (.) it's an ambiance,]
19  CHA:    &montrer l'patrimoine,*
            &show the heritage,
                        --->*
```

As he reformulates the proposal (4), the Chairman looks at the audience, but also looks back at BLF in a precompletion position, his turn being prosodically formatted as a request for confirmation, addressed to her. She confirms by repeating the first part of her proposal, but engages in a repair of the second part, with some hesitations (5). During these hesitations, the Chairman performs several pointing gestures towards the audience (Figures 3.37 and 3.38), scanning, perusing, and searching the audience for possible incipient disagreements. He then looks and points back at BLF as she continues without hitches and is about to complete her turn, nodding on the last part of her turn. He holds his parallel gesture in the air (Figures 3.38 and 3.39), first looking at the audience (Figure 3.38) then looking back at her (Figure 3.39), finally looking and pointing at her (Figure 3.40), as she does not complete her turn, but COL collaboratively does so (8).

Overlapping with COL, the Chairman explicitly seeks the agreement of the audience (9), reformulating the proposal (10). During this reformulation, he holds the pointing gesture and other gesticulations towards the audience. However, he also turns to the whiteboard, as he suspends the formulation (*c'est un lieu:* 'it's a pla:ce' 10), showing the relevance of the orientation to one of the thematic sections of the board (*usage* or *ambiance*) for its continuation. He then turns back to BLF, referring to her proposal as emanating from 'this group' (17), turning again to the audience when reformulating the body of the proposal and submitting to it.

In this case, the formulation is not stable: the joint authors continue to reformulate and repair it collaboratively, and the Chairman's reformulation is not definitive and remains tentative. Retrospectively, BLF's repairs and COL's collaborative attempts also bear traces of previous discussions and misalignments within the small group; they mix two different lines within COL's notes (*thème 'histoire'* + *patrimoine* and *valoriser les* ≠ *ambiances*; Figure 3.14(b)). Prospectively, the Chairman, turning to the inscription space, shows the constraints of the written version for the choice of the definitive formulation. As the elaboration of the proposal expands, the negotiation of the proposal with the authors and the orientation to the audience's response is carried out at the same time, the Chairman switching back and forth between them.

3.4   Conclusion: the Embodied Production, Elaboration, and Reception of a Proposal

The analyses of the various proposals produced during a meeting within a participatory urbanistic project show that the production of a proposal is deeply embedded in the ecology of the specific activity in which it takes place. The ecology matters in different ways as the sequence unfolds:

(a) Participants are constantly being situated within a space. The selection of the proposer situates him or her within a particular place in the room, within a 'table' treated as a specific 'participation unit'. This makes the next speaker a spokesperson speaking on behalf of a group, materialized as a 'table'.
(b) The proposal is addressed to the Chairman and produced by integrating references both to past exchanges and future inscriptions. Past discussions and negotiations are sedimented in private and 'collective' notes, which are held by the participants when formulating their proposals. Future inscriptions are taken into account by looking at the board or by integrating the normative constraints of their written and spatial organization.

(c) Once formulated, the proposal is ratified in either an immediate or delayed way by the Chairman, who repeats it (when he considers it to be adequate) or reformulates it (when he adapts it to the written constraints). At this point, the Chairman's action adopts a double orientation, visible in his body-torque position: towards the source of the proposal and towards the audience to which it is readdressed. Here, he orients to the audience as a whole, i.e. as constituting one party.

(d) Once the proposal has been voiced to the audience, the latter is scrutinized by the Chairman by spotting possible agreements, but also disagreements, identifying possible divergences and inviting the participants to choose. Here, the audience is oriented to through a circular gaze and circular gesture; they are treated as a composite group, as a multi-party, and as composed by potential imminent speakers.

During the moment-by-moment unfolding of the sequence in which a proposal is made, various details of the local ecology are made relevant:

  – The relevant structure of the environment is configured by the bodily postures of the Chairman, alternatively oriented to the wall or to the room, making relevant either the inscription space or the interactional space, depending on the sequential phase of the activity.

  – The body orientations of the Chairman also work to manage individual turn-taking and participation, which structure the interactional space at multiple levels. On the one hand, he manages the selection of the next speaker, the search for respondents, as well as opportunities for various speakers to talk, either simultaneously or chorally. On the other hand, he manages the relevance of various voices, orienting to their different statuses (as sources, authors, responsible spokespersons). Through the management of both aspects, he builds multiple participation frameworks, dynamically and flexibly structured as individuals, parties, groups, allies, observers, etc.

  – The bodily postures and gestures also make relevant different kinds of artefacts – especially textual artefacts – through the way in which they are produced, manipulated, read, written during the session, and pointed at, as well as quoted and oriented to as far as their structure and their constraints are concerned. So, artefacts are also oriented to for the normativity they materialize, such as the constraints of the written form, the genres associated with it, and the specific spatialization of texts on the whiteboard.

  – Last but not least, the linguistic structure of the proposal is itself deeply embedded in the local ecology, being reflexively achieved by orienting to the above-mentioned dimensions, as they are made relevant in the course of the action. In this sense, the proposal's formulation is situated, being both recipient-designed, sensitive to past and future versions, integrating different voices, and readjusting to multiple and flexible participation frameworks evolving as the activity unfolds.

Thus, we can say that the proposal is a polyphonic action which is sensitive to the distribution of voices at different layers of the ecology of action: voices are distributed among the participants, who can act and talk under different and mutable categories; they are also distributed within the material environment, inscribed in various places, such as the whiteboard and its rubrics, or personal notes, as well as other available documents. Different voices mobilize specific linguistic resources, oriented to informal vs. formal contexts of discussion, spoken vs. written formulations. Successful voices will migrate across other ecologies, not only within the inscriptional space of the whiteboard but also in the notes of the organizing staff and the Chairman acting as a consultant for the City Hall, in the protocols of the sessions and in further official documents. The material ecology persists after the local ecology of the interaction has been dissolved; nevertheless, the former crucially emerges from the latter.

By visibly pointing at precise locations within the room, the Chairman makes relevant the distribution of participants within the room. In contrast, he exploits the spatial structure of the environment to manage turns to speak, to make visible his action, and to assign speakers to a certain location within the room. Turn-taking thus becomes spatialized.

The detailed analysis of the situated production of an apparently simple utterance, and the way in which it is deeply rooted in the local ecology of the activity, shows the articulation between linguistic and multimodal resources, the organization of interaction, and its embodied integration into the local and global context. The ecology of interaction integrates both the spatial configuration of the interaction and the way in which it is made relevant by the embodied action of the participants. The detailed way in which it is organized through the emergent organization of turns to speak and the embodied organization of the participants' action shows the importance of observing it in the context of 'ecological data', i.e. recordings that are not orchestrated by the researchers but naturally unfold within their context.

Transcript Conventions

Talk has been transcribed according to conventions developed by Gail Jefferson. An indicative translation is provided line per line, in italics. Multimodal details have been transcribed according to the following conventions (see Mondada https://franzoesistik.philhist.unibas.ch/fileadmin/user_upload/ franzoesistik/mondada_multimodal_conventions.pdf):

* *	delimit descriptions of one speaker's actions
+ +	delimit descriptions of another speaker's actions
*–>	action described continues across subsequent lines
*–>>	action described continues until and after excerpt's end
–>*	action described continues until the same symbol is reached
>>–	action described begins before the excerpt's beginning
. . .	action's preparation
,,,,,	action's retraction
cha	participant doing the action is identified in small characters when he is not the current speaker or when the gesture is done during a pause
fig	figure; screen shot
#	indicates the exact moment at which the screen shot has been recorded

4   Approaching Language in Urban Interactions Ecologically: the Case of Spanish in Lima*

Juan Carlos Godenzzi

4.1   Introduction

Our approach to language in urban interactions may be called *ecological* in the sense that it emphasizes multiplicity, diversity, and interconnectedness. This conception of *ecology* as 'a complex open system of relations and dependencies' is detailed in Chapter 1, this volume, especially in regard to the distinction between different types of *foundation* or interdependency relationships – on the basis of Husserl – on horizontal and vertical axes as well as the differentiation of three levels, the micro-, middle, and macro-ecologies. The issue of urban level Lima broached in this chapter can be regarded as a middle ecology.

A key dimension in ecology is *space*. There are many kinds of spaces: places, areas, territories, networks (Lévy and Lussault 2003: 332); and each study chooses the space scale for its subject of research. Mondada (Chapter 3, this volume), for instance, focuses specifically on the micro-space level, and thus on the different relations of interdependencies on the level of discourse. This chapter, instead, is devoted to three urban areas or neighbourhoods, on a middle-space level; and will require a notion of space related to urbanity and to language. Generally speaking, space can be defined in *positional* or in *relational* terms:

There is probably no more decisive difference among thinkers than the position they are inclined to take on space: Is space that *inside which* reside objects and subjects? Or is space one of the many connections made by objects and subjects? In the first tradition, if you empty the space of all entities there is something left: space. In the second, since entities engender their space (or rather their spaces) as they trudge along, if you take the entities out, nothing is left, especially space. (Latour 2009: 142)

* This chapter has been translated from Spanish by Sara Smith. I am grateful to the Freiburg Institute for Advanced Studies (Language and Literature), Albert-Ludwigs-Universität, for the Senior Fellowship (October 2009) which permitted me to elaborate on the ideas presented in this chapter. I would also like to thank the Social Sciences and Humanities Research Council of Canada, whose financial support made my research in Lima possible. Finally, I would like to thank Michel DeGraff and Anna Babel for their comments, and to Sara Smith and Helena Rodriguez for their collaboration in the analysis of some of the interviews.

As a relational concept, space can be conceived of as the expansion of waves from an organizing point (Thom 1980),[1] or as a collection of properties that are defined by certain functions (Pilares 1995: 433; Lévy and Lussault 2003: 325). In this sense, language is not an activity that is *inside* a space (environment or context), but rather an interconnecting practice that produces its spaces as it trudges along in a semiotic way.[2] Among the multiple types of language spaces, we can single out the *urban language space*, which can be defined by the connections between language features or properties, and urbanity features or properties.[3]

Adopting this ecological and spatial perspective, this chapter focuses on the urban language space of Lima, Peru, paying attention to particular *language features* (mixing, variation, and stability) and to their interdependencies with particular *urbanity features* (density, diversity, and mobility). We also take into account the Spanish spoken by three people living in three *distinct* neighbourhoods of Lima: Huaycán, a lower-class area in East Lima; Los Olivos, an emergent area in North Lima; and Pueblo Libre, a traditional middle-class area.[4] We argue that a description of the connections between these features will allow us to understand the ways in which a language organizes its systemic make-up and the ways in which it takes part in urban dynamics.

From a population of 645,172 in 1940, 1,652,000 in 1961, and 7,765,151 in 2005 (Meneses 2009: 32), Lima has now grown to a city of more than 8 million inhabitants, one-third of Peru's population. The most determinative factor of this growth has been rural exodus from different regions in the country's interior.[5] In this way, the City of Lima is being reconfigured not only through

[1] 'Je verrais volontiers l'archétype fondamental de la notion d'espace, l'*Urbild* de la spatialité, dans l'image d'un point centre organisateur, qui s'étoile en une configuration sous-tendant tout un espace associé' ['I would gladly view the fundamental archetype of the notion of space, the *Urbild* of spatiality, as the image of an organizing center point, which scatters to form an underlying constellation of an entire associated space'] (137; our translation).

[2] The semiotic mechanism of language includes the interaction between planes of expression and contents. These planes are demarcated by a perceiving body that positions itself in a world of meanings, defining the boundary between what the order of expressions will be and what the order of contents will be. The relationship between an element of expression and an element of content produces meaning. Meaning, therefore, is tied to unity, regardless of the size of that unity, with discourse being the optimum unit (Fontanille 1998: 20–22).

[3] For another approach to urban space, diversity, and mobility, as well as its connections with language repertoires and patterns of language use, see Blommaert and Dong (2010).

[4] The three interviews on which the present work is based belong to a corpus that was gathered in the context of my research project 'Spanish in Lima: Sociolinguistic variation in the context of urbanization'. From 2005 to 2008, this had the financial support of the Social Sciences and Humanities Research Council of Canada.

[5] It has been estimated that the current migrant population living in Lima represents 56 per cent (4,348,484) of the city's total population (Meneses 2009: 32).

an increase in its population density, but also through the ethnic, cultural, and linguistic diversity of its inhabitants.[6]

Because this chapter is not based on a representative sample of the city's different sectors, our objective here is neither to identify different types of groups nor to categorize linguistic varieties. Rather, we aim to describe the way in which each of the three speakers makes connections with different entities, such as places, times, groupings, habitats, identities, and representations. They themselves bear witness to their urban experiences and draw out their movements and connections. By retracing these sketches we are able to work out how the city is constructed and transformed, as well as how language varies and restructures itself.

4.2   Language and Urbanity Properties

4.2.1   Mixing, Variation, and Stability

Languages arise by way of interaction and mixing (Baudouin de Courtenay 1897/1972: 213; Van Coetsem 2003: 30); and they evolve and change in the same way. Language *mixing* is, therefore, the rule, not the exception, because it is an intrinsic part of language itself (Mufwene 2001: 19; Van Coetsem 2003: 31; Chapter 1, this volume). In new contexts of contact, language mixing phenomena may be conspicuous (characterized as 'overt' by Kriegel, Ludwig, and Salzmann, Chapter 7, this volume); however, when languages have already been integrated and normalized, these phenomena tend to be less obvious ('covert'). In either case, there is mixing. *Variation* is another property of language, not an external or accidental one, but one that is immanent and continuous (Deleuze and Guattari 1980: 123, 130; Van Coetsem 2003: 32). Variation is always present, whereas the effects of standardization are derivative. Continuous language variation makes the emergence of so-called *social varieties* and *standard varieties* possible. *Stability* is a third property of language: while the lexical item (the word) is less stable, the relationship (the rule) is more stable. In other words, the lexicon is an ephemeral part of language, while grammar and phonology are more durable (Van Coetsem 2003: 32). Mixing, variation, and stability are interrelated, and the specificity of this relationship likewise depends on their relationships with other factors, such as, in our case, those related to urbanity.

---

[6] Quechua, Aymara, Shipibo, Ashaninka, and Awajun are among the most widely spoken languages in the country. The percentage of the population whose first language is indigenous stands at, at least, 4 million people. In the case of Lima, while a large part of the population speaks Spanish and Quechua, the languages that migrants *cultivate* 'represent all the existing cultures in the country' (Meneses 2009: 54).

4.2.2   *Density, Diversity, and Mobility*

The city is an organized spatial configuration made up of three fundamental components: density, diversity, and mobility. *Density* is the relationship between the mass of a localized substance in a given space and the size of this space (Lévy and Lussault 2003: 237); for our study, what applies is population density. *Diversity* is the relationship between the level of heterogeneity among co-present realities and the level of heterogeneity that exists in a space that serves as a point of reference (Lévy and Lussault 2003: 274); for our study, what applies is ethnic, cultural, and idiomatic heterogeneity. *Mobility* is all that is tied to the movement of humans and of material or immaterial objects in a given space (Lévy and Lussault 2003: 622); for our study, this includes immigration, relocation within the city, private or public transportation, and technological communication. Density and diversity are related to co-presence, that is, to the proximity of topographic contact, as a response to the problem of distance. However, as human agglomerations in cities increase, the problem of distance arises once again, which mobility tends to solve. By re-establishing contact in a minimal or immediate amount of time, mobility makes way for urban expansion and, as such, weakens density and, often, diversity (Lussault 2007: 269–270). Both as a result and cause of urbanization, mobility is expressed in population movements, in instant communication and the circulation of products, in images, and in information (Lussault 2007: 302; Augé 2009: 7–8). Urbanization must therefore not be thought of as a new kind of human settlement, but as new forms of mobility (Augé 2009: 21).

4.3   Producing Urban Insertion

Speaker A, at 25 years of age, is married with two children and works as a *combi*[7] driver. He was born in the Province of Huamanga (Ayacucho) and currently lives in Huaycán, a human settlement founded in 1984 and located in the Ate Vitarte district of East Lima. The district's population stands at 100,000 residents and comprises both migrants who were displaced by terrorist violence during the 1980s and poor families coming from 'ghettoized' neighbourhoods of the metropolitan city.

4.3.1   *Rural Background and Urban Experience*

Speaker A has moved through diverse spaces, from Pomabamba, which is highly rural, to Lima, a highly urban one, passing through Huamanga, the

---

[7] Minibus used for public transportation in Lima.

capital of the Department of Ayacucho, an intermediate point on the cline of urbanization. These spaces, which constitute very diverse habitats, are linguistically and axiologically marked. In effect, the interviewee distinguishes between: (i) predominantly Quechua-speaking, monolingual places, such as Pomabamba; (ii) bilingual places in which a regional Spanish variety is spoken, like Huamanga; and (iii) predominantly Castilian-speaking, monolingual places, such as Lima. The higher and lower levels of urbanization continue to correspond to the relatively high or low visibility levels of Quechua. These spaces, furthermore, form the environment in which conflicting opinions occur: Speaker A views his Andean village as a peaceful place, although it is affected by violence and terror. However, he also evokes another perspective, one that has been integrated into Peruvian society since colonial times and which undervalues and discriminates against indigenous peoples, their spaces, cultures and languages. This can be confirmed, for example, by the recommendation that the interviewee receives from his grandfather: 'if you don't speak Castilian ... they will insult you', thus highlighting the strong linguistic discrimination existing in urban interactions.

In the imaginary of Speaker A, Lima appears as the Promised Land. For him, a move to Lima represents the possibility of 'getting ahead' (*surgir*), which implies accessing more urbanized spaces, i.e., leaving the mountain 'village' to find work in the capital. Lived experience, however, doesn't always coincide with imagined space and he soon realizes that Lima is, for him, a tough place, full of suffering and rivalry, where he is expelled from one place only to take refuge in another, and where he experiences ridicule and contempt, particularly for the way he speaks Spanish.

He recounts that, while nobody ever ridiculed his Castilian in Huamanga, in Lima people would deride him and tell him '*serrano*, speak properly'.[8] The contrast between his village and Lima, which Speaker A alludes to, allows us to establish a relationship between a type of space and the level of ethnic, sociocultural and linguistic discrimination inherent to it. The Andean village, small in size and with low density and diversification, constitutes a sphere in which linguistic discrimination is almost inexistent. On the other hand, Lima, enormous in size and with high density and diversification, is a sphere that is particularly sensitive to even minor differences and engenders ethnic distances and linguistic discrimination, which, as it applies to Speaker A, is also linked to a particular spatial ideology and politics. The mountains are often considered to be an obstacle to progress, as they are perceived as an archaic, barbarous, and backwards place. Consequently, their products, people, and

---

[8] In this context *serrano* literally translates as 'mountain man' or 'man from the mountains'. In Peru, it has a pejorative sense akin to, but much stronger than, *hillbilly* or *hick*. It is in order to preserve this connotation that I have left the term in Spanish.

languages are devalued and viewed in a pejorative light (Orlove 1993: 321). As such, to call someone a *serrano* evokes all of the sociohistorical connotations that this term has entailed since colonial times; the term is thus used to implicate social distance and to establish ethnic and sociocultural boundaries.

Speaker A relates that he uses his mother tongue, Quechua, with some members of his family in particular circumstances, for example, during the celebration of a traditional festival from Ayacucho, now replicated in Lima. Speaker A thus makes reference to a specific time and place in which the link between a particular Andean linguistic and cultural tradition, that of Ayacucho, may be reinforced and celebrated. Participating in that sphere of affinities, affects, and values proves to be gratifying to him ('it is a pleasure to speak there'). However, the gratification is only short-lived and contrasts with the harshness and communicative difficulty that he experiences in his new habitat ('I can't [have a conversation in Quechua] with my friends because they only speak Castilian. They think they're from Lima now'). Speaker A's account also reveals the existence of *inter-spatiality*: people from Ayacucho residing in different places in Lima move to a place along the Avenida Argentina to recreate a festival normally celebrated in Ayacucho. One place redirects to other places. One place contains other places. The Lima of migrants begins to fashion itself as an agglomeration of networks that link diverse parts of the city to each other, and these to other places in the country's interior.

The urban experience of Speaker A is thus characterized both by the particularity of his mobility (migratory, residential, and quotidian) and by the manner in which he inhabits the city's co-presence (density and diversity). First he moves from a rural habitat to another, less rural one and, later, to another highly urban one (migratory mobility). Likewise, he moves from one poor neighbourhood to other poor neighbourhoods, until he finally establishes himself in an equally poor settlement, although now as a landowner (residential mobility). Moreover, as a driver of a transport vehicle, he moves daily throughout various sectors of the city, coming into contact with diverse residents of the city (quotidian mobility). On the other hand, his residence and trajectory in the city occur in environments with particularly high population densities in which there is also cultural, ethnic, and language diversity.

4.3.2   *Language Use and Linguistic Features*

Speaker A uses Quechua, his first language, to establish privileged connections with the network of Quechua-speaking migrants from the southern Andean plateau, especially if these are from Ayacucho. Meanwhile, he uses Castilian to establish connections with other actor-networks in the city. He himself is conscious of such a diversity and creates his own categories: on the one hand, there are people who 'think they're from Lima' (monolinguals born in Lima of migrant parents); and, on the other hand, there are people who speak like him (bilingual migrants).

Speaker A's Spanish reflects characteristics of both a Castilian spoken in the Peruvian mountains, with a strong Quechua influence, and the popular speech of the coast. The former include the double marking of the locative (1), gender neutralization (2), a double possessive (3), a particular use of the clitic *lo* (4), and the use of direct quotation, followed by the form *diciendo* 'saying' to tie sentences together (5):

(1)   Nadie hablaba el castellano *en allá*.
        nobody used.to.speak the spanish *in there*
        'Nobody used to speak Spanish *there*.'

(2)   En la capital *mismo*.
        in the capital(FE) *itself* (MS)[9]
        'In the capital *itself*.'

(3)   Me caí del tercer piso de *su* casa *de* mi tía.
        RF i.fell from.the third floor of 3P house *of* my aunt
        'I fell from the third floor of my aunt*'s* house.'

(4)   Por eso *lo* dicen ticti [a las alverjitas].
        for that 3O.MS.SG they.say ticti [to the beans (FEM.PL)].
        'That's why they say "ticti" to the beans.'

(5)   Mi – amá . . . vámonos allá a surgir *diciendo*.
        my [m]um . . . let's.go there to.get.ahead *saying*.
        'My mom said we should go there to get ahead.'

Features of the coastal popular speech include the weakening or disappearance of the intervocalic /d/ (6), the elision of the /s/ at the end of a word (7), the omission of the first consonant (8) and/or of the last syllable (9).

(6)   Hasta un día nos han *bota-o* de su casa.   [compare **botado**]
        'Until one day they've kicked us out of their house.'

(7)   Pero ahí *nomá-* llegué a tener mi familia.   [compare **nomás**]
        'But then I had a family.'

(8)   Por los mismos problemas, mi *-amá* tenía miedo de mí.   [compare **mamá**]
        'For the same problems, my mom was afraid for me.'

(9)   No, yo *pa'* regresarme *pa'* allá.   [compare **para**]
        'Me, I'll never go back there.'

---

[9] The abbreviations employed in this section are as follows: FE: feminine, MS: masculine, SG: singular, PL: plural, 3: third person, P: possessor, O: object, RF: reflexive.

4.3.3   A Mixed Urban Language

Speaker A mixes structural elements of two languages (Spanish and Quechua); likewise, he mixes features of two different varieties (that of the indigenous highlands and that of the lower-class speakers of the coast). This mixed Spanish is related to his mobility (migratory, residential, and quotidian), to his multiple associations, and to his dense and heterogeneous cohabitation. In effect, while he maintains some features of the Andean speech mode, he filters others out, particularly those that most directly indicate his rural background. Examples of this might be the instability of the use of the vowels *e/i* and *o/u*,[10] the refashioning of his accent, or the monophthongization of diphthongs. Thus, the features of Speaker A's Castilian are related to his ruptures and continuities, to his biography of spatial relocations and to his new habitat's networks.

In summary, we can identify the following *language features* of A: (i) some stability that is more or less guaranteed by the rules of two languages; (ii) notable inter-linguistic mixing, resulting from the first-language influence of Quechua and its 'interference' in the rules of the second language, Spanish; (iii) notable inter-dialectal mixing, between the highland and coastal varieties; (iv) a unique style of speech, with precipitates, retentions, innovations, and adoptions. Likewise, we can enumerate *urbanity features* that are related to A: (i) residence in lower-class urban neighbourhoods, which are densely populated and culturally heterogeneous; (ii) the strong effects of migratory mobility; and (iii) daily mobility that diminishes topographical distances minimally (owing to slow and unreliable public transportation). The interconnection of all these features, which have their origins in the speaker, creates a specific *urban language space* in which A operates and produces urban integration.

4.4   Building a 'Good' Place

Speaker B is a young woman who, at the time of the interview (2005), was 18 years old. She was born in El Rímac, the historic city centre, where she completed her primary education. Her secondary education was completed in her new place of residence, Los Olivos, where she was living with her parents. Los Olivos, considered 'the capital of North Lima', is a peripheral municipal

---

[10] Speaker A remarks that, when he arrived in Lima, he found the Castilian pronunciation difficult: 'mi lengua no me soltaba para el castellano' ['with Castilian, my tongue wouldn't loosen up']. Since then, he has rather successfully 'loosened up' his tongue, even though some features that index his migrant origins persist. In fact, the most perceptible feature of rural Andean Castilian, the instability of the pronunciation of medium and high vowels, practically does not exist in Speaker A's speech. An undifferentiated *e/i* appears only once: 'me dicían [compare *decían*] agarra periódico' ['they told me to grab a newspaper'].

district of Metropolitan Lima. Founded in 1970, and with a population of around 240,000 inhabitants, it is considered an 'institutional leader in the improvement of standard of living and in the promotion of economic, ecological and social development in the district' (Municipalidad Distrital de Los Olivos 2006). It houses one of Lima's largest malls, which has become a symbol of the district's economic progress.

4.4.1   Escaping from Density

Speaker B is not a migrant and neither are her parents, though her grandparents and other family members are. She left El Rímac, a densely populated although relatively homogeneous area, to live in Los Olivos, within a highly diversified population originating primarily from the country's interior. As such, her residential mobility has taken her to a safer, less dense place, at once confronting her with increased ethnic and cultural diversity. In her own words:

yo vivía en El Ríma – era una zona populosa – onde toda la gente es limeña, la gente es más avispada, avivada, ¿no? pero acá la gente era diferente, más sana, amable ... eh ... es es otro tipo de vida ... la vida del provinciano es, este, más sana me parece, ¿no?, hasta su ... hasta incluso su misma alimentación, la manera de expresarse, de formar a sus hijos, ¿no? es totalmente diferente.

[I used to live in El Rimac, it was a populated zone where everyone is from Lima, people are sharper, livelier, no? but here people were different, healthier, nice ... um ... it's, it's a different kind of life ... The provincial's lifestyle is, um, healthier I think, no?, even their ... even their diet, the way they speak, raise their children, no? it's totally different.]

Urban areas articulate diverse *places*, defined as smaller spaces of social life. A *place* is a discrete unit in which *inside* and *outside* enter into play (Lévy and Lussault 2003: 561–562). Speaker B discursively constructs this fold that separates the inside (here) from the outside (two blocks from here) to organize the experience of 'tranquillity' and 'insecurity'. She assigns calm people to an inside and unproblematic place, while she characterizes the external as the place of 'gangs' and insecurity. Well settled into her place, and feeling relatively secure, Speaker B elaborates on her life plan: to have a nice, completed, four-storeyed house, where her mother can stay. In other words, she wants to act in a way that might one day produce a 'good' space, which, in turn, might lend her a mark of distinction.

The urban growth of the last decades has made the city difficult to represent, as the old downtown is no longer the centre. Areas that were formerly designated as 'marginal' and which evoked poverty and precariousness are in reality new centres with their own peripheries. Speaker B's description of contemporary Lima makes constant reference to the factors related to the density, diversity, and mobility of the population. Some peripheral districts present high density, demographic diversity, and relative mobility: the people occupy streets and move through them, while also using public transportation to connect with other places. In contrast, the San Isidro district, one of the more prestigious sectors of Lima, appears in her account as a less dense and diverse space, but with high and individual mobility. Forms of mobility that correspond to this prestigious district include the automobile, that 'moving-place' that makes walking in the streets unnecessary, while residential Internet allows for an immediate connection to be made with the world. As Speaker B puts it, the people of San Isidro 'have everything in their home, so they stay there'.

All of this produces the redefinition of categories of identity. Speaker B distances herself from the 'provincials', but also from Lima's elites in her process of identification. In response to the question of whether she feels more like a Limeñan (i.e. resident of Lima) or more like a provincial, first she states that she had never before asked herself the question. Later she expresses a tension with regard to her being Limeñan and being *Chola* (*I feel like I'm a Chola, ¿no? I'm a Chola-Limeñan*). Finally, she resolves the tension in favour of feeling more like a Limeñan (*anyway I feel more like I'm a* Limeñan). However, it is clear that she does not consider herself to be a Limeñan in the traditional sense, as opposed to a provincial or a *serrana*, but rather a Limeñan who is connected to the provinces and to the mountains. Her urban experiences are characterized by her residential mobility, which have taken her from a very dense place in historic Lima (El Rímac) to another less dense place, situated in the new Lima of the northern periphery (Los Olivos). Likewise, her urban experience is conditioned by the means of her daily mobility: she has at her disposal relatively frequent public transportation services, compared to that which exists, for example, in Huaycán. However, compared to the people from San Isidro, she does not possess other means of mobility, such as an automobile, a cell phone, or residential Internet.

4.4.2   Ways of Speaking Castilian

Regarding the modes of speaking Castilian in her diverse surroundings, Speaker B distinguishes between the speech of first-generation Limeñans (children of migrants) and that of second-generation Limeñans such as herself (grandchildren of migrants). Some of the forms used by first-generation Limeñans greatly irritate her, such as double-marking the possessive, or the use of the article before a proper name. She tells us, moreover, that when she hears her friends use forms that she considers provincial or vulgar, she draws attention to them and corrects them, but without 'getting into race', that is to say, without making allusion to their place of origin, given that she knows that for Limeñans geography is racially marked and stratified. For example, she'll say to them, 'Speak properly! Hey! What's wrong with you?' However, she never says, 'Hey! *We're in Lima*, speak properly!' Introducing a spatial reference would, then, be a racist and discriminatory act. Speaker B, therefore, reveals that space is not neutral; rather, it is a factor that can also instigate discrimination and racism.

Some of the characteristic features of Speaker B's Castilian include the following: regarding her pronunciation, there is a tendency to omit the dental consonant /d/ or /t/ in word-final position variably. That is, while sometimes this consonant is produced (10a), it is usually omitted (10b–h).

(10)   a. Pero no, de *verdad* es que todo ha cambiado ¿no?
           'But no, really it's that everything has changed, no?'
       b. Mayoría tiene *Interné-* en su casa.   [compare **Internet**]
           'Most have Internet at home.'
       c. Mi *edá* ¿no?   [compare **edad**]
           'My age, no?'
       d. Pero la *comunidá* como te digo no se mete.   [compare **comunidad**]
           'But, like I said, the community doesn't get involved.'
       e. La *verdá* es que depende de cada familia.   [compare **verdad**]
           'It really depends on each family.'
       f. En la *unidá* vecinal del Rímac.   [compare **unidad**]
           'In the Rímac neighbourhood unit.'
       g. Hay *movilidá* para todos lados, eso sí.   [compare **movilidad**]
           'There are means of access to all places, that yes.'
       h. Estudiando en una *universidá* particular.   [compare **universidad**]
           'Studying in a private university.'

Likewise, one can observe an alternation between the retention and omission of the consonant /d/ in the intervocalic position (11).

(11)   a. Le han *robado* a un chico, le han *pegado*
           'They have robbed a boy, they have hit him.'
       b. Le han *quita-o* la zapatilla.   [compare **quitado**]
           'They have taken the sneaker from him.'
       c. Era una *zona* populos*a –onde* toda la gente es limeña.   [compare **donde**]
           'It was a populated area, where everyone's from Lima.'

Likewise, there are instances of velarization of the voiced bilabial occlusive /b/ before the diphthong *ue*, as well as the velarization of the voiceless bilabial occlusive /p/ in syllable-final position (13).

(12)   a. Acá a la *güelta* hay una iglesia evangélica.   [compare **vuelta**]
           'There's an evangelical church around the corner.'
       b. Ah, *güeno*.   [compare **bueno**]
           'Ah, good.'
       c. Porque mi *agüelita* trabajaba todo el día.   [compare **abuelita**]
           'Because my grandmother used to work all day.'

(13)   a. *Adactan.*   [compare **adaptan**]
          'They adapt.'
        b. Me gusta la música dancing, el . . . el *latin poc.*   [compare ***latin pop***]
          'I like dance music . . . Latin pop.'

Although the pronunciation of the /s/ in final position predominates, elisions of this phoneme are not absent, as shown in (14).

(14)   a. Lo*s* vecino*s* no son problemático*s*, son *tranquilo.*   [compare **tranquilos**]
          'The neighbours aren't a problem, they're calm.'
        b. Son gente *pue* provinciana.   [compare **pues**]
          'They're, like, provincial people.'
        c. Los *Olivo*, Los *Olivo*, ah, qué bonito Los *Olivo.*   [compare **Olivos**]
          'Los Olivos, Los Olivos, oh, Los Olivos is so nice.'

There are also frequent cases of consonant elision. In almost all of them, *también* is produced as *tamién*, eliminating the /b/ (15). Furthermore, in the case of the cluster /ks/, this is simplified to a velar fricative /x/ (16a) or an alveolar fricative /s/ (16b).

(15)   La mayoría *tamién* son hijos de provincianos ¿no?   [compare **también**]
          'Most are also children of provincials, aren't they?'

(16)   a. *Ejisten* los *pandilleros.*   [compare existen]
          'There are gangs.'
        b. Y el *prósimo* presidente que entre, y el *prósimo.*   [compare **próximo**]
          'And the next president that's elected, and the next.'

Some cases of syllable elision are also attested. While in (17) the initial syllable is omitted, in (18) it is the final one that is.

(17)   a. Para en carro, *-toces* va a las zonas principales.   [compare **entonces**]
          'He has a car, so he can go to the main zones.'
        b. Hace – *proximadamente* mi eda-, ¿no?   [compare **aproximadamente**]
          'It's been about the same amount of time as my age, no?'

(18)   . . . ya *pa-* cuando yo tenía creo diez años.   [compare **para**]
          'At the time I was about 10 years old, I think.'

Speaker B's variety of Castilian does not present Quechua linguistic substratum as does Speaker A's. Moreover, Speaker B's Castilian has features that are associated with the lower class, whose members do not possess an important educational capital, for instance, *agüela* (*abuela*), *-toces* (*entonces*), *descriminación* (*discriminación*), *nadies* (*nadie*). On the other hand, it is evident that B's linguistic performance reflects her effort to filter out Andean provincial features and appears to be socially mobile. In her interview, B represents herself as measuring distance, making distinctions, correcting her friends' speech, dreaming of finding a distinguished place in the world.

In summary, we have identified the following *language features* in B's speech: (i) guaranteed stability through the use of a single language, Spanish; (ii) absence of inter-linguistic mixing; and (iii) consistent use of 'vernacular' speech. Likewise, we have identified the following *urbanity features*: (i) residence in a district of emergent and growing prestige, with medium density and high diversity; (ii) absence of the marks of migration; and (iii) relatively fluid day-to-day mobility (frequent public transport and the best network of routes). The interconnection of all these features, whose point of origin is the speaker, creates an *urban language space* in which B positions herself – moving in 'good' areas and at a 'good' distance from the others.

4.5   Seeking a Safe Place

Speaker C is 57 years old and a long-standing urban Limeñan who has always lived in traditional Limeñan places. He attended a private school and carried out his post-secondary studies in administration at a private university. He has four children, all of whom have had post-secondary education.

4.5.1   *The Great Urban Divide*

Speaker C describes and explains the changes that Lima has undergone. From his point of view, which is that of the traditional urban zones (downtown Lima, Magdalena, Pueblo Libre), these changes are negative. For him, migrants are the cause or *operators* of this transformation. He builds *before* and *after* into his discourse and claims that these changes coincided with the arrival of 'people who are not from this place' and who 'have not been raised in the same place'. The Lima that he had inhabited before the arrival of the migrants presented attributes that he holds in high esteem. He recalls that Lima was a city with calm, serene, honest, sociable, and communicative people. The streets were clean, with few cars, little pollution and garbage, and no street vendors. In contrast, *today's* Lima, which hosts many migrants and their descendants, is allegedly a violent, bellicose, unsafe, and dirty city. Regarding the District of Magdalena in particular, he says:

antes [la gente] era muy tranquila, las casas, este, eran solariegas, ventanas abiertas y con mucha confianza, la gente podía dejar abierta la puerta de su casa, ¿no? cosa que no se hace ahora, ¿no? todo está, todo está lleno de rejas.

[before, people were very calm, the houses, um, belonged to good families, windows were open and people could confidently leave their doors unlocked, no?, something that isn't done now, no?, everything, everything is covered with bars.]

The connections that Speaker C favours are those that are likely to engender calm and safe spaces, avoiding density and diversity. When the population of downtown Lima, where he first lived, began to increase, he moved to quieter districts: Magdalena and Pueblo Libre. These spaces belong to what he calls the 'traditional urban zones', which in turn are contrasted with the new urban area that surrounds them: 'Lima is larger and much different from what we imagined ourselves to be living in, in the traditional urban zones' (our translation). Speaker C paints a generalized picture of Lima's urban landscape, as a series of differently sized spatial relationships: (i) the local sphere, that of the home, and the neighbourhood; (ii) the urban area in which one moves about and encounters people one knows; (iii) the other areas that form an unknown and unimaginable horizon, situating there the roots of violence and delinquency.

4.5.2   Preserving the Spanish of Old Lima

The interviewee signals that, in Lima, there are invisible places and networks where Quechua, Aymara, and other indigenous languages are spoken. This description suggests that a conflictive game exists between spaces of different magnitudes, statuses and levels of visibility. It is through the conflict between these spaces that multilingualism in the city is organised: Castilian is omnipresent and dominant, while indigenous languages are limited to informal settings and are used in peripheral spaces of the city. This multilingual context, primarily produced by intense migration during the second half of the 20th century, makes for possible substrate influences and, consequently, for an increase in the varieties of Castilian that are spoken in Lima. Speaker C distinguishes between, on the one hand, traditional Castilian, inherited from older Limeñans, which he calls the 'living language' and, on the other, divergent forms of Castilian that are present in Lima's periphery, which tend to irritate him. He gives the example of the Castilian used in the mass media:

por decir, a través de los medios de comunicación, llámese radio o televisión, hay programas, eh … que los conductores tienen un lenguaje de aceptación, es decir, no lo sentimos estraño, es decir, aceptamos que su manera de hablar es como la que nosotros tenemos. Sin embargo, hay otros con, hay otros, este, conductores, principalmente de radios de lo conos, donde sus mensajes son gritando, se habla rápido, se habla en forma violenta.

[let's say, through the communication media, be it radio or television, there are programs, ah … that the hosts speak a common language, that is, we don't find it weird, that is, we accept that their way of speaking is like ours. However, there are others with, there are others, um, hosts, primarily of radios from the cones [outskirts], where they shout their messages, they speak quickly; they speak in a violent manner.]

Let's look at the characteristics of Speaker C's Castilian. With regard to his pronunciation, he tends to omit the dental consonant /d/ or /t/ in syllable- or word-final position. While he sometimes pronounces this consonant (19), he often omits it (20):

(19)   a. Tienen que enfrentar una, una ***realida[d]* muy diferente.**
           'They have to face a, a very different reality.'
        b. La *juventu[d]* actual.
           'Today's youth.'

(20)   a. En el centro de la *ciudá-.*   [compare **ciudad**]
           'In the city centre.'
        b. La recuerdo con *claridá-.*   [compare **claridad**]
           'I remember it clearly.'
        c. Quizá por limitaciones de *oportunidá-.*   [compare **oportunidad**]
           'Maybe because of little opportunity.'
        d. Nosotros jugábamos a las escondidas, el *fú-bol.*   [compare **fútbol**]
           'We played hide-and-seek, soccer.'

In some cases, the /d/ is omitted in the intervocalic position (21), the /g/ in the final position of the syllable (22), and the /s/ in the pre-consonant position (23).

(21)   a. Un estudio de *aboga-o.*   [compare **abogado**]
           'A lawyer's office.'
        b. Debería mejorarse *to-avía* más.   [compare **todavía**]
           'It needs to get even better.'

(22)   a. Colegio Claretiano de *Ma-dalena* del Mar.   [compare **Magdalena**]
           'Claretiano de Magdalena del Mar School'.
        b. Nos mudamos a *Ma-dalena.*   [compare **Magdalena**]
           'We moved to Magdalena.'

(23)   a. He tenido la oportunidad de *e-tar* en, eh, casi en todo el
           Perú.   [compare **estar**]
           'I have had the opportunity to be in, ah, almost all of Peru.'
        b. *Pue* podría ser en San Borja, eh, La Molina.   [compare **pues**]
           'um, it could be in San Borja, ah, La Molina.'

There are also some cases of simplification of the consonant-cluster /ks/, as in example (24):

(24)   No lo sentimos *estraño.*   [compare **extraño**]
        'It didn't feel strange to us.'

This series of features frequently occurs in the spontaneous speech of Limeñans from traditional urban zones; and these are not negatively valued. Some studies referring to Lima, for example, have indicated that the intervocalic /d/ is disappearing, even in formal speech (Caravedo 1986). They also indicate that the /s/ is weakening in the pre-consonant position among Lima's middle classes (Caravedo 1983, 1987).

To summarize, we have identified the following *language features* in C's speech: (i) stability guaranteed by the rules of a single language, Spanish; (ii) absence of inter-linguistic mixing; and (iii) consistent use of formal speech. Likewise, we have identified the following *urbanity features* in relation to C: (i) residence in various traditional Lima neighbourhoods, of lesser density and diversity than the peripheral zones; (ii) absence of the effects of migration; and (iii) relatively fluid day-to-day mobility (his own vehicle, relatively fluid transportation routes). The interconnection of all these features, which have the speaker as their origin, creates an *urban language space* in which C seeks security in his traditional manner of speaking, acting, and living.

4.6   Overview

The urban experience of each one of the interviewees is tied to a particular make-up of the urbanity features previously considered. As we have seen, Speaker A is connected to densely populated and diversified areas and has neither fast nor fluid mobility. Generally speaking, migrants like A move to Lima by land transport vehicles, often taking difficult routes. Once in the city, they use public transportation to move around and are obliged to make long trips with various transfers. Their access to communication and information media is limited. For her part, Speaker B is connected to less dense, though diversified areas, and has somewhat fluid mobility. In fact, the district where Speaker B lives has more important bus routes, more numerous public trans- port lines, and phone and Internet outlets. Finally, Speaker C is connected to less dense and relatively less diversified areas, but has faster and more fluid mobility: he moves around mostly by automobile and has greater access to communication and information technologies. Density, diversity, and mobility are related in a way that generates socially differentiated and ethnically stratified spaces in the city; and each of these spaces is at the same time related to the speakers' speech peculiarities. Thus, a language feature may become an operator of social categorization and discrimination, not because of some intrinsic property of its own but because of how it is multiply related to other factors and functions.

The language features that are associated with Speaker A's urban space are strongly related to two particular kinds of mixing, one that occurs between Quechua and Castilian and one that occurs between the Andean variety of Castilian acquired as a second language and the costal Limeñan variety of the lower class.[11] Speaker A's Spanish, therefore, appears to be a *hybrid variety* that involves a weak *work of purification*,[12] as it constitutes a place where

---

[11] Two works on linguistic contact phenomena in Lima that are relevant to this discussion are Escobar (2007) and Klee and Caravedo (2005).

[12] I borrow this concept from Latour (1997: 107–108) to convey the idea that variation, in all its heterogeneity, is a central state of affairs (and a primary resource) and that the construction of norms or standards is the result of an act of separation (in Latour, the work of a 'purifying *cracking*') by which one selects only those forms that one considers correct and/or prestigious.

encounters between heterogeneous linguistic forms occur. This variety builds bridges between very differentiated, even antagonistic, linguistic and cultural traditions. In some way, this erases the abyss that, since the Spanish Conquest, has developed between the *nation of Europeans and their descendants* and the *nation of Indians*, although it simultaneously makes way for new forms of differentiation and segregation.

While Speaker A's language shows mixing and variation, this does not mean it is unstable. As in any language, phonology and grammar in Speaker A's Spanish are more stable than his vocabulary. This greater stability of relations (rules) is both guaranteed by Castilian and, to a certain measure, Quechua. Speaker A's stability is identical to that of the other speakers, but the difference lies in the regularity formed by new rules, which are more or less convergent between the two languages. Unlike Speaker A, the linguistic features associated with Speaker B's and C's urban spaces do not display this kind of mixing, though they differ among themselves, within the framework of traditional Limeño Spanish. In fact, the features associated with Speaker B's space contain certain peculiarities that are considered 'working-class' (*populares*) or 'uneducated' (*no culto*) by Speaker C. Likewise, Speaker C does not allow features associated with Speaker B's space, let alone Speaker A's, into his speech.

Finally, the connections established between the urbanity and language features of a particular speaker create a space in which a specific dynamic is instated: while A deploys his dynamism to integrate into a new habitat, B does this to attain a place of distinction for herself, and C to defend his safety and preserve his own traditions. Table 4.1 summarizes these assessments.

We may thus say that each speaker finds him/herself articulated to a series of urbanity and language features, from which his/her own *urban language space* is generated. Inhabiting this space, each speaker develops his/her own *idiolect*, that is to say 'an individual speaker's system of a language' (Mufwene 2001: 2). But idiolects are in contact, are osmotic, and change: 'Contact among idiolects and the ensuing competition and selection in the means available to their speakers become the default causation for change' (Mufwene 2001: 15). Thus, the multiple speakers' changing idiolects contribute to the transformation of the Spanish sociolects spoken in Lima.

Taking a metaphor from Sloterdijk (2005: 52), we might imagine urban language spaces as permeable bubbles that form a mountain of foam and glide over and/or under each other. They are thus 'ni véritablement atteignables ni effectivement séparables' ('neither truly attainable nor completely separable').

In regard to the linguistic features' separation, a competition-and-selection approach has been developed by Mufwene (2001: 57, 135; 2008).

Table 4.1 *Urban and Language Properties per Speaker*

Speakers	A	B	C
Urbanity features	de, di, ((mo))	(de), di, (mo)	((de)), ((di)), mo
Language features	– *Mixing*: apparent mixing between Quechua and Spanish, and between Spanish varieties (bilingual Spanish/ Limeñan Spanish).	– *Mixing*: absence of apparent mixing between Quechua and Spanish, and between Spanish varieties (bilingual Spanish/ Limeñan Spanish).	– *Mixing*: absence of apparent mixing between Quechua and Spanish, and between Spanish varieties (bilingual Spanish/ Limeñan Spanish).
	– *Variation*: variation that doesn't include a strong work of purification (*hybrid variety*). (*habla 'motosa'*)	– *Variation*: variation that includes some work of purification. Some of Speaker A's features are filtered. (*habla popular*)	– *Variation*: variation that includes a strong work of purification. Some of Speaker A's and Speaker B's features are filtered. (*habla culta*)
	– *Stability:* The stability of the rules is not given only by a linguistic tradition (of Spanish) but also by the contributions of Quechua, making linguistic transfers possible.	– *Stability:* The stability of the rules is given (almost) unilaterally by a linguistic tradition, that of Spanish.	– *Stability:* The stability of the rules is given (almost) unilaterally by a single linguistic tradition, Spanish.
Urban dynamic	Activity leading to one's integration into a new milieu.	Effort to attain a place of distinction.	Effort to defend one's safety and to preserve one's own traditions.

* In the following table, *de* stands for 'density', *di* for 'diversity' and *mo* for 'mobility'. The absence of a parenthesis indicates a strong presence of the property. The single parenthesis (x) indicates a significant presence of the property, while the double parenthesis ((x)) indicates a weak presence of the property.

The whole linguistic space of Metropolitan Lima appears therefore to be an articulated complex (a mountain of foam) comprising a multiplicity of urban language spaces (bubbles). Here we can see, for the purpose of an urban linguistic ecology, a new way to interpret Husserl's concepts of *foundation* and of *parts and wholes*, the mountain of foam being the *whole*, the bubbles the *parts*, and the bubbles' relations the *foundation*.

4.7   Conclusion

Our linguistic approach towards the Spanish of Lima has taken into account a multiplicity of ecological elements that encompass both urbanity and language features. As such, we have been able to ascertain how multiple urban language spaces are created. An urban language space is not a physical and administrative expanse that contains speakers within it; rather, it is a grid-like, at times discontinuous space, in whose web of relationships the speaker acts and is caught. This way, the urban language space of each of the interviewees has been defined through the particular way in which density, diversity, and mobility, as well as mixing, variation, and stability relate to each other and are combined. In conclusion, by describing these relations and combinations made possible by the concept of *urban language space*, we have articulated something more about the way in which the Spanish of Lima varies, is restructured, and participates in the urban dynamic of the city.

Part III

On the Ecology of *Space* and *Time*: Traditions in the Formation of Macro-ecologies

5   The Historical Formation of a Macro-ecology: the Case of the Levant*

Cyril Aslanov

5.1   Introduction

In this chapter, I would like to discuss from a macroscopic perspective the constitution of a specific linguistic horizon in the Eastern Mediterranean throughout a long period, twelfth to twenty-first centuries, using the theoretical asset articulated in Chapter 1 of this volume. Based on my book *Le français au Levant, jadis et naguère: à la recherche d'une langue perdue* (2006a), I stress that the languages in contact in the Levantine macro-ecologic system are not necessarily endogenous languages. Some of them are western languages transplanted to the Levant. Therefore, the specific ecological linguistic horizon of Eastern Mediterranean functioned as a meeting point between languages that did not necessarily have opportunities to be in contact with each other as long as they were spoken in western Europe. Parallel to the mutual interaction that characterized the contact between various western languages transplanted in the Levant, each of those languages underwent a process of Levantinization due to intensive contacts with local languages: Arabic, Greek, Turkish, and Armenian to mention the most commonly spoken.

In *Le français au Levant* I suggested that the different phases of the development of French in Near-Eastern contexts were united by a striking continuity. Indeed, Cypriot Francophony is a direct continuation of the French that was spoken in Crusader polities until the fall of Acre in 1291. Even before that crucial event, the French knights of Cyprus stayed in constant contact with their counterparts in the Asian mainland. In turn, Cypriot Francophony, which ended towards 1489, when the Kingdom of Cyprus was annexed to Venice, is separated by few years from the restart of contacts between French and Levantines, with the signature of the Capitulations treatise between Francis I and Suleiman the Magnificent in 1536 (Aslanov 2006a: 25).

From an ecological linguistic perspective, the elitist character of French in the Levantine context may be considered as a constant of interactions between

* This research was carried out thanks to the funding of the Russian Science Foundation (project No 15-18-00062; Saint Petersburg State University).

this sociolect and co-territorial languages in the Levant, especially as far as the earliest phases of Levantine French are concerned (see Aslanov 2008). To be sure, some importations of an updated blend of the language spoken in France significantly renewed Levantine French. Although Cypriot Middle French preserved some features of Crusader Old French (Aslanov 2006a: 135–136), it was obviously influenced by the constitution of a new *état de langue* in France itself since the middle of the fourteenth century. However, the dynamism of French in Levantine contexts was greatly helped by the fact that this language was already part and parcel of the Near Eastern linguistic horizon. In a certain sense, Crusader and Cypriot French paved the way for the continuation of Francophony from early modern till contemporary times, i.e. from the sixteenth century to the first half of the twentieth century.

Given the analogies between the discontinuous phases of the development of French in the Levant, it is tempting to establish a parallel between three cases of contact each of which constitutes a different situation: Old French in the Crusader polities of Syria, Palestine, and Greece (twelfth to thirteenth centuries); Middle French in the Kingdom of Cyprus (fourteenth to fifteenth centuries); and Modern or Contemporary French in Ottoman and post-Ottoman contexts (sixteenth to twentieth centuries). Besides the attempt to create a unique model of coexistence throughout the various periods of Levantine Francophony, this comparison will help to bridge the gap between external sociolinguistics and internal linguistics.

5.2   The Implications of Transplantation: Old French in its Levantine Environment

5.2.1   *Old French in Syria–Palestine*

As said in the introduction, Crusader polities provided a rare opportunity for dialects or languages that had been separated or even landlocked (as long as they were spoken in Europe) to come in contact with each other. The results of the ensuing contacts are obvious. The variety of Old French that can be reconstructed from such pieces of evidence as those provided by an Old French–Arabic glossary from the middle of the thirteenth century (Aslanov 2006b) appears as an idiosyncratic koiné with linguistic features that can be traced back to the dialect spoken in the North-Eastern half of the realm of Oïl (mainly Walloon and Lotharingian, but also Picard and Burgundian) (see Aslanov 2006a: 52–76, 2006b: 149–150, 180–184).

The nucleus that consists in a selection of dialectal features from various parts of the realm of Oïl was strongly Italianized (see Minervini 2000: 398–407; Aslanov 2000: 1273–1281, 2006a: 92–101, 2006b: 164–167) and substantially Provençalized (Aslanov 2006a: 101–107, 2006b: 167–170).

Actually the impact of Italo-Romance dialects (from Genoa, Venice, Pisa, Amalfi and other places in Southern Italy) on Crusader Old French was far stronger than the impact of Provençal. The latter language may have exerted a stronger influence in the County of Tripoli, which was founded by the Occitan ruler Raymond IV of Toulouse. Besides, the fact that this political entity survived until 1289, that is, two years before the fall of Acre, the last stronghold of Crusader presence on the Asian mainland, may explain the nature of contact between Old French and Provençal in Levantine context. The Provençalization of the variety of Old French spoken in Acre may be due to the intense exchanges between the neighbouring territories, at least as long as the County of Tripoli was still in contact with the County of Toulouse, that is, until the demise of the dynasty of Toulouse in 1187 and the accession of the dynasty of Antioche-Poitiers to the throne of Tripoli.

By contrast, the impact of Arabic on Crusader French (Aslanov 2006a: 77–92, 2006b: 162–163) seems to be limited to an occasional reshuffling of the semantic fields within the language and to the integration of copies of foreign phonemes into the phonological system.[1] Before the levelling of the affricate [tʃ] to [ʃ],[2] it seems that contact with Arabic allowed the phoneme [ʃ] to strike roots in Crusader Old French, as shown by the use of the Coptic grapheme *shai* in order to represent the post-alveolar fricative [ʃ]. A word like *chubbec*, adapted from Arabic *šubbāk* 'window', is not considered an Arabic word any longer; it is integrated in the row of the Old French lemmas to be translated by the Arabic term of Persian origin *rawzān* (Aslanov 2006a: 79–81, 2006b: 101–102, 162–163).

This shows that from the vantage point of the Coptic transmitters who were themselves speakers of Arabic, *chubbec* was already perceived as part and parcel of the variety of Old French to which they were exposed in the Levant. Thus *chubbec* can be considered a prototypical example of a conventionalized and structurally integrated copy, in relation to the continua of integration defined by Kriegel, Ludwig, and Salzmann (Chapter 7, this volume).

To be sure, the integration of the phoneme [ʃ] within the phonological system of Crusader Old French may have been facilitated by the special blend of dialects that was responsible for the crystallization of Levantine koiné. As I have demonstrated in other places, Walloon and Lotharingian dialectal features seem to have played a determinative role in the process of koineization (Aslanov 2006a: 75–76, 2006b: 141–142, 149–150).

---

[1] For the term *copying* see Chapters 1 and 7, this volume.

[2] The fact that the Coptic spelling of words like *charpentier* 'carpenter', *chamel* 'camel', and *char* 'flesh' begins with the digraph *theta–shai* or *tav–shai* reveals that at the date of the compilation of this glossary (before 1258), the levelling had not taken place yet, at least not in the Levant (see Aslanov 2006a: 68). It is quite typical of colonial koinés to conserve archaic features that do not exist any longer in the Metropolis.

134   Aslanov

Now, Walloon and Lotharingian are dialects of Oïl in which the phoneme [ʃ] was attested even before the levelling of affricate [tʃ] to [ʃ] (Pope 1952: 134, 489).[3] This may have helped integrate *šubbāk* and the phoneme [ʃ] within the system of Levantine French.

To sum up, the conjunction of internal ecological factors (Walloon and Lotharingian components in Levantine koiné) and external ones (contact with Arabic) may explain the integration of post-alveolar fricative [ʃ] in the variety of Old French that crystallized in Levantine context.

Interestingly enough, Levantine Old French koiné, which was so receptive to its Italian, Provençal, and Arabic surroundings, exerted only a very little impact on Italian and Provençal, and even less on Arabic. This situation strongly contrasts with the massive borrowing of French lexemes into Modern Standard Arabic since the end of the nineteenth century and in the Levantine Arabic dialects spoken in Syria and Lebanon since the first half of the twentieth century. For reasons that may be connected to the hostility of the Arabic-speaking world towards the intruders[4] (whose aggressiveness did not even spare Arab Christians) and more specifically because of the specificity of Arabic diglossia, Medieval Levantine Arabic was quite impervious to Old French, at least as far as the written documents are concerned. The few occurrences of Old French terms in medieval Arabic are found in the books of Arab authors writing about the Crusaders. Ibn Munqidh (1095–1188), for instance, mentions the terms *burges* 'bourgeois' (Arabized as *burjāsī*) and *burgesie* 'bourgeoisie' (adapted as *burjāsiyyah*) (Usāmah ibn Munqidh 1999: 141; Aslanov 2006a: 42–43) whereas Al-Nuwayrī (who died in 1333) uses the word *faṣal*, an integrated form of the Old French word *vassal*.[5]

Since the high register of *'adab* (Arabic *belles lettres*) strongly stuck to the norm of *fuṣḥā*, the written Arabic was preserved from the contamination of the western invaders whose terminology was probably used at a lower level of diglossia whenever it was really untranslatable into Arabic. Since high standard Arabic was sometimes receptive to lower strata of Arabic diglossia, some echoes of the code-hybridization, which is likely to have occurred at a vernacular level, are occasionally recognizable in literary Arabic texts when they happen to deal with Frankish issues. Whatever these indirect infiltrations might have been, they were part of a metalinguistic discourse on a foreign terminology rather than a real integration of Old French words. Whereas the

[3] Examples of Walloonisms or Lotharingianisms are the words *tixerant* 'weaver' spelled with Coptic *shai* and *cruix* < Latin nominative form *crux* 'cross' where the Coptic phoneme *shai* represents the post-alveolar [ʃ] (see Aslanov 2006a: 68–69).
[4] This is the opinion expressed by Amin Maalouf in *Les croisades vues par les Arabes* (1983: 281–282).
[5] See 'Abd al-Wahhāb al-Nuwayrī, *Nihāyat al-'arab fi-funūn al-'adab* (1924–1942: 260–261), Aslanov and Kedar (2010: 278–279).

westerners were unable to perceive the difference between high and low Arabic,[6] the Arabic diglossia that can be reconstructed for that period and that area reflects a clear-cut contrast between the imperviousness of literary Arabic and a probable openness of spoken dialects to the immediate linguistic surroundings, especially in the territories where the Muslim peasantry was ruled by Frankish lords.

5.2.2   Old French in the Hellenic World

The same diglossic explanation holds true as far as the contact between the Greeks and the Franks is concerned. As long as the Byzantine chroniclers used the high variety of Greek, they did not allow words from western languages to violate the purity of their literary language. Anna Comnena (1928) even complains about the barbarian sonorities of Frankish names (that is, Old French and Provençal names) in a reflexive excursus of the *Alexiad*:

I had got as far as this and was toiling with my pen about the time of lamp-lighting, when I noticed that I was dozing a bit over my writing, as the subject was losing its interest. For when it is absolutely necessary to make use of the barbarian names and to narrate various successive events, the body of my history and the continuity of my writing is likely to be cut up into paragraphs; but my kind readers will bear me no grudge for this. (337–338)

On the other hand, the demotic texts produced in the Crusader polities established in Greece at the expense of the Byzantine Empire are totally invaded by Romance words.[7] It is likely that the very structure of demotic Greek, as it is spoken to date, has been influenced by the contact with Romance languages, especially Italo-Romance ones (see Horrocks 1997: 273–276). Thus, such an important innovation as the development of an analytical perfect consisting of the auxiliary verb ἔχω 'to have' and a verbal noun in -ει/-εῖ (itself an avatar of the infinitive in -ειν/-εῖν) may be due to an imitation of the Romance forms, which continued Vulgar Latin *habere* + PAST PARTICIPLE. Although the first attestation of this construction goes back to the Roman period and is, therefore, attributable to a Late Latin rather than to a Romance influence, its reactivation in medieval demotic Greek is probably due to the contact with Romance vernaculars in the aftermath of the Fourth Crusade (Horrocks 1997: 78–79, 273–274).

Whatever the exact delimitation between structural and lexical influences might be, medieval demotic Greek was strongly marked by the contact with

---

[6] This is evident from a passage of the *Historia Francorum qui ceperunt Jerusalem* by Raymond d'Aguilers, an Occitan cleric who took part in the First Crusade. There, the Arabic language in general is called *vulgariter* 'vulgarly speaking'.
[7] On the linguistic hybridization in demotic texts produced in Frankish-dominated areas, see Aslanov (2006a: 119–131, 2007: 37–48).

Romance languages, whereas the high language preserved by the tradition of Byzantine humanism was almost hermetic to such interference.[8]

5.2.3   A Comparative Approach: Old French in Arabic, Greek and Armenian Settings

In the aforementioned cases, Crusader Old French stayed in contact with two languages, Arabic and Greek, which have in common a strong diglossic regime.[9] The analogies between the two kinds of linguistic contact cross the boundary between Frankish political entities on the Asian mainland (Syria–Palestine) on the one hand and the Greek-speaking territories conquered from the Byzantine Empire on the other hand.

Interestingly enough, the impact of both Arabic and Greek on Old French transcended the difference between high and low language varieties, whereas the impact of Old French on Arabic and Greek was strictly limited to the low language variety.

As far as Arabic is concerned, the adaptation of anthroponyms, toponyms, and *Kulturwörter* to Levantine Old French displays an interesting oscillation between literary Arabic as it is read and vernacular Arabic as it is heard. Thus, the name of Saladin, *Ṣalāḥ al-Dīn*, is sometimes transliterated as *Salaheldin* instead of *Salahadin* or *Salahdin* in chronicles probably influenced by Levantine French. In this form, the contact between [l] and [d] is represented graphically although the pronunciation of Arabic assimilates the [l] of the article *al* to a following dental (Aslanov 2006a: 89–90). Likewise, the paraetymological link between *al-zahr* 'dice' and the Syrian toponym *Al-'Azāz* shows that the two terms have been confounded on the basis of a false reading of the grapheme ز [zāi] as ر [rā'] (Aslanov 2006a: 87–88).

Conversely, other popular etymologies reveal that sometimes and perhaps most of the time, the mediation was the spoken dialect of Arabic rather than the literary language. Thus the Frankish chronicler William of Tyre (*c*.1130–1184) tries to link the Arabic name of Tyre (*Ṣūr*) with the name of the Syrians (*Sūriyyin*) in spite of the phonological difference between the emphatic sibilant [ṣ] of *Ṣūr* and the [s] of *Sūriyyin*. Such a neutralization of the emphasis is typical of the Levantine dialects of Arabic, especially in the mouths of Christians (Aslanov 2006a: 86–87).

---

[8] For the distinction between *esoteric* or *hermetic* languages, on the one hand, and *exoteric* or *contact-open* languages on the other, see Chapters 1 and 9, this volume. Thus creole languages for example can be considered as particularly contact-open languages, see Ludwig (2010).

[9] The very term *diglossia* was coined in 1885 by the Greek writer Emmanuel Rhoidis. On the invention and diffusion of the term *diglossia*, see Fernández Rodríguez (2005: 447–464).

A similar oscillation between high and low language varieties is perceptible in the Frankish reception of Greek in the aftermath of the Fourth Crusade (1204). Thus, in Henri de Valenciennes's *Histoire de l'empereur Henri de Constantinople*, the toponym *Thebes* is mentioned most of the time in the learned form *Thebes* (Valenciennes 1948), which had been popularized by Benoît de Sainte-Maure's *Roman de Thebes*, written in the second half of the twelfth century, long before the Crusaders started to conquer territories on the Greek mainland. This use of *Thebes* shows that Henri de Valenciennes was aware of the identity between the classical toponym Θῆβαι (*Thebae* in Latin; *Thebes* in Old French) and its modern avatars: either the classical form Θῆβαι pronounced [θíve] or its modern avatar Θήβα (pronounced [θíva]) (Aslanov 2006a: 115).

On the Asian mainland, we find both attitudes represented, that is, the learned reminiscence of the name in Classical sources on the one hand and the adaptation of the toponym as pronounced in the epichoric languages on the other hand. Thus, the name of Naplouse (*Nābulus*) was *Naples*, because the Crusaders were aware of the Greek etymology (Νεάπολις) of this toponym. However, this reflex did not function with the toponym *Tiberias* that was adapted to Old French according to its pronunciation in Arabic (both literary and vernacular), that is, *Tabarie* < *Ṭabariyyeh* rather than through the Latin name *Tiberias* (Aslanov 2006a: 84–85).

By contrast, the Middle Armenian spoken in the Kingdom of Little Armenia was eminently receptive to Old French, as shown by the integration of many words to the very core of the language. When the legal text of *Livres des Assises d'Antioche* was translated into Armenian by Smpad Sparaped ('Smpad the Constable', 1208–1276), Old French terms were adapted to the morphophonemic system of Armenian rather than really translated into genuinely Armenian terms. Even some verbs were simply copied and adapted: *chalengier* 'to challenge', *chastier* 'to punish', *defendre* 'to defend', *faillir* 'to fail', *plaidier* 'to plead', *saisir* 'to seize' were adapted as *jalenjel, jastel, tefendel, failel, blait'el, saizel* (Hübschmann 1897: 390–391; Karst 1901: 40–41) in a way that is strongly reminiscent of the adaptation of Anglo-Norman verbs to the morphophonemic system of Middle English. To be sure, these terms were loaded with a very precise juridical meaning, which may explain why the Armenian translator did not want to take the risk of adapting them by means of genuinely Armenian words. Smpad's resorting to these Armenized equivalents of the Old French forms implies that his readership was able to understand those terms either because Armenian aristocrats had some knowledge of Old French due to their intense contact with Crusader polities or because they were integrated into Armenian even before Smpad used them.

The successful integration of a big amount of Old French words in a text that belongs to a relatively high stratum of medieval Armenian diglossia may reflect a situation of genuine Old French–Armenian bilingualism among the Armenian aristocrats of Cilicia. Interestingly enough, the receptiveness of Armenian to Old French loanwords was not compensated by a symmetric penetration of Armenian lexical borrowings in Old French. The asymmetry observed above on the relationship between Old French on the one hand and Arabic and Greek on the other, was felt here again, but in an opposite direction: this time, the local language was receptive to the language of western intruders and not the other way round.

5.3   Fourteenth- to Fifteenth-century Cyprus: a Linguistic Melting Pot?

The variety of Middle French preserved in the Cypriot administrative documents edited by Jean Richard (1962) and studied by Aslanov (2006a: 131–141) and Baglioni (2006) displays an astonishing interpenetration between French and Italo-Romance dialects (Venetian, Genovese, common *scripta* 'administrative written language'). At the beginning of the period, in the fourteenth century, the Middle French elitist sociolect was occasionally Italianized in a way that is reminiscent of similar processes in the varieties of Old French spoken on the Asian mainland before 1291. The hesitation of the same notary between the French and Italo-Romance terms within the same text (*scire/cere* 'wax', *dihme/dezima* 'tithe', *houtuvre/outovrio* 'October', Richard 1962: 245; *vigneor/vignadur* 'vinedresser', ibid.: 257) reveals that, at least from the Hellenic perspective (indeed, those documents seem to have been written down by Cypriot Greeks), there was no real difference between the two Romance languages. The different Romance languages were rather perceived as an indistinct entity (Aslanov 2002).

However, it is likely that the indistinctiveness between the various Romance languages has been integrated by the native speakers themselves. After all, the aforementioned vacillation between an Italianized Middle French term and its Italo-Romance counterpart reflects a language variation that is attested in Venice itself and, with a different dialectal colouring, in the Angevin Kingdom of Naples. Throughout the thirteenth century and at least until the beginning of the fourteenth century, the literary language of those places of contact between Old French and Italo-Romance dialects had been a strongly Italianized Old French. This bilingual diglossia is attested by the diffusion of Old French epic and courtly romances in Northern Italy or the use of French by Marco Polo (1254–1324) in his *Devisement du monde*. To be sure, the oldest texts edited by Jean Richard go back to the second half of the fourteenth century, when a monolingual diglossia (*volgare illustre*/Italo-Romance vernaculars) was already replacing the previous bilingual diglossia (French/Italo-Romance dialects) in Italy itself. However, the relative isolation of Cyprus, the most remote stronghold of the Crusader presence in the Eastern Mediterranean after the fall of Acre in 1291, may explain why situations that were already obsolete in Italy were still found on the island. Thus, a bilingual diglossia in which Middle French and Italo-Romance coexisted was preserved for a longer time in Cyprus than in Venice itself.

Therefore, the gradual Italianization of Cypriot Middle French, which previously used to be a castolect, may be conceived of in diastratic terms rather than only in terms of diatopy (the factor of contact between two Romance languages transplanted in the Levant) or diachrony (the evolution of the languages brought into contact). The deterioration of cultural standards and the rise of the Venetian and Genoese bourgeoisie at the expense of aristocrats of French origin may explain why the low language (Venetian and Genoese) eroded the high language (Cypriot Middle French). The linguistic hybridization that occurred within the texts is just the intra-linguistic reflection of processes that took place in the comprehensive ecological linguistic system, itself an expression of the social dynamics that occurred on the island.

As for the contact between French castolect and epichoric Greek, it is difficult to evaluate it as far as French aristocracy is concerned. From the Hellenic perspective, however, things are clearer: the highest strata of the Greek segment of the Cypriot society were perfectly bilingual. They were able to write in French, as shown by their role in the composition of the aforementioned documents written in a mixture of Middle French and Italo-Romance. Sometimes they inserted whole sentences in Greek, but they transliterated them in Romance letters (Aslanov 2006a: 139–140). This particularity may hint at the fact that the local Franks (the French and Italian merchants) were probably able to understand spoken Greek but unable to read the language in the original alphabet.

The receptiveness of Cypriot Greeks to Old French and Italo-Romance is abundantly illustrated by Leontios Makhairas's chronicle (Makhairas 1932). This text is so full of Romance loanwords that sometimes it appears as a variety of Greek relexified with French and Italo-Romance words. Actually, neither the Greeks nor the Franks were closed to the language of their respective neighbours. The linguistic symbiosis between Greek and Middle French may be illustrated through a specular symmetry by dint of which the Greek title κῦρ 'sir' was adopted as *Quir* in Cypriot Middle French (Richard 1962: 30; Aslanov 2006a: 139; Baglioni 2006: 237) whereas its Middle French equivalent *sire* was Hellenized as σίρ in Makhairas's (1932) chronicle (paralleled by the Armenization of the same as *sir* in the above mentioned corpora, Karst 1901: 16). This mutual copying may be explained by means of the concept of Levantine sociability, according to which the neighbouring communities were able to at least engage in polite small talk with each other. The Gallicized Greek title *Quir* was used by the Franks in order to address or to refer to a Greek, whereas its parallel σίρ was reserved for the Franks when addressed or referred to by Greeks. In spite of the etymological difference between them, the users of the neighbouring languages probably aware of the fortuitous likeness between κῦρ and *sire* and they may have attributed this to a putatively common etymology.

The reciprocal contact between Italianized Middle French and demotic Greek occurred mostly at an intermediate stage of the Frankish–Hellenic diglossia. Such Levantine Old French texts as *Livre des Assises de Jerusalem, Livre des Assises des bourgeois*, Philippe de Novare's *Estoire de la guerre des Ibelins contre les Impériaux, Chronicle of the Templar of Tyr*, which were recopied in Cyprus throughout the fourteenth century and integrated into a book bearing the symptomatic name of *Geste des Chiprois* ('Deeds of the Cypriots') correspond to the high stratum of Old French diglossia. Precisely because of their archaism they were held in high esteem as the last echo of a vanished world, the Crusader possessions on the Asian mainland, including the Kingdom of Cyprus, claimed to be the continuation. On the other hand, the charts edited by Jean Richard were infra-literary documents without any pretension to elegance. Instead of reverberating the voice of the past, they were just registering the prosaic present and the ecological conditions of Lusignan Cyprus, where the contact with Greek prompted a relativization of the difference between Middle French and Italo-Romance. As for Leontios Makhairas's chronicle, it was perceived as a low genre from the vantage point of Greek purism. First of all, it was written in the local demotic and not in the high standard of humanist prose. Second, it was pervaded with foreignisms. And lastly, it was more akin to the genre of the chronicle in Old French vulgar exemplified by the texts compiled in the aforementioned *Geste des Chiprois* than to atticist Byzantine chronography.

Both Cypriot Middle French and Gallicized demotic Greek disappeared quite soon. The first was gradually superseded by Venetian in a process of withdrawal that is paralleled, during approximately the same period, by the absorption of Anglo-Norman by Middle English. In both cases, the disappearance of French has something to do with the rise of the bourgeoisie at the expense of the aristocracy. As for the Gallicized register of demotic Greek, it did not survive the annexation of Cyprus to Venice in 1489, let alone the conquest of the island by the Ottomans in 1571. The situation in which Middle French, Italo-Romance, and demotic Greek coexisted was replaced by another trilingualism in which demotic Greek coexisted with Venetian and Turkish, the languages of the two rival powers in the Eastern Mediterranean in early modern times (sixteenth to seventeenth centuries). It is quite symptomatic that in modern times Levantine Francophony reappeared in places other than Cyprus. In that island, it was buried for good after the disappearance of the socio-political conditions that had enabled its flourishing.

5.4 French in its Ottoman and Post-Ottoman Setting

5.4.1 The Ottoman Period

The spread of French in the Ottoman Empire was not a direct consequence of the signature of the Capitulations between Francis I and Suleiman the Magnificent in 1536. Rather, it resulted from the arrival of French traders and technicians in Turkey by the eighteenth century when the ruling class felt the need to modernize the obsolete structure of the Empire, which started its decline after the Battle of Vienna in 1683. One of the fields in which those French professionals were needed was the naval construction. This may explain the shift from Greek, very much used in the Ottoman navy and shipping until the Tanzimat era at least (Kahane, Kahane, and Tietze 1958; Ortaylı 1999: 165), to French as a result of the transition from a traditional shipping to a modernized one. Likewise, the French merchants from Marseilles flooded the Ottoman markets and established emporia in the famous 'Échelles du Levant' (Eldem 2006, especially pp. 311–317).

This time, French did not function as a conservative elitist sociolect, like in the Crusader polities or in Lusignan Cyprus. It was rather a vector of modernization, associated with the rise of non-Muslim minorities as a result of the Tanzimat process (1839–1876). The Levantinization of French foreigners who set roots in Istanbul and Smyrna had a counterpart in the westernization of non-Muslim minorities (first of all the Greek, Syrian, and Armenian Catholics, then the Orthodox Greeks, the Apostolic Armenians, and the Jews). Very soon, this convergence process took place within family units, since many Levantine Frenchmen married with local Christians (Greek Catholics and Armenian Catholics in Istanbul and Smyrna; and Greek Catholics or Chaldean Catholics in Syria). In this context, French assumed a double function: it was the vehicular that made it possible to short-circuit the Turkish language as a vehicular language between the neighbouring communities; it was also the language of communication with the outside world.

Moreover, the convergence process described above had another consequence: since Levantine Frenchmen were native speakers of French, their integration in the Christian quarters of Istanbul and Smyrna and the marriages they contracted with local Christian women led to a vernacularization of the French vehicular. The foundation of missionary schools in Istanbul and Smyrna was both a cause and a consequence of the appropriation of French as the native language of Christian Ottoman bourgeoisie. The first French school of Istanbul, the Lycée Saint-Benoît, was established as soon as 1783, before the Tanzimat era, at the time of the arrival of the aforementioned French technicians and merchants. Other Stambuli schools like Sainte Pulchérie, Notre-Dame de Sion, and Saint-Joseph were founded during the Tanzimat period as a result of the appropriation of French as a native language by the urban Christian minorities who just gained access to important functions in the Ottoman administration, as this was being modernized according to French standards. (The process included the frequent adoption of French as a chancellery language.) Thus, French either acquired new functions at the expense of Turkish (in the domains of administration, diplomacy, banking, and international business) or assumed roles that Turkish was never able to fulfil (lingua franca for communication with the outside world; language used in modern forms of mundane sociability in non-Muslim milieus).

In this latter function, French coexisted with the indigenous languages of the non-Muslim communities, i.e. Greek, Armenian, and Judeo-Spanish. As far as Greek and Armenian were concerned, the structural differences that distinguished them from French hindered fusion. In the salons of the Greek and Armenian elite in Istanbul and Smyrna, French was used as the acrolect, with little interference from Greek and Armenian. In other words, there were occasional manifestations of alternation between clearly distinct languages, but there is very little evidence of linguistic hybridization.

The situation was very different in the contact between Judeo-Spanish and French.[10] As both of these languages belong in the same family, the interference process was far more intense, so that a continuum was constituted where Gallicized Judeo-Spanish met Levantine French, that is, a blend of French influenced by Turkish through the mediation of a Turkicized variety of Judeo-Spanish (Wagner 1914: xi). Since the contact between Spanish and Turkish dated from the first years of the Sephardic presence in the Ottoman Empire, a process of fusion between Turkish and Judeo-Spanish was able to take place. In other words, the interference and hybridization followed a logic of transitivity. Turkish did not directly influence Levantine French, but it did shape Judeo-Spanish (due to the long term contact between both languages). In turn, Turkicized Judeo-Spanish was able to Turkicize Levantine French. However, the contact between Judeo-Spanish and French was reciprocal. If Turkicized Judeo-Spanish had a huge impact on vernacular or vehicular Levantine French, the latter contributed itself to the reshaping of Judeo-Spanish and to its rise as a language of secular culture (distinct from Ladino, the traditional written language used in the translations of the Bible and some parts of the Oral Law and Jewish liturgy).[11]

The huge lexical influence of Turkish on Judeo-Spanish on the one hand and the structural influence of French on Judeo-Spanish on the other hand created

---

[10] For the parameter of structural–typological distance or relatedness, see Chapter 11, this volume.

[11] On the structural impact of French in modern Judeo-Spanish (I deliberately avoid using the controversial term *Judezmo*), see Quintana Rodríguez (2006: 315–316) and Aslanov (2006a: 172–183).

a situation where Sephardic Jews were mixing the three languages (Varol Bornes 2008, 2009). This triglossia is quite similar to the Cypriot situation described above. There, two Romance languages (Middle French and Italo-Romance) coexisted with epichoric Greek, which resulted in a strong intertwining between all the three. By the same token Levantine French and Judeo-Spanish influenced each other with Turkish in the background.

To sum up, the contact of Levantine French with Greek and Armenian, the two most important Christian minorities in Ottoman society, did not lead to the crystallization of a mixed register. This happened only because Judeo-Spanish started its process of modernization after it became a collateral language of French.[12]

5.4.2   Post-Ottoman Contexts

Similar processes of hybridization occurred in the Post-Ottoman contexts of Egypt and Lebanon. In both places, the process of linguistic hybridization is due to specific reasons: In Egypt, a secessionist Ottoman province, more exposed than the core of the Empire to the impact of western influence (at least in Cairo and Alexandria), many speakers of French came with their own variety of French, that is, the Levantine French spoken by Sephardic Jews in Salonica, Istanbul and Smyrna, by Armenians and Greek bourgeois in the urban centres of Asia Minor, by Syrian Catholics and Melkites in Aleppo and Beirut. In Egypt and Lebanon French was not the imposition of Metropolitan French even though ramified educational networks contributed to the upgrading of local varieties of French in the frame of a local diglossia where the hypercorrect language taught in school coexisted with Levantine vernacular French. Thanks to the previous process of adaptation of French to the local conditions, the top and the bottom of Levantine Francophone diglossia influenced each other, so that the high variety of French was Levantinized whereas Levantine vernacular was most of the time more correct than Hexagonal vernacular. This led to the coexistence and occasional mixing of the two registers of French (Gueunier 2000: 757–761).

However, since the end of the nineteenth century in Egypt and for several decades in Lebanon, English competed with French in all the social and communicative functions implied by its contact with the world abroad. Moreover, English was traditionally associated with particular ethno-religious groups in the Egyptian and Lebanese landscapes: in the former country, the Copts were exposed to English rather than to French, whereas in the latter, English was traditionally associated with Orthodoxes and Druzes, owing to

---

[12] On the concept of *collateral language*, see Jean-Michel Éloy (2004).

their rivalry with Francophile and Francophone Maronites (Aslanov 2006a: 211–212). Once again, the triglossia that characterized Cyprus (involving Middle French, Italo-Romance, and epichoric Greek) and Sephardic milieus of the Ottoman Empire (Levantine French, Gallicized Judeo-Spanish, and Turkish) seems to apply also to the two European languages competing with each other in the shadow of Arabic diglossia. The only difference is that unlike in Lusignan Cyprus and in Ottoman Sephardic urban contexts, there were not two Romance languages in contact, but a Romance and a Germanic one. Therefore, the structural and typological difference between French and English prevented them from hybridizing with each other.

As far as the contact between French and Arabic is concerned, it must be stressed that Arabic exerted a deep impact on the top and the bottom of today's Levantine French diglossia, especially in Lebanon (Aslanov 2006a: 214–219). In Egypt, however, the dynamic of interpenetration does not pertain to speakers who are still living in the country. It primarily affects transnational diasporas mainly constituted of confessional minorities who gradually left the country after the rise of Nasserism: Jews, Syrian Catholics, Armenians. Nevertheless, a remainder of Francophony is still represented by those ethnico-confessional minorities who maintained their presence in the country even after the departure of the main bulk of non-Muslim minorities.[13]

While the Egyptian and Lebanese vernacular varieties are heavily influenced by Arabic, the latter is relatively unaffected by its contact with French. In Egypt, French lost most of its visibility after 1956, with the massive exodus of 'non-national' Egyptians. Beside a quasilectal[14] use of some formulas like *madame, merci*, and *mon chéri/ma chérie* and apart from some French lexical borrowings totally integrated into the morphophonemic scheme of the language,[15] Egyptian Arabic seems to be impervious to French structures, the last echoes of which vanished almost completely on the shore of the Nile. The example of *mon chéri/ma chérie* is interesting because it exemplifies a relation of mirrored symmetry between Levantine French and Egyptian Arabic. Indeed, the forms *yā ḥabībī/yā ḥabībti* 'my dear' are copied into Levantine French, whereas *mon chéri/ma chérie* is embedded within Egyptian Arabic (Aslanov 2006a: 205–206). This specular distribution is reminiscent of what we stated above about Lusignan Cyprus where *sire* 'sir' was adapted to local Greek as σίρ whereas κῦρ 'sir' was Gallicized as *Quir*.

---

[13] For the role of French in the urban ecology of Cairo, see Chapter 9, this volume.
[14] On the notion of *quasilect*, see Glinert (1993).
[15] As seen in the classification of nominal schemas of Egyptian Arabic in Woidich (2006: 90–110.)

5.5   Conclusion

At this stage of our survey of the nature of Levantine Francophony in its alloglot surroundings, some general statements are in order, so that we may determine what is common between the different avatars of French in the Eastern Mediterranean. Over the centuries, French became more and more integrated in the local ecological linguistic system. The almost two hundred years of Frankish presence in Syria–Palestine (1099–1291) were not sufficient for Old French to fully acclimatize in the Levant. After the departure of the last Franks, almost nothing of Old French was left in the ecological linguistic horizon of the area. Even in the Crusader polities founded on Greek soil, the impact of Old French was strong only as long as these political entities lasted, that is until the fifteenth century. The Principality of Achaia, where the *Chronicle of Morea* was composed, survived until 1432, the Duchy of Athens until 1444, and the Kingdom of Cyprus until 1489. However, in the last phases of their developments, that is, in the fourteenth century and at the beginning of the fifteenth century, the Principality of Achaia and the Duchy of Athens underwent a strong Italianization due to the role of Venice as a major political and economic power in the Greek world.

Texts such as the *Chronicle of Morea* or Leontios Makhairas's *Recital* are the reflection of a cultural and linguistic symbiosis that was interrupted once the only western presence in the Eastern Mediterranean was Venetian or Genoese. On the other hand, what made Francophony so strong in the Ottoman and Post-Ottoman space was precisely the fact that the spreading of French was not connected with any political domination. Apart from the brief period of the French Mandate in Syria–Lebanon (1920–1946), Francophony was the corollary of an economic and cultural supremacy in the last phases of the Ottoman Empire and beyond. The success of French in the Ottoman Empire and in the countries which maintained certain forms of Ottoman legacy is due to a process of convergence that brought together Levantinized French and westernized Levantines in the high society or in the middle class of a multi-cultural space. When modern nation-states emerged in the region (Kemalist Turkey, Israel, Nasserian Egypt, Ba'athist Syria), the situation that was associated with the Ottoman legacy was replaced by a striving toward monolingualism, which relegated French to the status of a language of an obsolete past.

The only places that somehow maintained the Ottoman legacy of Levantine Francophony are Lebanon, which is a mosaic of competing ethnoreligious groups rather than a fully-fledged nation-state, and the virtual place constituted by transnational diasporas that had been compelled to leave Egypt after the triumph of Nasserian nationalism in 1956. Ironically enough, the language of the first nation-state, the revolutionary France, has hardly survived the emergence of political entities inspired to a certain extent by its conception of a nation. However, it is not sure that Levantine French was really connected with the French nation-state. It was rather part and parcel of the Ottoman ecological linguistic system, where the linguistic particularism of alloglot minorities was transcended and sublimated by the use of a European language thoroughly acclimated to Levantine horizons.

The ecological linguistic analysis adopted in this chapter also affords us with some conclusions relevant to the framework of this book. To begin with, it appears impossible to understand today's linguistic situation of the Levant without understanding its historical constitution. Different degrees of openness to contact are associated with the different languages of the Levant ecology. Here, psycholinguistic parameters (of competence) and social parameters (of valuation) coincide. Different forms of hybridization show different degrees of conventionalization and structural systemic integration.

6 Spanish Anthroponomy from an Ecological Linguistic Perspective: the Antillean Society in the Early Sixteenth Century

Silke Jansen

6.1 Introduction

On 12 October 1492, after a two-month voyage which turned out to be the first journey to the 'New World', Christopher Columbus went ashore on a little island that he called San Salvador, in today's Bahamas. There, he encountered peaceful and friendly people who offered him food, parrots, and local artefacts in exchange of which the Spaniards provided trumpery. Soon afterwards, the exchanges, which involved not only merchandise but also words and cultural practices, were to become an integral part of interactions between Europeans and the local population. The first element to be exchanged in every one of those encounters probably was something so obvious that surprisingly it was hardly ever mentioned in the colonial sources: *personal names*.

The fact that humans bear names and exchange them in contact situations seems to be an anthropological constant. And yet, the structure, allocation practices, and usage of names may vary considerably between different linguistic communities, according to the specific ecological conditions in which they are embedded. As the arrival of the Spaniards profoundly altered the environmental situation of the Greater Antilles, establishing a completely different economic system and social organization as well as diffusing the Spanish language, we would expect to find these changes reflected, among other things, in the naming system.

The present study offers an ecological linguistic perspective on the names used by Spanish settlers to refer to the Antillean indigenous population in the first half of the sixteenth century. It demonstrates that the anthroponymic system traditionally employed by the indigenous people in the Antilles differed significantly from the naming practices in sixteenth-century Iberian Peninsula. Soon after the establishment of the colonial system (*encomienda*) in the Antilles, a new Iberian-based naming system developed, which was shaped both by the particular social factors within the early colonial society and the persistence and influence of pre-Columbian naming customs. This makes the Antillean anthroponymic system in the early sixteenth century especially informative about the interrelatedness of society, environment, and language within the theoretical framework of linguistic ecology.

6.2   An Ecological Linguistic View on Proper Names

6.2.1   *The Theory of Proper Names*

Traditionally, linguists have distinguished between *proper names* (also called *proper nouns, nomina propia*) and *common nouns* (also *nomina appellativa*). Proper names are used to identify unique entities (for example *Juan Carlos, Cuba, Ozama*) and differ from common nouns, which denote classes of entities sharing some characteristics (such as *rey* 'king', *isla* 'island', *río* 'river'). Thus, a common name like *perro* 'dog' denotes a class of animals, while *Lassie* identifies a singular and definite member of this class. Therefore, according to some philosophers of language, proper names are supposed to refer but not to have meaning.

This well-established distinction was challenged especially by Lévi-Strauss in his anthropological linguistic approach. His seminal work *La pensée sauvage* (1962) unmasked the Eurocentric perspective inherent in the conventional views. Although it is true that proper names often do not have meanings in the European tradition of lexical-semantics, they are, nevertheless, projections of symbolic thought that help to shape and define human reality; they are not merely labels attached to individuals. In addition to their identifying function, they classify individuals within the society according to criteria that are meaningful to a given human group at a given time. The widespread practice of differentiation between male and female names in western societies is a particularly illustrative example of the classifying function performed by personal names. In most cases, the given name automatically conveys information about the sex of its bearer, functioning as an index of the social category of gender. In non-western societies, these categories may be based on other socially relevant criteria, such as the fertility of the name bearer's mother in the case of the Lugbara, who use special personal names for twins, for children born from supposedly sterile women, and for the first children born after a series of still births (Lévi-Strauss 1962: 238). A widespread criterion for social classification in western and non-western societies is family group membership as reflected, for example, in European family names, which indicate the bearer's relationship to other individuals within the society, either diachronically (the descent from a certain parental lineage) or synchronically (the current affiliation to other individuals as expressed by the change of the name after marriage, divorce or widowhood). Lévi-Strauss (1962) refers to these names as 'noms / appellations claniques'.

The classifying function of proper names raises an issue about the widespread assumption that they do not possess meaning. As personal names display socially meaningful categories, we can regard them as *indexical signs* that link their bearer to socially relevant groups (see also the notion of 'termes relationnels' used by Lévi Strauss 1962: 254). The categories inherent in a given naming system are social artefacts (although they may have, as in the case of gender or parentage, a biological basis). They generally reflect social, cultural and ethical values and are often subject to modifications when these values or the organization of the society change (van Langendonck 1996: 1231). Today, in many European countries the synchronic aspect of family membership has become less important. Thus, for example, spouses may opt to keep separate surnames. At the same time, the diachronic aspect of relationship remains significant, which is reflected in the fact that by law every child is to receive either its mother's or its father's surname.

The reason why anthroponomy is a particularly suitable field for ecological linguistic research is that it constitutes a domain in which linguistic practices, social categories as cultural artefacts and, at least in part, biological conditions external to language come to interact with each other. The structure and development of naming systems, especially under the conditions of language and culture contact, cannot be understood by means of analysing language structure alone. They must be interpreted from a wider perspective that takes into account the interdependence between language, society, and habitat. The ecological linguistic paradigm proposed in Chapter 1 of this volume, considering language and language use in terms of the Husserlian concepts of *wholes–parts* and *foundation*, provides an appropriate frame for this kind of analysis.

6.2.2   The Ecological Linguistic Paradigm and the Study of Proper Names

Ecological linguistic thinking originates from a broad context of philosophical and linguistic theories of the nineteenth and early twentieth century and can already be found in the essays of Humboldt, Haeckel, Saussure, and Sapir (see Chapter 1, this volume). As an explicit research paradigm, ecological linguistics is intimately linked to Einar Haugen's work in the 1970s. In his programmatic article 'The ecology of language' (1972), Haugen defines the approach as 'the study of interactions between any given language and its environment' (1972: 325; see Chapter 1, this volume). While Haugen primarily focuses on a social and psychological understanding of *environment*, scholars following his approach employ this term in a broader sense. A more complex understanding of linguistic ecology has generated two different research frameworks. One of them applies the concept of ecosystem as a research metaphor, i.e. as a methodological tool to explain different kinds of factors external to a language that bear on its vitality and structural changes that it undergoes (Mufwene 2001, 2008). The other one addresses the question of the significance of language in the emergence of different environmental and social problems such as racism, sexism, extinction of species and languages, etc., as well as the issue by what means it could be prevented (Halliday 1990/2001; Mühlhäusler 1996b; Mühlhäusler and Peace 2006).

Following the general lines of ecological linguistic research as set out in Chapter 1 (this volume), the present chapter considers language as *part of a whole* that interacts dynamically with both internal (cognitive, universal) and external (social and physical environment) factors (see postulate1 in Chapter 1, p. 00). The linguistic ecology embraces not only the natural environment such as the physical and biological surroundings of a particular population, but also the social organization and the ideological background of human societies, as well as the mental constitution of human beings in general. Language systems represent projections of language use in concrete communication situations and are based on historically embedded communication patterns that, nevertheless, remain permanently transformed by communication practices. Environmental conditions, in the broadest sense, are supposed to play an important role in the formation of the linguistic structures and practices in a particular speech community. This suggestion enables us to interpret language change as a reaction of language to alterations of these conditions. However, we have to consider multiple causes leading to language change, as well as the very dynamic and complex nature of language itself: as a consequence of the dynamic character of language systems (see postulate1 in Chapter 1, p. 00), linguistic structure and language usage in concrete communication situations not only represent the speaker's reality, but are an integral part of it. This is especially true regarding the interconnectedness between language and cultural artefacts, especially because naming practices do not mechanically reflect pre-established social categories but contribute to creating and shaping them.

The interdependence between naming systems and different ecological factors can best be illustrated by the hierarchical model proposed in the first chapter of this volume. In this model, Ludwig, Mühlhäusler, and Pagel (Chapter 1) distinguish between the historically constituted macro-ecology (e.g., the Levant and the Spanish-speaking world), the intermediate ecological levels (e.g. urban ecologies, colonial ecologies), and the discourse ecology or micro-ecology (speech situations). Each level depends on the next higher and the next lower by means of *foundation* (in the Husserlian sense). Our study focuses primarily on the intermediate ecological level, i.e., the development of new naming practices in a specific ecology, the Antillean colonial system, trying to explain its emergence from the interaction of macro- and micro-ecological factors.

Whatever the ecological context, anthroponyms are expected to exist in every human society, because the use of personal names is a universal characteristic of human populations and as such a fundamental component of humankind's macrocultural competence, independent of space, time, speakers, or languages. At the same time, the indicated social categories may vary considerably across different speech communities. We assume that personal names are directly linked to the patterns of how different types of ecological relations are organized and perceived within the group and that these patterns of social and linguistic organization are a part of historically constituted macro-ecologies. When languages come into contact and hybridize, different macrocultural parameters (in our case, the western and the Antillean naming practices) interact with each other through speakers' discourse in micro-ecological contexts (see postulate5 in Chapter 1, p. 00). The importance of the micro level becomes obvious when we consider the fact that naming systems are rooted in concrete performative speech acts of naming by which, as we will see, individuals are linked to a particular space, situation, or social setting.

Shortly after the first encounter between Columbus and the indigenous populations of the Bahamas, the Greater Antilles faced the emergence of a completely new, ethnically mixed type of society, where European and Native American cultural patterns coexisted. In the following sections, this essay focuses on the transformation of the Spanish naming practices when challenged by the transplantation into a new ecology, with the emergence of a different social organization and intense language and cultural contact.

6.3   The Spanish Naming System in the Sixteenth Century

Today, all Spanish-speaking communities share a tripartite naming system of one or two given names (*nombres*) and two hereditary family names (*apellidos*). Generally, the first surname is the father's first surname and the second is the mother's first surname. At first glance, this may resemble the Roman tripartite naming system consisting of given name, clan name and family name. And yet, it is not a legacy of the Latin system, but developed relatively recently.

From the decline of the Roman Empire up to the Middle Ages, people in Europe used one given name only. It was not until the eleventh century that bipartite names, e.g. a given name and an inheritable family name, appeared. In the twelfth century, family names spread among the urban and rural population, even among bonded peasants and marginalized groups, such as vagrants or minorities (García Cornejo 1998: 172; Iglesias Ovejero 2003: 107–108). This usage had become systematic by the end of the Middle Ages (Kremer 1992: 463). In the Iberian Peninsula, a tripartite naming system developed during the sixteenth and seventeenth centuries. The first half of the sixteenth century therefore represents a crucial period in the formation of new naming patterns; and an unstable Spanish naming system, whereby tripartite names were still an exception, was brought to the Antilles, when Spaniards and Taino Indians lived together and the colonial society was born.

In order to understand the reasons for the development of complex personal names in Europe, we shall look at a variety of social and linguistic changes during the eleventh century from an ecological perspective. Demographics are a key factor affecting the dynamics of the European naming systems: population boomed during the high Middle Ages, and there was a strong pressure for urbanization. At the same time, the European population became more and more Christian, and – as a consequence of this important attitudinal (and institutional) change – there was an increasing emphasis to venerate the saints of the Roman Catholic Church in given names. On a micro-ecological level, name givers felt more and more drawn to choose names of saints (often from local cults), so that the traditional pagan names ran out of fashion and were gradually abandoned. Population growth, urbanization and the popularity of saints' names led to a situation in which a relatively small number of different names was given to an ever-increasing number of individuals within the same community. Consequently, names were no longer able to successfully fulfil their identifying function (see Kremer 1988a: 96, 1988b: 1588ff.).

In order to properly identify namesakes in concrete utterances, people started combining given names with surnames. This practice originated at the micro level and ultimately led to the formation and development of Spanish family names (*apellidos*).

Spanish *apellidos* could basically originate from four different sources. The most widespread procedure was to employ a patronym, based on the father's name or the name of another male ancestor, as *Martinez < Martín, Rodriguez < Rodrigo, Gonzalez < Gonzalo, Jimenez < Jimeno*, etc.[1] The *apellidos* could also reflect the occupation of a person, such as *Ferrero* 'blacksmith', *Zapatero* 'shoemaker', *Alcalde* 'mayor', *Molinero* 'miller', *Labrador* 'peasant', etc., or nicknames, mostly referring to some physical or mental characteristics (*Cano* 'grey-haired', *Crespo* 'curly-haired', *Delgado* 'thin', *Bermejo* 'ginger', *Calvo* 'bald-headed', *Leal* 'loyal', etc.). They also contained toponymic elements, such as *Alameda, Salazar, Burgos, Valverde, Villanueva*, etc. (see Kremer 1992: 463; García Cornejo 1998: 179ff.). Strictly speaking, a surname could not be considered as such until it had become heritable and was used as an index of family membership, without reference to actual attributes or qualities of its bearer.

---

[1] Typically, Spanish patronyms end in the suffix *-ez*, which means 'hijo de'. Although its Visigoth origin seems to be undisputed, the history of its development still remains to be clarified.

From an ecological linguistic point of view, the addition of the second element to the given name represents the adaptability of the language to changed ecological circumstances, where existing linguistic practices (use of one single name) were no longer able to fulfil social needs sufficiently and to identify individuals in complex urban societies. Heritability of the second element was not, however, an essential prerequisite to assert the identifying function of the name. It would have sufficed just to add any kind of surname as long as it made it possible to distinguish, say *Juan Calvo* from *Juan Crespo*.[2] We may therefore assume that the increasing ambiguity of given names in the context of urban growth was not the only ecological factor contributing to the emergence of a new system, but that some further reason made it necessary to classify individuals according to lineage.

It seems reasonable to attribute the desire to denote lineage in names to new attitudes and values that arose at the end of the Middle Ages. According to García Cornejo, this period brought about important changes in the way individuals perceived themselves as members of society:

La 'invención' de un *nomen paternum* no es una respuesta técnica al empobrecimiento onomástico sino que traduce la exigencia de una nueva relación en el mundo y en la sociedad, es la equivalente a la adopción de un estado civil. Es un momento en el que la sociedad entra en ebullición y en el que el individuo se reconoce como heredero, adquiere conciencia social e histórica, reflejándose en el uso del apellido. (1998: 172)

[The 'invention' of a *nomen paternum* is not a technical answer to the onomastic impoverishment but translates the demand of a new relationship in the world and in society, it is the equivalent of the adoption of a civil state. It is a moment when society gets mixed up, and when the individual recognizes himself as an heir, gathering a social and historical consciousness, which is reflected in the use of the family name. (my translation)]

It was the nobility who first emphasized their noble descent and the connection to the land they possessed by a surname. Accepted by larger segments of the population, the use of family names grew into an essential requisite of civil society, which gained importance in the Early Modern Period (Iglesias Ovejero 2003: 107). In the course of the sixteenth and seventeenth centuries, the *apellido* ceased to be confined only to the father's side. The mother's surname became heritable as well, probably motivated by a desire to mark not only the paternal, but also the maternal descent and legacy (Kremer 1992: 467f.; García Cornejo 1998: 178). Thus, important demographic developments and

---

[2] Cf. the modern naming system in Iceland, where the second component of the name changes in every generation. For example, if Jón is Guðmundur's and Sigríður's son, he may be called after his father *Jón Guðmundursson*, or after his mother *Jón Sigríðarson*. Jón's children may use *Jónsson* as a second name element (see Kvaran 2007: 314–315).

changes in social attitudes and values in the particular ecology of the medieval and early modern society generated the Iberian name system as a typical *système clanique* (Lévi-Strauss 1962). The function of proper names to denote social categories indexically served in the first place to convey the lineage.[3]

When the Spaniards landed in the New World, they encountered an astonishing diversity of indigenous societies. Their naming practices, like many other aspects of their languages and cultures, remained obscure to Europeans. The information provided by Spanish chroniclers such as Bartolomé de las Casas or Ramón Pané about indigenous naming systems are rather sparse. However, if we look more carefully at the Spanish and French texts from the late fifteenth to the seventeenth centuries, we can gain some insight into how indigenous people in the Antilles used personal names to identify individuals and to classify them according to socially relevant categories.

6.4   The Indigenous Naming System in the Antilles

Looking at the Caribbean archipelago in 1492, two important linguistic and cultural areas should be taken into consideration. The Greater Antilles were settled by an indigenous group known in Spanish as *taíno*, while the inhabitants of the Lesser Antilles used to be called *caníbales* or *caribes* in colonial times, nowadays referred to as *Island Caribs*. The language of the latter is relatively well known thanks to the work of the French Dominican missionary Raymond Breton (1609–1679). On the other hand, the scarcity of written sources on the Tainos prevents a full linguistic description of their language. They were decimated during the first half of the sixteenth century, before the Spaniards started to describe Native American languages in so called missionary grammars. As a result, only a few hundred words and toponyms are documented in Spanish chronicles. Nonetheless, the little documentation there is has let Americanist linguists to conclude that both languages belong to the Arawakan family rather than the Carib.

Various Spanish and French colonial texts show that indigenous people in the pre-Columbian Antilles only used one personal name. However, their names changed several times during their lifetime, depending either on changes in the social status of their bearers or on other important events. Nothing suggests that these names were hereditary. Besides, Taino, unlike European languages, does not seem to have had a fixed inventory of lexemes

---

[3] Cf. Iglesias Ovejero (2003: 105): 'Así pues, en el sistema de identificación onomástica vigente en España, todos los apellidos son, en principio, marcas de filiación.' ['Thus, in the onomastic identification system valid in Spain, all family names are, originally, filiation markers'] (my translation).

used only as proper names. Only one of about eighty anthroponyms of clear Taino origin (for example, *Guacanagarí, Caonaboa, Mayobanex, Anacaona, Cuaorocaya, Yahureibo, Haniguayaba, Manicaotex, Aerumeyro, Ayamanuex, etc.)* mentioned in the Spanish documents from the sixteenth century was borne by two different individuals.[4]

Taino names, unlike Spanish names, probably had denotative meanings. For example, according to the *Relación acerca de las antigüedades de los indios* (1493), the mythological hero *Caracaracol* owes his name to the circumstances of his birth:

la qual donna essendo morta di parto, l'aprirono, e cauarono fuori i detti quattro figliuoli, & il primo, che cauarono, fu Caracaracol, che uuol dir rognoso, il quale Caracaracol hebbe nome … gli altri non haueuano nome. (Rodríguez Álvarez 2008: 303)

[that woman died before giving birth, they opened her, and pulled out the aforementioned quadruplets, and the first they pulled out was Caracaracol, that means mangy, this child was given a name … the other ones did not have a name. (my translation)]

Although the word *Caracaracol* is not fully analysable due to our limited knowledge of the Taino language, it appears to contain the Arawakan root *uda* or *ura* 'skin' and therefore seems to denote a central physical characteristic of its bearer (cracked and itchy skin due to the prolonged stay in the mother's uterus). Both Las Casas and Peter Martyr d'Anghiera translate *Caonaboa*, the name of one of the five mightiest *caciques* that ruled the island of Hispaniola at the time of the arrival of Columbus, as *casa del oro* 'house of gold'. Unfortunately, the chronicles do not provide further details on its meaning, but we can assume that it is related to the bearer's biography and/or his living conditions. Lévi-Strauss calls this kind of name formation *syntagmatic* and distinguishes it from the European patterns, which are essentially *paradigmatic*, except for nicknames or animal names that can be freely invented and possess a denotative meaning (Lévi-Strauss 1962: 273).

According to historical sources, Taino names could be borrowed from other individuals who were not necessarily blood relatives but with whom the bearer shared a kind of ritual kinship that the Tainos called *guatiao*. As reported in Spanish chronicles, during the *guatiao* ritual, two people – generally dignitaries – could interchange their names to reflect their respect

---

[4] However, there may be a particular reason for this, as the two individuals sharing the same name are brothers: 'En 12 de julio de 1527 se depositaron en Juan de Orozco dos indios que se dicen, el uno, Gaspar y en Cubahaguabana Birex, y el otro, García y en Cubahaguabana Birex, hermano del dicho Gaspar, naturales del dicho pueblo del Guanabo de la provincia de Guamohaya.' ['On 12 July 1527, two Indians were given to Juan de Orozco, whose names are, for the first, Gaspar and in Cubahaguabana Birex, and for the second, García and in Cubahaguabana Birex, the brother of the afore mentioned Gaspar, both of them natives of the afore mentioned village of Guanabo, in the province of Guamohaya'] (my translation) (Mira Caballos 1997: 419).

and solidarity for each other. Spanish conquerors often engaged in *guatiao* rituals to form strategic alliances with Taino chiefs. Las Casas provides an illustrative example that shows a *guatiao* ritual as an effective means to resolve conflicts. In 1503, Nicolás de Ovando, governor of Hispaniola, ordered Juan de Esquivel to repress a Taino rebellion under the leadership of the *cacique* Cotubano. After days of arduous fighting, an armistice was declared by way of a *guatiao* ritual:

> Este trueque de nombres en la lengua común desta isla se llamaba ser yo y fulano, que trocamos los nombres, guatiaos, y así se llamaba el uno al otro guatiao. Teníase por gran parentesco y como liga de perpetua amistad y confederación. y así el capitán general y aquel señor quedaron guatiaos, como perpetuos amigos y hermanos en armas. Y así los indios llamaban Cotubano al capitán, y al señor, Juan de Esquivel. (Las Casas, *Historia de las Indias*, 1994, II, cap. 8, p. 1324)

> [In the common language of this island, this exchange of names was said to turn me and such-and-such into *guatiaos,* and so they called each other *guatiao*. It was considered [an expression of] close kinship and of a relationship of perpetual friendship and confederation. And so the general leader and this *señor* were *guatiaos,* as perpetual friends and brothers in arms. And so, the Indians called the leader Cotubano and the *señor* Juan de Esquivel. (my translation)]

According to Spanish sources, a lot of Taino chiefs carried Spanish names, but no Spaniard seems to have ever used an indigenous name after taking part in a *guatiao* ritual.

Apart from adopting the name of a *guatiao*, Tainos could also change their names at critical moments in their lives, for example, after having survived a grave illness. This is reported about Guahagiona, another mythological hero in the *Relación de las antigüedades de los indios*, who adopts the name *Biberoci* after having been cured from smallpox (Rodríguez Álvarez 2008: 299). The changing of names was performed in two steps: first, two anthroponyms were used simultaneously, the old name following the recently adopted one. After a certain time, the old name was given up for the new one only, as is illustrated by the names referring to different mythological characters in the *Relación de las antigüedades de los indios*:

Guahagiona	→	Biberoci Guahagiona	→	*Biberoci
Caracaracol	→	Dimiuan Caracaracol	→	*Dimiuan
*Cahuuaial	→	Inrire Cahuuaial	→	Inrire

It appears that Taino anthroponyms were not permanent and could be linked to other people, events, or circumstances that were in some way important in the life of any given individual. Such names can be characterized as *termes relationnels* in the broadest sense of the word, because the Indigenous naming system does not necessarily regard an individual on the level of kinship or other social relationships only, but can take into consideration all kinds of different aspects of the ecology he or she has lived in.

While Spanish anthroponyms are inherited and definite, the Tainos could change their names several times during their lives, each name highlighting an aspect of its bearer's life which was perceived as important at a given point in time, but not necessarily essential to the individual as such. The Spanish and the indigenous naming system therefore represent two fundamentally different approaches to naming, as described by Lévi-Strauss:

> Nous sommes donc en présence de deux types extrêmes de noms propres, entre lesquels existent toute une série d'intermédiaires. Dans un cas, le nom est une marque d'identi-fication, qui confirme, par application d'une règle, l'appartenance de l'individu qu'on nomme à une classe préordonnée (un groupe social dans un système de groupes, un statut natal dans un système de statuts); dans l'autre cas, le nom est une libre création de l'individu qui nomme et qui exprime, au moyen de celui qu'il nomme, un état transitoire de sa propre subjectivité. (1962: 240)

> [We are therefore facing two extreme kinds of proper names, between which there is a series of intermediate cases. In one case, the name is an identity marker that confirms, by the application of a rule, the membership of the named individual in a predetermined class (a social group within a system of groups, a natal status within a system of status); in the other case, the name is a free creation of the individual who names and who expresses, by means of the person he or she names, a transitional state of his or her own subjectivity. (my translation)]

6.5   Studying Spanish Anthroponymy in Sixteenth-century Antilles

6.5.1   The Encomienda System

In order to understand the ecological context in which new naming practices emerged under the Spanish colonial rule, we shall take a look at the organization of colonial society in the Greater Antilles in the first half of the sixteenth century. In 1502, the Spanish Crown imposed the so-called *encomienda*, a kind of labour system that gave Spanish colonists (*encomenderos*) the responsibility for a certain number of indigenous people and the right to employ them in various areas, generally in gold mining. In return, *encomenderos* were obliged to protect their *indios encomendados*, provide them with food and clothes and instruct them in the Catholic faith (see Mira Caballos 1997).

Colonial society under the *encomienda* system was characterized by a strongly hierarchical organization (Mira Caballos 1997: 81ff.). On the one hand, there was an imbalance of power and status between the Spaniards and the Tainos. On the other hand, the colonial indigenous populations inherited significant status differences as a relic of pre-Columbian social hierarchy. The *caciques* formed the top of Taino society, followed by the *nitaínos* who seem to have been a kind of local elite.[5] The *naborías*[6] and slaves stood at the very bottom of the social pyramid. While the *naborías* were subjects of the Spanish Crown, and therefore legally free, the slaves were in the possession of their masters. They were acquired as prisoners of war, probably from the so-called *indios de guerra*, members of the more belligerent tribes living in the Lesser Antilles. The *cimarrones* who had tried to flee from the *encomienda* were also enslaved. The living conditions of both the *naborías* and the *esclavos* were practically identical.

6.5.2   *The* Cédulas de Repartimiento

The distribution of the local indigenous population among Spanish *encomenderos* was recorded in the so-called *cédulas de encomienda* or *repartimientos*. These documents are extremely useful for the study of colonial anthroponymy because, given their particular function, they contain a large number of personal names. Las Casas describes the practice of the *repartimiento* and the linguistic form of *cédulas* as follows:

Y porque [en] cada pueblo de indios se hacían munchos [*sic*] repartimientos dando a cada español cierto número – como es dicho – dellos, con el uno dellos asignaba que fuese el señor o cacique y éste daba al español a quien él más honrar y aprovechar quería. A los cuales [el Rey] daba una cédula de su repartimiento que rezaba desta manera: A vos, fulano, se os encomiendan en el cacique fulano cincuenta o cien indios para que os sirváis dellos en vuestras granjerías y minas y enseñaldes [*sic*] las cosas de nuestra sancta [sic!] fe católica. Item, decía otra: A vos, fulano, se os encomiendan en el cacique fulano cincuenta o cient indios, con la persona del cacique, para que os sirváis dellos en vuestras granjerías y minas y enseñaldes [*sic*] las cosas de nuestra sancta [*sic*] fe católica. (Las Casas, *Historia de las Indias*, 1994, II, cap. 13, p. 1346)

[Because in every Indian village there were a lot of *repartimientos,* where every Spaniard was given a certain number of them [the Indians], as has been said, and one of them said who was to be the lord or *cacique*, and that one gave them to the Spaniard he wanted to honour and whose profit he wanted to increase most. And the King gave them a bond that read as follows: To you, such-and-such, will be given under the cacique such-and-such fifty or a hundred Indians so that you can take advantage of them in your farms and mines and teach them our Holy Catholic Faith. And another one read:

---

[5] Spanish sources usually translate *nitaínos* as 'nobles'.
[6] Spanish sources do not provide a conclusive explanation of the meaning of the term *naboría* nor of the role these people played in pre-Columbian and colonial societies.

to you, such-and-such, will be given under the cacique such-and-such fifty or a hundred Indians, together with the cacique, so that you can take advantage of them in your farms and mines and teach them our Holy Catholic Faith. (my translation)]

Every formula exhibits at least two anthroponyms, one of the Spanish *enco-mendero* and one of the *cacique*. In most cases, the *cacique* was the only indigenous person explicitly referred to by his personal name. People under his rule were usually identified as *indios* or *naborías*, with the occasional specification of their sex, age, or occupation. The names of common people were recorded systematically in the so-called *libros de la visitación*, but unfortunately none of these books has been preserved. Nevertheless, in certain cases the *cédulas de repartimiento* also contain the names of some *naborías* and slaves. This happened, for example, when slaves or *naborías* were assigned to another *encomendero* who was not their *cacique*.

The sources employed in the following analysis of colonial naming practices represent various *Cédulas de encomienda* and *repartimientos* from the *Repartimiento de Albuquerque*, also known as *Repartimiento de la Isla Española* (1514, Arranz Márquez 1991).[7] Another extremely informative source containing a number of slave names is the 'Relación de los esclavos',[8] a document on brand marking and the public sale of indigenous people. Additionally, the anthroponyms documented in works of Columbus, Las Casas, and Oviedo are also taken into account.[9] In order to compare naming practices within the *encomienda* system, on the one hand, and general naming patterns in sixteenth-century Spain, on the other, we also consulted copious literature on anthroponomy in the Iberian Peninsula, as well as Peter Boyd-Bowman's (1985) *Indice geobiográfico de más de 56 mil pobladores de la América Hispánica (1493–1519)*.

6.5.3   The Database

A database with 785 records (= individuals or tokens) was obtained through a detailed study of the above-mentioned historical sources. It contains not only personal names and their variants, but also information about the sex, origin, and social position of the name bearers. In 648 out of 781 (83 per cent)

---

[7] It contains a variety of the *Cédulas de encomienda and repartimientos* dating from 1514, 1515, 1519, and 1523 published in Mira Caballos (1997).

[8] *Relación de los esclavos que se herraron a las personas que los sacaron en almoneda de los que se vendieron y truxeron del armada de Su Alteza que esta a cargo del capitán Juan Ponce de León, Adelantado de Biminy e isla Florida* (1515).

[9] Ramón Pané's *Relación acerca de las antigüedades de los indios* (1498), which is considered the earliest and undoubtedly the most important text on Taino culture, will not be used in this analysis, because the text only contains names used by the Tainos themselves and not by the Spaniards.

cases, individuals are clearly referred to as *cacique/cacica, nitaíno, naboría o esclavo/esclava*. In the remaining 133 cases, the context did not provide enough information on their status. 61 per cent of the indigenous people documented in the sources are *caciques* or *nitainos*. This percentage does not give an accurate representation of the Taino population and should be understood in connection with the text type *cédula de repartimiento*, in which dignitaries were mentioned much more frequently than common people. A profile of people according to the different social categories can be summarized as follows:

- 191 women, 589 men, 1 not specified
- 38 female and 402 male chiefs (*caciques/cacicas*)
- 39 nitaínos (seem to be exclusively male)
- 69 female[10] and 79 male *naborías*
- 15 female and 4 male slaves

The vast majority of those registered were adults. Only six children are mentioned in the studied colonial documents, four of them were slaves.

Different types of naming patterns can be distinguished from a structural point of view. *Indios encomendados*' names could consist of one, two, or even three components. This study will refer to them as first, second and third name components in order to avoid confusion with conventional connotations and functional categorizations inherent in terms as *Christian name, family name* or *surname*, and *middle name*. Looking at the etymologies of the names, we note that they are of either Spanish or Taino origin. They sometimes contain additional elements, such as toponyms or the name of a *cacique*. In other cases, personal names are modified by diminutive suffixes or honorifics. In the following sections, we will analyse the name inventory in greater detail and try to show how it reflects ecological linguistic conditions of the early colonial society.

6.6   *Naming Practices in the* Encomienda *System*

6.6.1   *Number and Origin of the Name Components*

Two facts about the colonial name system as applied to the indigenous people of the Greater Antilles are particularly striking: firstly, nearly three quarters (74 per cent) of the *indios encomendados* bore only one single name, 25 per cent had two, and a small minority (1 per cent) three names.

---

[10] One woman referred to as *criada* 'housemaid' was classified as *naboría.*

This clearly differs from naming customs in sixteenth-century Spain, where it was common to bear at least two and sometimes even three names. Second, the predominance of single names *cannot* be explained by the fact that the Spaniards frequently used indigenous names when referring to their workers. An overwhelming majority of the Tainos were registered under a Spanish name; indigenous names constitute only 9 per cent of the elements that appear as the first component or as the only name in the corpus. In this respect, the Antillean colonial society reproduces a pattern that can be observed in many situations of language contact and in virtually all Spanish colonies. The more powerful the group, the stronger is the tendency to impose a new naming system, rather than to adopt the names of those conquered (Patterson 1982: 54–55; Löffler 1996: 1297). The fact that the conquered people are often renamed when being subjected to the conqueror's domination as slaves or servants is well documented throughout European history; French and English colonists treated their African slaves in a similar manner. Although the assignment of new names to slaves of foreign origin may be explained by practical reasons because, in comparison to indigenous names, Spanish names were easier to pronounce and to retain for the colonists, it represents, in the first place, a statement of power (Patterson 1982: 55).

To sum up, about seventy indigenous names are documented in the corpus:

Abey, Acanaorex, Aconex, Aerumeyro, Agüeibana, Aimanio, Anacaona, Anaorex, Anípana, Antrabaagures, Apadinla, Araguay, Aramana, Ayamanuex, Bacafex, Barahona, Baraona, Behechio, Beninepex, Cacimar, Caguas, Canobana, Caonaboa, Çapiaguex, Capitanex (?), Çarrafaya, Caseçan, Cayey, Çayguan Guaraba, Cotubanamá, Cuaorocaya, Goayrabo, Guacanagarí, Guanabax, Guarionex, Guatiguana, Guayama, Guevaya, Haniguayaba, Humacao, Incagueca, Mabodomoca, Macote, Manicaotex, Manyguatex, Marien, Masupa Otex, Mata Boronex, Matutino, Maxaguan, Mayaguamaça, Maybona, Maymotonex, Mayobanex, Nibagua, Ochoyra, Orocobiz, Queban, Simenex, Urayoán, Uxmatex, Xamayta, Xinahueça, Yaguaço, Yaguahán, Yahureibo, Ynamoca

We can easily recognize their Arawakan phonetic form (especially, the extremely regular syllable structure KVKV) and the suffix *-ri(x)* or *-ex*, which was probably a noun marker for the features [+MASCULINE] and [+HUMAN] (Granberry and Vescelius 2004: 102). The individuals who carried such names were exclusively *caciques* and very often important protagonists in the history of the conquest, as told by Columbus, Las Casas, and Oviedo. For example, indigenous dignitaries such as *Guacanagarí, Caonaboa, Mayobanex*, or *Anacaona* established a close contact with the Spaniards prior to the establishment of the proper colonial society. Their leading position and prominent role in the *Conquista* may explain why the chroniclers referred to them by their indigenous names rather than assigning them Spanish names or just calling them *indios*. The only exception to this rule is the rebellious *cacique* Enriquillo who retained his Spanish name probably because he was raised by Franciscans. Colonial sources described him as an *indio ladino*, i.e. a culturally and linguistically assimilated indigenous person.

Apart from the imposition of new names after the conquest, we can also distinguish another means of representing power relations onomastically. According to a secular European tradition, the number of constituents in a name, and especially the presence or absence of a clan name, indexes the free or bonded status of its bearer. In the Middle Ages, subordinate people, unlike free ones, bore only single names. Similarly, slaves in Ancient Rome also bore a single name (*praenomen*), contrary to free citizens who had tripartite names consisting of a first name, a clan name, and a family name (Löffler 1996: 1297).

In compliance with the function of family names as markers of lineage, the absence of a family name underscores the bonded person's 'natal alienation' (Patterson 1982: 5) and his or her lack of any rights or privileges attached to birth:

[Authority and the control of symbolic instruments] is achieved in a unique way in the relation of slavery: the definition of the slave … as a socially dead person. Alienated from all 'rights' or claims of birth, he ceased to belong in his own right to any legitimate social order. All slaves experienced, at the very least, a secular excommunication. (Patterson 1982: 5)

In most parts of Europe, including the Iberian Peninsula throughout the Middle Ages, not only enslaved or bonded people, but also servants, women, children and other legally and economically dependent individuals who were not in possession of full civil rights were deprived of family names (Kremer 1988a: 104; Löffler 1996). However, as European societies in the Early Modern Period shifted away from feudalism and serfdom, the distinction between free and non-free people became less important, and the use of surnames spread into broader segments of society. In sixteenth-century Spain, family names were already commonly used, except for people of marginal social status (for example, vagabonds, beggars, criminals, etc.), as a relic of the old restriction to people of high social class.

Contrary to the above, the birth of colonial society in the Antilles, together with the establishment of the *encomienda* system, created ecological conditions that favoured the reactivation of the ancient European pattern. The new, culturally heterogeneous society developing in the sixteenth-century Antilles was ethnically highly segregated. Being indigenous automatically entailed subjection to forced labour and bonded social status. No wonder that the naming system reflected this social development. The deep-rooted European tradition to regard different degrees of complexity of the name as a means of distinction between people from the various strata of the social pyramid was reactivated. The descent of the indigenous people was not important to colonial rulers and, from a naming perspective, not even for the Taínos themselves, since their naming system emphasized current social relationships to other people rather than filiation. In the Antillean context, single names not only referred to the bonded status, but, at the same time, to the ethnic origin of their bearers, since only indigenous people lacked family names.[11] Therefore, anthroponyms of different degrees of complexity were simultaneously social *and* ethnic classifiers. This phenomenon emerged within a specific ecological frame of the colonial society due to a spatial–temporal contiguity of social position and ethnic membership. Leaving aside the question of family names, let us now look at the lexical elements that could be used as given names for the *indios encomendados*.

6.6.2   First Name Component

6.6.2.1 Name Types

While structural differences between masters' and servants' names reflect a traditional European pattern, this is only partly true for lexical elements chosen as given names. In European Antiquity, slave names were generally derived from Greek or Latin and not from the ethnic languages of slaves. However, different name repertoires were used for free and non-free people (Löffler 1996: 1297), so that the exotic touch of the names of the slaves could serve as a social classifier revealing the bonded status and possibly intended to stress the 'otherness' of the subordinate group. This custom was later adopted by the French, English, and Spanish in the context of the African slave trade in the Caribbean. So, French slave names from Saint Domingue were typically chosen from biblical, mythological, or historical sources (with some irony in many cases!), though some slaves bore names denoting days in the calendar or geographical places. (Patterson 1982: 56–57; Fouchard 1988: 228ff.; Löffler 1996: 1299).

An examination of the first component of Antillean Natives' names reveals that they are not different from Spanish names at all. Spaniards preferred the same names for their *indios encomendados* that were most popular on the Iberian Peninsula and in other parts of the Spanish colonial empire at that time. The following lists compare the ten most popular names in different Spanish-speaking areas.

---

[11] Spanish settlers without a second name are absent in Boyd-Bowman's (1985) 'Indice geobio-gráfico'.

Andalusia (1493), García Cornejo (1998)	Carmona/Sevilla (16th century), Álvarez, Ariza, and Mendoza (2000)	Mexico (1540), Spanish colonists, Boyd-Bowman (1970)	Antilles (1509–1523), native men Corpus Jansen
1 Juan	Juan	Juan	Juan
2 Alonso	Pedro	Diego	Diego
3 Pedro	Alonso	Francisco	Pedro
4 Antonio	Francisco	Pedro	Alonso
5 Bartolomé	Antonio	Alonso	Francisco
6 Diego	Diego	Antonio	Gonzalo
7 Martín	Hernando	Luis	Martín
8 Gonzalo	Cristóbal	Hernando	Antonio
9 Francisco	Gonzalo	Cristóbal	Cristóbal
10 Hernán	Bartolomé	Baltasar	Hernán

Despite some slight differences, all of the studies show similar preferences for a relatively small number of names such as *Juan, Pedro, Alonso,* and *Francisco.* A clear-cut tendency in the Greater Antilles, just as in Spain and Mexico, to use only a limited repertoire of different Christian names generated a situation where greater segments of the society shared an identical name (Boyd-Bowman 1970: 16ff.; Kremer 1992: 464). Of the men, 15 per cent in my corpus are called *Juan,* while the five most frequently used names belonged to 54 per cent of the male individuals and the ten most popular names even cover 70 per cent of them.

Female names display a similar distribution, although the rank order is less stable in comparison with the male names. *Isabel, Inés, Catalina, María* and *Leonor* are clearly the most preferred names among both Spanish and indigenous women in Spain and in the colonies.

Andalusia (1493), García Cornejo (1998)	Carmona/Sevilla (16th century), Álvarez, Ariza and Mendoza (2000)	Mexico (1540), Spanish women, Boyd-Bowman (1970)	Antilles (1509–1523), native women Corpus Jansen
1 Catalina	Ana	María	Isabel
2 Isabel	Inés	Isabel	Inés
3 Marina	Isabel	Ana	María
4 Mari	Juana	Catalina	Catalina
5 Ana	Marina	Beatriz	Beatriz
6 Antonia	Catalina	Leonor	Elvira
7 Leonor	Elvira	Juana	Magdalena
8 Juana	María/Mari	Francisca	Luisa
9 Teresa	Gracia	Inés	Leonor
10 Elvira	Guiomar	Luisa	Juana

Isabel, the most popular female name in the Greater Antilles, is shared by 14 per cent of the indigenous women. The five most frequently used names are borne by almost half (49 per cent) of the women, while the ten most frequently used names are borne by almost 80 per cent of them.

The first component of the name demonstrates an evident continuity of the naming practices from the Iberian Peninsula to the American continent, independent of social status or ethnic membership. The lexical choice did not fulfil a classificatory function in the Spanish *encomienda* system, contrary to the naming patterns in European Antiquity and in many colonial slave societies (Patterson 1982: 57–58). The social segregation between masters and servants, which corresponded directly to the ethnic separation between Spanish and Tainos, was represented onomastically only by the number of components, e.g. by the presence or absence of a *nom clanique*. Similar patterns of naming have been observed in other Spanish colonies, e.g. in the Canary Islands (Lobo Cabrera 2010: 212), the Viceroyalty of Peru (Zúñiga 2010: 194), and Cuba (Pérez Díaz 2006).

This finding, which may appear striking at first sight, can plausibly be explained within the ideological framework of the Spanish colonial enterprise, which considered the conversion of the indigenous population as one of its most important aims (Mira Caballos 1997: 78). Traditionally, the concept of a complex ritual of baptism has included the allocation of a Christian name as an emblem of joining the Christian community. Indigenous people taking on *Christian* names were identified as members of the Christian community, while differences in ethnic affiliation and social status were expressed by other means.

At the same time, pre-Columbian naming practices probably facilitated the adoption and use of Spanish names by the Taino. As it emerges from the sources at hand, it was natural for the Natives to change their names when their lives took a new direction; and this practice was perfectly compatible with the Christian ritual of baptism. Las Casas even reports that the Tainos were fond of taking on Spanish names:

Estuvieron allí en fiestas y conversación amigable los unos con los otros algunos días; y unos dellos convidaron [*sic*] al señor del pueblo, que se llamaba Alonso o don Alonso (no supe si los religiosos aquel nombre le pusieron, o quizá algunos cristianos que por allí habían de antes pasado, porque los indios comunmente son amigos de tener nombres españoles), convidáronlo, digo, a él y a su mujer. (Las Casas, *Historia de las Indias*, 1994, II, cap. 33, p. 1897)

[There they were on some days, engaged in parties and friendly conversation with one another; and some of them invited the chief of the village, who was called Alonso o don Alonso (I never knew if the clergymen gave him that name, or perhaps some Christians who had come along before, because the Indians generally are fond of having Spanish names), they invited him, as I've said, him and his wife. (my translation)]

The sources also reveal that the Tainos used different Christian names at different moments in time:

el cacique Anton de la Yaguana, que se decía antes Cristóbal. ('Repartimiento de la Isla Española', 1514, in Arranz Márquez 1991: 227)

[the cacique Anton de la Yaguana, formerly called Cristóbal. (my translation)]

una india que se dice Beatrizica y ahora Constanza Puacayma. ('Fragmento del juicio de residencia tomado a Gonzalo de Guzmán en 1530', in Mira Caballos 1997: 418)

[an Indian woman called Beatrizica, and now Constanza Puacayma. (my translation)]

This suggests that they may have continued pre-Columbian naming patterns even when using names of Spanish origin, though these were actually supposed to be definitive. These examples and Las Casas's report show that it would be too simplistic to regard the naming practices of the *encomienda* as the mere imposition of new anthroponyms by the conquerors as a statement of power. Rather, the open and dynamic character of the indigenous naming system must be considered as an essential ecological factor which fostered the adoption of Spanish names by the Natives.

6.6.2.2 *Diminutive Forms*
The high frequency of diminutive forms in the structure of the first name components is particularly striking, too. Nearly one quarter of the names of the entire corpus contains a diminutive suffix. More than half of them represent the names of *naborías* and slaves (53 per cent) and 4 per cent are the names of *caciques* and *nitainos*. They include: *Alonsico, Alonsillo, Francisquito, Juanico, Tomasico, Isabelica, Isabelita, Isabelilla, Inesica*, and *Leonorica*, among others. Children's names are exclusively diminutives. The suffix *-ico/-ica* is the most common one for both sexes and is used in 84 per cent of the female and 72 per cent of the male diminutive names. Apart from this suffix, *-ito* often appears in male names (17 per cent) followed by *-illo* (11 per cent). Female names are also built by means of the suffixes *-illa* (13 per cent) and *-ita* (3 per cent). This development demonstrates continuity with a general usage of diminutives in Spain up to the sixteenth century, where *-ico/-ica* was the suffix usually combined with proper names (Náñez Fernández 1973: 172).

At the end of the Middle Ages and during the early modern period, diminutive suffixes in personal names served several purposes. On the one hand, they were used to express affection, a feature we can still observe in modern Spanish. The complete absence of affective forms like *Pancho* for *Francisco, Pepe* for *José*, etc. in the corpus leads to the conclusion that the main function of the diminutive suffixes in sixteenth-century colonial society was not, however, to form terms of endearment. Otherwise, we would expect the diminutive names to alternate with other types of hypocorisms.

Another important function of diminutives in Spain was to distinguish individuals sharing the same name. The custom to name children after older relatives created a common situation where identical names existed within the same family or even reflected family traditions in the choice of given names.[12] When two family members bore the same name (e.g., father and son or two siblings of different age), the younger one was usually called by a diminutive form (see Gonzales Ollé 1962; Buesa Oliver 1988; Kremer 1992: 472). Therefore, the suffix simultaneously performed an identifying function (distinction of two people with identical names) and a classifying function with respect to an individual's age (diminutive as indexical sign for younger age).

The case of the Antilles shows discontinuity with the metropolitan tradition to choose identical names for family members. In the cases where the historical sources reproduce names of several members of the same indigenous family, generally siblings or parents and children, they always bear different names, e.g., *Inesica* and *Leonor* (sisters), *Marica, Elenica* and *Juanica* (sisters), *Perico* and *Andresico* (brothers), *Gaspar* and *García* (brothers), *Perico* and *Francisquito* (father and son), *Beatriz, Juanica*, and *Elvirica* (mother and two daughters). In contrast to Spain, the use of the same given names within a family was not common among the *indios encomendados*. A disambiguation of the diminutive forms was unnecessary, since there was no need to distinguish different family members, although a tendency to use diminutive forms with children was quite common.

The fact that diminutive forms were also employed in adult names in sixteenth-century Spain is best illustrated in the picaresque novel (*novela picaresca*), a popular literary genre which depicts the adventures of a roguish, picaresque hero with a low social background in a satirical and humorous way. The protagonist and other characters of 'Lazarillo de Tormes', the first Spanish picaresque novel, bear diminutive names, like *Guzmanillo, Estebanillo, Pablillo,* and *Justinillo*. Alonso (1982: 204–205) suggests that diminutive names used in this type of novel, especially those formed with *-illo* and, to a lesser degree, with *-ico* or *-ito,* characterize their bearers as *pícaros* and people from *germanía* (low class criminals). In other words, the diminutive names identify their bearers as members of a socially marginalized group and, therefore, can be seen as social classifiers in the sense explained by Lévi-Strauss. This classifying function of the suffix in personal names appears to have originated in different metonymic extensions of the original diminutive meaning. When applied to an adult, the meaning of names with *-ito, -ico* or *-illo* could oscillate between affection and negative attitude. This feature made them particularly appropriate to refer to picaresque anti-heroes

---

[12] Not only family names, but also Christian names could become heritable and function as *noms claniques* in medieval and early modern Spain.

whom the *novela picaresca* usually depicted with a certain sympathy in spite of their criminal way of life.

Be that as it may, we are concerned with the following question: which function did diminutive names perform in the colonial naming system as applied to the Natives? Undoubtedly, the expression of affection and disambiguation, two central functions of diminutives in the Iberian Peninsula, has no parallel in the Antilles. We may speculate that the Antillean context provided a favourable sociocultural ecology for the diminutive to develop as a social classifier whose function was to mark different social categories within the indigenous segment of the population. As mentioned above, such a development was probably generated by a particular function of diminutives, such as marking a low class and marginal social status, as expressed in the *novela picaresca*. Their function as social classifiers becomes especially clear when we look at the distribution of diminutive and non-diminutive names among *caciques* and *nitainos* on the one hand and among *naborías* and slaves on the other:

	caciques and *nitainos (%)*	*naborías* and slaves (%)
Juan	non-diminutive form: 90	non-diminutive form: 21
	diminutive form: 10	diminutive form: 79
Diego	non-diminutive form: 100	non-diminutive form: 64
	diminutive form: 0	diminutive form: 36
Pedro	non-diminutive form: 96	non-diminutive form: 0
	diminutive form: 4	diminutive form: 100
Alonso	non-diminutive form: 96	non-diminutive form: 0
	diminutive form: 4	diminutive form: 100
Francisco	non-diminutive form: 95	non-diminutive form: 11
	diminutive form: 5	diminutive form: 89
Gonzalo	non-diminutive form: 100	non-diminutive form: 17
	diminutive form: 0	diminutive form: 83
Martín	non-diminutive form: 80	non-diminutive form: 25
	diminutive form: 20	diminutive form: 75
Antonio	non-diminutive form: 100	non-diminutive form: 50
	diminutive form: 0	diminutive form: 50
Cristóbal	non-diminutive form: 100	non-diminutive form: 75
	diminutive form: 100	diminutive form: 25
Hernán	non-diminutive form: 78	non-diminutive form: 0
	diminutive form: 22	diminutive form: 100

The study of female names reveals similar results. None of the 38 *cacicas* recorded in the database is called by a diminutive form, while 38 per cent of the *esclavas* and female *naborías* have diminutive names.

Despite some irregularities, we can clearly observe a complementary distribution of non-diminutive and diminutive forms among *caciques* and *nitainos* on the one hand and among *naborías* and slaves on the other. Hence, the classifying function was realized by marking affiliation with one group or another in a hierarchical social world order. This development can only be properly understood within the organization of the colonial society and the *encomienda* system, since social categories as *caciques* and *naborías* were inherited from pre-Columbian times and did not exist on the Iberian Peninsula. However, we cannot exclude that the continental tradition to apply diminutive forms to individuals who either were not considered to be full members of the society or belonged to socially marginalized groups (*pícaros*) might have helped to shape a new function as a social classifier in the conditions of the *encomienda* system. Usage of simple and complex names as ethnic classifiers originated in congruity with different social factors, such as age, position in social hierarchy, and degree of legal and economic autonomy within the contemporary ecological frame.

6.6.2.3 By-names and Nicknames

We have already determined that the first component of the name was virtually always a Spanish lexical item. Nevertheless, it did not necessarily have to be a traditional personal name. Some of the *caciques* (but none of the *naborías* or slaves) bore names that originally denoted Spanish military and navigation ranks, as well as noble, academic, or religious titles, such as *Capitán* (also *Capitanico, Capitán del Rey*), *Almirante* (also *Almirantico*), *Doctor, Contramaestre, Adelantado, Alguacil, Mayordomo, Comendador, Padre*, and *Fray*.

Two reasons explain the use of titles as personal names among *caciques*, one of which has to do with the indigenous custom of taking the name of another individual either as a result of the *guatiao* ritual or baptism. For example, Las Casas reports that a Cuban *cacique* chose the Spanish word *Comendador* as his Christian name, obviously misinterpreting a Spanish military title, as a personal name:

El nombre del cacique: « Comendador », lo hobo [*sic*] desta manera: que, como de los españoles que por allí venían supiese que era bien ser cristiano baptizándose [*sic*] y pidiese el baptismo [*sic*], no supe quién lo baptizo [*sic*] más de que, cuando el nombre se le había de dar, preguntó que cómo se llamaba el señor grande de los cristianos que aquesta isla Española gobernaba; dixéronle que se llamaba « el Comendador », y entonces dixo que aquél quería que fuese su nombre. (Las Casas, *Historia de las Indias*, 1994, III, cap. 24, p. 1859)

[The name of the cacique: 'Comendador' was given to him in the following manner: When he learned from the Spaniards who came here that it was good to be a Christian and to that he should ask for baptism, I didn't find out who baptized him, apart from the fact that, when he was about to be given a name, he asked for the name of the important ruler of the Christians who controlled that Island of Hispaniola; they told him that he was called 'el Comendador', and so he said that he wanted to be called like that. (my translation)]

Boyd-Bowman (1985) does not record any Spanish settlers with surnames such as *Capitán, Almirante*, and *Comendador*, and the adoption of these items as names appears to have happened because of some confusion between nominal forms of address and personal names, as described by Las Casas.

At the same time, ostensibly honorific names such as *Almirante* and *Capitán* could also be interpreted as nicknames assigned by the Spanish to the indigenous chiefs with ironical intent. This conclusion is supported by the following example from Las Casas, who reports that Spaniards often derided the Indian chiefs by calling them all kinds of names:

Aquel rey e señor de las dichas // sierras y tierra hasta la dicha mar, tenía por nombre Mayomanex [*sic*]; por otro nombre le llamaban los españoles el Cabrón, no sé otra causa sino por escarnio, como solían poner nombres a los señores, vituperiosos como los hallaron desnudos. (Las Casas, *Historia de las Indias*, 1994, I, cap. 120, p. 987)

[That king and leader of that sierras and territories up to that sea, had the name of Mayomanex; with another name the Spaniards called him 'el Cabrón' [= the billy goat, used in Spanish as a derogatory term], I don't know any other reason than for derision, as they used to call the nobles names, blaming them because they were naked. (my translation)]

This evidence, together with the frequent use of diminutive forms, especially *Almirantico* and *Capitanico*, lends support to the idea that a good portion of the nicknames were used in an ironic and derisive way. Honorific or religious titles for *caciques* (e.g. *Don Sancho, Don Diego, Don Juanico de Acasa, Don Juan,* and *Doña María*; perhaps also *Maese Pedro, San Pedro, San Juanico, Fray Juan*) should be understood similarly. Indigenous chiefs were officially allowed to take honorific titles in very exceptional cases. For example, the rebellious *cacique* Enriquillo was given the title of *Don* after the peace treaty in 1530. The general tendency to use ironic nicknames for indigenous people developed parallel to the habit of referring to members of the *germanía*, e.g., criminals, beggars, and prostitutes as *Don* or *Doña*. Picaresque novels used this means to underscore the comical effect (Alonso 1982: 208). The name *Capitanex* provides another interesting example of this practice, as it seems to be a cacography based on the combination of Spanish *capitán* with the typical Taino suffix *-ex*.

At the same time, nicknames that reflect physical or mental characteristics of their bearers are rather exceptional in the corpus. Only two examples, *Peinado* 'combed haired' and *Melenas* 'maned', refer to their bearers' hairstyle. The nickname *Doctor* given to one of the *caciques* reveals an important aspect of his personality. According to the text, this by-name was given 'porque era el que más sabía de todos' ('because he was the one who knew most of them all', my translation) (Mira Caballos 1997: 109). Another nickname (*Barbero* 'barber') refers to a professional title.

Contrary to traditional Spanish personal names such as *Juan, Diego*, and *Alonso*, nicknames show parallels with indigenous names, since both are descriptive and, therefore, have denotational meanings, although in official documents such as the *cédulas de repartimiento* they are used primarily to identify individuals. An ecological linguistic approach requires a closer look at the semantic fields from which nicknames developed. As they generally reflect – in the eyes of the name giver – the most salient or most important qualities or attributes of the bearer, they enable us to gain insights into values and patterns of perception in a given speech community, and to identify group-specific attitudes and values that characterized the linguistic ecology. In this respect, we shall emphasize that the practice of giving nicknames to indigenous chiefs does not show many similarities with traditional Spanish sources for the *apellidos*. Spanish nicknames, as well as family names, are generally derived from parents' names, toponyms, job titles, and epithets that describe physical and mental properties. It appears that these semantic fields were perceived in the Antillean context as inappropriate source domains to create nicknames for indigenous people – maybe because physical appearance, customs and occupation of indigenous people made a relatively uniform impression on the Spaniards. Especially during the first years after the arrival of the conquerors and colonists, encounters between the indigenous populations and the Spaniards took place primarily in the context of military conflicts. This important ecological factor in the early communication setting had a certain impact on the way in which Indian chiefs were perceived and nicknamed by the Spaniards.

6.6.2.4 Additional Elements

In the *cédulas de encomienda* personal names are sometimes used together with other lexical items. In most cases, the additional elements are toponyms (e.g. (*natural*) *de Samaná, de Baytiqueri, de la ysla de Guadalupe, de Higüey*, and *de Turquino*) and other anthroponyms, generally names of the *caciques* to whom a *naboría* or slave in question belonged (e.g. *del caçique Humacao, del caçique Abey, del cacique Françisco Caçibona del Aymanio, de Ayabibix*, and *de Ayaybex*). Cases where personal names are accompanied by words associated with the bearer's profession, typical activity (*pescador* 'fisherman', *barbero* 'barber', and *contador* 'book keeper', *paje* 'page') or physical characteristics (*el viejo* 'the old', *el tuerto* 'the one-eyed', and *la coja* 'the lame') are rather rare. In only one case a Taino woman is identified by the name of her father: *Isabel, hija de Culebrix*. Given that historical documents from Spain dating from the same period demonstrate a high frequency of the expression *hijo de* (Álvarez, Ariza, and Mendoza 2000: 157), we can consider these results as further evidence in favour of the fact that the genealogical descent of indigenous people had little significance for the colonial rulers. The only evident reason that explains the addition of similar specifications is the need to unequivocally identify the *indios encomendados* in the *encomienda* documentation. As noted above, given names alone were not sufficient to fulfil this purpose; the situation is thus strikingly similar to that in medieval Europe, when family names were introduced, among other reasons, to preserve the classificatory function of anthroponyms.

However, the manner in which specifying elements are embedded in the texts does not justify considering them as parts of personal names in a linguistic sense. Generally, additional specifications such as professional titles and adjectives that describe physical appearance are written in small initial letters and separated from given names by a comma. It suggests that the writers perceived them as *nomina appellativa*. Unfortunately, the indigenous people disappeared from the Antilles within a few decades after Spanish conquest, leaving us no option other than to speculate whether this kind of specifying expressions could have evolved into a new complex naming system, as it happened in Europe.

6.6.3   *Second and Third Name Component*

The use of complex names was relatively rare among indigenous people and only *caciques* and *nitainos* seem to have enjoyed this privilege. While only 8 per cent of the *naborías* and slaves bear a second name, this is true for at least 38 per cent of the caciques.[13] Structural variation in the representation of complex names allows us to distinguish between two etymological patterns. On the one hand, the first component may be Spanish and the second of indigenous origin (e.g. *Gasparico Guahuyuex, Bartolomé Zemcubadahaguano, Diego Guacoquex, Violante Ateyba, Rodrigo Çicuyabey*, and *Francisco Caçibona*). This mixed pattern was typical for both *naborías* and *caciques*. On the other hand, the entire name may be entire Spanish (e.g., *Martín López, Catalina Méndez, Juan Bravo, Alonso Gomez, Alonso Velazquez, Gonzalo Maldonado, Luisa Ramírez*, and *María Alonso*). In this case it was impossible to determine by the name alone whether the name-bearer was indigenous or Spanish. Completely Spanish names were used exclusively by Taino chiefs.

On the other hand, the existence of mixed names may reflect the practice to use Spanish and indigenous names simultaneously in different social contexts. The following passage from one of the documents in the corpus illustrates this

---

[13] This number refers only to the *caciques* with a Spanish first name. *Caciques* with an indigenous first name, which was as a rule their only name, are not included here.

practice. An indigenous woman with the Spanish name *Mendoza* kept using her native name when she went to Cubagua:

En 28 de septiembre de 1527 se depositó a Juan Millán, vecino de esta ciudad, a Mendoza, india que se dice en Cubagua, a Aguancybenençoca Oratohaba, natural del pueblo del caguahano, de la provincia de Guantanabo, naboría que fue de Alonso Muñoz, difunto. (Mira Caballos 1997: 420)

[On September 28, 1527, Mendoza was given to Juan Millán, parishioner of this town, [she was] an indigenous woman called Aguaneybenençoca Oratohaba in Cubagua, native from the village of Caguahano, from the Province of Guantanabo, and had been a *naboría* of Alonso Muñoz, deceased. (my translation)][14]

However, the fact that the indigenous element is exclusively found in the second position appears to reflect the pre-Columbian practice of transitionally using two names simultaneously before giving up the old one. Thus, what may formally look like a family name from a European perspective was in fact the previous indigenous name of the individual (see the above-mentioned examples from the *Relación acerca de las antigüedades de los indios*).

Indigenous women often acquired a Spanish family name when they married a Spaniard. Complex combinations of two or three Spanish components in male names are likely to have emerged from the name exchange between Spanish and indigenous people during the *guatiao* ritual. Spanish colonial texts display numerous cases of indigenous people, especially *caciques*, who took names of Spanish conquerors or colonists. According to Las Casas, Spanish conquerors and colonial officials such as Diego Marque, Juan de Esquivel, and Juan Ponce de León gave their names to Indian chiefs. A comparison of the complex Spanish names in our corpus with the names listed in Boyd-Bowman's (1985) *Índice geobiográfico de más de 56 mil pobladores de la América Hispánica (1493–1519)* demonstrates that one and sometimes even several Spanish settlers who bore the same name can in many cases be identified as possible name-givers (e.g., *Pedro Velázquez, Francisco Mejías, Gonzalo Maldonado, Juan Dominguez*, and *Francisco de Rivera*).

The Spaniards usually made no use of the new indigenous names they received in the *guatiao* ritual. On the other hand, they treated the new Spanish names of their *guatiaos* as the official ones; otherwise such names would not have appeared in the *cédulas de repartimiento*. An indigenous element was naturally incorporated in the Spanish practice of name allocation. However, the particular ecology of the sixteenth-century Antilles altered the function of the second name component within the system. The original function as a *nom clanique* was lost and another frame became the norm. Traditional Spanish

---

[14] Likewise, African slaves in French plantation colonies seem to have used African names alongside French ones (Fouchard 1988: 229).

family names such as *Velázquez, Domínguez*, etc. could be applied to indigenous people as a consequence of the *guatiao* ritual, but they did not entail filiation in this case. The main emphasis was placed on the relationship to another member of the society who was not necessarily a family member in a biological sense. This practice reflects partial survival of the Taino relational system.

The adoption of full Spanish names by Taino chiefs is baffling from a functional point of view, since it is incompatible with both the identifying and the classifying function of anthroponyms. A real exchange of names did not take place and had a one-sided character, so that the *guatiao* ritual contributed to an increasing homonymy between the names of individuals as well as to confusion between two ethnic groups. As we have seen, bearers of complex names could not be classified as being Spanish or indigenous by their name alone. However, only 17 per cent of the Natives registered in the corpus bore a complex Spanish name. Their number must have been even smaller in relation to the entire indigenous population in the colonial society, as only the *caciques* participated in *guatiao* rituals.

6.7   Conclusion: Anthroponyms from an Ecolinguistic View

The discovery and colonization of the Americas made a profound and lasting impact on the political, economic, social, and cultural systems of both indigenous and European people involved in the colonial context. The conquest of a new habitat by the Spaniards and the emergence of new social and economic concepts reshaped the entire ecosystem. A natural consequence of these transformations was the development of linguistic patterns that were able to meet specific needs of the speakers in the emergent colonial society.

We have studied the interdependence of ecological conditions and language as it is reflected in the anthroponymic system. Special emphasis was placed on classifying the function of proper names, a useful tool to gain insights into the particularities of an organization of a given society. In this respect, the European and the Antillean naming systems presented considerable differences on a macro-ecological level. The Spanish anthroponyms classified individuals according to pre-established social categories such as sex and family group membership. The core of the indigenous *système relationnel* was based on the concept of the synchronic way of being and relating, and was realized by syntagmatically formed anthroponyms. Personal names did not mark immutable properties of their bearers in an essentialist way; rather, they reflected their relationship to the ecology in which they lived.

At the beginning of the sixteenth century, one of the most prominent features of the first stages of Spanish settlement in the Antilles was the introduction of the *encomienda* system, which generated a different social order with complex class distinctions on the levels of ethnicity and status. The anthroponymic system was particularly sensitive to this new experience. The most evident realization of the new world order was the renaming of indigenous people with Spanish personal names, consistent with an ancient European macro-ecological tradition wherein slaves and other bonded people were assigned new names as a statement of the colonizers' power and a verbal sign of their new status. At the same time, the pre-Columbian macro-ecological conditions (especially the open and change-able character of names) fostered the adoption of Spanish names by the Tainos. On a micro-ecological level, renaming often took place in the context of the Christian baptism ritual; at the same time, pre-Columbian patterns of name allocation persisted, as is illustrated by the existence of Spanish *guatiao* names and of names of mixed Spanish and indigenous origin among the Natives, as well as by the fact that they may have substituted one Christian name for another. As renaming was an integral part of their anthroponymic practices, the baptism ritual may have been quite natural to the Tainos, and they probably often adopted Spanish names consensually, not necessarily by force.

The colonial naming system rapidly developed ways of distinguishing between the (free) Spanish and (bonded) indigenous population by the pres-ence or absence of an *apellido* 'family name'. During the early modern period, European societies shifted towards a more egalitarian and less hierarchically structured social organization. The use of family names emerged as a visible sign of a new social and historical consciousness. Contrary to this, the emer-gent colonial society in the Antilles was highly hierarchical. The Spanish naming system could not provide adequate linguistic means to express new social categories that emerged as a result of the subjugation of the Tainos and the introduction of the *encomienda* system. To meet this challenge, the anthroponymic system had to resort to the reactivation of a linguistic pattern that was already in decline in Spain: the use of single names as opposed to complex names in order to distinguish between free and bonded individuals. The power status, which was automatically linked to ethnic origin under the conditions of the colonial society, explains why the presence or absence of a second component in the name served as an additional ethnic classifier. This function was unknown on the Iberian Peninsula, where status differences did not necessarily ensue from ethnic origin. When adopted by indigenous people, as was the case based on the *guatiao* ritual, Spanish *apellidos* were not hereditary and did therefore not fulfil the same function as in the continental *système clanique*, e.g. to mark the affiliation with a family and, from a wider perspective, with a civil society. Rather, they were used to express social relationships (*guatiao*) in compliance with pre-Columbian naming practices.

At the same time, linguistic means already present in the Spanish system were reanalysed and acquired new functions in the American setting under the pressure of new ecological conditions. The labelling of people from marginal groups of society by means of diminutive forms, which represented another typical strategy of anthroponymic classification in sixteenth-century Spain, was expanded in the Antillean context to embrace different levels of subordination.

Several factors facilitated these developments. On the one hand, the colonial naming system made use of the inherent feature of proper names to express social categories indexically. On the other hand, the colonial society was able to develop a spatial–temporal contiguity between traditional categories such as master/slave or dependent/free and newly introduced categories such as ethnicity or the *cacique/naboría* status opposition. Finally, in the context of culture contact, the macrocultural frame of the Taino naming system fostered the adoption of Spanish names, even if they were often used according to pre-Columbian cultural logic. Although at a first glance the anthroponymic system of the *encomienda* seems to be essentially Spanish in character, it is in fact the result of culture contact and hybridization.

One important detail distinguishes the naming patterns in the *encomienda* system from the traditional custom to create slave and servant names. Contrary to practices in the Roman Empire and, later, in the plantation societies during the colonial era in the Caribbean, the Spanish did not give exotic names to the *indios encomendados*. This trend appears to have developed due to the highly prominent role of Catholicism in the Spanish colonial enterprise. The Spanish conquest was largely understood as a missionary campaign and the conversion of the indigenous population to Christianity was one of the most important political aims of the *encomienda* system (Mira Caballos 1997: 78). Intimately linked to the baptism ritual, the act of giving Christian names to the indigenous people implied their admission to the Christian community and, in a broader sense, their affiliation to the Spanish colonial society. In contrast, African slaves in French or English plantation societies were often not baptized and acquired names primarily for practical purposes (Durand and Logossah 2002: 34), which contributed to the development of distinct lexical paradigms for master and slave names.

Unfortunately, the Antillean indigenous population became extinct fewer than forty years after the first encounter with Columbus. We can venture the suggestion that the colonial naming system would have otherwise experienced further important transformations. This study provides only a snapshot of Spanish-indigenous language and culture contact in changing ecological conditions, on which future research will undoubtedly shed more light.

Part IV

On the Ecology of *Language* and *Speaker*:
the Hybridization of Language and Discourse

7   Reflections on Discourse Ecology and Language Contact: the Crucial Role of Some Scalar Terms*

Sibylle Kriegel, Ralph Ludwig, and Tabea Salzmann

7.1   Introduction: Ecological Frames, Contact Phenomena, and Discourse Analysis

In this chapter we examine the special relevance of the discursive micro level to ecological linguistic investigation, before going on in the following to stress all three levels of the model of linguistic ecology articulated in Chapter 1, this volume. Drawing on examples from two corpora, we focus on some specific ecological parameters, especially aspects of language contact such as the competences of the interactors in different codes, the importance of contact languages, and the different discursive functions of *hybridization*. The main focal point is, however, language contact itself. We will take up established terms of contact linguistics like *code-mixing, code-switching, borrowing, calquing* etc., point out their inadequacies (section 7.2.1), and propose their replacement with a coherent terminology based essentially on a development of Lars Johanson's concept of *code-copying* (e.g. Johanson 2002a, 2002b, 2005, 2008) (section 7.2.2). We then transfer this terminology to a scalar definition, introducing three complementary scales that we believe are apt theoretical and empirical–descriptive tools. These allow us to note different forms of copies and their degree of *conventionalization* and *system integration* (section 7.3). The conceptual proposals and their use in analysis become particularly apparent in contrasting two contact ecologies: Mauritius (section 7.4) and New Delhi, India (section 7.5). In both ecologies North Indian languages and English are in common use. The examples used are conversations in educational contexts: the Mauritian example contains teachers conversing informally in school, while the example from New Delhi is of a teacher conversing with his students before class.

* We would like to thank Fabiola Henri, Anu Bissoonauth, and Florence Bruneau-Ludwig for essential help in transcription and translation of our recordings from Mauritius. We owe many thanks to Anu Bissoonauth, without whose competent help as mother-tongue speaker of Bhojpuri the translation and interpretation of the example from Mauritius would not have been so fertile. Some of the ideas of this chapter have been developed in collaboration with Florence Bruneau-Ludwig and Fabiola Henri.

7.2   Descriptive Concepts in Contact Linguistics: Some Theoretical Reflections and Terminological Proposals

7.2.1   *Some Terminological Issues*

Traditional approaches have used a long series of terms to describe contact phenomena. Many of these are binary: *code-switching* as opposed to *code-mixing*, *matrix language* to *embedded language* (Myers-Scotton, e.g. 2006a), *nonce borrowing* to *sedimented borrowing* (Poplack and Sankoff 1988; Auer 2007a), and *structurally integrated* to *structurally not integrated borrowings*. The distinctions between these are not always clear-cut, however, for which reason several problems arise. In the next sections, we adopt a scalar approach instead (see section 7.3).

The first problem concerns describing and labelling the relation between two languages in contact situations involving *mixing* of the languages. One option in this case is to distinguish between the *matrix language* and *embedded language*, a distinction introduced into contact linguistics by Myers-Scotton (2006a). This approach raises the question of defining the intersection between the two languages, as it requires there to be always one dominant language, the *matrix language*, which provides the frame for the incorporation of elements from the dominated language, the *embedded* language. Muysken (2000) criticizes the need for this distinction and proposes the term *alternation*, which does not suggest such a hierarchy.

In our analysis, we show that the distinction between matrix and embedded languages remains very useful in many cases. That being said, there also exist examples of more or less balanced alternations between languages. Consequently, our proposed continuum provides the possibility of a progressive transition between *balanced alternation* and *macro-structural copying*, as we show in the next section. We would like to call to mind that examples of 'balanced' alternation are also known in the history of language contact, although they are less common. Indeed, the *Serments de Strasbourg*, the oldest document involving the French language, is an instance of balanced alternation between two languages on the same level; Charles the Bald and Louis the German took their oath in both French and German to ensure intelligibility for the soldiers in both armies.

A second difficulty in the description of language contact processes arises from the distinction between *mixing* and *switching*, which is deeply entrenched in contact linguistics. Gardner-Chloros (2009, 2010) provides a review of the development of the terminology and related arguments. Poplack and Sankoff (1988) are responsible for one of the most cited and discussed list of differentiation criteria, which is adopted in, for example, Díaz, Ludwig and Pfänder (2002). Nonetheless, the debate remains unresolved with a variety of proposed solutions (see for example Clyne 2003: 70ff.). Defining a precise division between switching and mixing is difficult, because the more an element is integrated into micro-structural text levels, the easier systemic assimilation becomes on the cognitive linguistic level. Due to the problem of distinguishing between the two phenomena, some linguists have proposed to generalize one of the terms; for example, Kelkar-Stephan (2005) generalizes *switching*, while Muysken (2000) generalizes *mixing*.

Closely related to this problem of differentiation between code-switching and code-mixing is that of the distinction between these notions and what are usually called *borrowing* and *calquing*. Borrowing is often considered as the transfer of phonological shape and structure, whereas calquing does not involve the phonological shape at all. In contrast, some approaches use *borrowing* as a hyperonym covering *calquing*. Matras and Sakel (2007), Sakel (2007) and Matras (2010) distinguish between *MAT* (*matter*) and *PAT* (*pattern*) *borrowing*. They speak of MAT-borrowing when morphological material and its phonological shape are copied, and PAT-borrowing when only the patterns of the other language are replicated. For our analysis, we find it useful to make similar distinctions but we avoid the term *borrowing*.

7.2.2   The Concepts of Code-copying and Alternation

The concepts of *copying* and *alternation,* introduced by Johanson (2002a, 2005, 2008), can at least partially resolve the terminological problem sketched above. They are designed to avoid the blur between definitions and their inadequate connotations in 'traditional' contact-linguistic terminology:

The term 'borrowing' is already based on a deceptive metaphor. Nothing is borrowed in language contact: the 'donor language' is not deprived of anything; and – more importantly – the 'recipient language' does not take over anything identical with anything in the 'donor language'. Terms such as 'transfer' pose the same problem, since they also suggest identicality of originals and copies. Non-identicality of originals and copies is a fundamental principle of our framework.

The term 'interference' is inadequate because of its connotation of 'unserious' development, undesired deviation from monolingual norms, causing impaired communication, e.g. the negative effects of a first language (L1) on the acquisition of a second language (L2). Such terms may contribute to prejudices against contact-influenced varieties seen as 'mixed' or 'contaminated'. The term 'code-copying' implies no more than the insertion of elements copied from one code within the context of another code, without specifying the degree of acceptability at a given stage of development. (Johanson 2002a: 288)

The idea of non-identity expressed in this quotation is also outlined and stressed even more in later publications:

Copies are never 'imported' or 'transferred' foreign elements and never true replicas of their models. There are always dissimilarities in substance, meaning, contextual applicability and frequency between models and copies. (Johanson 2008: 62)

In terms of copying, Johanson consistently distinguishes between the following four aspects: *substance* (mainly referring to phonetic substance of encoding), *meaning* ('content', which – in our interpretation – comprises lexical–semantic to grammatical meaning and structure), *combinational properties* ('word-internal and word-external combination patterns', Johanson 2002a: 293) and *frequency* (regarding occurrence and use). In what he calls *global copying,* a model is copied in all four aspects. *Selective copying,* on the other hand, involves only individual aspects.

These aspects do not appear to be on the same level. Lexical, semantic, and grammatical meanings and their structures can be copied with or without using material encoding of the model or model language. Some combinational elements that are part of the original meaning are even part of the structure, and therefore cannot be separated. The fact that the meaning can be purely structural is very important for our approach, which includes the possibility of copying complex text structures.[1] In other respects, combinational properties and frequency are characteristics of language use that change precisely through the copying process. These tend to be the two aspects that most often show the difference between copy and original – one of Johanson's central claims – and the fact that copies are gradually integrated into the code that copies. For this reason we fully incorporate combinational properties and frequency (not just partially as Johanson does) in the scales introduced below.

The following well-known and simple example can demonstrate this point. The German word *Wolkenkratzer* is a lexical copy of the English *skyscraper.*[2] This copy nevertheless shows clear alterations compared to the original. To begin with, the meaning is copied without the phonetic material. Also, the original metaphor undergoes metonymic change, in that the determinate is no longer *sky,* rather it is *clouds.* Part of the copied basic metaphor in the German copy is the unchanged structure Determinatum < Determinans, i.e. *sky < scraper.*

For this reason we narrow our terminology to substance and meaning, and consider various types of meaning and structure as part of meaning.[3]

---

[1] Johanson himself refers to grammatical copying: 'Copies may include grammatical markers such as voice, aspect, mood, tense, case and number markers, articles, pronouns, junctors for word- and clause-combining, or ordering patterns relevant for word-formation, phrase-, clause and sentence formation, clause combining, text construction, text subdivision, other morphosyntactic or morphosemantic structures, and patterns of pragmatic organization' (2008: 66).

[2] We quote this example because it is often used to illustrate what a calque is. This is a term we do not use but is translatable into our terms.

[3] An elaborate debate of *semantics* or *meaning* is not our goal here. An interesting attempt to integrate the various types of meaning was made by the German speech act theorist Dieter Wunderlich (1976). We adopt a large view of the scale of meaning–functions and – potentially or really – copied elements, including for example what others call 'pragmatic borrowing' (Andersen 2014).

Consequently, we use *copying* as a hyperonym and adopt Stolz and Stolz's (1996) distinction between *overt copies* ('overte Kopien') and *covert copies* ('koverte Kopien'), which are patterned on Whorf's (1945) distinction between *overt* and *covert categories*. This is our equivalent to Johanson's central features of *global copy* and *selective (semantic) copy*. *Overt copies* copy both phonetic encoding and lexical–semantic and/or structural–grammatical information, and *covert copies* contain only lexical–semantic and/or structural–grammatical information from the model. Considering our example then, *Wolkenkratzer* is a covert lexical copy. This differentiation of *overt copies* and *covert copies* also comes close to Matras and Sakel's distinction between *MAT* (*matter*) and *PAT* (*pattern*) borrowing mentioned above (see section 7.2.1; Matras and Sakel 2007; Sakel 2007; Matras 2010).

Next to this central differentiation we also consider the possibility of material copies. These are copies of pure material of encoding. This additional term is especially useful when considering phonic suprasegmentals in contact processes. A well-known example of this in the history of French is the copy of the Franconian accent of force by the Romanized population of northern Gaul after the Franconian conquest (see von Wartburg 1946/1971: 63–67).

Johanson defines *alternation* in the following manner:

> Code-copying is to be distinguished from code-alternation: The latter mode of code interaction means shifting from one code to another, juxtaposing elements belonging to different systems. Many cases of so-called 'code-switching' imply alternate choices of codes. (Johanson 2002a: 286)

Despite its compactness, this quote includes fundamental elements of definition: specifying that alternation implies a situational shift from one code to another. This is a cognitive act of 'system shift' on the part of the speaker in a situation of interaction. The question of the speakers' permanent linguistic competence in both codes or languages is thus secondary at most. Similarly, (non-)congruence of the languages and the manner in which the speaker deals with these differences and perceives them cognitively is secondary.[4] In his notion of alternation, Muysken (2000) also emphasizes the fact that two or more codes or languages are separated cognitively in their linguistic realization.

7.3   A Scalar Approach

7.3.1   Scalar Approaches in Linguistics

As suggested above, some authors neutralize terminological oppositions such as *mixing* vs. *switching* given that no clear-cut distinction is possible. One step

---

[4] For congruence, see Mufwene (2008); Besters-Dilger et al. (2014).

towards solving this problem here was suggesting clearer and simpler terminology. Another part consists in transferring these terms into scales.

Although a scalar interpretation of linguistic categories and evolutionary processes has a long tradition in modern linguistics, such notions have increased in use from the 1970s onwards. But as Pagel (2015) demonstrates, continuous conceptions of contact-induced language change had already prevailed in the early contact-linguistic contributions by William D. Whitney (1881) and Hugo Schuchardt (1884). Pagel goes on to propose a cohesive scalar conception of contact-linguistic phenomena that may resolve some urgent contemporary problems in contact linguistics. Similarly, Mufwene, and Vigouroux (2012: 130) emphasize the role of scalar and scale-grounded notions in sociolinguistics and creolistics. Important here is the fact that scales can better describe theoretical–terminological issues as well as capturing a linguistic–empiric status quo. One well-known example is scales of grammaticalization. On the one hand, these allow the description of a status quo (the fact that a linguistic element is grammaticalized only to a certain extent); on the other hand, they describe a linguistic development and allow projections for the future paths of grammaticalization to be made. This applies likewise for the well-known continuum from *basilect* to *acrolect*, terms coined by Stewart (1965) and further developed in creolistics, especially by DeCamp (1971) and Bickerton (1973).[5]

In the following sections, we introduce three continua: a *Code hybridization continuum* (CHC) (section 7.3.2), a *Conventionalized systemic integration continuum* (CSIC) (section 7.3.3), and a *Structural systemic integration continuum* (SSIC) (section 7.3.4). The CHC aims to resolve what we perceive as a futile discussion concerning a clear-cut distinction between code-switching and code mixing. The CSIC may resolve the problem of a lucid distinction between *nonce borrowing* and *sedimented borrowing*. The CSIC is frequently, but not obligatorily, linked to the SSIC. It serves to capture phonological and morphological consequences of copying processes. But even if it is evident that conventionalization often goes hand in hand with structural integration, structurally integrated copies may not necessarily be conventionalized.

7.3.2 *Code Hybridization Continuum (CHC)*

We propose the continuum in Table 7.1 reproduced from Kriegel, Ludwig, and Henri (2009). Following the three-level model laid out in the first chapter of this volume and the basic importance of linguistic interaction, this first continuum mainly relates to the synchronic pragmatic–grammatical description of

---

[5] Mufwene even affirms that all creoles (or, in a sense, all languages) are continua, and criticizes the association of the continuum with *decreolization* (Mufwene 1994, 2005).

Table 7.1 *Code Hybridization Continuum (CHC)*

Balanced systemic alternation (between languages A and B)	Interlectal/inter-lingual copying			
Alternation	*Macrostructural copying*			*Microstructural copying*
Alternation between partial texts of languages A and B quantitatively and hierarchically more or less equivalent	Partial texts more important/ hierarchically superior in the embedded language	More and more reduced partial texts, growing syntactic integration	Embedding of isolated elements/ isolated techniques	Embedding of agglutinated morphemes of a small semantic unit
Prototypical switching 1: cognitive separation between the systems, same status of the two languages on the cognitive level	Prototypical switching 2: cognitive separation of the two languages/ predominance of one of the languages on the cognitive level			Prototypical mixing: cognitive deletion of the boundary between the systems/the embedded element merges cognitively into the system of the matrix language

texts in situations. The upper part of the schema contains our terminology, while the lower part aims to establish a connection between alternation/copying and traditional terms, so as to make the traditionally established terms and our terminology relatable.

This schema suggests the following.

Balanced alternation vs. matrix language/embedded language: we assume the existence of a continuum between two extremes: at one end stands *balanced systemic alternation,* while at the other stands the *strict integration of an embedded element – a copy – in the matrix language.* We consider embedding to be a gradual phenomenon. This will become clearer in the following chapters. Cognitive separation of linguistic systems here is problematic, though necessary, and prompts the question of the point at which something is considered a copy, an alternation or part of the system. Evidently, this separation is easier to perceive on the level of alternation than on that of copying. Note that this scale does not include the possibilities of mixed languages and creoles.

In this chapter we would like to introduce the concept of the *partial text* in our schema, and the idea of an organizational hierarchy of texts. A partial text is a linguistic application of Husserl's (1913) general term *part of a whole*, which, although developed primarily for text linguistics, can also be used in discourse analysis. Accordingly, a conversation would be a (part of a) whole structured into turns, which are made up of *turn constructional units*.[6] In other words, a partial text can comprise more or less complex turns. This idea of connecting code hybridization and the organization of the text on different levels of partial texts, from macrostructure to microstructure, has at least two theoretical consequences:

1. Placing balanced systemic code alternation next to macrostructural copying suggests that there is no balanced alternation at the level of microstructural elements. This is more likely to happen with partial texts at the macrostructural level. Thus, it is conceivable that while turns or sentences alternate in a balanced manner, isolated words do not.
2. The textual hierarchization allows for an easier description of a common phenomenon: the co-occurrence of contact phenomena on different levels. An example of this is the possible balanced alternation between A and B, while A and B themselves include copies (see section 7.4.3.1).

Applied to the concept of code-alternation, this results in two different types of alternation. First, an alternation may appear inside a unique complex turn; in this case it is produced by one and the same speaker (type A). Second, the alternation may coincide with turn changes; it is then produced by at least two speakers (type B). Therefore, the referential frame of the code alternation concept is the text or the communication situation, not the speaker.

Code copying, however, does not appear to be suitable to cover the whole field of code alternation; therefore, the term should only be used to describe the transfer of an element into a matrix language. In our CHC *copying* often refers to overt copies, that is, transfers of the 'form and semantics-structure' unit as well as the occurrence of purely semantic-structural copying, that is covert copies. Our example of the German *Wolkenkratzer*, if it were to appear in a German text, would be a covert copy near the pole of *microstructural copying*. Distinguishing between overt and covert copies raises interesting issues for the code hybridization continuum. For one thing, it can be assumed that covert

---

[6] Conversations as wholes also constitute partial wholes, since they are parts of series of conversations and/or of other larger units of social interaction. For *discourse analysis, turn* and *turn-taking*, see Sacks, Jefferson, and Schegloff (1974). Further relevant references may be found in Chapter 3, this volume.

copying is more likely to occur near the right end of the scale in the above table. Additionally, it is an open question whether covert copies integrate into the system of the matrix language more quickly than overt copies.

7.3.2.1 Genetic and/or Typological Distance

The proposed continuum is not limited to hybridization processes between different systems of historical languages. It is sometimes difficult, however, to decide whether we are dealing with an opposition between languages or dialects (see for example Chambers and Trudgill, 1998). Although we agree that French and Chinese are different languages, that opposition is more difficult to draw, for example, between French and Vulgar Latin of the ninth century. Even if we consider Mauritian Creole in our first example as an autonomous language and in no way a dialect of French, the mesolectal data on which our work is based sometimes do not permit the drawing of a clear-cut line between the two varieties (see section 7.4.2, especially the speech of Mr Bunsy).

The separation between linguistic systems is weaker where congruent and possibly genetically related languages are concerned than between not congruent, typologically different languages. This raises an issue over the hypothesis that copying processes are facilitated, and therefore appear more often between genetically and related strongly congruent languages.

On the other hand, our second example from India implies that copying processes can also be frequent between less congruent codes if the social framework provides the necessary conditions. This is a hypothesis we find in the work of Thomason:

> Typological congruence . . . is just one of many factors that help us move toward weak predictions of the linguistic results of language contact. Together with most other historical linguists, I do not believe in the possibility of making strong predictions about linguistic change, including contact-induced change, primarily because of the impossibility of discovering and weighing all the social factors that affect the outcome of a change process. Like other predictions about contact-induced change, the linguistic factor of typological congruence can be, and often is, trumped by social factors. (Thomason 2014: 216)

Despite the fact that Hindi and English are two typologically different and incongruent languages, the mixing of overt and covert copies on different levels sometimes makes it difficult to decide which part of a statement can be assigned to which language of origin.

For this reason, we do not support an *a priori* distinction between languages and dialects, and rather think that the term *code* covers the totality of the terminological field.[7] Also noteworthy is the fact that although it is certain that

---

[7] Regarding the difficulty of distinguishing languages see the examples from the Pacific region in Mühlhäusler (1996a: 3ff., 282ff.).

Table 7.2 *Conventionalized Systemic Integration Continuum (CSIC)*

Extreme 1: Situational–pragmatic process/ resource not established in the langue = *situational transfer*	→	Growing conventionalization process of 'propagation' (Croft 2000: 147)	→	Extreme 2: *Systemic stage independent of particular situational pragmatic factors/ conventionalized resource = transfer into the* langue
Interactional copying (particularly of microstructural elements)				Conventionalized copy (overt or covert copies)

typological proximity or distance between languages in contact can influence the nature of code hybridization considerably, our schema does not include this factor.

7.3.3   Conventionalized Systemic Integration Continuum (CSIC)

Phenomena of code hybridization considered as processes or situational acts have to be distinguished from the conventionalized copy as a systemic achievement. The conventionalized copy is the result of multiple hybridization processes, namely general repetitive copying acts and therefore increasing frequency of use are involved. This leads to the propagation of the copied element and thus increased conventionalization. Classifying a linguistic element as a conventionalized copy implies that the transfer has been completed and that the copy is part of *la langue* in Saussure's sense of the term. Conventionalized copies can nonetheless be used as copies in a pragmatic sense. Since we are concerned with pragmatics, we still refer to matrix and embedded languages when speaking of conventionalized copies. Our example *Wolkenkratzer* is one such conventionalized copy that has found its way into standard German dictionaries and which many Germans no longer perceive as copy.

Concepts comparable to our idea of conventionalized copy are presented in Auer (2007a), for example, with the exception that here it is termed *borrowing*. According to Auer, 'there is a continuum of insertions with ad hoc (nonce) borrowing at one extreme, and sedimented borrowings (words which are habitually used by a certain speaker or even in a bilingual community) at the other extreme' (2007a: 327). Similarly, Johanson (2002a) talks about 'habitualisation and conventionalisation', and according to Mufwene (2008: 125), 'the spread of innovations ... from a few idiolects to the communal language also represents another aspect of selection in the life of a language'.[8]

[8] Important mechanisms of the process of propagation are forms of accommodation and identity projection (the desire of speakers to identify themselves overtly with a social group through the use of certain linguistic variants), see Auer and Hinskens (2005) and Auer (2007b).

In order to grade copies on our scale (Table 7.2), we adhere to the following criteria, which are drawn from Pagel (2010), who in turn elaborates on Winford (2003):

1. The frequency of use of a copied element in monolingual speakers: circumstances in which monolingual speakers resort to a copy indicate that what is considered equivalent is not merely situation-bound and interactionally conducted; rather, it can penetrate into the customs of a group.
2. The vitality of a language in a societal context: if a formerly vital contact language is currently extinct in the speaker group, then copies in the present language are necessarily at least partially conventionalized.
3. The availability of functional synonyms in the receiving or matrix language: the absence of structural equivalents in the matrix language justifies the need for copying and for partial or full conventionalization.[9]
4. The availability of alternatives that represent different grades of integration: for example, the Spanish noun *problema* 'problem' has been copied into the Rapanui language of Easter Island but coexists there with the indigenized variants *probrema, porobrema*, and *poroborema*, which are morphonologically system-integrated in Rapanui. This suggests that the more structurally system-integrated forms *probrema* etc. are not yet (completely) conventionalized.[10]

In this last case, structural systemic integration can be an indicator of conventionalization, in that the further a copy is conventionalized the more it appears to be structurally integrated into the system. We consider *structural systemic integration*, discussed below, to be a continuum in its own right, though it may be an indicator of an advanced degree of conventionalization.

7.3.4   Structural Systemic Integration Continuum (SSIC)

Copies can formally and/or semantically be more, or less, integrated into the matrix language (Table 7.3).

The relevant criteria are therefore:

1. morphophonemic integration;
2. semantic and grammatical adaptation to the matrix system's rules and principles, as illustrated below.

The more a copy is structurally integrated into the system, the less cognitively salient it is, and therefore the less likely it is to be recognized as a copy. There

---

[9] Availability of synonyms is, for example, given for many Spanish elements in the Chamorro language, spoken on the Mariana Islands (Pagel 2008, 2010 chapter 10, this volume).

[10] Pagel (2008: 175). A similar case in the same contact situation involves the Spanish word *Chile*, copied and morphologically adapted into Rapanui as *Tire* (Pagel 2010: 214). Aslanov, this volume, provides other examples, such as the word *chubbec* in old Levantine French, a conventionalized and structurally integrated copy of Arabic *šubbāk* 'window'.

Table 7.3 *Structural Systemic Integration Continuum (SSIC)*

Systemic non-integration:	→	*Systemic integration*:
a copied element is not adapted to the dominant morphonological and morphosyntactic rules of the matrix language		a copied element is adapted to the dominant morphonological and morphosyntactic rules of the matrix language

might also be a connection here to frequency: the higher the (type- and token-) frequency of a copy, the more system integrated and less salient (in the sense of the single code) it becomes (see Cheshire, Kerswill, and Williams 2005). As observed above, there is a clear connection between the degree of conventionalization and the degree of structural integration; the more a copy is integrated structurally, the more conventionalized it often is. Note, however, that this correlation does not always hold up; that is, such a structural adaptation can also vary according to idiolects and situations. There are several examples that can illustrate this structural systemic integration.

The first of these is essentially semantic–grammatical, but it is accompanied by morphophonemic integration. In Chilean Spanish, the German word *Kuchen* is a conventionalized copy. In contrast to the German word, however, in Chilean Spanish the words *pastel* (pie), *torta* (gateau), and *queque* (cake) narrow the denotation of *kuchen* (flan or tart). Grammatical integration becomes obvious here in that the copy conforms to the processes of pluralization dominant in Spanish: in addition to the universally unmarked German plural *los kuchen*, the marked Spanish plural *los kuchenes* is also used (Morales Pettorino, Quiroz Mejías, and Peña Alvarez 1986, III: 2558). This latter form is an instance of system coherent marking in (Chilean) Spanish.

A second example, provided by our informants, comes from Ecuadorian Spanish.[11] Here, the more conventionalized English copy *man* (pronounced /man/ in Ecuadorian Spanish), meaning 'guy', is integrated consistently into the grammatical morphosyntactic rules of Ecuadorian Spanish to mean 'man' and 'men'. It is also used in the feminine, an amplification that does not exist in English, but this is made possible by the fact that gender marking in loanwords is morphologically the same in Spanish for masculine and feminine. The only gender marking in this case is given in the article: *el man, la man, los manes, las manes*. This amplification is probably also modelled on the Spanish *el tipo, la tipa*. A copy that is structurally somewhat less integrated is the Salvadorian Spanish *man* (pronounced /meng/), which is used only as a reinforcing exclamation particle: *¡meng, qué calor hace!* 'phew, how hot it is!'.

---

[11] P.c. Emilia Portaluppi, Carmen Gonzalez, Camila Weffer.

Structural integration and conventionalization can go hand in hand, especially when the integrated copy is used more and more frequently and if it undergoes semantic–structural change; in the case of 'man', there is lexical–semantic *demarcation* (Ludwig 2001) and pragmaticization. We can also observe some correlation, albeit as a tendency, between scales 1 and 3, in that it seems easier to integrate micro-structural copies.

Nevertheless, as Gardner-Chloros underscores, an apparent morphonological integration of a copy does not necessarily imply conventionalization:

Both *ad hoc* code-switched nouns and verbs, as well as more established loans, can take the morphophonology of the borrowing variety, as examples from many language combinations have shown: e.g. French-Alsatian *déménagiert* ('moved house'), from French *déménager* (Gardner-Chloros 1991); English-Maori *changedngia* ('to change') (Eliasson 1990); English-Spanish *coughas* ('you cough') (Zimman 1993); German-English *gedropped* ('dropped') (Eppler 1991); etc. (2010: 196)

To illustrate our theoretical approach we present two examples. The first from Mauritius especially sheds light on questions of the first continuum (CHC), while the second example from India will provide particular insight into processes of the second (CSIC) and third (SSIC) continuum.

7.4   Example 1: Communication in Mauritius

7.4.1   *The Ecological Frame: Mauritius as Macro Area*[12]

The linguistic ecosystem on the island of Mauritius is a multilingual environment in which French-based Mauritian Creole is the dominant spoken language[13]. The main written languages are English and French. Although the official status of languages is not stipulated in the Mauritian Constitution, the dominant language of the parliament is English. This is unsurprising given that Mauritius was a British colony from 1814 to its independence in 1968. It should be noted, however, that both written and spoken Englishes are largely restricted to the political arena, with English playing only a minor role in the everyday life of Mauritians. According to an official census in 2011, Mauritian Creole is used as a home language by about 80 per cent of the population, and Bhojpuri, an Indo-Aryan language that has been imported from North India with indentured labourers since 1835, is the home language of about 5 per cent[14] (although *Ethnologue* gives a much higher figure).

---

[12] Having introduced a model with different levels of ecological spaces, which we named the Levant and Francophony as examples of the highest level, the macro ecology, we are well aware that the island of Mauritius must probably be considered as fitting on a slightly lower, intermediate level. Nevertheless, Mauritius is a macro ecology in comparison to the intermediate ecologies of just regions and cities.

[13] For creolization in ecological perspective, see Ludwig (2018).

[14] www.gov.mu/portal/goc/cso/ei977/pop2011.pdf

According to a recent sociolinguistic study of language shift in Mauritius, despite the fact that 'ancestral languages [including Bhojpuri] are steadily declining and being replaced by creole and French in the domestic domain, they are nevertheless still maintained by the older generations and through favourable educational policies' (Bissoonauth 2011: 421).

The Mauritian polyglossia and the frequent instances of code hybridization play a major role in the identity of Mauritius. Following the analysis of Kriegel, Ludwig, and Henri (2009: 205), we distinguish between two main tendencies of language alternation within this community:[15]

1. Rural alternation: in rural areas Bhojpuri speakers alternate between creole and Bhojpuri. French and English are also present, but to a lesser extent.
2. Urban alternation: educated speakers in urban contexts alternate between creole, French and English, and to a lesser extent also Bhojpuri.

In this chapter, we focus on the second domain, that is urban alternation, and still more specifically on interactions in educational contexts. This scenario has been specifically chosen to allow an easy comparison with our later Indian example.

7.4.2   *The Transcription: Communication in an Educational Context*

7.4.2.1 *Comments on the Situation*

The audio recording of this conversation took place in a college in Port Louis, the capital city. Fabiola Henri, a Mauritian herself, played the leading role in the conversation. She worked as a teacher in St Bartholomew's College and invited five of her colleagues to have a discussion on the different languages of Mauritius. Ralph Ludwig and Sibylle Kriegel were also present, but were primarily involved with controlling the technical equipment for recording and did not participate in the conversation.

Venue:	Port-Louis, St Bartholomew's College
Date:	16/03/2005, 14h30
Participants:	Hélène Woomed, 47 years, PGCE (Postgraduate Certificate in Education), Quatre-Bornes
	Nirmal Bunsy, 32 years, BA (Hons) Humanities
	Sanjeet Ujoodha, 40 years, PGCE, Vallée des Prêtres
	Peerbalkumar Ramdanee, 54 years, PGCE, Camp Thorel
	Diksha Ramnarain, 22 years, Higher School Certificate, Saint Pierre, Moka
	Fabiola Henri, 27 years, teacher and doctoral student, Quatre-Bornes
Recording:	Sibylle Kriegel, Ralph Ludwig
Transcription:	A. Bissoonauth, F. Bruneau-Ludwig, F. Henri, S. Kriegel, R. Ludwig
Translation:	A. Bissoonauth

---

[15] For the differentiation between *urban* and *rural* in the context of *hybridization*, see Salzmann (2014).

7.4.2.2 Text: Teachers in St Bartholomew's College
Transcription:

(…)	not transcribed
[…	simultaneous
' … '.	Quotes from Bhojpuri
Bold letters:	examples analysed in section 7.4.3

01   MR R *(…) Mais en, di, disons on va parler bhojpouri la, en quoi disons kamyon ki, on dit 'kamyon jaye, kamyon larou plat ho gal, kamyon ke larou plat ho gal'. Larou c'est français*
But, we say let's say we want to speak Bhojpuri, we are talking let's say 'a lorry, that hum … lorry goes, the lorry has a flat tyre, the lorry's got a flat tyre' 'larou' is French

02   MR U *kamyon c'est français, larou aussi c'est français*
'Camion' is French, 'larou' is also French

03   MR R *plat, plat*
flat, flat

04   MR U *[plat aussi c'est français*
flat is also French

05   MS R *[Plat aussi*
Flat also

06   (…)

07   MR R *'**kamyon ke larou plat ho gal**'. 'Kamyon' français, 'larou' français, 'plat ho gal'. Il y a [que quelques mots*
The lorry's tyre is flat, 'camion' is French, 'la roue' is French, got flat. There are some words

08   MR U *[en enn fraz*
There is a sentence …

09   MS H *ena enn fraz ?*
There is a sentence?

10   MR U *ena ena enn fraz koum sa mo rapel kan enn gran pret indou ti pe fer lapriyer, li'nn koz enn fraz an bhojpouri, bhojpouri kreol. Li dir '**montagn ke bor me, pistas plantal ba**'. 'Montagn' li pe koz kreol la, enn kreol fran, enn kreol morisyen, 'montagn'*
there is a sentence like this I remember when a great Indian priest who was praying, he said one sentence in Bhojpuri, Creole Bhojpuri. He said 'at the foot of the mountain, peanut [trees] have been planted'. 'montagn' (mountain)', he is speaking creole, a French Creole, a Mauritian Creole, 'montagn' (mountain) …

11   Mr R li *pe koz bhojpouri ?*
He is speaking Bhojpuri?

12   Mr U *li pe koz bhojpouri. Li dir 'montagn' c'est français. 'Ke bor'
sa ve dir 'près de la montagne', 'Ke bor me' 'pistas', 'pistas' c'est
français, 'plantal', 'planter' c'est français. Sa ve dir si nou get dan sa
bhojpouri la ena bizin dir katrovin poursan bann mo ki an franse*
He is speaking Bhojpuri. He is saying 'montagne'. That's French.
'Ke bor' means near the mountain, 'ke bor me' 'pistas' 'pistas' is French,
'plantal', 'planter' is French. It means that if we take the Bhojpuri for
instance, we could say that eighty percent (80%) of the words are French.

13   Mr R *Il y a que deux mots bhojpouri 'ke'*
There are only two Bhojpuri words 'ke'

14   Mr U *'ke ba' e remarke dan la plipar kan nou koz bhojpouri se sa mo
'ke' la li euh, wi li*
'ke ba' and note that when we mainly speak Bhojpuri it is that word
'ke' , it yes it …

15   Mr R *bhojpouri c'est tout à fait comme en hindi, hindi est comme ci
latin. En latin tous les verbes viennent après, à la fin, à la fin de la
phrase comme ça.* **Les verbes viennent après, in, it's the last word in
latin. So in Hindi also, in Bhojpuri also, the verb, l'action que vous
montrez ou l'état d'esprit ça vient après.** *Hein la façon dont c'est en
latin. Alors, il y a, il y a quand même ça. Mais je pense que maintenant
on a une grammaire de bhojpouri sinon c'était un dialecte*
Bhojpuri is just the same as Hindi, Hindi is like Latin. In Latin, all the
verbs come after, in, it's the last word in Latin. So in Hindi also, in
Bhojpuri also, the verb, the action that you show or the state of the mind
comes after. Humm that's the way it is in Latin. So there is, there is also
that. But I think that now we have a Bhojpuri grammar, otherwise it was
a dialect.

16   Mr U *Dialecte*
Dialect

17   Mr R *(…)* **Parce qu'on demande moi** *si le gouvernement entraîne à
disons, à faire des lois qu'on va imposer l'étude du créole et bhojpouri à
Maurice. Nous sommes un pays très isolé. Hein, vous pouvez constater,
c'est un, c'est une île, cons, isolée dans la mer. Nous n'avons pas de pays
tout de suite comme ça et nos informations, l'éducation nous viennent à
travers les grandes langues, les grandes langues de l'Europe.* **Il y a l'
anglais mem**, *il y a le français. A la rigueur on pourra avoir un peu de
mandarin, mais ça ne fonctionne pas trop, mandarin ou hindi. Mais disons*

*qu'on va étudier le bhojpouri ou on étudie le créole. Où est-ce qu'on va aller avec ça ? Est-ce qu'on va parler bhojpouri ou créole en Europe ou ailleurs en, en, dans le monde? Il y a pas d'avenir, grand avenir à étudier bhojpouri mais disons on fait ça tout simplement pour une valeur culturelle, on va rende, **c'est tout ça, simplement, simplement décoratif, c'est décoratif, it's ornamental but it hasn't got you see any***

Because you ask me if the government goes on to have laws to make creole and Bhojpuri compulsory in Mauritius. We are a very isolated country. Humm you can see for yourself, it's a, it's an island, isolated in the sea. We do not have countries around us like that and our information, education come from the great languages, the great languages of Europe. There is English, there is French. If need be, we could have some Mandarin, but Mandarin and Hindi do not work so well. But let's say that we'll study Bhojpuri or creole. Where will this lead us? Are we going to speak Bhojpuri or creole in Europe or in some other places in the world? There is no future, no great future in studying Bhojpuri, but we can say that we do it only for cultural value, we'll make it, in fact it is ornamental, it's ornamental but it hasn't got you see any …

18   Mrs W *or sentimental*

19   (…)

20   Ms H *papa mama ti pe koz bhojpouri nou granper donk c'est enn parti nou lidantite*
        dad and mum spoke Bhojpuri our grand-father as well so it is part of our identity

21   Mr R **c'est ça, c'est ça, c'est plutôt sentimental c'est disons on veut simplement maintenir on veut disons keep it here living but it has got nothing more than this and spending lot of money on this sort of studies. I think it's a waste of time, a waste of money**
        That's it, that's it. It is rather sentimental, it's let's say simply to maintain we want let's say keep it here living but it has got nothing more than this and spending lot of money on this sort of studies. I think it's a waste of time, a waste of money

22   Mr B *[juste deux mots quoi, pour ajouter. En fait langage à l'île Maurice c'est enn enn, enn affaire byen byen sansib et fragile. Oke. A l'île Maurice nou koz enn ti pe listwar de langage mem koman sa finn evolue.* **Oparavan nou finn gagn bann Dutch, nou finn gagn bann franse, nou finn gagn bann angle, e nou finn gagn bann kouli bann Chinese ainsi de suite.** *Voilà la naissance de bhojpouri koman finn evolue à l'île Maurice. Lontan kan bann kouli ti pe vini, si quelqu'un pe*

*al kit manze dan enn karo dir e 'Madour ke ma kana leata'. C'est
purement indien. Il n'avait pas le français ni la créole dedans.*
just a couple of words to add. As a matter of fact languages in
Mauritius are a very sensitive and fragile issue. Okay, in Mauritius we can
speak a bit about the history of languages even how they have developed.
Long ago we had the Dutch, then we had the French, we had the English
and we had the coolies, the Chinese and so on. Here is how Bhojpuri was
born and how it has evolved in Mauritius. A long time ago when the coolies
arrived and someone brought lunch over in the field [one could] hear
'Madour's mum is bringing food'. It's purely Indian. There was no French
and no English in this sentence.

23   MR R *Oui*
        Yes

24   MR B *(...) Oke, alors, voilà le bhojpouri à Maurice. Maurice ena boukou
        bann komunote, meme so tamil, telegu, **chacun ena so prop fleo de
        langage, saken ena so prop dialek mais li enn sujet byen byen sansib et
        fragile ki pa kapav toucher....***
        Okay so here's Bhojpuri in Mauritius. There are several communities
        in Mauritius, even Tamil, Telugu, everyone has their own language
        varieties, everyone has their own dialect, but it is a very sensitive and
        fragile issue that cannot be raised.

7.4.3   Analysis

This interaction includes the four major languages spoken in Mauritius. Pro-
portionally, considering the whole conversation and not just the section here,
French seems to be the language most used, followed by creole, English, and
finally Bhojpuri. These proportions vary depending on the individual speaker.
The main speakers in the excerpt are Mr Ramdanee, Mr Bunsy, and Mr
Ujoodha, who all speak Bhojpuri fluently. Mr Ramdanee (54 years old) comes
from a rural area and thus Bhojpuri is most likely his first language. But in the
presence of several non-Bhojpuri speakers, the 'we code' is Mauritian Creole
and all have good competence in French (and also English, the 'they code').[16]
The presence of two European linguists as well as the institutional although
informal context, can perhaps account for the fact that the conversation is
predominantly in French with frequent alternations to creole and English,
which all the participants understand.

---

[16] See Gumperz (1982/2002); for a more detailed discussion of these terms in the Mauritian
ecology, see Kriegel, Ludwig, and Henri (2009).

7.4.3.1 The Code Hybridization Continuum (CHC)

Our analysis involves primarily the dimensions of the code hybridization continuum. However, in the first part of the transcription the speakers make metalinguistic reflections on language hybridization in the linguistic ecosystem of Mauritius: Mauritian Bhojpuri is the subject of the conversation and the passages in Bhojpuri are quotes to illustrate the hybrid character of the Bhojpuri variety spoken in Mauritius. This part therefore does not seem to be suitable for an illustration of the CHC. Instead the first part will allow us to illustrate our conventionalized systemic integration continuum (CSIC), with some remarks on the structural integration of the creole copies into Bhojpuri (SSIC) (7. 4. 3. 2). We will first concentrate our attention on illustrating the CHC by considering the second part of the transcription.

Balanced Systemic Alternation

Regarding the overall transcription, the fact stands out that the most common form of alternation in the communicative interaction is along the turn changes. But we also find alternations within single turns, as in examples (1) to (3). In our transcription, Mr Ramdanee (type A: same speaker, see section 7.3.2) produces balanced systemic alternations between French and English, the language he teaches at Bartholomew's College.

(1) *Les verbes viennent après, in,* it's the last word in Latin. So in Hindi also, in Bhojpuri also, the verb, *l'action que vous montrez ou l'état d'esprit ça vient après.*
 'In Latin, all the verbs come after, in, it's the last word in Latin. So in Hindi also, in Bhojpuri also, the verb, the action that you show or the state of the mind comes after'.

(2) *c'est tout ça, simplement, simplement décoratif, c'est décoratif,* it's ornamental but it hasn't got you see any
 'in fact it is simply ornamental, it's ornamental but it hasn't got you see any … '

(3) *c'est ça, c'est ça, c'est plutôt sentimental c'est disons on veut simplement maintenir on veut disons* keep it here living but it has got nothing more than this and spending lot of money on this sort of studies [I think it's a waste of time, a waste of money
 'That's it, that's it. It is rather sentimental, it's let's say simply to maintain we want let's say keep it here living but it has got nothing more than this and spending lot of money on this sort of studies. I think it's a waste of time, a waste of money'

Interlectal/Inter-lingual Copying

In Mr Ramdanee's turns French is almost always the matrix language. This is unsurprising as Mr Ramdanee predominantly speaks a strongly hybridized variety of French. In (4) and (5), we focus on microstructural copies from creole:

(4)   *Il y a l'anglais mem, il y a le français*
        'There is English, there is French'

The use of *mem* (NB: we chose to transcribe it with creole spelling conventions) is a copy from creole. In Mauritian Creole, this item is a highly frequent intensifier, the syntactic and semantic characteristics of the French adverb *même* being different. According to the French word order rules, the item should be preposed to the nominal phrase *l'anglais*.

(5)   *parce qu'on demande mwa*
        'because you ask me'

As Mr Ramdanee delabializes the item *mwa*, we again chose to transcribe it according to creole spelling conventions and qualify it as being an overt copy from creole. Our further analysis of example (5) is on a morphosyntactic level. Regarding its structural complexity, this is a partial text and must be situated in the middle of the Code hybridization continuum (CHC). As a morphosyntactic unit this is a covert copy, embedding the shorter overt copy *mwa* that is situated further to the right of the continuum. This construction does not conform with French grammar rules, which require the pronominal direct object to take the clitic form *me* and to be preposed to the verb: *parce qu'on me demande*. This deviation from French can be interpreted as being a copy from creole *and* English, because both languages show the same pattern of pronominalization: the postposing of *mwa* reflects the position the object pronoun takes in creole, viz. *paski (zot) deman **mwa***. In English, the object pronoun is also postposed to the verb, viz. *because they ask **me***. The example here may be the result of convergence (Mufwene 1996: 103; Kriegel, Ludwig, and Pfänder, forthcoming) between the creole and English structures.

Given that Mr Ramdanee works as an English teacher and that creole probably is his second language (after Bhojpuri), it is not astonishing that he copies the structure he knows from two of his more proficient languages into his French.

In the following example from Mr Bunsy, creole can be considered the matrix language of the turn, but we can easily identify some overt lexical copies from English (*Dutch, Chinese*), and an overt French copy at the end of the construction (*ainsi de suite*):

(6)   *Oparavan nou finn gagn bann Dutch, nou finn gagn bann franse, nou finn gagn bann angle, e nou finn gagn bann kouli bann Chinese ainsi de suite.*
        'Long ago we had the Dutch, then we had the French, we had the English and we had the coolies, the Chinese and so on.'

Interestingly, the English copies are structurally integrated into creole morphosyntax because they are preceded by *bann*, the nominal plural marker in Mauritian Creole.

7.4.3.2 Metalinguistic Reflections Made by the Speakers: Conventionalized, Structurally Integrated Copies in Mauritian Bhojpuri (CSIC and SSIC)

At the beginning of the transcribed discourse, the speakers emphasize the hybrid character of Mauritian Bhojpuri, which contains many conventionalized copies from creole. We start our analysis of the transcription with a closer look at examples given by the speakers themselves and at their metalinguistic reflections.

Mr Ramdanee starts to illustrate the hybrid character of Mauritian Bhojpuri with the following example:

(7) | Kamyon | ke | larou | plat | ho | gal |
      |--------|------------|-------|------|-----|-----|
      | Lorry | OBJ.MARKER | wheel | flat | BE | PP |

'the lorry's wheel/tyre is flat'

This example contains three conventionalized, overt lexical copies from creole (*larou, kamyon, plat*).[17] Besides the fact that our speakers seem to agree on their conventionalization, a check in Sewothul (1990, a small Kreol–Mauritian Bhojpuri dictionary), revealed that *larou* and *plat* appear as the Bhojpuri translations of the corresponding creole items. This fact can be considered as a material proof for their high degree of conventionalization.[18]

Example (7) also follows the morphosyntactic marking of Bhojpuri: in terms of the *structural systemic integration* (SSIC), the noun *kamyon* is marked by the Bhojpuri object marker *ke. Kamyon-ke* precedes the head noun *larou*, consistent with Bhojpuri word order rules (Mesthrie 1991: 254s.).

Mr Ujoodha gives another example of the hybrid character of Mauritian Bhojpuri by quoting an Indian priest:

(8) | Montagn | ke | bor | me, | pistas | plant-al | ba |
      |----------|------------|------|-----|--------|----------|-----|
      | Mountain | OBJ.MARKER | side | LOC | peanut | plant.PP | be.3SG.PRES(?) |

'at the foot of the mountain, peanut [trees] have been planted'

All content words here (*montagn, bor, pistas, plant*) are from creole, and can be considered conventionalized overt copies: as in example (7), a check in Sewothul (1990) revealed that all four items are given as the Bhojpuri translation of the creole words.

The word order (SOV) and the morphosyntactic organization employed here are from Bhojpuri (see SSIC). The object marker *ke* follows the noun *montagn*

---

[17] The speakers themselves interpret them as being French. In fact, the three elements also exist in French from where Mauritian Creole draws 90 per cent of its lexical items: *la roue* 'the wheel', *camion* 'lorry', *plate* (ADJ. FEM.) 'flat'.

[18] An entry *kamyon* does not exist in Sewtohul (1990).

according to the syntactic organization of Bhojpuri, as explained above. The complex local postposition *bor me* consists of the polyvalent locative marker *me* from Bhojpuri and the creole-derived element *bor* (< Fr. 'bord' 'side, shore'). The root or base of the verb *plant* is Creole, but the morphological marking comes from Bhojpuri.

Examples (7) and (8) illustrate our statement that structural integration (CSIC) and conventionalization (SSIC) often go hand in hand (section 7.3.4). They also demonstrate the non-identicality (Johanson 2002a) of originals and copies discussed in section 7.2.2.

7.4.3.3 Code Hybridization between Creole and French

We complete our analysis with an example on the material (phonetic–phonological) level. In all Indian Ocean French Creoles the opposition between post-alveolar and alveo-dental fricatives was lost during creolization, with only the alveo-dental fricatives maintained. The following evolutionary process can be posited, and is here illustrated with the word *saken*: [ʃ]→[s] and [ʒ]→[z] (for a perception study of those sounds by creole speakers, see Dufour et al. 2014).

(9)   *chacun ena so prop fleo de langage, saken ena so prop dialek mais li enn sujet byen byen sansib et fragile ki pa kapav toucher*
       'everyone has their own language varieties, everyone has their own dialect, but it is a very sensitive and fragile issue that cannot be raised'

While Mr Bunsy pronounces [ʃ] in the first occurrence of *chacun* 'everybody' as in French, he alternates to the creole pronunciation [s] *saken* in the second occurrence. Mr Bunsy pronounces [ʒ] in both *sujet* and *fragile* (French pronunciation), and [ʃ] in *toucher* (French pronunciation). In more basilectal creole he would have pronounced these words with [z] and [s], respectively.[19] This example allows the following statements: first, our transcription shows that variation within one and the same speaker, sometimes in the pronunciation of one and the same word, is common. Second, it illustrates the mesolectal character of our data. The participants in the conversation may be considered representative of the huge group of speakers of mesolectal creole (see e.g. Mufwene 2005: 79ff.). These varieties are a challenge to the code hybridization continuum (see section 7.3.2) if one differentiates between creoles and their base languages.

---

[19] Carayol and Chaudenson (1979: 131) illustrate the continuum between French and creole on Reunion Island by means of several variables. One of them is the realization of [ʃ]/[s] and [ʒ]/[z], the basilectal variants being [s] and [z].

7.5   Example 2: Communication in India – the Terminology of Copies

7.5.1   *The Ecological Frame: the Historical Constitution of the Hindi Macro Area in India*

English has been the language of higher-level bureaucracy and commerce as well as higher education in India since its colonization by the British. According to Kapoor:

> It is to be noted however that while Hindi and English are both functionally more potent languages of wider communication in India as together they cover more than half of the entire bilingual population, their nature of functionality drastically differs. While Hindi serves more in the domain of mass entertainment, public contact, low-level trade and commerce, places of public transport etc., English is employed in the field of science and technology, higher education, and all those domains of activities, which involve prestige. (Kapoor 1994: 105)

An indigenized English variety known as Indian English (sometimes with pejorative connotations) has developed through various processes (such as language contact), which in pronunciation as well as grammar shows significant differences from British English. Like any national language variety, Indian English is by no means a uniform one. It is rather an umbrella term of varieties spoken on the Indian subcontinent (see e.g. Sailaja 2009; Sedlatschek 2009).

In northern India a heavy influence of Hindi[20] can be noted, especially on the grammar of local English. Here we focus on this northern Indian variety.

Hindi developed from Prakrit varieties with Sanskrit and Persian influences in the Moghul era, more or less at the time of the European Middle Ages. Later, in the course of nationalization,[21] Khariboli-Hindi was established as national language. During this politicization it was heavily re-Sanskritized, while Urdu on the other hand increasingly drew on the Persian lexis and the vocabulary of the Turc languages (see Dua 1992).

---

[20] The term Hindi is applied in three ways: Firstly, as a collective name for various indigenous northern Indian language varieties (for example Khariboli, Hindustani, Dakkhini, Urdu, Hariani, Awadhi, Bhojpuri, Maghai, Vajjika, Maithli, Bundeli and Braj); secondly, with the meaning of Khariboli-Hindi or high Hindi; and, finally, as an umbrella term for colloquial Hindustani and the superposed literary varieties of Hindi and Urdu. Hindi developed primarily out of Pali, the Prakṛt languages, Apabhramśa and Brajbhaṣa, but also Sanskrit as the language stage preceding these. Noteworthy is that due to the mentioned politicization the vocabulary of current Hindi is considerably nearer to Sanskrit than to the mentioned middle Indian languages (see Oberlies 2005; Bechert 1993: 33ff.).

[21] English was added to the Constitution as a national language only in the 1970s when it had to be admitted that English was still very much alive in India. Previously, it had been assumed that Hindi would take over the positions English held and English would die out.

Our explanations here are based on Khariboli-Hindi and Hindustani (within the limits of our knowledge), although the legitimacy of using Khariboli-Hindi as pattern of explanation can be questioned, since it is hardly ever spoken as a mother tongue and only educated Indians are proficient in it. A speaker's mother tongue is typically their regional Hindi variety or rather Hindustani (which is more frequently spoken in everyday life), which exerts some influence on their competence in Khariboli-Hindi.

7.5.2   *The Intermediate Level: New Delhi – Jawaharlal Nehru University*

The transcripts and their respective recordings analysed here are within the context of university communication at the Jawaharlal Nehru University. The analysis of this kind of setting as part of ecological linguistic studies has shed significant light on a number of topics in contact linguistics, because in most countries written and spoken language, regional and global intellectualism, etc. meet here. Jawaharlal Nehru University (JNU), is one of the few state universities in India, and the one most closely allied to the government. It is also reputed to be one of India's best universities.

Although students of diverse cultural and linguistic backgrounds from all over the country attend JNU, most of them are from the north. Regarding the language of communication here, we have a situation that is probably not difficult to find elsewhere, though is more common and evident in university contexts. The main languages of communication are Hindi (Khariboli as well as Hindustani) and Indian English[22] (which is also the medium of teaching), as well as Urdu. Students of Hindi and Urdu backgrounds usually use these languages for their everyday communication.[23] Those from other linguistic backgrounds tend to use a mix of English, their mother tongue, and Hindi, depending on the composition of the group in the setting of interaction.

The English varieties used by Hindi-speaking students vary noticeably from those produced by speakers of other languages, as suggested above. In parts of India where Hindi is the lingua franca, it appears to exert the most influence on English. Therefore, Hindi-influenced English differs more from British English than the varieties spoken in parts of India where English or another

---

[22] The frequent use of English outside institutions like the university is an urban phenomenon.
[23] In certain circles, e.g. religious Hindu groups and groups promoting Hindi nationalism, a heavily Sanskritized Hindi is preferred to Hindustani, which is usually more Persian-influenced and therefore nearer to Urdu. This choice depends largely on one's subject of study and political attitude, since, due to the political position of JNU, politics also play an important role for the students. For the last five decades JNU has been a platform for all the political parties, above all the left wing and left wing extremists. Supporters of the conservative right wing tend to use a more Sanskritized Hindi, whereas the language of leftist individuals is predominantly influenced by Persian and Urdu. A representative variety of Hindi on the streets would mostly include Persian rather than Sanskrit loanwords but would be altogether more balanced.

regional indigenous language is typically spoken; for example in the south, where Hindi is of almost no consequence. In Southern India, Tamil, Telugu, Kannada, and English are the major languages.

7.5.3   The Transcription

7.5.3.1 Problems and Conventions of Transcription

The transcription undertaken by Salzmann turned out to be slightly diffi-cult, as everything was written down for European readers in Latin letters, even though two of the three languages involved have their own writing system: Persian in Arabic letters and Hindi in Devanagari. Since there are different conventions for and ways of transcribing these three languages, a choice had to be made, especially in the transcription of peculiarities in the pronunciation of English.[24] Seeing that here we are concerned with a conversation held in English and Hindi, a transcription following the Eng-lish conventions might be the best solution.

7.5.3.2 Comments on the Situation

We are convinced that a given language situation can be well understood only by taking into consideration the general ecological background. This conversation takes place at JNU before the beginning of a Persian class. The teacher Mumtaz, a Ph.D. student (in his mid-thirties and a Muslim who speaks Urdu as mother tongue), and six other students, all of them male (between 18 and 22 years old) except for one foreign (German) female student, are in the classroom. Everyone is from a different faculty, because this Persian class is an elective extension course open to students of all specializations.

While they are waiting for other students to join the class, they engage in several conversations. The teacher tries to find out where Tabea, the foreign student, wants to travel in India after the end of the semester and gives tips. The main participants in the conversation are the teacher and three other Indian students, one of them called Nazim. These students comment on the teacher's contribution to the conversation and the teacher responds. After about two minutes, communication becomes polycentric, splitting into three separate discussions: the teacher talks to two students at his desk in a hybrid Hindi–Urdu variety; at one desk further back, two students converse

---

[24] For Persian and Hindi there are both scientific versions of transcription not widely known and colloquial phonetic notations. The latter conventions differ, though, according to which language the transcriber speaks.

alternating between Urdu and Hindi; and at one desk much further back and nearest to the recording device, an Indian student still discusses travelling throughout India during the holidays with Tabea in English. In the latter case, the focus is the trip a group of students are planning to the Himalaya. As English is the language in which classes are taught at the university, all the participants have some competence in it. Urdu is the mother tongue of at least half the class, as are various other northern Indian languages for the rest.

7.5.3.3 Transcription: 'Before Class Begins'

(…)	not transcribed
--	pause
[…	simultaneous speech
Bold:	examples explained below
Cursive:	non-textual utterances (laughing)
TlwgTypewriter:	Hindi

01   MUMTAZ   Don´t go there. **You are foreigner.** And e::h, **dey can understand easily ki from where you are coming**.

02   MUMTAZ   **To:: –   – Dont go northeast or north e or Himalay region**
       NAZIM   Delhi
       STUDENTS   *(laughing)*

03   MUMTAZ   [(…   )   Eh?
       STUDENT Y   [**She´s going in Himalay**   **She´s going to Himalaya**

04   NAZIM   visit or not (…) dey will give you and then dey will demand

05   NAZIM   And from your [house *(laughing)*
       MUMTAZ   [Vidit a::ll de places   What?
       STUDENT Y   from your house.

06   MUMTAZ   She ( )is( )speak English
       TABEA   ya:, sure
       NAZIM   *(laughing)* she will she will get arrest(ed)

07   NAZIM   they(´re) from Tabea's ho[use
       MUMTAZ   [Tabea's, how dhow do you know where she´s li –
                    from?
       STUDENTS   *(laughing)*

08   STUDENT Y   Just go and enjoy, **go for outing**. we´ll be going on – ahm trek, I mean

09   STUDENT X   where do you go?   who walks it?
       STUDENT Y   trek, for trek

10   STUDENT Y   **we go, we walk, we trek and only 2000 rupees**. the (…)scene is re:lly fantastic

ca. 1:25 start of class, meanwhile there are two other conversations, two students in front of Tabea as well as Tabea and student Y next to her continue their conversation.

11   MUMTAZ   **calo calo jaldi**

7.5.4   Analysis

7.5.4.1 Global Discourse Functions of Language Selection and Hybridization – the CHC

Basically, English is the matrix language for this conversation. A detailed examination on the basis of the spectrum of code hybridization seems necessary all the same. The institutional frame of the setting, especially the actual classroom, determines the general choice of language. As explained above, English is the medium of instruction at JNU. In the informal opening, English additionally serves to integrate Tabea, the foreign student. We have some alternates to Hindi (in the macro-structural range), mostly from Nazim.

In a purely informal setting, these participants, including the teacher, would not necessarily converse in English, aside from conversations actively including Tabea (though she does speak Hindi too). Despite the use of English, some spontaneity, partial informality, and interpersonal communicative closeness are maintained by a relatively high occurrence of interjections in Hindi by the students, as well as numerous, even extensive copies by Mumtaz. Hindi as lingua franca in northern India is particularly suitable here because it represents the Indian folk culture more adequately than English, the language of the former colonizers, and acts as a unifying language almost free of ethnic or religious connotations, unlike languages such as Urdu.

The permanent Hindi–English contact situation, the apparent hybridization of both languages and the imperfect learning of English are the reasons for the large number of not only interactive but also conventionalized copies from Hindi into English. Regarding Mumtaz's hybrid variety, he apparently prefers to use a Hindi tinged with Persian rather than a Sanskritized Hindi. This comes closer to his mother tongue Urdu and with it he can possibly project an Islamic identity.

7.5.4.2 Conventionalized System Integrated Copies (CSIC) and Structurally System Integrated Copies (SSIC) in Indian English

Many of the copies in this conversation are covert copies or copies that combine overt and covert copies. At the same time they combine copies that are localized at various points of the three continua. Often a conventionalized copy is also structurally more system-integrated and goes hand in hand with a less conventionalized copy. This can be attributed to the long-term language contact between English and Hindi in Northern India. In Indian English many copies from the autochthonous languages have been conventionalized, and the resulting code thus shows many signs of convergence (Kriegel, Ludwig, and Pfänder, forthcoming) making further situational copies easier to integrate.

> (10)   They can understand easily ki from where you are coming.
>   To . . .

This example contains several interesting features. In Hindi, subordinate question clauses that are triggered by the verb in the main clause are marked with the clause complementizer *ki*. The sentence structure is *main clause + clause complementizer ki + subject + question word + VP*. In Standard English the structure for this kind of sentence is either *main clause + preposition + question word + subject + VP*, or *main clause + question word + subject + VP + preposition,* i.e., there is no clause complementizer. As such, Hindi to English is mapped as null in translation or copying situations. Since this speaker is more at home in Hindi than in English, he feels the necessity to overtly introduce a clause complementizer and therefore copies *ki* from Hindi. In terms of structure, in situations of orality in current Standard English, the more common structure in usage involves the preposition *from* in the sentence final slot. The other structure is felt to be more adequate for written academic contexts, and even there, it can be seen as antiquated. In Hindi on the other hand, the semantic information offered by the English preposition is already contained in the question word and therefore given in the same structural slot. The clause complementizer *ki* also contains structural information for the subordinated sentence it heads: *ki + subject + question word + verbal clause* (e.g. *ve pataa sakte haî ki tum kahā se a rahi ho* – you can know where she is from). As the speaker is competent in English in an academic context he would not use the same structure in an English sentence and thus produce **they can know ki you from where are coming*. But the structural–semantic information combined with the fact that the question word in Hindi does not need a second slot for a preposition induces the speaker to use *from where* together, but to otherwise retain the common use English structure. The resulting *ki from where you are coming* can therefore be understood as a combined overt and covert copy, in which the covert copy is modified. This hints at the fact that the combining of the overt copy *ki* with a covert structural copy is often used and therefore more conventionalized. The structural system integration in this case depends on the function with which *ki* complies. Later in the conversation the speaker uses a very similar construction, this time adhering to the more common Standard English *How do you know where she is from?* As he does not use a clause complementizer here – because the main clause is a question – there are no further structural copies contained and he can separate the question word and preposition and follow the Standard English word order.

The complementizer or conjunction *ki* has various uses in Hindi that correspond to different semantic meanings and therefore constructions in English (for further information, see e.g. Sinha and Thakur 2005). Using *ki* in Indian English is a phenomenon observed frequently as it facilitates filling or replacing structural slots in English that would otherwise have to be realized quite differently in Hindi. Hindi speakers in situations of imperfect learning of English and for reasons of cognitive facilitation and adherence to (for them) unmarked structures often prefer using *ki*. Copying *ki* into Indian English can then be considered a conventionalized copy, especially when structural convergence between Hindi and English facilitates the copy. As both an overt and covert copy this ranges in the middle of the CHC.

The use of *coming* in the present continuous tense instead of simple present tense in semantic contexts defining national, cultural or regional origin is expected neither in Hindi nor in British English. It must therefore be considered an innovation, which might point to confusion between two semantic patterns, origin and ablative, in situations of cognitive overload.

Discourse markers are transferred overtly and become quite conventionalized copies despite being at the microstructural end of the CHC; for example, the copy *to* 'so, then' from Hindi is used quite frequently in this variety of Indian English to introduce new sentences or new contents.

(11)   She's going in Himalay ... She's going to Himalaya

Directional markers are apparently open to long term change through copies. The student sitting next to Tabea states: *she's going in Himalay*. This is a covert morphosyntactic copy from Hindi because Hindi itself does not have an allative marker comparable to the English preposition *to*, although it does have a postposition encoding the opposite ablative (Kriegel, Ludwig, and Henri 2009). Hindi has a postposition *ko* corresponding to English *to* as in *give a book to*. This, however, is purely a marker for recipient or benefactive and cannot be used as a directional marker, unlike the English *to* (*ko* also marks the direct specific object while the direct unspecific object stays unmarked; Agnihotri 2007: 143). So in Indian English the allative is realized in the pattern of Hindi, namely with a null marker (as in *don't go Himalay region*) or with the prepositions *in* or *at* and the like. An important reason for this peculiarity is that English *to* is also associated with functions other than allative, such as to mark the indirect object or the infinitive, or to introduce complements of verbs such as the modal *have* and *invite*. In the repetition of his phrase (*she's going to Himalaya*) the student nevertheless corrects himself towards Standard English both in the use of preposition and pronunciation of *Himalaya*.

Another indicator that this is a copy is the fact that the geographic name *Himalay* is overtly copied from Hindi. English would use the equivalent form *Himalaya,* which corresponds to the Sanskrit original. Mountains in Sanskrit are always masculine (while rivers are feminine); a typical ending for masculine in Sanskrit is 'short *a*' which in Hindi always disappears. In this case the construction probably makes even more sense to the speaker since the foregoing *don´t go northeast or north* are geographic directions (*north* and *north-east*) and therefore do not need a preposition even in Standard English. For the same reason the definite article is omitted. This specific case involving the Himalaya might be a conventionalized copy as the Himalaya is historically a very important cultural and religious landmark, and as a synonym for 'North' gains value as a cardinal direction. In addition, Hindi does not have definite articles. The coexistence of both forms, *Himalay* and *Himalaya* (as observable in the repetition) might imply that it is not yet completely conventionalized; but the specific parameters of the situation, especially regarding the historic coexistence of English and Hindi, could explain a conventionalized coexistence similar to situations in the Spanish-speaking world.[25]

> (12)   you are foreigner, just go and enjoy, go for outing,
>   we'll be going on trek

A common copy from Hindi is the bare noun; i.e. not using any article, as in *go for outing*. In British English *go on an outing* would be correct, but in Hindi there are no articles. This example also shows that prepositions in contact situations are among the first morphological features prone to change. This is due to the cognitive complexity of nuances in the various meanings and uses of prepositions.

This use of bare nouns seems to be rather common, and might be interpreted as conventionalized and system integrated copies. Examples such as *you are foreigner* (instead of BE *you are a foreigner*) and *we'll be going on trek* (for BE *we'll be going on a trek*) are typical of this kind of construction. In this last example the intonation could even be interpreted in the following way: between *on* and *trek* is a kind of faltering pause as if the speaker felt that really there should be something there but still ends up not using an article because he or she is unsure. In all three examples an indefinite article would be expected in British English, as otherwise the reference here would be interpreted as nonspecific or generic. Yet, in this context only one of three examples (i.e. *you are foreigner*) has generic reference.

---

[25] For further explanations on such phenomena in Spanish see e.g. Klee and Caravedo (2005).

Phenomena emerge in language contact situations that are conditioned by parameters of orality and informality. These phenomena are not necessarily direct copies, but rather follow the necessity of lightening the cognitive load by reducing markedness and thus showing universal tendencies.

(13) *we go, we walk, we trek*

As a possible, indirect and already highly structurally adapted copy from Hindi, we have the paratactic sequence *we go, we walk, we trek*. Stringing together three short clauses with intransitive verbs produces both intensification of the movement and specification of the kind of motion: Since *go* alone would be unmarked, it would not necessarily denote the physical movements of walking or the duration and distance denoted by *trek*. In addition, *go* denotes spatial motion and in the second instance the temporal distance to be covered to the location of *hiking* (in the holidays). As is generally known, verbs of motion such as *go* and *come*, are regularly co-opted for grammaticalization; in several languages they head the serial verb constructions in which they are used as markers of direction or other notions of deixis.[26] Moreover, familiar from Hindi are compound verbs in which a special semantic meaning is conveyed by stringing verb stems together with only the last inflected. Just as in serial constructions, in Hindi the fixed, non-variable verb or predicate is characteristically selected from a limited group. Typically, these are verbs that contextualize the situation temporally and spatially as well as verbs of movement (e.g. *go, come, stay, sit, stand, start*) (see Agnihotri 2007: 202ff.). This example involves a more advanced stage on the scale of structural systemic integration without being very conventionalized. This interpretation is also suggested by the intonation contour, which constitutes a relatively monotone, slightly stretched unit. Had the speaker intended a separate meaning for every single verb in the construction, he would most probably have broken the intonation into three parts, each of which would have a falling pattern as is typical of Hindi and Indian English.

(14)   and only two thousand rupees

Strong reductions of markedness are typical for situations of orality and language contact. An example of this can be found in the construction *only two thousand rupees* without a verbal phrase. In Standard English an explicit verb would be

---

[26] An instance of this can be found in French creoles from Guadeloupe and Dominica which Ludwig (1996: 236-295) analyses in detail. For more recent analysis see Aboh (2009) and Winford (2008: 31ff.).

expected (*it is/costs only two thousand rupees*). Here, *only two thousand rupees* is considered a complete sentence despite the fact that neither a subject, copula verb nor verbal phrase is used. Null-subjects can be used in Hindi, but there is only one semantic-syntactic context in which the copula verb can be dropped, namely in a negation in the imperfective present tense (*nahi* 'not'; *it/ there isn't – nahi hai -> nahî*), and here it is replaced by nasalization of the end vowel (see for example Snell and Weightman 2003: 64). Dropping just the subject and keeping the copula (i.e. **and is only two thousand rupees*) probably did not sound right for the speaker. Moreover, dropping both the subject and verb might reflect influence from another possible construction. In Standard English this kind of construction could be possible if it were not a complete sentence, but rather connected with a preposition to the previous sentence such as *we go, we walk, we trek, and for only two thousand rupees*. Hindi does not have prepositions – it uses postpositions. Since it would sound very wrong to use the English preposition at the end of the sentence the speaker chose not to use any.

      (15)   calo, calo, jaldi

Interestingly, the serial combination of discourse markers in *calo, calo, jaldi* constitutes an amalgamation of interactional and conventionalized overt copies. The conventionalized discourse marker *calo*, reduplicated in the present case, is often used to state the end of a unit of meaning or change to another topic, particularly in telephone conversations where *calo* ends the conversation, much as for example *ok, then, talk to you later*. This effect of structuring discourse is enhanced here by the interactional copy *jaldi* 'quickly'. The copies are overt in this case without any structural systemic integration. Although some are highly conventionalized, the scale of structural systemic integration is of no consequence here, because the copied markers comply with universal tendencies in almost every language to structure discourse in situations of orality, and are therefore easy to copy.

7.5.4.3 Code Hybridization between English and Hindi

Finally let us make some remarks on the material level. Strong hybridization catches the eye from the very beginning on the phonetic–phonological level. Mumtaz's pronunciation of English, as well as that of the students, is heavily influenced by Hindi and Urdu, especially when the copies are very short or language usage favours code alternation. Thus, he is inclined to substitute /d/ or /f/ for /θ/ and the retroflex /ɖ/ for /d/ in word-final position. He also unrounds the English round vowels.

    As already shown by Gumperz (1982), the intonational patterns of Indian English differ greatly from those of British or American English. Unlike

British English, in which one drop and lift would most probably be distributed over a whole sentence with the main emphasis on the contextually most important word, short coherent entities that can consist of only one word are marked by one lift and one drop of the voice. Intonation can therefore be quite decisive for the concrete meaning of the statement in the particular context.

In comparison to our example from Mauritius, the situation here in terms of deeply rooted local varieties is clearer: although various conversations are held at the same time in different languages, in the conversation we analyse there are no alternations to another language. Instead, many copies are inserted on the microstructural level with varying degrees of structural integration and conventionalization, resulting in a hybrid code. These copies range form lexical overt copies to structural covert copies and are occasionally triggered by overt copies. They also include material copies in the suprasegmental area such as mixed pronunciation and a melodic phrasing closer to Hindi. The language use remains very flexible, allowing the integration of small nuances according to changes in parameters of the situation. The resulting code is more convergent with Hindi, and as a variety of English lies closer to it than, for example, to British English (from which it evolved). It becomes apparent that the general sociohistorical frame, a frame that has become very differentiated in its use of linguistic codes over a long period of time, is very much part of the ecological situation and affects the emergent language use.

7.6   Conclusion

It is important to conclude by drawing connections between the body of this chapter and the general approach of linguistic ecology and language contact, and pointing out its relevance to that theoretical frame. Let us pick up on two central ideas from Chapter 1, this volume:

1. In general, linguistic ecology means to examine connections of foundation. This refers not only to language in its specific historical, social, and cognitive connections but also to the foundation relations that pertain to various languages or codes that meet in a society or a specific situation of interaction. In this respect, contact linguistics following Haugen (1972) is a genuine, privileged part of an ecological approach to language.
2. According to our three-level model, empirical analysis revolves around authentic, situational interaction. This is precisely the type of situation that clearly reflects the manifold relations of the foundation of language in terms of both social groups and more global, historically founded reference levels.

In this chapter we have been concerned with developing theoretic–terminological instruments of research on language contact. We developed these tools to enable us to encompass the complex interrelations in situations of language contact arising from situation-grounded linguistic interaction.

To this end we took up Johanson's term *code-copying* and developed it further to comprise three continua: the *code hybridization continuum*, the *conventionalized systemic integration continuum*, and the *structural systemic integration continuum*. To illustrate our theoretic–terminological approach we analysed two cases of situational linguistic interaction in the multilingual context of education, one from Mauritius and one from India.

Finally we must underscore some arguments by means of examples. Consider the phrase *they can understand ki from where you are coming*, taken from our second case (see section 7.5.4.2, Example (10)); as a Hindi copy in English we can first of all simply detect a copy. This can then be specified as possible 'grammatical–structural' *covert* copy headed by a grammatical–lexical overt copy *ki*. We also have the opportunity to evaluate it as a complete, partial, or non-conventionalized copy, or to identify it as partially conventionalized, and then separately determine its degree of structural systemic integration (here a copy well integrated). Taking this approach, we avoid rashly presupposing a specific analytical interpretation as using the terms *borrowing* or *calquing* would imply. Depending on the author, these terms include the aspects of covert or overt conventionalization or non-conventionalization in their definition. This significantly complicates the analysis of more complex examples such as that just given.

Also, the hierarchical formation of parts and wholes in our code hybridization continuum renders possible an understanding of how interaction can contain code alternation at turn boundaries or within turns. In addition, alternations can include large-scale copies that themselves comprise microstructural copies. The relatively short example *parce qu'on demande mwa* (see section 7.4.3.1, Example (5)) illustrates why it is necessary to consider various levels of text and the relations of parts and wholes: on the level of the turn, French is the frame language with a longer covert creole copy embedded in it. This copy again contains a short overt copy: *mwa*. The whole turn is then part of a communication showing many alternations at turn boundaries.

On the one hand, this model can deal with occurring complex phenomena using a consistent and coherent terminology that can be specified as necessary. On the other hand we accommodate the terminology to natural linguistic behaviour and its multifaceted discourse functions and general ecological parameters using a scale. In contrast, the more conventional terminology is often as complex as it is blurred and is generally conceptualized as binary and thus somewhat limited in its accurate descriptive power.

Using our examples of transcription from Mauritian and North Indian intermediate ecologies, we hope to have aroused interest anew for spaces that can be appreciated as creating a privileged field of study for linguistic ecology.

8   Language Mixing and Ecology in Africa: Focus on Camfranglais and Sheng

Anne Schröder and Philip W. Rudd

8.1   Introduction

In the introductory chapter to this volume, Ludwig, Mühlhäusler, and Pagel present a hierarchy of ecological levels, placing urban ecologies at the inter-mediate level, between historically constituted macro-ecologies on the one hand and discourse micro-ecologies on the other (Figure 1.1). It is this intermediate level of linguistic ecology that is the focus of the present chapter. Urban ecologies and urban languages, not so unlike koinés (Hinskens, Auer, and Kerswill 2005: 12), should perhaps be considered the consequence of language contact par excellence, as cities offer greater potential contact among greater varieties of language coupled with greater potential instances of internal and external motivation and competition.

    Language evolution is the result of language change in the mind (Weinreich 1953), and what changes in the mind is the idiolect. The idiolect evolves as the individual speaker interacts with other speakers and makes selections from the various options available in the linguistic feature pool.[1] Idiolects, in Mufwene's framework (2001, 2008), are organisms that together make up populations; they have histories and experience movements. These movements lead to contact. Population movements and language contacts foment feature competition and engender selection (Mufwene 2008: 31). The sole trigger for language evolution then is inter-idiolectal contact (Mufwene 2001). This conception of language evolution has many side effects, but all of them, though they occur in the minds of the speakers, have the communal level as their point of ignition. It is on this intermediate ecological level in the urban space (Ludwig, Mühlhäusler, and Pagel's *hic*) that the speaker, and thus her/ his idiolect, vacillates the most.

    When discussing the connection between language contact, language variation and linguistic ecology, linguists seeking to establish a link between

---

[1] According to Mufwene (2008), 'An idiolect is of necessity a hybrid from various idiolectal inputs' (120).

structural language analysis and its historical and sociocultural ecology, quickly realize that

> language contact is a multidimensional, multidisciplinary field in which interrelation-
> ships hold the key to the understanding of how and why people use language/s the way
> they do ... *Languages in contact are*, after all, *the result of people in contact*. (Clyne
> 2003: 1, our emphasis)

This position is consistent with the theoretical assumptions of this volume, outlined in the introductory chapter by Ludwig, Mühlhäusler, and Pagel. However, the result of language contact, most notably the mixing of languages (or 'conventionalized hybridization', according to Kriegel, Ludwig, and Salzmann, Chapter 7, this volume), has usually been seen negatively, frequently ridiculed, chastised, or proscribed by language purists. This is particularly true for so-called 'mixed' languages, which are more often than not denied the status of 'true' languages, because they are perceived as corrupt and aberrant versions of their contributing languages (Winford 2003: 1).

In this chapter, however, we will argue in agreement with Winford (2003: 2) that '[f]ar from being deviant, language mixture is a creative, rule-governed process that affects all languages in one way or another'. We thus hope to contribute to the current discussions on the concept of linguistic ecology by presenting the cases of two African mixed languages, Camfranglais and Sheng, the first spoken in Cameroon and the second in Kenya, and the amazing creativity expressed in them. For this, however, we need to establish the type of languages discussed within a broader context of language contact and types of contact languages.

8.2   Types of Contact Situations and Contact Languages

According to Winford (2003: 11ff.), three types of contact situations can be distinguished:

(a) situations marked by language maintenance,
(b) situations resulting in language shift, and
(c) situations leading to the creation of new contact languages.

However, as Winford correctly points out, there are also many 'fuzzy' cases, which may, for instance, be characterized by the interplay between maintenance and shift (2003: 11).[2] In the context of the present chapter, situations leading to the creation of new contact languages are of particular interest, as these involve extreme restructuring and/or pervasive mixing of linguistic structures. The type

---

[2] See Winford (2003: 23–24, table 1.2.) for a detailed overview on the major outcomes of language contact classified according to these three types of contact situation.

of contact languages created in these contact situations are, on the one hand, pidgins and creoles and, on the other, mixed languages that are neither pidgins nor creoles.

According to Winford (2003: 24), mixed languages are languages incorporating 'large portions of an external vocabulary into a maintained grammatical frame', while pidgins are '[h]ighly reduced lingua francas that involve mutual accommodation and simplification' and are 'employed in restricted functions such as trade'. Creoles are then defined as languages 'with grammars shaped by varying degrees of superstrate and substrate influence, and vocabulary drawn mostly from the superstrate source' (ibid.). Thus, while in pidgins and creoles the greatest part of the lexicon usually comes from one lexifier language only (hence we speak, e. g., of English-based, French-based, or Spanish-based creoles), their grammars can usually not be traced back to a single (and identifiable) source language. With mixed languages, however, the lexicon and the grammar can be traced back to the different source languages, from which they are taken in large chunks (Thomason 2001a: 196–198). Therefore, in many cases, a mixed language can be defined as '[a] language in which the morphosyntax of one language is matched with the vocabulary of another language' (Bakker and Muysken 1995: 41) or as a 'language which has lexical morphemes from one language and grammatical morphemes from another' (ibid.). The lexical items are usually taken without significant (morphological) changes and frequently occur in large bundles.

Another difference between mixed languages, on the one hand, and pidgins and creoles, on the other, lies in the type of contact situations in which they evolve. While pidgins and creoles typically develop in contact situations without widespread individual bi- or multilingualism, which makes the creation of a lingua franca as a medium of communication necessary, mixed languages are created in language situations with widespread bi- or multilingualism. They are therefore not really needed as media of communication but 'arise instead within a single social or ethnic group because of a desire, or perhaps even a need, for an in-group language' (Thomason 2001a: 198), and frequently they are 'deliberate and conscious creations' (Matras 2000: 81). Finally, as with pidgins and creoles, mixed languages escape genetic classification and therefore 'cannot be placed in a genetic tree' (Bakker 2000b: 29). The differences and similarities between these three types of languages are summarized in Table 8.1.

Furthermore, Thomason (2001a: 203ff.) distinguishes between *mixed languages in persistent ethnic groups*, where a gradual loss of ethnic–heritage language leads to heavy borrowing/interferences from the dominant language (e. g. Anglo-Romani), and *mixed languages in new ethnic groups*. The latter type develops when, because of intimate cultural and linguistic contact between ethnic groups, a new ethnic group develops, which uses the newly created mixed language as a symbol of its new ethnic identity that separates its speakers from the source groups (Thomason 2001a: 207ff.).

Table 8.1 *Typology of Contact Languages*[3]

Pidgins and creoles	Mixed languages
Lexicon usually taken from one source language; frequently involving semantic changes	*Grammar* and *lexicon* taken from each source language in large chunks without significant changes
Grammar cannot be traced back to one source language	
Arise in contact situations with limited contact and individual *bi-* or *multilingualism*	Arise in contact situations involving *widespread individual bi-* or *multilingualism*
Need for a medium of communication/*lingua franca*	*No* need for a medium of communication/*lingua franca*
Genetic classification impossible	

It is this latter type of mixed language that we are concerned with in this chapter, and we will now turn our attention to two case studies on Camfranglais and Sheng.

8.3   Mixed Languages in Africa

8.3.1   Camfranglais

8.3.1.1 The Ecological Frame

The ecological frame is the econiche that a particular language occupies, including the language itself, related dialects/varieties, and other languages or species.[4] Cameroon, a West-Central African country located on the Bight of Biafra, between Equatorial Guinea and Nigeria is, even by African standards, an extremely multilingual country. In addition to the two official languages, French and English, there are approximately 280 indigenous languages spoken at the local level, out of which some eight languages, including Cameroon Pidgin English (CamP), have attained the status of regional lingua francas, but none of which has been accorded the status of a national language (Schröder 2003a).

These languages serve communicative functions on various levels, a situation which can best be described by the following, modified version of Bamgbose's (1991) three-language-model:

---

[3] Table based on Thomason (2001a: 196–198).

[4] Begon, Townsend, and Harper (2006), cited in Chapter 1, this volume, list these levels of ecology as the organism, the population, and the community, respectively. Mufwene (2008) analogizes this linguistic econiche to a highway traffic in which each vehicle has the others as part of its ecology.

Table 8.2 *The Linguistic Situation in Cameroon*[5]

Local level	Indigenous languages; CamP (urban areas)
Regional level	CamP; other languages of wider communication (e. g. Fulfulde, Duala) (French)
National level	French English CamP
International level	English French

Most urban centres show a great multilingual and multicultural complexity, in which local indigenous languages (IL), languages of wider communication (LWC), and the two official languages English and French interact. And it is in these urban centres that we observe the creation of a new and highly mixed code to which several names, such as *langue des bandits de Douala, Pidgin French, Pidgin Makro, Franglais, Camspeak*, and *Camfranglais* have been given (Schröder 2007). All these labels indicate that it is a highly hybrid and complex language, which incorporates features from the official languages, the ILs, and LWCs (including CamP). *Camfranglais* is the term used in this chapter, because it is the most widespread and accepted label. The language variety is believed to have its origin in a secret language spoken among criminals from the city of Douala in the early 1970s (Tiayon-Lekobou 1985).

8.3.1.2 Structural Aspects

Unsurprisingly, the Camfranglais lexicon is highly mixed. Lexical items are primarily drawn from English, French and the ILs, such as Ewondo, Bassa, and Duala. However, it is often difficult to ascertain the etymology of a lexeme, as it may be attributed to several sources. For example, the word *boulou* 'to work' has possibly been selected from Bassa *bolo* or Duala *ebolo* (both signifying 'to work'), but a French influence from the noun *boulot* 'work' seems also probable (Tiayon-Lekobou 1985: 90).

Concerning the grammatical structure of this language, according to Tiayon-Lekobou (1985), one can distinguish two types of Camfranglais, one 'via French syntax' and another one via 'CamP syntax'. The following examples illustrate this observation.

(1a)   *Kikman*   **dem**   *flop*   *fo*   *Douala.*[6]
         Thief   **PL**   many   for   Douala

---

[5] Table adapted from Schröder (2003a: 121).
[6] All examples for Camfranglais are taken from Tiayon-Lekobou (1985).

(1b)   *Tifman*   **dem**   *plenti*   fo   *Douala.*
        Thief   **PL**   many   for   Douala
        'There are many thieves in Douala.'

Thus, focusing on pluralization strategies in Camfranglais, note that *Kikman* in (1a) is pluralized with a postposed plural marker *dem*, similarly to (1b) in CamP. The same is true for Camfranglais 'via French syntax':

(2a)   ***Les***   *wa*   *vs.*   *une*   *wa*
        ART.DEF.**PL**   girl   NUM   girl

(2b)   ***Les***   *filles*   *vs.*   *une*   *fille*
        ART.DEF.**PL**   girl.PL   NUM   girl

The pluralization of *wa* ('girl') with the preceding definite article in example (2a) keeps the essence of Standard French plural marking. As illustrated in (2b), in French the singular and the plural are differentiated typically by the pronunciation of the preceding article, the singular and the plural form of the noun not being distinguished at the phonological level in the vast majority of cases. The omission of the redundant plural marker on the noun in the Camfranglais example can therefore be explained by the fact that Camfranglais is a predominantly oral phenomenon.

Tense and aspect in CamP are marked by four preverbal markers: *di* for IMPERFECTIVITY, *don(g)* for PERFECT or PERFECTIVITY, *bi(n)* for PAST, and *go* for FUTURE.[7] As examples (3a), (4a), (5a), and (6a) show, Camfranglais makes use of the same set of preverbal markers as CamP, for which the glosses, as provided in (3b), (4b), (5b), and (6b), are the same:

(3a)   *A*   *no*   ***di***   *nyolei*   *tudai.*
        1SG   NEG   **IPFV**   drink (alcohol)   today

(3b)   *A*   *no*   ***di***   *drink mimbo*   *tudai.*
        1SG   NEG   **IPFV**   drink alcohol   today
        'I am not drinking today.'

(4a)   *Ma*   *reifrei*   ***dong***   *nye.*
        1SG.POSS   brother   **PRF**   come

(4b)   *Ma*   *broda*   ***don(g)***   *kom.*
        1SG.POSS   brother   **PRF**   come
        'My brother has come.'

---

[7] See Schröder (2003b) and Schröder (2012) for details.

(5a) *I*   ***bi***   *jong*   *and*   *hi*   *koupou*   *kik*   *hi*   *dou.*
      3SG   **PST**   drink   and   3SG.POSS   friend   steal   3SG.POSS   money

(5b) *I*   ***bi(n)***   *drunk*   *an*   *i*   *kombi*   *tif*   *i*   *moni.*
      3SG   **PST**   drink   and   3SG.POSS   friend   steal   3SG.POSS   money
      'He got drunk and his friend stole his money.'

(6a) *A*   ***go***   *gi*   *yu*   *nyol.*
      1SG   **FUT**   give   2SG.OBJ   drink/alcohol

(6b) *A*   ***go***   *gif*   *yu*   *mimbo.*
      1SG   **FUT**   give   2SG.OBJ   drink/alcohol
      'I am going to offer you a drink.'

However, in Camfranglais, verbs also take the same verbal inflections as in French, as is evident from their French translations. Thus, the verb *aimer* 'to love' in example (7a), inflected for present tense and the third person plural, has exactly the same form as in the French translation in (7b).

(7a) *Les*   *Bami*   ***aiment***   *boulou.*
      ART.DEF.PL   Bami(leke)   **love.3PL.PRS**   work

(7b) *Les*   *Bamilekes*   ***aiment***   *travailler.*
      ART.DEF.PL   Bami(leke)   **love.3PL.PRS**   work
      'Bamileke people like working.'

The same holds for verb forms in the *passé composé* (8) and verb phrases indicating future tense (9) using an inflected form of the verb *aller* 'to go' followed by an infinitive:

(8a) *La*   *reimei*   ***a***   ***kuk***   *l'atanga bred.*
      ART.DEF   mother   **AUX**   **cook.PTCP**   bobolo

(8b) *La*   *mere*   ***a***   ***cuisiné***   *du*   *bobolo.*
      ART.DEF   mother   **AUX**   **cook.PTCP**   bobolo
      'Mother has cooked bobolo.'

(9a) *Je*   *vais*   *kousa*   *ce*   *soir.*
      1SG   **go.1SG.PRS**   **dance.INF**   ART.DEF   evening

(9b) *Je*   *vais*   *danser*   *ce*   *soir.*
      1SG   **go.1SG.PRS**   **dance.INF**   ART.DEF   evening
      'I am going to dance tonight.'

Finally, copula constructions in Camfranglais appear to be patterned on CamP syntax, with the equative copulas *na* and *bi* used in both language varieties:

(10a) *Pigmis*   ***na***   *nabs*   *dem*   *ol.*
      Pigmies   **COP**   midget   PL   all

(10b)   *Pigmis   dem   **na**   smol   pipul.*
        Pigmy   PL   **COP**   small   people
        'Pigmies are small people. /Pigmies are all midgets.'

(11a)   *Ma   mbok   **bi**   Jane.*
        1SG.POSS   girlfriend   **COP**   Jane

(11b)   *Jane   **bi**   ma   kombi.*
        Jane   **COP**   1SG.POSS   friend
        'Jane is my girlfriend.'

The same accounts for the use of the existential/locative copula *dei*, as in (12a) and (12b), and for the use of predicative adjective constructions, as in (13a) and (13b):

(12a)   *Mburu   **dei**   fo   ma   kwa.*
        Money   **COP**   for   1SG.POSS   bag

(12b)   *Moni   **dei**   fo   ma   bag.*
        Money   **COP**   for   1SG.POSS   bag
        'There is money in my bag.'

(13a)   *Da   nga   **ndjugsa**   wowo.*
        DET   girl   ugly   a lot

(13b)   *Dat   gel   **wowo**   plenti.*
        DET   girl   **ugly**   plenty
        'That girl is very ugly.'

In Camfranglais, the above structure is incidentally the same as that of Standard French, as illustrated in (14a) and (14b):

(14a)   *Sa   shoud   **est**   ndjugsa.*
        3SG.POSS   girlfriend   **BE.3SG.PRS**   ugly

(14b)   *Son   amie   **est**   laide.*
        3SG.POSS   girlfriend   **BE.3SG.PRS**   ugly
        'His girlfriend is ugly.'

As the Examples (1)–(14) amply illustrate, Camfranglais has not developed morphosyntactic patterns of its own but instead co-opted patterns of CamP or French. It can therefore be referred to as relexified CamP or relexified French and as a primarily lexical phenomenon, which is highly marked by slang vocabulary.

8.3.1.3 Ecological Functions
However, as with other mixed languages, there is more to this language, as it fulfils important functions in the ecological linguistic environment of urban

centres in Cameroon. In agreement with the model presented in the introductory chapter by Ludwig, Mühlhäusler and Pagel (Figure 1.2), various ecological parameters, in our case most notably the SPEAKER dimension, i.e. group-specific competences and attitudes, play a major role in the development and persistence of Camfranglais. As we mentioned above, quoting Thomason (2001a: 198), mixed languages typically arise out of a social group's desire or need for an in-group language. In fact, as Biloa (1999: 150) points out: 'le camfranglais n'est pas le résultat d'interférences linguistiques, au sens strict. Il est né de la volonté des initiés de créer un code qui serait incompréhensible aux non-initiés' ['Camfranglais is not the result of linguistic interference, in a strict sense, but is born from a desire of the initiated to create a code which is intended to be incomprehensible to the uninitiated' (our translation)].

This interpretation is confirmed by informants interviewed in 1999 and 2000.[8] For example, a high-school principal in Yaoundé, the capital city of Cameroon, makes clear that Camfranglais is an in-group language for adolescents who would like to distance themselves from adults:

A: Principal, Francophone (Yaoundé)
le franglais, c'est, il y' a une espèce de plaisir, n'est- ce- pas. Ils sont contents de parler un peu cette langue-là. Un peu, vous savez, c'est comme *une espèce de code pour que les adultes* qui sont à côté *ne comprennent pas ce qu'ils disent*. Bon, ils parlent le... ce franglais.

[Franglais, that's, that's a kind of fun they have. They are happy to speak this language a bit. It's a bit, you know, like having some kind of code, so that the grown-ups who are with them do not understand what they are saying. So they speak this Camfranglais. (our translation)]

Or, as a high-school student from the same school puts it, Camfranglais is part of the cultural production of young people in Cameroon as it is closer to them than, for example, Standard French:

B: High school student, Francophone (Yaoundé)
Le francanglais c'est ... quand on est par exemple *entre nous. Entre camarades de classe, entre amis*, là on parle francanglais.
[...]
Parce que ça fait *partie de la culture des jeunes* actuellement. Ça vient tout seule.
[...]
Oui, le francanglais au Cameroun, l'argot au Cameroun, est *plus proche des, des jeunes que le français*.

[Francanglais, it's ... when we are among ourselves. With our classmates, with friends, then we speak Francanglais ... Because really that's part of the youth culture. It comes

---

[8] See Schröder (2003a) for details on data collection and analysis.

naturally . . . In fact, Francanglais in Cameroon, this Cameroonian slang, is closer to, to young people than French. (our translation)]

Thus, for Cameroonian adolescents, this language serves as an informal language for intimate communication on the one hand and as a secret code on the other. Its primary function is identification with peers and non-communication with non-group members. However, as the group of urban adolescents in Cameroon typically comprises people from different ethnic backgrounds, it is a means of inter-ethnic and intra-group communication at the same time. For these young people the official languages leave a void as they are inadequate means of communication at the local level and in informal settings. This void, however, cannot be filled by ILs either, because of the heterogeneous linguistic background of the group members on the one hand and the lack of proficiency of the young people in these languages on the other.

The phenomenon of a highly mixed code reflecting the multilingual and multicultural reality of young urban Africans is not unique to Cameroon. In fact, similar developments can be described for other African countries, as we will illustrate with a second case study from the Eastern part of the African continent.

8.3.2   Sheng

8.3.2.1 The Ecological Frame

Languages in East Africa must vie for resources in their econiches as well. Kenya, bordered by the Sudan and Ethiopia in the north, Somalia and the Indian Ocean in the east, Tanzania in the south, and Lake Victoria and Uganda in the west, has the distinction of being one of very few countries where three major African language families intersect: Nilo-Saharan, Afro-Asiatic, and Niger-Congo. The country has a population of over 35 million, speaking approximately 61 languages (Gordon 2005). Nearly 65 per cent of the languages are Bantu (of the Niger-Congo family), about 30 per cent Nilotic (of the Nilo-Saharan family), some 3 per cent Cushitic (of the Afro-Asiatic family), and the remaining 2 per cent represent non-African languages, such as English and Hindi, among others (Heine and Möhlig 1980). Table 8.3, corresponding to Table 8.2 for Camfranglais, displays the communicative purposes of these languages at various levels in Kenya.

The national language and the official language are the only languages that have been supported by the government. The latter is English, the language of colonization and of world trade; the former is Swahili, which has been perceived to be a politically neutral language, the ideal candidate as a national

Table 8.3 *The Linguistic Situation in Kenya*[9]

Local level	Indigenous languages (Upcountry Swahili); Swahili/English/Sheng (urban areas)
Regional level	Swahili; other languages of wider communication (e. g. Luo, Kikuyu, Kamba, Luyia) (English)
National level	Swahili English Sheng
International level	English Swahili

symbol[10] in a post-Independence attempt to make Kenya less colonial. Sheng, a Swahili-English hybrid, is the name of the then-emergent urban variety, which has come to symbolize the non-elite urban dweller of Nairobi.[11] It began to be noticed shortly after Independence in 1963 when increasing numbers of migrant Kenyans began moving to and settling in Eastlands, the eastern part of the capital city.

8.3.2.2 Structural Aspects of Sheng

Rudd (2008: 123) gives a basic vocabulary analysis of Sheng, using a composite of the Swadesh 100-word and 200-wordlists, containing a total of 207 words (Trask 1996: 408–409), and shows that 52 per cent of the items are from Swahili, 32 per cent from English, and 16 per cent from other sources. The division in Sheng is remarkably similar to that of the core lexicon of Michif: 'the "nec plus ultra" of mixed languages' (Papen 1987, cited by Bakker and Mous 1994b). In the language of the Métis, 52 per cent of the core items are French, 30 per cent are Cree, and 18 per cent are both French and Cree (Bakker 2000a, 2003: 122). Croft (2003: 66–67) contends that 'an exact correlation between the act of identity and the primary source of basic vocabulary' exists but that as 'a new society is created … the basic vocabulary comes from multiple sources'. As is clear, the core vocabulary of Sheng is from multiple sources, reflecting a new society.

[9] Table is from Rudd (2010) and emulates Schröder (2003a: 121).
[10] On 4 July 1974, President Jomo Kenyatta, the first president of the Republic of Kenya, decreed Swahili to be the country's national language. Incidentally, a new constitution upgraded the language to co-official status next to English on 27 August 2010.
[11] Sheng is not now an exclusively Nairobi phenomenon; it is associated with urban dwellers in other parts of the country as well. Moreover, as described by Abdulaziz and Osinde (1997: 45), the youths of the wealthier Westlands mix their languages and create what is called *Engsh*. In contrast to Sheng, Engsh is based primarily on English grammar.

The evidence that suggests that Sheng's grammatical structure is mixed lies in the existence of both early system morpheme convergence and late system morpheme convergence. Early system morphemes are generally morphemes for case, gender and number and are selected (albeit indirectly) by speaker intention. They are often significant in determining how an incipient mixed language is formed, and are of less consequence to the establishment of a fully crystallized mixed language. Late system morphemes, conversely, are pertinent because they are less determined by speaker choice and are more system driven. These late system morphemes are categorized as bridge morphemes and outsider morphemes. Bridge system morphemes integrate other morphemes into a constituent and have their formation directed from within their maximal projection. Outsider system morphemes are influenced from beyond their immediate heads. The presence of alien bridge system morphemes signals that a turnover of the matrix language has already begun (Myers-Scotton 2002: 244), while the reason that late outsiders are significant is that their presence implies that the matrix language frame has already been altered (Myers-Scotton 2002: 248).

The early system morpheme convergence in Sheng is evident from the morphemes for PLURAL, determiners, and derivational affixes. The nominal (NOM) prefixes are essentially singular and plural markers. The demonstratives (DEM) are determiners, placing them into the category of early system morphemes. The derivational morphemes are a third type of early system morpheme, one of which is the HABITUAL marker (HAB), an aspectual morpheme, which sets Sheng clearly apart from Swahili. The late system morpheme convergence in Sheng is evident from the Adjective (ADJ), Subject (SUB), Object (OBJ), Possessive (POSS) and Relatives (REL) affixes, which are all agreement markers. Late outsider morphemes receive information for their form beyond the head of their maximal projections. The Prepositional (PREP) prefixes are late bridge system morphemes for they are conjoiners.

The examples in (15) to (17) show the agreement affixes of one noun class indexing the nominals of another. Whereas standard Swahili requires the *ya-* SUB prefix, Sheng uses *zi-*, the CL10 SUB as in (15):

(15) CL6 NOM with CL10 SUB

u-me-vut-a rosta mpaka **ma**-cho **zi**-me-kuwa hivi[12]
2SG/SUB- hemp PREP CL6-eye C10/SUB- ADV of
PRES PER- until PRES PER- manner
pull-FV BE

'You have smoked pot until your eyes have become this way.'

[12] All examples for Sheng are taken from Rudd (2008).

Examples (16)–(17) demonstrate the conflation occurring in Sheng, as CL7-8 is being marked by the CL9-10 affixes. The modifier in (16) is marked with a zero affix in Sheng, but in Swahili it would be prefixed with a CL7 concord (*ki-*).

(16)   CL7 NOM with CL10 ADJ

Alafu	u-na-ju-a	**ki**-tu	ø-moja[13]
ADV/then	2SG/SUB-NONPST-know-FV	CL7-thing	CL9-one

Halafu unajua kitu **ki**moja. (Swahili)

'Then you know one thing.'

(17)   CL8 NOM with CL10 DEM & SUB

Mlami	ni	mlami.Si	huko	ndio	**hizo**	vi-tu	zi-li-tok-e-a.
CL1/ADJ-tar	COP	CL1/ADJ-tar	NEG/COP	DEM/LOC	EMP/DEM	CL10/DEM	CL8/NOM	CL10/SUB-PST-come from-APPL-FV

Mzungu ni mzungu. Si huko ndiko hivyo vitu vilitokea.

'A whiteman is a whiteman. That place indeed is where those things came from.'

In Example (17), we see the CL 10 demonstrative *hizo* and the N-N SUB marker *zi-* co-indexing nouns of the *ki-vi* class, signalling that the early system morpheme and late outsider system morpheme of CL7-8 have lost productivity in Sheng and are being replaced.

Another category of an early system morpheme in Sheng is the habitual marker, which is the only deviation from the derived verbal affix paradigm of Standard Swahili. Sheng has the *hu*-prefix of Swahili but it also uses one of its own suffixes, which it prefers two-thirds of the time. An illustration of HAB *-a (n)g* usage[14] in Sheng follows. The suffix in (18) shows the progressive sense of the Bahati (BB3) subjects' (CL2, 3PL) current desire/habit.

(18)

Na	siku hizi	vile	wa-na-pend-**ag**-a	hiyo	ø-game
CONJ/and	CL10/NOM-CL1/NOM-day-CL10/DEM/these/ADV/TIME	CL8/DEM/ADV/MANNER	3PL-NONPST-like-DER-FV	CL9/DEM	CL9/NOM/game

'na siku hizi vile **hu**penda huo mchezo'. (Swahili)

And nowadays the way they love that game.

---

[13] Numerals 1–5 and 8 in Swahili are prefixed as adjectives and must be in agreement with the noun.

[14] A relic of *-ang-* is found in the Swahili verb *kufinyanga* 'to knead' which likely derived from *kufinya* 'to pinch'. Its alternate *-ag-* form is in *kumwaga* 'to spill' and *kukanyaga* 'to tread on'. Polomé (1967: 77–78) claims this is actually the ultimate source of the Swahili nominal derivational suffix *-aji* as in *mwindaji* 'hunter' from *kuwinda* 'to hunt'.

The -a(n)g- in (18) too seems to add to the sense of the continuous earnestness of the footballers when it comes to playing. That this affix has salience[15] over the native Swahili prefix is indicated not only by Sheng speakers' choice to employ it but also by its imposition[16] as a documented transfer[17] into non-standardized varieties of the non-bantu language Luo,[18] demonstrating that the external ecological factor of frequency makes it unmarked. HAB selection in Sheng reflects the paragon of the intermediate ecological level of contact–choice.

Subject, Object, Possessive, and Relativizer affixes are late outsider system morphemes because they mark agreement with elements outside of their immediate constituents. NOM, DEM, and HAB are early system morphemes, but what has not been explained yet in this exploration of Sheng's system morphemes is the set of concords found in the last two examples. No *ka-* or *tu-* concordial prefix, as seen in (19) and (20), exists in the paradigm of Standard Swahili. These two concord markers form the nominal class CL12–13, which no longer exists in Swahili. Nurse and Hinnebusch (1993: 338–339) reconstruct only CL12 for Proto-Northeast Coast (PNEC) Bantu, as CL13 had already been replaced at that point by CL8 (Contini-Morava 1994).

(19) Sasa   u-na-**ka**-on-a   **ka**-ki-tu   **ka**-dogo   huku.
      ADV   2SG-NONPST-   CL12/NOM-   CL12/ADJ-   DEM/LOC
              CL12/OBJ-see-FV   CL7/NOM-thing   small   this here
      'Now you see it, a small thing here.'

(20) Huu   mzee   ana   **tu**-ndevu hu-peleka hii   ndiga yake   mdogo mdogo
      3SG/CL3 old   has   CL13-   HAB-   CL9/   car   CL9/   CL9/   CL9/
      DEM   person   beard   convey   DEM   POSS   slow   slow
      'This man with the small beard drives this car of his slowly.'

The *ka-tu* class (CL12–13), the subsystem of diminutive markers, whose function has been taken over by CL7–8 in Swahili, is found in the Thagicu and Masaba–Luhya subgroups of Bantu. Sheng, like most of the Bantu languages of Kenya today, has the *ka-tu* subsystem in its agreement marker system. In (19), *ka-* is employed as OBJ in *unakaona* 'you see it', NOM in *kakitu* 'thing' and ADJ in *kadogo* 'small'. In (20), *tu-* is used only as a plural noun marker in *tundevu* 'beards'. As this subsystem is truly foreign to Swahili, it provides

---

[15] Prominence has many extra-linguistic determinants, making prediction a daunting task (Hinskens, Auer and Kerswill 2005: 45).

[16] Van Coetsem (1988) contends that the language that imposes on another has an 'agentivity' role.

[17] Second language acquisition studies would employ 'transfer' instead of imposition.

[18] Stafford (1967: 2) illustrates the Luo -ang- use with *Aparo**nga** Maseno* or 'I always remember Maseno'.

evidence that late system morphemes from the embedded language are found in the composite matrix language. Furthermore, this non-convergence towards the standard usage with respect to the diminutive formation in Sheng could be a substrate[19] effect from the Thagicu and Masaba–Luhya languages.

A final point should perhaps be made about OBJ and REL morphemes. Sheng appears to be losing or to have already lost the subsystems of the object prefix and the nominal relative prefix.[20] The code simply juxtaposes two clauses to form a relative clause. 'Good Swahili got on for years without ... ' the *amba-* complementizer (Perrott 1951: 64). Sheng seems to continue that tradition, but takes it a step further. It requires neither a relative pronoun nor a prefix. These system–morpheme surface differences are completely alien to Standard Swahili and demonstrate a new set of well-formedness conditions on the abstract level. Constraints foreign to the set of late outsider morpheme requirements of Standard Swahili indicate that some stage of a matrix language turnover has already occurred in Sheng.

To summarize, Sheng has both foreign early system morphemes and foreign late system morphemes. Because it has a core vocabulary consisting of a nearly half-and-half split (i.e., 52 per cent Swahili and 48 per cent non-Swahili words), because it contains early system morphemes alien to Swahili (e. g., the imperfective *-a(n)g-* suffix) and because it contains late outsider system morphemes alien to Swahili (e. g., the affixes from CL12–13 or *ka-tu* nominal class of diminutives), Sheng can legitimately be called a 'mixed language' from the perspective of morphosyntax as well as lexicon.

8.3.2.3 *Ecological Functions*

As with other urban vernaculars of Africa, it is not easy to define Sheng. The appellation has been claimed to be a blend from Swahili-English (Mazrui 1995: 171). However, a description with more explanatory power is argot reversal, a transposition of the two syllables in English, from *Eng-lish* to *lish-Eng* with a reanalysis of the *li-* as a Bantu CL5 prefix on *Li-Sheng*, which is dropped as it is no longer productive in Swahili. Therefore, the name *Sheng* comes from a transposed version of the colonial language, symbolizing an emergent speech community with a new code that derives its value from neither its origin in colonial administration nor its mother-tongue status for a particular ethnic group.

---

[19] Following Mufwene (2008: 134), we employ the term *substrate* for convenience: 'several speakers sharing the same substrate language or typologically related ones transferred the same features into what would evolve into a new variety'.

[20] We are not claiming that the adverbial relatives of time, manner, and place, of CL16–18, do not exist in Sheng, only that the nominal classes CL1–14 do not generally affix REL particles onto verbs.

Paradoxically, Swahili, the national language, was a communicative hindrance both for the poor and the elite in the country. The nouveaux riches would have had a mastery of English, while the *wananchi* 'citizens' would have spoken mostly one or more of the local indigenous languages. Even though there had long been an unavoidable, definite, and widespread use of Swahili as an interethnic mode of communication, these exchanges had been on a rather basic level with much interference from the speakers' first languages, as emphasis was on communicating in any way rather than abiding strictly to Swahili norms of grammaticality (Harries 1976: 160). Moreover, more of the higher-level civil service positions required literacy in English and were occupied predominantly by educated Kikuyu speakers, giving them motivation to promote English (Parkin 1977: 204; Laitin and Eastman 1989: 52). An amendment in 1975 solved the problem for the elite by making parliamentary proceedings bilingual, permitting the use of either English or Swahili (Mbaabu 1996: 137).

That Kenyans were uncertain about Swahili is reinforced by the fact the national language remained neither a testable nor a compulsory subject on the national examinations for primary and secondary schools until 1985.[21] In that year, Swahili finally reached some true political status across the nation and began to be required for social advancement. But the twenty-two-year interim from 1963, the year of Independence, to 1985 was also the genesis of Kenya's first truly independent, postcolonial generation, and these *wananchi* had had little or no schooling in Standard Swahili. This educational lapse halted any potential or de facto advergence[22] of Upcountry Swahili towards Standard Swahili in Nairobi and in Kenya in general; furthermore, it was an incubatory time leading to the emergence of a new identity, that of the modern Kenyan urbanite. Sheng resolved the issue for the *wananchi*.

8.4   Mixed Languages vs. Language Mixing and Linguistic Ecology

A question which is frequently raised when mixed languages are discussed is whether they are separate languages or should be regarded as instances of code-switching. However, as is pointed out by Kriegel, Ludwig and Henri (2009: 206): 'La terminologie du code-switching est l'objet d'un vaste débat, et les différentes définitions sont loin de faire

---

[21] The educational system of the new country was revamped, moving from a British to an American format, i.e., an 8–4–4 system in which education levels consist of eight years of primary, four of secondary, and four of university.

[22] This term is what Mattheier (1996), as cited in Hinskens, Auer, and Kerswill (2005: 2), uses to describe levelling or convergence towards a prestige variety, what Hock (1991) refers to as unidirectional convergence.

l'unanimité'[23] (see also Chapter 7, this volume). Frequently, code-switching is confused with or distinguished from concepts such as *code-mixing, language attrition, and borrowing/copying*. Myers-Scotton (2006b) also uses the concepts of *matrix language* and *embedded language* adopted in this chapter.

For the languages discussed in this chapter, we find that Ludwig, Henri, and Bruneau-Ludwig (2009) provide an interesting model for how they can be described. Along with them, we submit that these phenomena can be referred to as 'code hybridization':

> Nous partons donc du principe que les formes d'HYBRIDATION CODIQUE (terme impliquant le contact entre éléments linguistiques des deux langues/codes à l'intérieur d'un même texte) s'échelonnent entre deux pôles: l'ALTERNANCE systémique équi-librée – en fonction de laquelle des parties textuelles réalisées dans des codes différents alternent sans qu'il y ait hiérarchisation et fusion systémique – d'une part, et la fusion systémique et cognitive d'une microscopie d'autre part. (Ludwig, Henri and Bruneau-Ludwig 2009: 178)

> [We assume that forms of code hybridation (a term implying contact between linguistic elements of the two languages/codes within the same text) are spread between two poles: balanced system alternation – where the parts of the text in the different codes alternate without any form of hierarchy or systemic fusion – on the one hand, and systemic and cognitive fusion of a microscopy on the other. (our translation)]

In many ways this is similar to what has already been suggested by Rudd (2008: 86–87). Hence, one could situate Sheng and Camfranglais on a con-tinuum of bilingual speech from (1) classic code-switching to (5) fully crystal-lized mixed languages, as articulated in Table 8.4.

Development into a fully crystallized mixed language (Deumert 2005), though by no means certain, appears to proceed through five stages (Table 8.4). Both Auer's (1999) 'fused-lect' vision and Myers-Scotton's (2002) 'split-language' perspective assert that crystallization of code-switching allows the emergence of a new mixed language. Myers-Scotton (2002: 244) stresses that this grammaticalization be of late outsider system morphemes.

What can be concluded from this survey of languages is that the morpho-syntactic frame of a mixed language is a composite matrix language. This conclusion does not exclude Anglo-Romani and Ma'a for these languages include foreign late system morphemes. All late system morphemes in Anglo-Romani and in Ma'a are non-Romani and non-Cushitic respectively. The hypothesis remains testable for emerging mixed languages, such as Camfranglais and Sheng. Convergence creates a new morphosyntactic frame,

---

[23] 'The terminology of code-switching has been widely debated and there is no general agreement on how to define the term' (our translation).

Table 8.4 *Mixed Language Metamorphosis*

Stage	Examples	Pragmatics
		↓
1 Classic code-switching		↓
both intersentential &	El Barrio (Zentella 1997)	↓
intrasentential CS	Campus Swahili (Blommaert 1992)	↓
Serve a stylistic/rhetorical role		↓
2 Code-switching 1		↓
CS = unmarked choice	Turkish–Danish (Backus 2003)	↓
CS loses its social/stylistic role	Italoschwyz (Francheschini 1998)	↓
3 Code-switching 2		↓
More intrasentential CS	?	↓
Less intersentential CS	Kombuistaal (McCormick 2002)	↓
Some core vocabulary loans		↓
4 Incipient mixed language		↓
Fossilization of structures	Malti (Stolz 2003)	↓
Lexicon not yet quite 90%	Sinti Romani (Auer 1999)	↓
	Sheng; **Camfranglais**	↓
5 Fully crystallized mixed language	Petjo (Rheeden 1994)	↓
Lexicon–grammar bifurcation	Anglo-Romani (Thomason 2001a)	↓
Core vocabulary near 90%	Michif (Bakker 1997)	↓
Matrix-language turnover	Media Lengua (Muysken 1994)	↓
		↓
		Grammaticality

(Diagram taken from Rudd 2008: 87, adapted from Deumert 2005: 127)

and this reconfiguration is the method through which foreign system morphemes can enter a language. Myers-Scotton (2003: 244–245) states that the presence of late system morphemes is an indication of the start of a matrix language turnover. Moreover, fossilizations of turnovers can be plotted along a continuum from just a few morphemes to a whole morphosyntactic frame in its entirety. Any mixed language can be situated on a continuum of bilingual speech. Progression along this cline results from declining pragmatic use of code-switching due to ever-increasing grammaticalization. Classic code-switching, intrasentential, and intersentential, is primarily a pragmatic choice while 'composite code-switching' has the beginnings of grammaticalization. Composite code-switching (Myers-Scotton 2003: 105), which results from language convergence or language shift, manifests a bilingual complementizer phrase whose morphosyntax is a composite, meaning it has dual parentage. Smith (2000) classifies languages such as Camfranglais and Sheng as 'symbiotic mixed languages' and points out that there are two factors which 'qualify these "languages" for this title: a separate ethnic identity ... combined with a different set of basic lexical items' (Smith 2000: 123).

Language ecologies of this type evolve in response to poor language policy and inadequate urban planning, constituting disturbances in the ecological linguistic systems of urban residents and their offspring. Emergent groups or strata form ecologies in which an unmarked language gap separates the community.[24] In Cameroon's urban centres, Camfranglais hybridizes aspects of the indigenous languages, the languages of wider communication, and the two official languages. In Nairobi, speaking homeland languages is considered tribal behaviour, Upcountry Swahili provincial, and English colonial/elitist. Consequently, a new linguistic mix combines all three. In both countries, language mixing is an adaptation to the ecological linguistic niche.

8.5   Conclusion

The two mixed languages we presented in this chapter can clearly be defined as in-group languages whose speakers also know other languages and who are used as indicators of a newly developed and independent group ethnic identity. They display the interdependence/mutual foundation of several ecological parameters laid out in the introductory paper of this volume: linguistic competences, attitudes, and pragmatic functions,[25] as well as social or societal conditions, and structural factors. With such a view, one turns away from looking at the phenomena described as having an effect on the language system (e.g. the lexical or syntactic level) only. One thus proceeds to take into consideration sociolinguistic and ecological aspects and defines 'language' also as 'means of communication' and not just as an abstract system. Hence, language contact phenomena and the mixed languages discussed need to be described both from the perspective of their structural particularities on the various linguistic levels and according to the ecological functions they fulfil or the ecological dimensions by which they are shaped.

Although 'mixed languages do not offer a uniform language type, but are outcomes of diverse mechanisms' (Matras 2000: 96), we believe that the two languages presented here can be taken as similar to linguistic developments observed in other parts of the African continent. As the examples of *Tsotsitaal* in South Africa (see Slabbert 1994; Msimang 1987), *Hybridized English* in Ghana (see Ahulu 1995), and *Nouchi* in Ivory Coast (see Kube 2005) possibly indicate, similar ecologies of multilingual and multiethnic urban settings in

---

[24] 'Only the city, in Africa at least,' writes Mufwene (2008: 217), 'has come close to reducing them [ethnic languages and identities], acting like sugarcane plantations and rice fields of the Atlantic and Indian Ocean settlement colonies'.

[25] E.g. in the sense of Coulmas (2005: 171): 'A basic tenet of sociolinguistics is that language displays its speakers' identity', or Tabouret-Keller (1997: 315): 'The language spoken by somebody and his or her identity as a speaker of this language are inseparable: This is surely a piece of knowledge as old as human speech itself.'

developing African states seem to trigger comparable linguistic choices and developments. However, it must be kept in mind that

die in einem konkreten interkulturellen Milieu auftretenden Sprachkontaktphänomene in ihrer Gesamtheit ein einmaliges und damit lokal-spezifisches Gepräge aufweisen, und daß ein Vergleich mit anderen Kontaktphänomenen nur Ähnlichkeiten, aber keine Identitäten aufweisen kann. (Haarmann 1996: 845)

[that language contact phenomena occurring in one specific intercultural environment are unique to and entirely characteristic of this locally determined situation and that a comparison with other contact phenomena may only exhibit similarities without being identical. (our translation)]

Finally, as any linguistic structure may be copied, it is specific social and discourse–pragmatic parameters within the complex ecology of a language in contact that govern the linguistic choices of its speakers. Thus, we have examined the linguistic choices of the mixed codes in two urban African ecologies – each filling its own ecological niche.

9 Hybrid Speech of Francophone Groups in Cairo: from Macro-level Ecology to Discourse

Cynthia Dermarkar, Françoise Gadet, Ralph Ludwig, and Stefan Pfänder

9.1 Introduction: Linguistic Ecology as a Historically Founded Hierarchy of *Parts of a Whole* – from Macro-ecology to Discourse Ecology

Urban discourse, communication, and language contact in metropolises have come to the fore of linguistic and anthropological research in a world increasingly governed by the competing dynamics of globalization and individualization.[1] The need for mediating between traditionalism and modernity, group identity and cosmopolitanism is especially felt in metropolitan areas.

This chapter will show that the urban discourse of Cairo presents an excellent field of application for the ecological linguistic approach advocated in this volume. In Chapter 1 of this volume, Ludwig, Mühlhäusler, and Pagel explain their central ideas regarding linguistic ecology. Among these are the conceptions (based on ideas by Edmund Husserl) of linguistic ecology as an integrated whole, constituted by individual parts, and that of the interrelation or reciprocal 'foundation' of parts and wholes (Husserl 1913). Ludwig, Mühlhäusler, and Pagel propose a three-level model of linguistic ecology in which individual speech situations rank as the basic or micro-ecological level. They tie in with Goffman's 'encounter' (as a 'micro-ecological orbit', 1964: 133) and Hymes's (1972/1986) 'speech event' here. The opposite pole is constituted by the macro-ecology representing large cultural, social and historical entities, a dimension highlighted by Mufwene and Vigouroux (2012). Ludwig, Mühlhäusler, and Pagel propose an intermediate step and the integration of these three in a hierarchical model (Figure 1.1 in Chapter 1), which is basically in accordance also with contemporary models in biological ecology (see Begon, Townsend, and Harper 2006).

The social and linguistic relevance of the intermediate level and the mutual foundation relations between the three ecological levels are focused on in the

---

[1] For the sociology of the city in general, see, e.g. Castells (1975), Hannerz (1980), Calvet (1994), and Parker (2004). For urban linguistics and urban language contact in Latin America, see Chapter 4, this volume; Ludwig (2002); for the linguistic situation in London and in multicultural Paris, see Gadet and Guerin (2012). For the theoretical classification of metropolises as 'aires communicatives', see Gadet, Ludwig, and Pfänder (2009).

present chapter. In order to do so we will apply a discourse–analytical method to corpus data.

In accordance with the overall framework of this volume laid out in the first chapter, we will use the following terms to describe contact-linguistic phenomena: *alternation* for a 'switch' between two code systems and *copy* for the 'transmission' of an element from code A into code B. In the latter case, we distinguish between *overt copies* (phonetic encoding and lexical–semantic and/or structural–grammatical information copied) and *covert copies* (only lexical–semantic and/or structural–grammatical information copied).[2]

Let us start with the concept of the vertical, part-of-a-whole hierarchy. We argue that urban communication in Cairo cannot be understood without taking into account its historical macro level: the linguistic and cultural area of the Levant in the sense of Braudel's historical approach (1981–1982).[3] A fundamental tenet of the present chapter is that *the Levant functions as the macro ecology in which the linguistic systems and strategies of multilingual speakers in Cairo are grounded.* Cairo with its various groups of speakers thus constitutes an intermediate level of linguistic ecology in which the discrete communicative interactions are embedded. The latter constitute the basic or micro-level, as is shown in Figure 9.1 which takes up the model of linguistic ecology from Chapter 1, this volume; the horizontal arrows represent correspondences to other entities on the same level (e.g., in the case of this chapter, Levant-European francophony):

So far, we have been following a top-down direction in describing the linguistic evolution from the macro to the micro-level. In an analysis, however, a bottom-up approach should be given priority. All linguistic choices, strategies, patterns, and acts of identity have their place in the concrete speech situation, in the current dialogue. Linguistic ecological relations of foundation with intermediate and macro levels can only be ascertained from dialogical manifestations. You could even say that intermediate and macro-levels are produced and reproduced primarily in, by, and through discourse. As far as this vertical axis is concerned, the following question arises: is the current discourse ecology of Cairo based exclusively on the conventional historical macro-ecology or are influences of additional or alternative macro factors becoming apparent today?

In an ecological perspective, reciprocal relations emerge both between linguistic forms and functions and between (supra)national norms and diverse

---

[2] For the case of *material copy*, which is of lesser importance for the analysis of this chapter, see Kriegel, Ludwig and Salzmann (this volume).

[3] Lately, the notions *Levant* and *Levantine* have gone out of favour due to negative connotations originating from the colonial era. For the history of the term see Aslanov (2006a: 13-16, and in this volume).

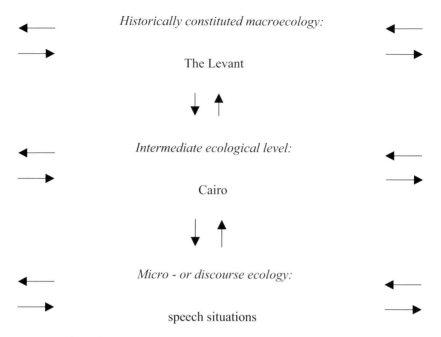

Figure 9.1 Three-level model of linguistic ecology

discourse strategies. Considering the plurality of social groups that is characteristic of contemporary metropolises, manifold interdependencies emerge.
Some parameters will turn out to be the most relevant in relation to the
conversations recorded in Cairo: the contact of various languages and
varieties, religion, social group, social class, social network, age, and gender.
The following analysis will focus on precisely these parameters.

Our tentative hypotheses for this analysis are the following:

1 The contemporary linguistic behaviour of Levantine francophones, their
  choice of register as well as the strategies of linguistic hybridization, is
  understandable only in its foundation in a historically based macro-ecology.
2 Francophone speakers in Cairo constitute an intermediate ecology, a heterogeneous environment hosting diverse social groupings whose speech
  behaviour is conditioned by various partly competing factors, such as
  group-formation, opening up towards other groups, in combination with
  varying linguistic competences in the codes used.
3 Depending on group affiliation, the linguistic behaviour in francophone
  Cairo encompasses contrasting strategies ranging from the poles of herme-
  tism/esoterism (Ludwig and Schwarze 2006; Chapter 1, this volume) to
  hybridization/exoterism (Kriegel, Ludwig, and Henri 2009). This range

explains two contrasted attitudes of societies in language contact: language communities can be more, or less, open to language contact; they can absorb or reject stimuli from contact situations. Moderate forms of hermetism/esoterism have been known in Europe through the different purist movements since the sixteenth century.

4 The contemporary linguistic intermediate ecology of Cairo goes beyond this historical foundation, if we take into account the role of English as a lingua franca, both historically and currently, with its additional impact on linguistic strategies within the complex environment.

The following section addresses aspects of the first hypothesis, namely the constitution of the historical macro-ecology.

9.2   The Levant Considered as a Macro-ecology: a Brief Overview

The countries of the eastern Mediterranean, referred to as *the Levant*, followed the evolution of Latin and later stages of Romanization without themselves being part of *the Romania* in the traditional sense of the term (Tagliavini 1982), i.e. historically Romance-speaking Europe. Around the beginning of the Common Era, a multitude of varieties of Latin must have been in use in the provinces of Syria, Palestine, and Egypt. Roughly a thousand years later a clash of cultures took place when the first armies of crusaders from western Europe arrived around 1096. During the roughly two hundred years in which crusader states existed, intensive contact of more than one 'oriental language' with several European languages took place. In fact, we have to imagine the Middle East in the eleventh and twelfth centuries as a conglomerate of polyglot petty states. Together they formed a linguistic landscape in which native speakers of Greek, Armenian, Arabic, and Coptic encountered foreigners, primarily soldiers and tradesmen, who brought with them a colourful mix of different varieties of vulgar Romance: the most widespread were the *parlers d'oïl*, followed by the Italo-Romance dialects, as well as Occitan and Catalan varieties (Aslanov 2006a).

A consistent Levantine French did not exist then. Most likely, the conception of لسان الفرنج (*lisān el faranğ*) = *lingua franca* came about through the predominantly arabophone Orientals calling the languages of all Europeans 'language of the Franks'. Over the centuries, a tightly knit web of trading posts developed along the trade routes of the eastern Mediterranean beginning in the early modern age. It was the zenith for big cities such as Constantinople and Alexandria which absorbed Oriental and European cultures likewise.

French became increasingly important in the Levant under the 'Capitulations' of the Ottoman Empire, a series of bilateral acts contracted from 1500 on to regulate trade relations with Europeans in the Mediterranean.

These endowed the French merchants with concessions and privileges for commerce in the ports under Ottoman control.

When Napoleon Bonaparte's troops and his academic entourage reached Egypt in 1799, the French language had already taken roots there, though it was to remain a marginal variety in the area. That expedition, which ended in 1801 in a military fiasco after three years, was clearly more successful in the cultural domain. Educational, archaeological, and scientific institutions established during that period were intended to bring the French language and culture home to the Egyptians. The Ottoman Vice Roy, Muhammad Ali, who reigned in Egypt from 1805 to 1848, sought to import western knowledge to modernize the country, thus providing continuity and cultivating an intensive exchange with France.[4]

Today, the most widespread foreign language in Egypt is English. This occurred despite the fact that the Anglicization of Egypt had barely begun after the British occupation (1882–1922) in the 1930s,[5] as the occupying force did not succeed in imposing its culture in the country. In his *Dictionnaire amoureux de l'Égypte*, Robert Solé is surprised to find that the British colonial administration did not take notice of the Egyptian elite: 'Curieusement, la Grande-Bretagne néglige les élites égyptiennes' (2006: 187 and the chapter 'Occupation britannique', 338–340), and a contemporary observer summarizes the situation as follows:

En Égypte, l'Angleterre avait une armée, les Français avaient une idée. L'Angleterre occupait le pays, la France avait une philosophie claire en matière d'éducation ... ce qui n'était pas le cas des anglais, le crayon français a toujours été plus puissant que l'épée anglaise. (quoted from Gérard-Plasmans 2005: 251)

[In Egypt, Britain had an army, the French had an idea. Britain occupied the country, the French had a clear philosophy in terms of education ... which wasn't the case for the British, the French pencil has always been more powerful than the British sword. (our translation)]

In the course of the nationalist movement, politically acted out in the revolution of 1952 and especially in the Suez crisis 1956, the colonial languages, namely French, Italian and English as the most prominent ones, were suppressed as 'politically undesirable' by the regime.

It was not until the second half of the twentieth century that competition from the English language set in and Arabic became increasingly important in the course of the nationalist movement for independence. Not until the 1970s,

---

[4] For the cultural impact of the Napoleonic expedition, see Solé (2006: 303–336).
[5] See also the chapters in Solé (2006) on the school system in Egypt at the beginning of the twentieth century (ibid.: p. 100), the impact of the Entente Cordiale of 1904 (ibid.: p. 137), and the passage about the 'Guerre des langues' (ibid.: p. 245).

when Egypt opened up to the West, did the influence of American culture and language on public life gather pace. English continues to thrive due to the strong American presence in cultural media: in music, television, and cinema.

Today, in the early twenty-first century, French is still holding its ground in the big urban centres of Cairo and Alexandria as the language of a middle class conscious of their family tradition and education.[6]

9.3 Francophone Groups in Cairo Today as an Intermediate Ecology

9.3.1 Demography and Social Framework

In its latest statistical update 2010, the Organisation Internationale de la Francophonie (OIF) counted a proportion of 0.4 per cent of French speakers in the total population of Egypt (84.5 million inhabitants; OIF 2010: 14). While this ratio has remained unchanged since the previous survey (total population 74 million in 2005; OIF 2007: 16), the category *partially francophones* recorded a slight increase from 2.8 per cent to 3 per cent (2.5 million, corresponding to an increase of roughly 0.5 million) over the five-year period. This development can be attributed to the support programmes provided by the French government that range from sponsoring schools, founding universities as well as subsidizing cultural institutes with their local branches in the provinces.[7]

French degree programmes, which were implemented at Egyptian universities a couple of years ago, tie in with the traditional and long-standing educational possibilities offered at the schools. The *Centre Culturel CFCC* provides significant outreach for French culture with its language courses, libraries and theatre and film performances.

Of the formerly rich printed media landscape one Egyptian French newspaper has survived despite diminishing readership: *Ahram Hebdo*, the French equivalent of *Ahram Weekly*, supervened in the 1990s, and is holding its ground thanks to subsidies from the big Arabic newspaper of the same name. In this case, readership is not decreasing because the francophone population of Egypt is dwindling, but rather because of readers' predilection for electronic

---

[6] For the cultural motivations of language choice during the inter-war period, see Gérard-Plasmans (2005). For an account of the social ranking of non-Arabic languages in present-day Egypt, see Dermarkar and Pfänder (2010: 16–20).

[7] For an overview of official French activities in Egypt, see the website of the French embassy in Egypt, 'La France en Égypte'. The 'Atlas français de la coopération décentralisée et des autres actions extérieures', s.v. 'Egypte', lists all current projects on the regional and communal scale as well as a table revealing that the subsidies have been considerably cut down owing to the political upheaval since 2010.

media to access information, as for example the Cairo issue of the international online newspaper *Le Petit Journal* (www.lepetitjournal.com).[8]

The TV station *Nile International* has several time slots where news and documentaries are broadcast in French, alternating with English programmes, for instance, 'Bonjour l'Egypte, Revue de presse, Autour du monde'. The channel's website is trilingual: English, French, and Hebrew (http://nileinternational.net). A very successful experiment is *La Radio du Lycée Français du Caire,* broadcast by the students themselves from the school's own studio. The archive on the website of the radio transmitter accumulated since 2005 is very extensive (www.radiolfc.net).

The high demand for local labour with expertise in French by the branch offices of firms from France and Québec cannot be ignored. The prestige of these job positions again increases the stimulus to learn French. This assessment is consistent with the OIF 2010 report, which observes an increasing educational commitment to French due to economic advantages, to complement, as it were, the Anglo-Saxon option (OIF 2010: 112–115).

Éducation is a central term in the value system of francophone Egyptians. Education is a key concept for professional success and social advancement. Several of our respondents led us to understand that they see the mastery of one or more world languages as a 'back-up' in view of the precarious political future of the country.

9.3.2   Speaker Attitudes and Strategies of Interaction: General Features and Hypotheses

Ecologically, certain speaker attitudes and strategies of interaction of the francophone population of Cairo become apparent in their discourse, as articulated in the examples discussed below. We can distinguish two groups: traditionalists and innovators, according to their different attitudes towards language usage.[9]

The traditionalists have a native-speaker-like competence in French with two conspicuous features. Their French falls clearly within the Levantine tradition. Distinctive characteristics include a slower tempo than European speakers tend to have, a trilled apical /r/ and prosodic peculiarities that reflect

---

[8] The time-honoured French-language newspaper, *Le Progrès Égyptien,* founded in 1893, has ceased to appear in print, instead it has shifted to an up-to-date Internet presence on Facebook (checked 30 December 2016).

[9] The 'traditionalists' vs. 'innovators' dichotomy replaces the former distinction between *anciens* and *modernes* used in our earlier publications not only to avoid allusions to the historical literary *querelle*, but also because we agree that these terms describe the nature of the contrast more accurately.

a long-time Arabic influence.[10] This group shares a 'conservative' linguistic attitude, especially as regards the specific contact situation in Cairo: its speakers seem to systematically avoid copies from Arabic or from English, the more recent of the two contact languages.

The innovators are more difficult to pinpoint, given that they feature a number of tendencies, one of which being, at least in some cases, a decreasing proficiency in French. Rather than adhering to the Levantine type of pronunciation, they tend to aim at the Parisian style. In many cases these speakers have been affected by the discontinuity in the tradition of French in Egypt as a result of the Suez crisis in 1956 with all its political consequences, such as the banning of foreign languages from school curricula and the expulsion of all foreigners, including Egyptians of foreign descent. Their usage of French includes extensive code alternation and copying from Arabic such as the covert syntactic copy *mon frère il travaille officier de police* ('my brother he works Ø police officer').[11]

Francophone speakers in Cairo in general can be further characterized with respect to the parameters mentioned in section 9.1. We first explain these parameters in relation to the francophone social groups in Cairo. The specific consequences regarding their linguistic competences, choices, and strategies will be demonstrated in the examples in section 9.4.

- *Contact of various languages and varieties*: altogether French has the status of a language of ethnic minorities in Cairo, the dominant contact languages being Egyptian Arabic and English. By dominant contact languages we mean languages that are well represented (socially and demographically) in the contact constellation and which can thus potentially induce language change.[12]
- *Religion*: formerly, French was spoken primarily in the various Christian communities of Egypt, whereas nowadays the percentage of Muslim 'innovators' is clearly increasing. The confessional distinction among those

[10] A systematic study of the prosodic features in Levantine French has as yet remained completely unexplored, which leaves us with these dissatisfyingly few terms to describe its peculiarities.
[11] This and all the examples given in this chapter are taken from the corpus of Dermarkar and Pfänder (2010), collected within the framework of the project CIEL-F (Corpus International Écologique de la Langue Française). The recordings are available online in the database: www.ciel-f.org. For a report of the project, see Gadet et al. (2012). Several instances of copies formed after the same model are quoted in Solé's *Dictionnaire amoureux de l'Égypte*: 'on *travaille comptable* (ou ingénieur), on *laisse cadeau* un objet, on *habille* son veston, ou plutôt sa *jaquette*' (2006: 186, original italics).
[12] Non-dominant contact languages in Cairo are for example Armenian, Italian, and German, and in Alexandria also Greek: these languages are unlikely to influence the social extension or structural form of the 'larger' languages in the area, i.e. Arabic or French. For the conceptual difference between dominant and non-dominant contact languages see also Gadet, Ludwig, and Pfänder (2009).

younger group members seems to be dissolving. So we can presume that it is still observable in the speech of some speakers, though gradually losing its social relevance.

- *Social group/class/social network*:[13] the francophone population is markedly educated middle class. In particular the 'traditionalists' like to point out that they are descendants of the 'old bourgeoisie', such as the families of the former Ottoman dignitaries.

- *Age*: in principle the average 'innovators' are younger than the 'traditionalists'. However, even children can be assigned to the latter, if they are raised in a corresponding traditionally oriented, francophone household.

- *Gender*: a significant number of respondents told us that there seems to be an implicit understanding that girls go through a francophone school education whereas boys (even of the same family) attend British or American schools. See for example the statement of an experienced school secretary in a French Lycée:

```
01   MY      il y a une conception depuis tout le temps . le francais
             c'était la langue du salon . le francais c'est la langue pour
             les jeunes filles . l'anglais c'était pour les garçons parce
             que c'est la langue des affaires . et ça ça ... c'était l'idée
             qui existe depuis longtemps .

        [translation Dermarkar and Pfänder (2010): 80: 'there has always been
        a conception: French was the language of the 'salon'. French is the
        language for young girls. English was for boys because it is the
        language of business. And that was the idea that has always
        existed.']
```

9.4   Discourse Ecology

9.4.1   *Discourse as Place of Production and Reproduction of Communicative and Social Positioning*

Now we will turn to the question of the way ecological levels and parameters and their implicit discourse strategies manifest themselves in communicative acts (see especially hypotheses 3 and 4). We have already emphasized that communication embedded in situations is the place where linguistic resources are mobilized and selected, and also where social bonding and social boundaries are produced and reproduced. In the following, this concept will be developed in a detailed comparative study of three different conversation excerpts. A number of precise questions need to be answered.

---

[13] For applications of the sociological concept of *social network*, see e.g. Milroy and Wei (1995). For a recent application of social network analysis to urban discourse and contact, see Salzmann (2014).

- Can the formation of the higher ecological levels, which have been postulated by means of a historical and language-external approach, be substantiated at the micro level, i.e. in the current dialogue?
- Can any clues be found that would question, correct, and/or broaden the categorizations outlined so far?
- Is the potential linguistic–cultural contact ecology of Cairo (and more precisely of the francophone groups) realized through hermetic or rather hybridization strategies?
- What other communicative–textual functions do certain French language resources and hybridizations fulfil?
- What cognitive parameters intervene in the intermediate or – more manifest – in the micro level? Specifically: what communicative impact may linguistic competence have? What is the impact of differences in linguistic competence when there are several participants in a conversation?

9.4.2   French as an Unbroken Levantine Tradition

Transcription

The following transcript reproduces a narrative passage from a conversation with an elderly gentleman who recounts his life. An interlinear English translation is provided for both the French and the Arabic parts.

SPEAKERS: Pierre (PI), aged 71; Cynthia (CY); primary competence in French and Arabic (and several other languages)
DATE: 22.11.2007
PLACE: At his home, living room

```
2   CY      e:t vous êtes donc de: famille syro-libanaise
    [transl. so you are from a Syro-Lebanese family]

3   PI      je suis de famille s' MOI(.) syriENNE
    [transl. I am from a family me Syrian]

4   PI      mais ça aurait pu être aussi syro-libanAISe parce que les
            deu:x=ethnies se:
    [transl. but it could also have been Syro-Lebanese because the two
            ethnic groups]

5   PI      écoutez c'est la même lANgue la même gastronoMIE la m'
            pratiquement la même religion malgré (les)
    [transl. listen it is the same language the same cuisine the s/
            practically the same religion despite (the)]

6   PI      la mosaïque de RITes
    [transl. the mosaic of rites]

7   PI      euh de chrétiens orientaux etcétéra
    [transl. of the Oriental Christians etc.]

8   PI      e::t 'voilà. (1,0)
    [transl. and that's how]
```

```
 9     PI      c'est comme ça mais MOI écoutez(.) mon cas est un peu unIQue
        [transl. it is like this but me listen. my case is somewhat unique]

10     PI      euh j'ai beaucoup aimé le lANgues donc j'ai fait carrière
                dans l'amba' l'ambassade d'EspAgne
        [transl. I loved languages a lot so I made a career at the Spanish
                embassy]

11     PI      dans la: hh traductiO:n
        [transl. in translation]

12     PI      l'interprétariAt?=mais pas(.) pas beaucoup ou pas du tOUt?
                l'interprétariat de cabINe (et) la consécutive etcétéra?
        [transl. translation but not (.) not much or not at all simultaneous
                translation in the booth(and) consecutive, etc.]

13     PI      et::
        [transl. and]

14     PI      la traduction surtOUt?
        [transl. mostly translation]

15     PI      et voilÀ;
        [transl. and so]

16     PI      et maintenant je me repose Cynthia. (laughs)
        [transl. and now I am relaxing C.]

17     CY      c'est bien?
        [transl. that's fine]

18     PI      (laughs)

19     CY      vous avez l'air reposÉ aussi
        [transl. you look relaxed too]

20     PI      il faut bien se reposer (à) un moment donné dans la vIE
        [transl. you have to rest at some point in your life]

21     PI      'oui ou non;
        [transl. yes or no]

22     CY      mais oui
        [transl. yes (certainly)]

23     PI      e:t je regrette beaucOUp de n'avoir pas appris deux langues
                de n'avoir pas ajouté deux langues à ma
        [transl. and I very much regret not having learned two languages not
                having added two languages to my]

24     PI      à ma hARPe de langues (...)
        [transl. to my harp of languages]

25     PI      c'est le tURque?(.) et le hongrOIs.
        [transl. that is Turkish and Hungarian]
```

Analysis

Speaker Pierre is of Syrian descent but was born in Cairo; the conversation takes place at his home in Cairo, and he talks about his active professional life as a translator at the Spanish embassy. This speaker can be assigned to the group of 'traditionalists'. Three characteristics are especially evident. The variety he uses bears all the features of Levantine French, such as the specific prosody, speech tempo, trilled apical /r/, all of which are not apparent in the purely orthographic transcript, but are clearly noticeable in the recordings (see n. 11). Morphosyntactically, negation with the particle *ne,* as in line 23 *(de n'avoir pas),* is still productive in contemporary Egyptian French, whereas it has almost disappeared in the European varieties.

Moreover, the word order in the same example, *de n'avoir pas* (l. 23) is considered refined style in written French and has fallen into disuse. This speaker has a predilection for metaphoric creations that appear archaic, though his style sounds sophisticated, as with *la mosaïque de rites* (ll. 5–6) and *ma harpe de langues* (ll. 23–24). These constructions are clearly marked by the repairs or repetitions that precede the metaphors, viz., *les/la mosaïque* and *à ma/à ma harpe*. Furthermore they are prosodically prepared by a subtle hesitation before he comes to the focal point of the phrase.

To sum up, we observe that the traditionalist speaker takes a markedly hermetic–puristic attitude to position himself within the melange of urban discourse, experienced as excessively influenced by contact phenomena. Speakers in this group tend to confine their usage to the principle of 'one language at a time', probably as a result of an old-style school education and their adherence to ideals of linguistic and stylistic correctness. This means in particular: next to no copies from contact languages, i.e. Arabic or English.

9.4.3 Intermediate Ecology Between Tradition and Accommodation: the Role of Alternation and Hybridization

Transcript

This conversation was recorded during a business lunch in a restaurant on the Nile with three gentlemen and the interviewer. It is an example of how speakers adapt to varying situational conditions. The conversation had so far been conducted in Arabic with occasional alternation with English. Now, the narrator (OM), recalling the interviewer's original interest ('When and with whom do you speak French?'), turns to CY to tell a hunting anecdote in French.

SPEAKERS: Omar (OM), aged 63; Hosni (HO), 60; Bachir (BA), 51; Cynthia (CY)
DATE: 30.10.2007
PLACE: Restaurant on the Nile, noisy surroundings ; business lunch

(reproduced from Dermarkar and Pfänder 2010: 67–71)

```
26    OM       euh <mAr:a 3ala 7ka:yet> ronflement
               [transl. <mAr:a 3ala 7ka:yet = once on story+GEN (,talking of')>
                       snoring]

27    OM       ((towards CY)) les chassEUrs. rOnflent
               [transl. the hunters snore]

28    CY       pourquoi
               [transl. why]

29    OM       jE ne sais pas (.) <by definition/> (.) un chasseur (.)
                       rOnfle
               [transl. I don't know . by definition . a hunter snores]
               [comm.   <by definition/> English pronunciation]

30    OM       bon (1.2)
               [transl. well]

31    HO       donc i(l) y en a deux qui (...)
               [transl. so there are two who <(...)> Arabic intonation,
                       incomprehensible]

32    OM       al(ors) <(...)>
               [transl. so]

33    OM       <fa ana> (.) Ana:/ je ne ronfle pas
               [transl. <fa ana = so I> I/ I don't snore]

34    OM       <kollena wa:hed> [(...) ah non (...) ronfle pas]
               [transl. <kollena = all of us>; <wa7ed = one> oh no(incomplete
                       phrase) don't snore]

35    HO       [ah non pas du tout. a:h=(j')ai très bien dormi. a:h oui]
               [transl. oh no not at all. oh I slept very well. oh yes]

36    OM       <we Hosni we F.> ronflent pas. <we> M. ne ronfle pas.
               [transl. <we ... = and (+ proper names)> don't snore. <we = and> M
                       doesn't snore]

37    OM       alors. quand on avait bâti la: la <estera:7a>-là
               [transl. so when we had built the <estera:7a = resting place>
                       there]

38    OM       on avait dit nous les trois/ on a/ sEpt chambres
               [transl. we said the three of us/ we have (got)/ seven rooms]

39    OM       personne n'approche? on ne ronfle pas? on est ensemble on est
                       heureux? pErsonne n'approche.
               [transl. nobody gets close? we don't snore? we are together we are
                       happy? nobody gets close]

40    OM       alors un jour il y avai:t=euh. un tAs de gens un tas
                       (d'autres invités) ils nous ont dit écoutez vous avez quAtre
                       lits dans votre chambre vous prenez quelqu'Un
               [transl. so one day there were many people many (other guests) they
                       told us listen you have four beds in your room you take
                       somebody with you]
```

```
41   OM      quelqu'un dort avec vOUs. vous êtes trOIs/ à trois il y a
             quatre lits/ quelqu'un dort avec vous.
     [transl. somebody sleeps with you. you are three of you/in a threesome
             there are four beds/ somebody sleeps with you]

42   OM      alors nous les trois on s'est mis à regarder un peu qui était
             là/
     [transl. so we three we started looking a bit who was there]

43   OM      On a trouvé un gOsse/
     [transl. we found a boy]

44   OM      de quinze ans c'est(...)
     [transl. fifteen-year old it is]

45   OM      c'était l'ami de: euh he was he was R'.s friend, T's friend.
             <Sa7ib T.>.
     [transl. it was the friend of (...) <Sahib T. = friend-GEN;SG (name)
             (,the friend of T'.)>]

46   OM      alors on lui a dit/ tOI/ tu viens dormir avec nous
             aujourd'hui. parce qu'il était <petI:t> (i)l était jeune
     [transl. so we told him/ you/ you come to sleep with us today. because
             he was young]
     comm.    <petI:t>: probably synonymous to ‚young', as in Arabic
             Se3'i:r صغير 1. ‘small', 2. ‘young'.

47   OM      (...) va pas ronfler
     [transl. (…) will not snore]

48   OM      alors il s'est mis sur les lits d'en haut/ parce qu'il y
             avait (.) d:EUx lits/ l'un au-dessus de l'autre/
     [transl. so he took the top bunk(s)/ because there were two beds/ one
             over the other]

49   OM      M. dormait toujours (.) [dans le lit d'en dessous/
     [transl. M always slept in the lower bed]
     [comm.   (restaurant phone rings)]

50   OM      lui c'etait le lit là?
     [transl. he it was the bed there]

51   OM      moi dans un côté avec un lit seul. 0
     [transl. me on one side with a bed alone. 0.]

52   OM      onze heures. on est rentrés?14 on s'endort
     [transl. eleven o'clock. we have retired we fall asleep]

53   OM      vingt minutes après vingt-cinq minutes près ils commencent
             vraiment à dormir (.)] et tOUt soudainement/ on entend
             quelqu'un hurler
     [transl. twenty minutes later twenty-five minutes (later) they really
             begin to sleep . and all of a sudden/ we hear someone scream]
```

---

[14] The verb *rentrer* here does not mean 'to go home', as in European French, but 'to retire (to bed)', in this context used as a copy on the Egyptian Arabic model *da7'al(na)*: '(we) went into', i.e. 'went to bed'.

```
54   OM      ((hushed, fading)) <7Ara:mi: 7Ara:mi> (1.1 s)
             [transl. <7Ara:mi = thief-NOM;SG>]

55   OM      on se lève tOUs/ hein/
             [transl. we all get up/ (all right)]

56   OM      chAcun. tire son révolvE:r/
             [transl. everyone draws his gun (revolver)]

57   OM      on allume la lumière?
             [transl. we turn on the light]

58   OM      celui-là. il est debout sur son lit
             [transl. that one. he is standing on his bed]

59   OM      en disant 7ara:mi 7ara:mi 7ara:mi et il s'endort
             [transl. saying thief thief thief and he falls asleep]

60   HO      (il est) somnambUle/
             [transl. (he is) a sleepwalker]

61   OM      ((high-pitched)) ouI
             [transl. yes]

62   HO      ah il était somnambule
             [transl. oh he was sleepwalking]

63   OM      <ba3daha b(e)nous:=sa:3a> (.)
             [transl. <ba3daha b(e)nous:=sa:3a = after this by half an hour>]

64   OM      ((in a high pitched, wailing voice)) <il7a2i:ni ya mA:ma (.)
             ya ma:ma>
             [transl. <ba3daha ... = half an hour later>; <el7a2i:ni ... = save me,
             Mummy! Mummy!>]

65   OM      <el le:l kol:ou (.) ad:enA: 3al=zift dawwat/>
             [transl. <el le:l kol:ou = the whole night> < ad:enA: = we spent>
             <3al=zift dawwat/ = with this plague>]15

66   OM      <we houwwa f=koll rub3 sa:3a yeTla3lena be2iSSa>
             [transl. <we houwwa = and he> < f=koll = in every> <rub3 sa:3a =
             quarter of an hour> < yeTla3lena = comes up (to us)> <be2iSSa
             = with a story>]

67   OM      <we dA=lle 7'adna:(h) 3achan ma bi cha7':arch(e)>
             [transl. <we dA=lle 7'adna:(h) = and this one we had taken (him)>
             <3achan = because> < ma bi cha7':arch(e) = he doesn't snore>]

68   BA      <we:: eh=bi:=yetkallem we houwwa na:yem ya3ni/>
             [transl. <we:: eh = and what> <bi:=yetkallem = he talks> <we houwwa
             na:yem = while asleep?> <ya3ni/ = that means]
```

---

15 Arabic *zift* means 'tar, pitch'; here, in a figurative sense, 'plague'.

```
69   OM       <biyetkallem we biyEmchi>
     [transl. <biyetkallem = he talks> <we = and> <biyEmchi = walks
             around>]

70   OM       <biyetkallem we biyemchi we houwwa na:yem - biga3:ar>
     [transl. (he) talks and walks (around) while sleeping - < biga3:ar =
             he screams>]

71   OM       <bi2oul 7aga:t 3'ari:ba giddan>
     [transl. <bi2oul = he tells> <7aga:t = things> <3'ari:ba = weird> <
             giddan = extremely>]
```

Analysis

The anecdote is quoted in its entirety so that the reader may note how clear the structure of the narrative is, with a prologue (ll. 26–36) to describe the setting, a main part that deals with the action itself (ll. 37–64), and an epilogue with a summary and a comment (ll. 65–71).

The following general observations can be made:

- Unlike in the dialogue with the 'traditional Levantine' speaker Pierre, the main speaker here, Omar, exhibits various instances of code alternation and copying.
- The languages primarily involved in this process of hybridization are French, Arabic, and, to a lesser degree, also English. Still, the main (matrix) language of the narrative part is French. However, having finished the story proper, the speaker moves on to a commentary which he gives entirely in Arabic.[16]
- The French variety represented here, particularly by speaker OM, is not traditional Levantine in articulation and choice of vocabulary.

Focusing on the phenomena found in this usage of French and the hybridization in detail, note that the narrative starts with an Arabic copy (l. 26), which acts as a text-structuring signal, as a meta-communicative deictic that determines how the following speech chunk is received: *marra* 'once', functionally equivalent to 'once (upon a time)'. *3ala 7ekayet* ('about story+Gen') topicalizes the following subject.

---

[16] Cairo's language ecology seems to tolerate hybridization in all directions, unlike e.g. in Congolese, where speaking French with copies from indigenous languages is frowned at as incompetent, while it is acceptable to speak Congolese languages with copies from French (p.c. Salikoko Mufwene, November 2014). The acceptance of this hybridization practice in Cairo does in fact vary between the speaker groups outlined above (conservatives vs. innovators), but not with respect to the selected matrix language.

The negations in lines 29 (*je ne sais pas*), 33 (*je ne ronfle pas*), 36 (*we M. ne ronfle pas*), and 39 (*personne n'approche? On ne ne ronfle pas* ...) reflect the conventional Levantine norm (as opposed to generalized usage in Europe) which has retained the particle *ne*, as noted above. The English copy *by definition* in line 29 confirms the credibility of the speaker's statement. It appears to be multifunctional: it has a focalizing or attention-catching function; it indicates the selection of a more formal register generally attributed to legal and intellectual discourse, thereby allowing the speaker to position himself as a participant in the global western culture. This is one of many examples in the corpus indicating that the English language has become absorbed in the modern intermediate ecology, to the extent that it has found its way into the communicative repertoire of a considerable number of social groups within the urban ecology of Cairo.

In response to Hosni's insertion *donc il y en a deux qui* ... (l. 31), Omar focuses, in contrast to *deux*, on a new referent, himself, by copying the Arabic structuring particle *fa* 'so' (a conjunction) followed by the personal pronoun *ana* 'I' (see Woidich 2006 for a grammar of the spoken variety in Cairo). Grammatically speaking, he uses the Arabic disjunctive pronoun on the French model *donc moi, je* ... . This is made possible by congruence with Arabic syntax, which provides the same structure. This also holds for the copying of the Arabic conjunction *we* 'and', which is used to coordinate the three subjects in line 36.

Hosni's turn in line 35 reveals a French competence that abides by European norms, even in pronunciation and prosody. Having studied in Switzerland, his French seems to be devoid of traditional Levantine characteristics, although he remains within the traditional non-hybridizing language use. As he preserves the concept of 'pure' language for social identification, this identifies him more as a member of global Francophonia than as a Levantine.

The lexical copy <*estera7a*> (l. 37) is a de-verbal noun from the verb <estaray:a7> (colloquial Arabic form of 'to rest'), which can also mean 'hostel', 'resting place' or 'rest area'. This purely lexical copy is used in a system-integrated way, in that it is framed by the appropriate definite article (feminine singular) and the postposed demonstrative pronoun -*là* in French.

An interesting passage is where the speaker tries to explain who the protagonist of his anecdote is by pointing out his social relationship in three languages (l. 45): Omar changes from French (*c'était l'ami de* ...) to English (*he was/ he was <R'.s> friend, <T's> friend.*) and, after a short pause, to Arabic (*Sa7ib T.*). Each of these attempts is structured by repairs, running into the final rephrasing in Arabic (with an intonation that says 'anyway, briefly ... ') constituting a hinge to the dominant language of all the participants in his audience. In this passage an almost hypercorrect articulation can be heard on the recording. It reveals that the speaker seems to avoid specific Levantine features, presumably in order to identify with a European variety of French. This is made more evident by the lexical choice of the term *gosse* (l. 43, 'kid, boy'), which is markedly European French.

On the other hand, the same speaker also makes an unintentional, solely structural, therefore covert copy from Arabic by using the wrong preposition in *dans un côté* (l. 51, instead of the phrase *d'un côté*). This is obviously formed on the model of the analogous construction in Arabic with the preposition *fi* 'in'.

Later in the narrative, Omar quotes the protagonist's exclamation in Arabic:

et tout soudainement, on entend quelqu'un hurler : 7arami, 7arami! (thief-NOM;SG) on se lève tous, hein. (ll. 53–55)

Obviously, the quotation has a dramatizing effect by adding immediacy to this part of the narrative.

From line 65 onwards the dialogue opens out into a commentary in Arabic. Omar refocuses on the actual contents of the narrative by situating the story deictically:

<el le:l kol:ou (.) ad:enA: 3al=zift dawwat/> the whole night we spent with this plague (l. 65)

This alternation finalizes the narrative. The use of Arabic in this part is not restricted to sporadic insertions, as in lines 52–64; in fact the communicative motivation for the alternation can be explained in two ways: in terms of narrative structure, the epilogue is of a different order than the preceding speech. While the latter was adapted to accommodate the drama, action and a punch line, the conclusion comments on and evaluates the incident. By means of code alternation, the speaker takes advantage of his multilingualism to enhance the plasticity of his narrative account. But we should also take into consideration a kind of environmental rub-off: somebody is making a phone call in Arabic (l. 49), and the audible conversations going on in the immediate vicinity are also all in Arabic. From this point of view, the final alternation to Arabic can also be interpreted as the speaker's accommodation to the situational environment.[17]

The above analysis suggests the following conclusions, which complement the general observations at the beginning of this section.

Hybridization in this text consists typically of code alternations and overt copies of complete syntagms from Arabic into French. This kind of

---

[17] For this type of language alternation see Auer (1995: 125ff.).

hybridization is highly intentional, the aim being to fulfil various interactional functions such as focusing, text structuring, etc. Accordingly, non-intentional, covert copies like *dans un côté* are the exception.

Despite a purposeful and very productive use of alternation and copying, hybridization does not develop into an overriding communicative strategy. To a certain extent the speakers in this example still adhere to the traditional language culture of the Levant, including its hermetic and purist tendencies (as illustrated in our first example). However, this does not prevent them from taking the liberty of going beyond the conservative norm at discretion.[18] Then, the language norm referred to in terms of lexical choice, grammar and articulation is not that of traditional Levantine Francophonia but rather that of European francophonia culture.

9.4.4   *Forms of Alternation: Hybridization as Innovation within the Intermediate Ecology*

Transcription

The initial topic of the following interaction (also included in Dermarkar and Pfänder 2010: 41–45) is the galloping inflation in Egypt at the time (2008) and the newly imposed motor vehicle tax. The right column (ll. 74–85) represents Suzettes's conversation on the phone with a carpenter, conducted simultaneously with the ongoing conversation. From line 88 Suzette breaks in on the inflation/car topic in the ongoing conversation between Carine and Cynthia to comment on her phone conversation.

SPEAKERS: Suzette (SU), aged 71: L1 competence in French and Arabic;
                       Carine (CA), aged 37, daughter of SU: L1 competence in Arabic, L2 in
                       French and English; Cynthia (CY)
DATE: 15.05.2008
PLACE: At Suzette's home, living room

```
72   CA:      Si tu as une voiture de de trois cent, euh trois mille huit
              cents cc
     [transl. If you have a car of three hundred (…) three thousand eight
              hundred cubic capacity

73            tu paies, je sais plus trop quoi.
     [transl. you pay I am no longer sure what
     SU's cell phone rings.
```

CA

74   <we e7na>, on a deux voitures.
Comme ça moi j'ai acheté une
voiture il y a... <mch3arfa>
(...),...
[transl. <we e7na = and we> we
have two cars, so I I bought a
car (...) ago <mch3arfa = I don't
know>]

75   ...en janvier, février, peut-
être en mars
[transl. in January, February,
perhaps in March]

76   ...et trois, trois mille, trois
mille CC
[transl. and three three
thousand, three thousand cc]

77   mon mari m'a dit, on va payer
huit mille livres, à peu près
huit mille livres pour pour le
<da>
[transl. my husband told me we
are going to pay eight thousand
pounds about eight thousand
pounds for for the <da = this
one>]

78   quand son beau-frère..., quand
son frère est allé... Hier, il
lui a dit: <lessa> la loi n'est
pas encore faite.
[transl. when his brother-in-
law ... when his brother went …
yesterday he told him <lessa =
not yet> the law has not been
passed yet]

79   va les... va faire les voitures.
On a deux voitures, on allait
payer... <mch3arfa>(whispering).
Il m'a dit un nombre, vingt
mille, trente mille, <7aga keda
bass> pour faire les papiers des
voitures.
[transl. go ... go do the cars we
have two cars we were going to
pay ... <mch3arfa = I don't know>
<7aga keda bass = something like
that only>]

SU

<aywa. Ay aywa. ezzayak ya
Amir?> <7amdoulillah!> <merci
3al doulab ana et...>
[transl. <aywa. ay aywa = yes,
yes> <ezzayak ya Amir = how are
you, A.> <7amdoulillah = thank
God!> <merci 3al doulab ana et...
= thank you for the cupboard, I
...>]

<etlaba7't keda wana ba:7'od el
garayed baSSe:t la2e:t> (laughs)
[transl. <etlaba7't keda = I was
confused like this> <wana
ba:7'od el garayed = as I got
the newspapers> <baSSe:t la2et =
I looked I found ...>]

<la2et el doulab fi wichi>
(laughs)
[transl. <la2et = I found> <el
doulab = the bookshelf> <fi
wichi = in my face, i.e. in
front of me>]

<bass ma da7'altouch ya albi
(...)> (SU moves out of earshot
while she continues talking)
[transl. <bass = but> <ma
da7'altouch = you didn't carry
it inside> ya albi (...)= my
darling...>]

<Tayyeb>. (...)
[transl. all right]

80   il est allé <ba2a> aujourd'hui
     <Alli: *Ah lessa*>, *moi, j'ai fini
     j'ai fait... Il est ...*
     [transl. he went <ba2a = so>
     today <alli = Ah lessa = he told
     me: just a minute ago>: I, I
     have just finished, I did ... he
     is...]

81   il est très content qu'il a su
     les faire. Et on a trois ans
     <ba2a le3'ayet ma nedfa3 ta:ni>
     tout cet argent. Il les a fait –
     <bass>, tu t'imagines <ya3ni>.
     [transl. he is very pleased that
     he was able to do them and we
     have three years <ba2a le3'ayet
     ma nedfa3 tani = now until we
     pay again> all this money, he
     did/ made them <bass = only,
     but> can you imagine <ya3ni =
     that is>]

82   on a... on a payé... Ils ont   <ana ma reditch akallimak 3ala
     augmenté le benzine. On paye des   fikra 7'oft aSa7ik walla
     taxes et des taxes pour avoir   7aga>(...) <Tab Jayeb>.
     des voitures et <e:h> aussi on   [transl. By the way, I didn't
     paye...   want to call you, because I was
     [transl. we ... we paid ... they   afraid to wake you up (...) all
     raised the fuel, we pay taxes   right]
     and taxes to have cars and <e:h
     = what> also we pay…]

83   ...je ne sais pas qu'est-ce   <bessalama.>
     qu'... ya3ni comment ça marche,   [transl. <bessalama = have a
     je ne sais pas   good trip (and get back
     [transl. I don't know what... that   safely)>]
     is how it works I don't know]

84   <aho a:l>, il leur a dit,... Le   (...) <bessalama tigi (enta)
     président leur a dit *moi je vous   teda7'alou in cha2allah. >. Oké.
     donne une augmentation de trente   [transl. As soon as you are
     pourcent pour (...).* Vous savez   safely back (bessalama), you
     ça, n'est-ce pas?   will come (and) haul it in(to my
     [transl. <aho a:l = there he   apartment), God willing]
     said> he told them I give you a
     thirty percent pay raise for (...)
     you know that don't you]?
     CY: (...)

85   <we e:h> tout chose a augmenté   <in cha2allah.> OK. merci.
     de cinquante pourcent peut être.   (..)<ma3assalama.>
     [transl. <We e:h: = and what   [transl. <in cha2allah = God
     else (exclamation, rhetorical   willing> <ma3assalama> good bye]
     question)> everything has
     increased by fifty percent
     perhaps]

     End of phone call

```
86  CY:     donc les trente pourcent... merci, hein.
            [transl. so the thirty percent ... thanks (all right)]

87  CA:     Ah? là¹⁹ merci on les veut pas <ba2a>...
            [transl. oh there thanks we don't want them < ba2a = now>]

88  SU:     (gives a small cough) Le premier Égyptien qui travaille et
            qui fait ce qu'on lui demande et qui vient aux heures
            [transl. the first Egyptian who works and who does what he's asked and
            who comes on time]

89          ça, ça ne se trouve pas en Égypte. (claps her hands)
            [transl. that, that is not found in Egypt]

90  CY:     (laughs)

91  SU:     ça ne se trouve pas. C'est rare!
            [transl. that's not found. it is rare]

92  CY:     oui.
            [transl. yes]

93  SU:     <in cha2allah! In cha2allah!> (claps her hands) Et attends.
            [transl. God willing! God willing! (...) and wait]

94          mais celui-là? Il a dit, il est venu même avAnt le temps.
            [transl. but this one? he said he came even before the (scheduled)
            time]

95  CA:     (gasps) <bass da kan meTalla3 dinek essana llefatet>
            [transl. <bass = but> da kan meTalla3 dinek = this one had exasperated
            you> <essana llefatet = last year

96  SU:     <ma3..., Ah aywa>.²⁰
            [transl. <ma3...with> ..., yes, yes]

97  CA:     <...how:a we A. da...>
            [transl. <...how:a = he> <we A. da = and this A.]

98  SU:     pour faire toute la maison et tout ça <ya mA:ma>²¹.
            [transl. to do the whole house and all that <ya mA:ma = my darling>]

99  CY:     (laughs)

100 SU:     mais...
            [transl. but]

101 CA:     <how:a>, il lui a fait les le...
            [transl. <how:a = he> he made the... for him]

102 CY:     ... les moustiquaires, hm.
            [transl. the mosquito screens]
```

[19] The transcription reflects an interpretation as French interjection *ah* plus the demonstrative pronoun *là*. It was difficult to decide if the pronunciation of [Ah la :] couldn't also be interpreted as an Arabic exclamation *<Ah ? la :>* made up of *<Ah = yes>* (see also l. 96 and the corresponding note) and *<la : = no>*, which may seem unlogic, but is pragmatically acceptable in this situation: *yes* as consent to CY's previous remark, and *no* as attached to *merci*, blending to an Arabic-French 'no thanks'. This kind of 'contamination' is quite frequent in Cairo French and can provide ample material for a separate study.

[20] *Ah* and *aywa*, both denoting 'yes', correspond to different stylistic levels: *Ah* being considered as more 'vernacular' and *aywa* as standard colloquial.

[21] The expression *ya mA:ma*, frequently used by parents to children, seems to be an elliptic phrase, probably resulting from the omission of a genitive, like 'mummy('s darling)'.

```
103  CA:     ... les fait les... Ah les moustiquaires, hm.
     [transl. ... made the ... the mosquito screens
104  SU:     euh il a fait de nouv(eau)... de nou(veau)...
     [transl. and he did again]
105          ça, c'est nouveau!
     [transl. this is new]
106  CY:     oui.
     [transl. yes]
107  SU:     Il a fabriqué ça chez lui! Il est venu me les mettre!
     [transl. he made this at his place! he came to put them in for me]
108  CY:     oui.
     [transl. yes]
109  SU:     <ya3ni>, ça, ce n'est pas les vitres. Lui, il a emporté les
             vitres maintenant...
     [transl. <ya3ni = that is> this this is not the window glass. he he
             took the windows now]
110  CY:     Ah, où sont les vitres d'ailleurs? Ah, ah bon.
     [transl. oh where are the windows in fact?]
111  SU:     ...pour pour les faire...
     [transl. to to make them]
112  SU:     ...chez lui – et proprement – et me les amener. mais c'est qui
             est vraiment²²
     [transl. at his place and properly and bring them to me. but what is
             really]
113          un travail formidable. ni je salis la maison ni...
     [transl. wonderful work. neither do I dirty the house nor]
114  CY:     Oui.
     [transl. yes]
115  SU:     Il prend ce qu'il veut! je lui donne ce qu'il dit! et alors
             il travaille.
     [transl. he takes what he wants. I give him what he asks for! and then
             he works]
116          mille livres? mille livres. deux mille livres? oui, deux
             mille livres... hop!
     [transl. one thousand pounds? one thousand pounds. two thousand
             pounds? two thousand ... hop!]
117          (laughs) <bass>, travaille! <7'alas>. (laughs)
     [transl. <bass = enough>; <7'alAS = finished/full stop>]
```

22 We transcribed *c'est* (not *ce*, as would be expected to be grammatically correct), as SU clearly pronounces [e], not schwa. This is a case of conversational 'online' repair: there is a syntactic breach after *c'est,* because the speaker modifies her syntactic plan to continue with a relative clause (*qui est formidable*).

Analysis

As a general observation we can state that the two speakers represent different levels of language competence in French, the mother clearly belonging to the group described above as 'traditionalist'. Her daughter, Carine, obviously has to struggle to keep up with the demands of a conversation in that language. But is she simply a language 'learner' or can she be associated to the group of 'innovators'? The analysis will help us to distinguish the notions.

Talking about the imminent introduction of a new tax on car registration, Carine opens her statement in l. 78 with the copy *lessa*. This Arabic particle, meaning '(not) yet' anticipates its semantic counterpart in French, *pas encore*, in the subsequent phrase *la loi n'est pas encore faite* ('the law has not yet been passed'). Even if we interpret the intense recourse to Arabic structuring particles, core words, etc. as a consequence of her linguistic insecurity (as opposed to her mother's performance), there still remains a focalizing and a text structuring effect: In this example she launches the beginning of direct reported speech in its original Arabic version.

The all-purpose verb *faire* 'to make' or 'to do' is a convenient tool to convey all sorts of actions, as in *la loi n'est pas encore faite* (l. 78, for the *passing* of a bill) and in *va faire les voitures* 'go do the cars' (l. 79), in this context for 'to register', the French equivalent *immatriculer* obviously not being readily available. The recourse to vague expressions, as *faire*, is a universal mechanism in oral situations and even more so in contexts of contact. It is an economic device that spares the speaker having to search for the specific word or for appropriate copies in the other language. Carine draws heavily on this option, as with *moi j'ai fini j'ai fait* (l. 80, again in the context of car registration). All in all, there are twelve instances of this in this excerpt of roughly three minutes of conversation.

In l. 79, Carine uses two Arabic copies, *mch3arfa* (gloss.: NEG-know:1PRS;F, 'I don't know') and *7ag(a) keda bass* (gloss.: thing like that just/enough, 'just something like this'), in order to partially restrict the truth content of her assertion, more specifically an exact amount of money. It appears once more that the Arabic elements work on a different level, by structuring and pragmatically modifying the French utterances.

Elaborating on her account of the car registration, Carine carries on by saying *Il est allé ba2a aujourd'hui* (l. 80, 'so he went today'). The Arabic deictic particle *ba2a* ('so now') is a marker of the perfect, adding a resumptive hue to the narrative course. Together with the time adverb *aujourd'hui* it clarifies the reference.

Subsequently she alternates to a sequence in Arabic by quoting the dialog with her brother-in-law in the original language <*Ah lessa*> (gloss.: 'yes, just a minute ago'), the quotation is introduced with <*alli*> (gloss.: told:3PRF-me, 'he told me'). We find a similar quotation strategy later in l. 84, when Carine refers to the president's promise: *aho a:l, il leur a dit,. . . le président leur a dit. moi je vous donne une augmentation de trente pourcent pour (. . .)* (gloss.: *aho a:l* there said:3SG;PRF). The copy *a:l* marks the reproduction of the discourse: '[he] said', which is then paraphrased in French as *il leur a dit*, (the subject of the reported speech 'il' being the former Egyptian president Moubarak). By distinguishing the verbs according to their function in discourse – verba dicendi in Arabic, verbs in the narrative part in French – the speaker achieves a notable surplus of emphasis and profile.

With *ba2a le3'ayet ma nedfa3 ta:ni* (l. 81, 'so (now) until we pay again'), a whole phrase is copied from Arabic, with the deictic particle *ba2a* again at the head of the phrase. The subordinated direct object corresponds to the syntax of both Arabic and French, thereby providing an effect of structural congruence (Dermarkar et al. 2009: 122).

Two other structuring particles *bass* 'only, but', and *ya3ni* 'i.e., so', are copied from Arabic in the same turn: *bass tu t'imagines ya3ni. Ya3ni* can be considered as partially conventionalized or 'habitualized' in Johanson's (2008) terminology. Originally denoting 'this means', *ya3ni* has mutated through frequent use into a structuring particle that can mark (among other functions) an explanation adjunct, as in Suzette's turn *ya3ni, ça ce n'est pas les vitres* (l. 109). In this place though, *ya3ni* functions as a particle marking the end of a turn, as described in Dermarkar and Pfänder (2010: 23ff.).

However, later, in l. 83, *ya3ni* occurs at a point of repair, where it assumes the role of linking the rephrased part to the preceding fragment: *je ne sais pas qu'est-ce qu'... ya3ni comment ça marche, je ne sais pas.* The fact that it is also used in other languages spoken in Egypt, such as English or German, is indicative of the extent of its cultural conventionalization. As a result of progressive semantic bleaching, this marker has even acquired pragmatic significance to the point of assuming the functions of a speech-accompanying gesture, as shown in detail in Dermarkar (2014).

Carine's use of the word *benzine* (l. 82) instead of the standard French *essence* or *carburant* also deviates from the norm in her selecting the masculine article. *Benzine* is actually part of the French Levantine lexicon; it is either an archaic French usage or a copy from English or even from (Egyptian) Arabic, where it has been entirely absorbed as the common word for gasoline. This is only one of many instances where it is difficult to decide on the exact origin of a copy.

In her subsequent explanations, *on paye des taxes et des taxes pour avoir des voitures et e:h aussi on paye...* (l. 82), the particle *eh* could easily be mistaken for a repair of the coordinate conjunction *et*. In fact, the word takes an accent and is therefore identifiable as the Arabic interrogative pronoun (also employed as an interjection) *eh* ('what'). In this context the copy of Arabic behaves as an emotively modalizing extension 'and what else (you pay)!'.

The interjection reoccurs with the same meaning in l. 85 at the beginning of Carine's turn: *we e:h tout chose a augmenté de cinquante pourcent peut être,* viz., as an exclamative rhetorical question which results in a thematic focusing operation. However, the non-standard use of masculine *tout* with *chose* is typical of learners' language in contact situations. When in doubt, the unmarked category is preferred, in the present case, the unmarked masculine over the marked feminine. Here it becomes apparent how cognitive parameters become operative in the ecology of discursive contact situations.

To sum up the characteristics of Carine's discourse, we find that she makes abundant use of copied Arabic particles from the domains of modalization, discourse-structuring markers, and deictic setting, viz., *Ah? la(2)* 'yes? no' and *ba2a* 'now' in her statement: *Ah? la(2), merci on les veut pas ba2a...* 'yes? no thanks we don't want them now' (l. 87). We thus recognize that the insertion of Arabic copies at decisive points of the discourse deploys a highly text-structuring meta-communicative power.

Meanwhile Suzette has been talking on the phone with the carpenter; the conversation is entirely in Arabic, because the workman is monolingual. Here she conducts multi-centred communication, as she follows two different communicative goals. We refrain from analysing the entire phone call and turn directly to the moment when she hangs up and steps again into the conversation between her daughter and Cynthia. Here are her last two turns in the conversation with the carpenter:

```
84   SU      <bessalama tigi (enta) teda7'alou>
     Gloss.  with-peace you come you PRS;2SG-carry into-it:ACC;3SG
     Transl. As soon as you are safely back (bessalama), you will come
             (and) haul it in(to my apartment)
     SU      <in cha2allah>.. Oké.
     Gloss.  if wish-PRF;SBJV allah
     Transl. God willing. o.k.

85   SU      in cha2allah. oké. merci. (..)<ma3assalama.>
     Gloss.  with-peace
     Transl. good bye
```

This passage is particularly interesting because it shows that the selection of a language is accompanied by certain identity-related and cultural strategies. We can observe highly dialogic techniques of accommodation to ecological factors, viz. to conditions such as language competence (more specifically, the non-mastery of French on the part of the workman), the social situation, and the religious background of the interlocutor.

Suzette is getting ready to end the conversation with the craftsman. Her strategy to convey her central concern (viz., to make him haul the bookshelf inside the apartment) meets the requirements of the Islamic-majority society. *Bessalama* being the standard Arabic phrase to wish travellers *bon voyage* and a safe return, we can infer that the carpenter is giving reasons why he cannot carry out the task promptly. Suzette in turn pursues her aim by formulating instructions which she modalizes by arranging the set phrases *bessalama* and *in cha2allah* around the actual command, thereby framing it with culture-compliant forms of politeness.

The formula *in cha2allah* is mandatory in connection with any projection to the future; to dispense with it would be interpreted as irreverence. Its pragmatic role is to attenuate the rigour of the command by embedding it in the majority's cultural background. The hybridized complimentary close *oké* is an obvious borrowing from English, though it is also used by monolingual speakers of Arabic. Applying it in this context has a double effect: feedback and the closure of a conversation.

After hanging up, Suzette gives a slight cough and jumps into the ongoing dialogue by referring to her conversation with the carpenter. This is the point where she addresses the two different communicative causes governing her linguistic behaviour:

```
88-89 SU    Le premier Égyptien qui travaille et qui fait ce qu'on lui
            demande et qui vient aux heures. ça ça ne se trouve pas en
            Égypte. (claps her hands)
```

What follows is an illustration close to comedy of what one has to expect of workers in Egypt:

```
93-94 SU    in cha2allah! In cha2allah! (claps her hands).. et attends.
            mais celui-là? il a dit, il est venu même avAnt le temps.
```

In a prime example of polyphony, Suzette quotes again the Arabic invocation pronounced before on the phone, but this time reframing it ironically, as she alludes to stereotypes about Egyptian craftsmen: allegedly unreliable and late. With this strategy she repositions herself with her interlocutors, daughter and guest, and confirms her integration in the group of francophone Christians of Cairo, situated on the intermediate ecological level.

Her daughter objects in Arabic: 'but this one had exasperated you last year' (l. 95). The alternation to Arabic is a clue that it is the language of proximity between mother and daughter. From a situational-ecologic point of view, this language choice is tolerable, given that Cynthia also speaks Arabic.

Suzette in her reply spontaneously takes up the cue in Arabic, then alternates back and forth between French and Arabic: <*ma3. . ., Ah aywa*> ('with . . . yes yes'); *pour faire toute la maison et tout ça* <*ya mA:mA*> (gloss.: VOC-mummy, 'darling'). In doing so, she approves of the affective function of Carine's alternation to Arabic, but at the same time she re-establishes French as the framing language. This also reveals Suzette's preference to keep French and Arabic separate in this conversation, according to the different relations between the interlocutors.

The only time Suzette uses *ya3ni* as a structuring particle is in this turn: *il est venu me les mettre! ya3ni. ça, ce n'est pas les vitres.* (ll. 107–109). As opposed to her daughter who uses it much more frequently to cover a wider range of functions, Suzette's discourse strategy is deliberately selective and even hermetically and puristically shaped. We can interpret this as evidence that the integration of *ya3ni* in Cairene French is being increasingly conventionalized.

Suzette's summarizing statement is a further polyphonic arrangement deploying Arabic copies in order to confer more authenticity to her words:

```
116  SU       mille livres? mille livres. deux mille livres? oui, deux
              mille livres... hop!

117  SU       (laughs) <bass>, travaille! <7'alAs>. (laughs)
     transl.  <bass> enough; <7'alAS> finished/full stop.
```

At the same time this technique allows her to meet culturally different requirements in one and the same situational context.

The following overall picture of the speakers arises from the micro-ecologic interaction. The elder speaker, Suzette, rarely uses copies and alternations and, when she does, it is in a very reflective way and limited to a few specific functions, such as to parody local Arabic discourse, including direct quotes, cultural and identity-related bridging, and affective approval of her daughter's communicative initiatives. Covert, unintentional copies are (almost) absent, and copies of Arabic particles or markers are rarely used, not even to structure the text. There are, however, some exceptions, namely those copies that have a higher degree of integration or conventionalization in the French of Cairo.

Carine, the younger speaker, shows less competence in French. Consequently, she draws on Arabic structures and structuring markers more easily and frequently. It is precisely with regard to text-structuring, modalization, and the like that her intense use of Arabic copies and alternations becomes apparent. So, even if a competence gap is often responsible for this difference in hybridization behaviour, it nevertheless also accounts for a productive use of these techniques, which can fulfil a wide range of distinct functions.

9.5   Conclusions

The hierarchical language ecology model (Figure 9.1) is corroborated by the corpus data. Certain parameters prove to be particularly relevant to the ecology of Cairene French. All the parameters mentioned are primarily tangible on the micro-ecologic level. The main outcomes of our analysis can be related to the three ecological levels of our model:

> *Macro-level:* we have shown that the usage of French in Cairo is related to the cultural geographically relevant macro-level, i.e. the

historical communicative culture of the Levant. Nevertheless, the discourse activities of some speakers cannot be entirely understood through the foundation in a single macro-ecology (such as the Levant). Usage of French often goes beyond the scope of the Levant as a cultural frame of reference and is oriented towards a European (French) norm. The English copies observed in our analysis also conform with an orientation to a macro-ecological frame beyond the Levantine culture.

Intermediate level: Cairene French as the main empirical domain of the chapter relates to the intermediate level; several results can be summed up with respect to this domain. The relevant parameters on the intermediate ecological level include the social group, age, competence, and religion. Several ecological variables raise questions that cannot be answered here, such as gender. We noted that it is mostly schoolgirls or young women who develop relatively good competence in French in the course of their education, while schoolboys or young men (of the middle and upper class) rather attend anglophone, business-oriented educational institutions. The examples analysed confirm this observation. Transcript 3 is an instance of the francophone speech of a young woman in Cairo, whereas in transcript 2 it is precisely men (or businessmen) who use English hybridizations. However, those are just single examples that only allow for an inductive development of hypotheses. Hence, the parameter *gender* has to be investigated further. The same applies for the parameter *religion*, which turns out to be a factor that is not absolutely binding in the current intermediate ecology of Cairo, even if the 'traditional' francophones are likely to have a Christian background.

Hybridization techniques can be constitutive of group distinction in the sense of Bourdieu (1979), meaning that differences between social groups are symbolized by different kinds of behaviour (including linguistic behaviour). In our transcriptions, members of the educated middle class use European French and English hybridization to index their social and educational status. Two francophone groups emerge that differ in their discourse strategies: the 'traditionalists' and the 'innovators'. The 'traditionalists' align historically with the francophones of the Levant. They share some typical linguistic characteristics, which include the trilled /r/, the differentiating use of copies according to their function in discourse, and an eloquent, archaic speech style. The 'innovators', on the other hand, sometimes (but not always) have less competence in French. Their speech is characterized e.g. by frequent copying, alternations, and a striving for the norms of European French. By and large, the group of 'innovators' appears to be much more heterogeneous than that of 'traditionalists'.

> *Micro-level*: the micro-level can be understood as the domain of pragmatic techniques provided by language to adapt to varying conditions of text and situation. Code alternations and certain overt copies (such as marking quotations, particular structures, focusing, and intensifying particular parts of a narrative) have specific functions in the text. Furthermore, hybridization can bring together speakers with different attitudes and competences; it can even be a compensation strategy in view of varied multilingual competences.

10   The Opposite of an Anti-creole? Why Modern Chamorro is Not a New Language

Steve Pagel

10.1   Introduction

This chapter is about Chamorro (or Chamoru),[1] the autochthonous Malayo-Polynesian language of the Mariana Islands, situated roughly halfway between Japan and New Guinea in the western Pacific Ocean.[2] Chamorro has undergone significant contact-induced change ever since the European discovery of the Pacific in 1521, the major influences coming from Spanish and American English.[3] These changes can be interpreted as the transformation of an insular language ecology under the impact of European colonization, westernization, modernization, and globalization (see Mühlhäusler 1996a, especially pp. 105ff.). Contact with Spanish dates back to the first stage of the colonization of the Marinas, from 1565 to 1898, when the archipelago officially formed part of the Spanish kingdom (as did the Philippines). Diseases and warfare decreased the indigenous population from approximately 50,000, at the time of the founding of the first Catholic mission in 1668, to fewer than 4,000, only forty years later (Cunningham 1992: 170; Rogers 1995: 70–71; Mühlhäusler 1996a: 105–108). Modern Chamorro people, language, and culture emerged under various influences from the Hispanic colonial world (especially Mexico and the Philippines) during the eighteenth century. Chamorro–Spanish bilingualism was widely spread on the Marianas in the eighteenth and nineteenth centuries (Rodríguez-Ponga 1999). As a result of the 1898 war, Spain ceded Guam, the southernmost island, to the United States and sold the other islands to the German empire. American English was then quickly introduced to Guam and developed

---

[1] For a discussion on the 'correct' spelling see Pagel (2010: 31), Onedera (2011a), and Rodríguez-Ponga (2013).

[2] The archipelago consists of fourteen major islands of which only the southernmost four (from north to south: Saipan, Tinian, Rota, and Guam) are inhabited. Geographically, the Marianas form part of the island group of Micronesia.

[3] A third and equally important source are Philippine languages, a contact fold that has not been researched in detail yet (Blust 2000).

into the dominant language of the Mariana chain after the end of the Second World War, when the northern islands also came under US authority.[4] The local variety of Spanish disappeared with its last speakers in the 1990s at the latest; the last samples of Marianan Spanish were recorded by Albalá and Rodríguez-Ponga in the 1980s and are analysed in detail by Albalá (1997) and Pagel (2010).

The focus of the present chapter is on the contact between Chamorro and Spanish, leaving aside the equally important, and yet largely unstudied, contact with American English (see Pagel 2008). The two contact situations have taken different paths of linguistic change: while the overall direction of Chamorro in the contact with Spanish has been language maintenance with heavy copying from Spanish, that of the contact with English has been language shift. Unlike the Spaniards, who never officially promoted the use of Spanish in their colony, US administration has pursued a rigorous pro-English policy from the very beginning, banning Chamorro from public spaces by means of law. According to 2010 census data (United States Census Bureau 2013), 213,241 people live on Guam and the Northern Mariana Islands of which 72,283, roughly one-third, consider themselves as ethnic Chamorro. Some 37,646 people claim to speak Chamorro at home, making this the third-largest speaker group in the census after 'English only' and 'Philippine languages'. Indisputably, English is the major dominant language on the Marianas archipelago, and most ethnic Chamorros – virtually all on Guam – have primary competence therein. The use of Chamorro is restricted largely to intra-community communication and to private domains. In the Northern Marianas significantly more ethnic Chamorros claim to speak Chamorro at home (11,819 out of 12,902) than on Guam (25,827 out of 59,381). In addition, on Guam Chamorro is spoken considerably more often in the age groups of 35 and up. Most young Chamorros, especially in central Guam, have few or no competence in their ethnic language. Compared with the census data of the year 2000 (United States Census Bureau 2003, 2004), the ratio of Chamorro speakers to total population has further decreased, again especially on Guam. As Odo (1972) has shown, the language shift among the Chamorro on Guam was already well under way in the early 1970s (see also Underwood 1984, 1987). Revaluation of indigenous culture and language since the 1970s has, until present, not been able to outweigh cultural disintegration on the Marianas (Rapadas, Balajadia, and Rubinstein 2005; Pagel 2010: 40–45).

---

[4] To date, the Marianas have been divided into two political zones, of which the northern Mariana Islands (i.e., all except of Guam) represent a commonwealth in political union with the United States, while Guam is an unincorporated territory of the US.

10.2   Question, Aim, Procedure, and Method

The main question addressed in this chapter concerns the genetic and typological status of contemporary or *Modern Chamorro*. This term refers to the stage the Chamorro language entered in the eighteenth century (Pagel 2008, 2010; Rodríguez-Ponga 2013: fn. 13), when the remaining native population merged into an ethnic group comprising Chamorros, Mexicans, Filipinos, and, to a much lesser extent, Spaniards. Consequently, today's Chamorro displays numerous copies from Spanish at all levels of its system – a fact that in the past decades has led many linguists to argue that we are dealing with a 'new language', whose genetic affiliation and typological characteristics are no longer exclusively Malayo-Polynesian but also Romance.[5] Chamorro has also been characterized as a pidgin and a creole – views against which I argue below. I show that many of the established (and in part widely accepted) assessments of the status of this language are, in fact, highly questionable. A survey and contrasting of different studies that deal with the status of Modern Chamorro, their methods, databases, and scientific and theoretical backgrounds suggests that non-ecological approaches to complex situations of language contact can lead to substantially problematic results. Taking recourse to the data of my own analysis of the Spanish–Chamorro contact in Pagel (2010) I argue that, on genetic as well as on typological grounds, there is no reason to consider Modern Chamorro as a 'new language' in any other but the most general meaning of this term. Although today's Chamorro makes use of a vast number of Spanish copies, the language contact on the Marianas has neither led to the 'birth' of a 'daughter language' with an independent linguistic system, nor to a merging with Spanish or any other systematic hybridization that would question the status of Chamorro as a member of the Malayo-Polynesian language family.

From another perspective, this chapter challenges a common answer to the first of ten questions Haugen (1972) listed as crucial to understanding the ecology of a language: 'What is the language's classification in relation to other languages?' (1972: 336). In order to do so, other questions also mentioned by Haugen (e.g. regarding the domains of use, the users, their attitudes towards the language, concurrent languages, and institutional support) must be addressed. Consequently, I will follow the ecological approach to language and language contact as proposed in the first chapter of this volume. After addressing the notion of a *new language* in historical–genetic and in contact linguistics in section 10.3, I will summarize and update in section 10.4 my own results concerning the Spanish element in Modern Chamorro, published originally in Pagel (2010). This analysis is based on empirical data, collected in a

---

[5] Probably the latest example is Rodríguez-Ponga (2009: 41ff.) who groups Chamorro together with Chabacano, Papia Kristang, Tetun Dili, and others in a category called 'Nuevas Lenguas'.

corpus of spoken and written Chamorro between 2001 and 2011. It will provide the descriptive groundwork for a critical discussion in section 10.5 of previous evaluations of Modern Chamorro. Here, different classifications and arguments will be compared, while their plausibility will be measured against the background of several ecological parameters.

Referring to the theoretical apparatus given in Chapters 1 and 2 of this volume, the parameters most relevant for this endeavour are located in all four dimensions: *Speaker, Space, Time*, and *Language*. The empirical grounding of the analysis is provided by *natural data* as defined by Gadet and Pagel (Chapter 2, this volume; see also Chapter 3, this volume), that is, data taken from types of interactions that can be considered characteristic for a major portion of the Chamorro speech group and that are embedded in a three-level structure (micro-/meso-/macro-ecology). These include unmonitored face-to-face conversations at home, office or in classrooms, but also radio interviews, newspaper articles, and Internet conversations. The 'natural' environment of Chamorro interactions encompasses different spatial and temporal attributes, individual and group competences and attitudes, specific discourse traditions and code choices. These interactions are framed by what can be called the *discourse ecology*. In the case of Modern Chamorro, and due to the multiple historical and contemporary contact situations on the Marianas, this ecology is *founded* (in the sense of the term laid out in Chapter 1 of this volume) in several different meso- (e.g. Marianan, Guamanian, urban, rural) and macro-ecologies (e.g. Malayo-Polynesian, Asian, Anglo-American, Hispanic). Speakers of Modern Chamorro can situate themselves in and relate themselves to these ecologies (each of which has its own idealized spatial, temporal, linguistic, and other attributes) depending, among other things, on the semantic and pragmatic contexts of the interaction and by means of their choices in interaction. The paramount question of this chapter – regarding the relationship of Modern Chamorro to the Malayo-Polynesian and Romance language families, to the typological features associated with them, and to the defining criteria of several categories of language hybridization – rests, of course, primarily in the *Language* dimension. But it seems clear in the light of the ecological considerations laid out so far, and will become evident in the analysis in sections 10.4 and 10.5, that the other dimensions must not be excluded if a proper classification of Modern Chamorro is sought. Such an ecology-focused contact–typological classification will be given at the end of section 10.5, before final remarks are formulated in section 10.6.

10.3   What is a 'New Language'?

In order to answer this question, we must ask first: what is *a language*? Evidently, the phenomena subsumed under this term are not elements of the natural world but social constructs relating to highly abstract phenomena. Any definition (and study) of *a language* thus essentially depends on metaphors, analogies and other means of visualization (see Chapters 1 and 2, this volume). In Western linguistic thought biological analogues have a firm stand since at least the nineteenth century, although, as Noonan (2010: 52) observes, an explanation why language is apparently the *only* cultural artefact for which biological analogues are considered to be valid has yet to be given. Perhaps the most influential of these analogues is that of the *genetic relatedness* of languages, established as a scientific paradigm in the nineteenth century when wide-ranging similarities also between geographically very distant languages were discovered. Inspired by the biological sciences, historical linguistics conceptualized languages as unitary organisms and their genetic relation as the result of asexual reproduction (parthenogenesis) (see Pagel 2018). This conceptualization lies at the heart of the so-called *Stammbaum* or *family tree model* of genetic relationship, which is practically unrivalled until today, although interesting alternatives have been proposed (e.g. by Croft 2000 and Mufwene 2001, 2008 who argue for the conceptualization of languages as *populations*; see also Noonan 2010: 52, 55).[6] When we ask 'what is language X?', then the family tree model of genetic relationship, more than any other, is the central point of orientation: Spanish, for example, is said to be a member of the group of Romance languages in the Italic branch of the Indo-European language family. Within the family tree model, then

two languages are said to be genetically related if they descend from a common ancestor. Since it is at least theoretically possible that all languages descend from a common ancestor, languages are usually claimed to be related only if their relatedness can be established through the comparative method or some alternative procedure. (Noonan 2010: 52)

Genetic relationship is established primarily by means of *diachronic analysis*. Establishment can therefore be difficult if few or no diachronic data of the language is available. In principle, however, any natural, spoken language is thought to have genetic relationship: *a language X*, we can conclude at this point, is a construct (social, historical, cultural, and political) that is thought to be genetically related to other constructs of the same kind. If no genetic

---

[6] In fact, these two observations are connected: the scientific success of the familiy tree model must not be explained by its conceptual superiority but precisely by the dominance of the understanding of *a language* as an organism-like entity. The family tree model simply fits best for this understanding, and a different understanding of *a language* would necessarily result in a different model for relationship. In other words: concepts like *language family, genetic relationship of languages*, and also *language contact* mainly exist because Western linguistic thought conceptualizes *languages* as organism-like entities (see Toulmin's 1972 evolutionary model of conceptual change and the notion of *intellectual ecology*, Roggenbuck 1999, 2005 for interesting discussions on the importance of the tree metaphor in linguistics, and Pagel 2018 for a detailed history of the contact linguistic paradigm, which is inseperable from 19th century biologism in linguistics).

relationship to any other language can be established, this means that there is insufficient diachronic data and/or that the related languages are extinct or not yet discovered; until further evidence is adduced, the language in question is then considered to be an *isolate*.

With regard to Chamorro, there is sufficient agreement that the Marianas were settled from insular South-East Asia, most likely from the Philippines or the Sunda Islands, around 1500–1000 BC, and that Chamorro society and language developed in relative isolation from other Pacific societies and languages (Topping 1973; Denoon 1997; Blust 2000; Zobel 2002). In the historical–genetic framework, Chamorro language has been classified as an independent branch in the Malayo-Polynesian group of the Austronesian language family (Dyen 1965; Greenhill, Blust, and Gray 2008). Evidence for further subgrouping appears to be inconclusive (Blust 2000: 104), but attempts have been made to place Chamorro in a Western-Malayo-Polynesian subgroup (Blust 1977, 2000) and in a Sunda–Sulawesi branch of a Nuclear-Malayo-Polynesian subgroup (Zobel 2002).

After this outline of what the notion of *a language X* in the family tree model of genetic relationship conveys, we can explicate further what the notion of *a new language* indicates in the same framework. Noonan's (2010: 54) summary of the basic assumptions of the family tree model is helpful in this regard:

1 Languages are unitary systems: they are wholes, not entities defined by their parts (the unitary organism analogy).
2 Two languages are genetically related if they descend from a single common ancestor (the parthenogenesis analogy).
3 New languages can only be created by splitting off from an existing language (the parthenogenesis analogy).
4 Linguistic splits are final and produce independent linguistic systems (the parthenogenesis analogy).
5 No linguistic feature or set of features is required for genetic relationships to exist between two languages (though such features are required for establishing such relations) (the unitary organism analogy).
6 Language contact is irrelevant for determining genetic relationships (the unitary organism and parthenogenesis analogies).

According to assumptions 3 and 4 'new languages' come into existence only by splitting of from *one* existing language, and these splits are always final and irreversible. Assumption 5 adds that genetic affiliation is the result of common descent, not of (synchronically) shared inventory of features, and thus can never be changed. In Joseph Greenberg's words: 'a historical fact cannot be annulled. A language which is Germanic cannot "become" Romance' (1999: 355). But shared inventory of features is required for the establishment of genetic relationship; here the comparative method mentioned above comes into play. Finally, assumption 6 shows that possible effects of language contact on languages are not denied in the historical–genetic framework but considered irrelevant for the notion of genetic relationship.

If we ask then, with Noonan (2010: 49ff.), what precisely *genetic relationship between languages* means, the view expressed by the family tree model and historical–genetic linguistics follows a 'generational transmission approach':

> In this way of looking at things, assessing the genetic relatedness of languages amounts to assessing the history of the generational transmission of linguistic traditions. By 'generational transmission of linguistic traditions' I mean the acquisition by children of essentially the same linguistic system that their parents acquired as children. (50)

Concerning the main question of this chapter, we can state clearly at this point that Modern Chamorro, as opposed to Old or Pre-contact Chamorro, cannot be considered a *new language* in the classical historical–genetic meaning of that term. This would require the splitting off from another existing language, typically defined by regular structural (especially phonological) changes, and there is no evidence whatsoever for such a process. Since Chamorro has no indigenous writing system, documentation of pre-contact stages of this language is also very scarce (and in fact limited to the grammar and catechism of Father Sanvitores and some early wordlists). Analyses of these data (e.g. Burrus 1954; Rodríguez-Ponga 2013; Winkler 2013), however, confirm that we are dealing with essentially the same linguistic system and suggest that the differences between Old/Pre-contact and Modern Chamorro should be captured in contact linguistic rather than in historical–genetic dimensions.

This raises the question how *genetic relationship* can be interpreted if contact linguistic considerations are taken into account. Noonan adds to the 'generational transmission approach' expressed in the family tree model two other approaches he labels 'essentialist' and 'hybrid'. The 'essentialist' position

> maintains that there are certain linguistic features, consisting both of grammatical morphemes and characteristic morphosyntactic features, that must be transmitted along a genetic line for a language to be considered a member of a given taxonomic unit. This is not to say that these features over time cannot change. It maintains only that in assessing potential mother-daughter relationships, these features must be transmitted; language relatedness is assessed along chains of transmission of these features from mother language to daughter language. (2010: 50)

But only the third approach allows for true 'mixing' or 'hybridity' in the assessment of genetic relations between languages:

> A hybrid approach takes the position that a language is a collection of entities (morphemes, grammatical constructs, etc.) that may have multiple sources. At some point, the mixture of forms may become so great as to preclude the assignment of the language

to a specific taxon within a hierarchy of taxonomic levels, though it might still easily be placed within a higher level. Most linguists these days would concede that true 'mixed languages' exist, e.g. Copper Island Aleut, Michif, Media Lengua, etc., but would relegate them to a category outside the normal development of languages – that is, outside any genetic line. Others would include creoles in the category of hybrid languages, while still others would include in this category at least some non-creoles as well. (Noonan 2010: 51)

Contrary to the assumptions of the 'generational transmission approach', language contact can seriously blur genetic relationships and even create 'new languages', according to the 'essentialist' and the 'hybrid approach' to genetic relationship. These *mixed* or *contact languages* (Thomason 1997) cannot, by definition, be incorporated in any existing genetic line, because they have at least two parental languages, which is a contradiction to the parthenogenesis analogy constituting the family tree model (see above). This theoretical problem has been discussed in detail by Thomason and Kaufman (1988), who arrived at the conclusion that

> **mixed languages** do not fit within the genetic model and therefore **cannot be classified genetically at all; but most languages are not mixed**, and the traditional family tree model of diversification and genetic relationship remains the main reference point of comparative-historical linguistics. (3, emphasis original)

Although this exclusion of 'mixed languages' from the family tree model of genetic relationship is of a technical nature (see Thomason 1997), it suggests (and perhaps also reflects) an interpretation of these languages as somewhat 'abnormal' or 'unnatural' (see Chapter 2, this volume), given that this model dominates our understanding of language. In fact, 'mixed languages' have been treated as 'exotic', to say the least, in linguistics ever since the constitution of the historical–genetic paradigm in the nineteenth century (see, e.g., Müller's 1862 axiom of the unmixability of grammar, Thomason 2002 and Mufwene's response 2003, and especially Pagel 2018). Combined with the observation (made already by, e.g., Van Name 1869–70, Clough 1876, and Whitney 1881) that, due to their own long history of contacts, European languages such as English or the Romance languages display high degrees of 'mixture' themselves, such a distinction can be (and has been) interpreted as strongly Eurocentric. A more neutral model of genetic relationship with an explanatory power similar to that of the family tree model is, however, not in sight. The question of how much 'mixture' is needed to form a 'new language' should therefore be approached from the perspective of models of language contact.

    At least since Whitney (1881), most models covering the whole range of processes and outcomes of contact-induced language change comprise three distinct categories, labelled, for example, *language maintenance, language*

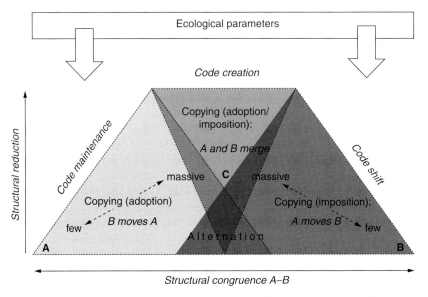

Figure 10.1 A continuous model of contact-induced change (Pagel 2015:167)

shift, and *language creation*. In modern versions (e.g. Winford 2003: 23–24) these categories are modelled as strictly separate; the first two typically encompass processes conceptualized as scalar (e.g., *borrowing* or *diffusion* in the first, and *interference* in the second), while the third category consists of three separated types of 'new' contact languages: pidgins, creoles, and bilingual mixed languages. The theoretical problems of autonomous categories, autonomous 'new language' types, and misleading metaphors in the conventional contact linguistic terminology are discussed in detail in Pagel (2015) where also an alternative model of contact-induced change is proposed. This model conceptualizes contact-induced language change as an essentially continuous space and proposes a more adequate terminology. I refer to this model in the following (see Figure 10.1). Its basic geometry consists of three overlapping triangles, each of which represents one mode of contact-induced change. From left to right, these are *code maintenance, code creation*, and *code shift*.

Three idealized codes – A, B, and C – serve as points of reference in these modes: code A represents one of two codes in contact (the one under scrutiny in a given investigation) and in the form of 'ideal maintenance' (speakers of A maintain unaltered A as their primary code) also one potential outcome of the contact; code B represents the other of two codes in contact and in the form of 'ideal shift' (speakers of A replace A with unaltered B as their primary code) another potential outcome of the contact; code C represents a code created in the contact as the result of A and B merging.[7] The continuous character of the model allows for any point in the space spanning between A, B, and the upper edge of the creation mode to be occupied by a given outcome of language contact at a given time.

The three modes are primarily *diachronic constituents* and must be set apart from the *processes* of contact-induced change. In order to achieve terminological clarity and adequacy (and following Johanson 2002a and Kriegel, Ludwig and Henri 2009; see also Chapter 7, this volume), I distinguish only two processes: *code copying* and *code alternation*. As laid out in detail in the mentioned contributions, these processes cover what has traditionally been called *borrowing, interference, transfer, calquing, code mixing*, and *code switching*. *Code copying* and *code alternation* represent synchronic strategies of the speakers in contact, and in the form of *conventionalized copies* also synchronic results of copying, propagation, and conventionalization at a later stage of contact. A major innovation of this model is that *code creation* is situated between *maintenance* and *shift* whereby the three modes are set in a precise relation to each other. Results of code creation such as 'new languages' can thus be understood as products of processes exceeding both massive copying through adoption in the maintenance of code A and massive copying through imposition in the shift to code B. In fact, the processes of adoption and imposition become indistinguishable in code creation, where, by definition, codes A and B merge. As a consequence, a 'new language' C can be interpreted from the perspective of both the maintenance and the shift mode. In the continuous space of the code creation mode prototypical 'new' or contact languages such as pidgins, creoles and bilingual mixed languages, and also less prototypical and borderline cases can be located and related to each other.

Finally, all outcomes of contact-induced change can be measured in two dimensions: horizontally, the structural congruence between A and B (always increasing relative to A and B prior to contact), and vertically the structural reduction involved (typically increasing relative to the *combined* features of A and B prior to contact). Influencing on the speakers' code choices and thereby activating certain processes of contact-induced change are a theoretically indefinite number of ecological parameters, in the sense laid out in Chapter 1, this volume.

---

[7] Note that this is a simplified view that has been adopted for the sake of clarity and transparency of the model. Most contact situations, especially those in which 'new languages' emerge, involve more than two participating codes. However, the processes responsible are identical, and the levels of explanation of this model are thus not affected. In principle, the model in its two-dimensional form can be extended by a third or fourth dimension, covering other languages in contact with A. See Pagel (2015) for further details.

We can sum up this section by stating that the notion of *a new language* is not the same in historical–genetic and in contact linguistics. The applicability of the historical–genetic meaning of this term for Modern Chamorro already ruled out, it is the contact linguistics understanding of *a new language* as well as the types that are traditionally subsumed under this term that will be in the focus of the subsequent evaluation of Modern Chamorro and its genetic and typological status.

10.4   The Spanish Element in Modern Chamorro

The following excerpt is from an article published in the *Guam Pacific Daily News*, Guam's largest and generally Anglophone daily newspaper, in February 2011 (Onedera 2011b). At the time of writing this section, it was the most recent lengthy example of written Modern Chamorro and was chosen for this purpose only. The transcript consists of three lines: the first and second lines represent the Chamorro text and translation as printed in the newspaper. The third has the text orthographically adapted, broken into morphemes and with Hispanisms underlined (dotted when uncertain):

Example 1: *Modern Chamorro (Ch.GPDN11-2)*

01 *Siempre lokkue′ ma monstra i gayera sa′ fotte este gi i kinalamten lao sin gambolet na manera.*

   Some will also present a demonstration of cockfighting as this is also considered a form of pastime, sans the gambling aspect.

   Siempre lokkue′ ma-monstra i gayera sa′ fotte este gi i k-in-alamten lao sin gambolet na manera.

02 *Manma hatsa lokkue′ sade′ gani siha ya i famagu′on duru manma dimimoria lalai, kanta yan baila siha ni′ u fanma prisenta gi dinanna′ huntan eskuela.*

   Chamorro huts will be constructed and many children are busy learning chants, songs, and dances that will be presented at numerous school assemblies.

   Man-ma-hatsa lokkue′ sade′gani siha ya i famagu′on duru man-ma-dimimoria lalai, kanta yan baila siha ni′ u-fan-ma-prisenta gi d-in-añā′ hunta-n eskuela.

03 *Manma baba i eskuela siempre ya manminagagu i famagu′on, manma′estra/tro yan emplehao siha gi tradisiunat na mestisa ya manma usa kadenan flores yan mantinihong nu i tihong tiniffok niyok.*

   Open houses will also be conducted and children, teachers and school personnel will adorn floral leis and the traditional mestiza as well as woven coconut hats.

   Man-ma-baba i eskuela siempre ya man-m-in-agagu i famagu′on, man-ma′estra/tro yan emplehao siha gi tradisiunat na mestisa ya man-ma-usa kadena-n flores yan man-t-in-ihong nu i tihong t-in-ifok niyok.

04 *Bula na lalahi mansinade′ ya manma katga lansa taiguihi i manansianu na gereron Chamorro siha.*

Many boys will also wear the sade' or loin cloth and will carry thick, long wooden sticks to depict the ancient Chamorro warrior with a spear in his hand.

Bula na lalahi man-s-in-ade' ya man-ma-katga lansa taiguihi i man-ansianu na gerero-n Chamorro siha.

05 *Siempre u guaha fina'estoria ginen manma'gas kumunidat yan manamko' ni' u ma empatte estoria put gera, hinengge put i taotaomo'na yan espiriton manansianu, put inamten amot Chamorro yan kontodu estorian lina'la' gi i sengsong yan lancho siha ni' manma chalappon gi enteru i isla.*

There will be storytelling with community leaders and elderly enlisted to share stories of war experiences, superstitious beliefs, herbal medicines and massages and other tales of life in the villages and ranches scattered throughout the island.

Siempre u-guaha f-in-a'-estoria ginen man-ma'gas kumunidat yan man-amko' ni' u-ma-empatte estoria put gera, h-in-engge put i taotao-mo'na yan espirito-n man-ansianu, put in-amte-n amot Chamorro yan kontodu estoria-n l-in-a'la' gi i sengsong yan lancho siha ni' man-ma-chalapon gi enteru i isla.

06 *Para u guaha misa, kuentos pumeska yan nabigasiunat, tinanna' yan fina'tinas inacha'ikak parehu lokkue' yan fina'huegu siha gi todu lugat […]*

There will be a liturgical celebration, navigational and fishing demonstrations and lectures, food tasting and culinary competitions as well as games of skills throughout the island.

Para u-guaha misa, kuentos p-um-eska yan nabigasiunat, t-in-aña' yan fina'tinas in-acha'-ikak parehu lokkue' yan f-in-a'-huegu siha gi todu lugat.

Contrary to copies from English, all Hispanisms in Chamorro must be considered conventionalized (instead of interactional/spontaneous/nonce) copies. This is due to the simple fact that Spanish, aside from being the first European language to have been introduced to the islands and used there for centuries, has not been widely spoken on the Marianas for more than a century, hence awareness as to the source of these elements is, as a rule, not given. A quantitative analysis of the excerpt above shows that of 188 tokens 55 are unambiguously of Spanish origin, and that another one is a very probable candidate (01, *kalamten*, see Rodríguez-Ponga 1995: 355 '¿< *calambre* "contacto eléctrico"?'). These 56 tokens make up roughly 30 per cent of the text. A more ambiguous case in the text is the definite article Ch. *i*, which could be derived from Sp. *el*, but the data is not conclusive with regard to this (Pagel 2010: 76–80). If we add all instances of Ch. *i* to the side of Hispanisms too, these would number 66 and make up 35 per cent of the tokens in the text. Both figures confirm to the results obtained in Pagel (2010: 53–60; see also Bowen 1971: 949). They conflict, however, sharply with observations made by Albalá and Rodríguez-Ponga (1986) and Rodríguez-Ponga (1995), according to which

En general … las palabras de origen español que usan los hablantes actuales del Chamorro constituyen entre un 50 y un 60% de su léxico. (Rodríguez-Ponga 1995: 92)

[In general . . . the words of Spanish origin used by the current speakers of Chamorro make up between 50 and 60 per cent of its lexicon. (my translation)]

As pointed out in Pagel (2010: 53–60), these figures may not be representative of the Hispanisms actually in use in Chamorro, owing to methodological inconsistencies in the way the data were obtained.[8] Nonetheless, they have been repeatedly decisive in the discussions of the genetic and contact-typological status of Modern Chamorro. I will return to this issue in section 10.5.

Regarding the quality of the data, Hispanisms in Chamorro can be subdivided into at least three groups, according to their level of significance in the overall system of the language (Pagel 2010: 131–133): a first group consists of Hispanisms that have become systemically indispensable, as they are highly grammaticalized and have no functional autochthonous alternatives. In this group we find determiners such as the indefinite article *un* (< Sp. *un*; for an insightful discussion, see Stolz 2010 and 2012); possibly the definite article *i* (< Sp. *el*?); the demonstrative *este* 'this' (< Sp. *este*); a number of prepositions such as *sin* 'without' (line 01, < Sp. *sin*) and *put* 'about' (line 05, < Sp. *por*), which gave the traditionally agglutinating morphology of Chamorro a more analytical character; the grammaticalized marker for irrealis modality or future tense Ch. *para*, and the adverb or second future tense marker *siempre* (lines 01, 05, 06, < Sp. *para* 'for, in order to', Sp. *siempre* 'always'; for a recent discussion on their status see Chamorro 2012); and, to mention just one more, the comparative construction Ch. *mas . . . ki* 'more . . . / . . . -er than' (< Sp. *más . . . que*).

The second group consists of Hispanisms that have become important to Chamorro's system but are not entirely indispensable, as they alternate with autochthonous or other non-Hispanic alternatives. Here we will find, e.g., a number of discourse markers, competing in modern speech with equivalents from English, and quantifiers like *todu* 'all, whole' (line 06, < Sp. *todo*) and *kada* 'every, each' (Sp. *cada*). But it is above all the numerous lexical Hispanisms that make up this second group, as many of these have more or less synonymic autochthonous counterparts (e.g. *buenu* [Sp. *bueno*] vs. *maolek* 'good', *bida* [Sp. *vida*] vs. *cho'gue* 'do', *lengguahi* [Sp. *lenguaje*] vs. *fino'*, Salas Palomo and Stolz 2008: 245).

The third and last group comprises Hispanisms that are rather marginal in the system, because they represent optional operations and, in general, have not become productive on autochthonous stems. Here we find, e.g., fossils of

---

[8] The most important ones are that a dictionary and not actual texts were the primary source used, and that it was thus a quantitative analysis on the level of lexical words only and not on the level of morphemes constituting a text. In other words, 'non-natural' data, in the sense laid out in Chapter 2, this volume, has been consulted.

the Spanish gender system, as in line 03: *maestra/-o* 'female/masculine teacher'. Grammatical gender agreement, as in Spanish, is rarely found in Chamorro, and in fact seems to be restricted to a handful of copied pairs (especially with *bunitu/-a* 'beautiful' as in *i isla bunita* 'the beautiful [FEM.] island [FEM.]'; but see line 05 *gi enteru i isla* 'on the whole [Sp. MASC.] island [Sp. FEM.]'). Other members of this last group are diminutive and augmentative suffixes (e.g. *-itu/-ita*), which are, by and large, restricted to vocabulary copied from Spanish, and the plural suffix *-(e)s*, which is maintained in form and function in a few pairs covering mostly units of measurement such as *ora/oras* 'hour/-s' (< Sp. *hora/-s*) or *metro/metros* 'meter/-s' (< Sp. *metro/-s*), or is simply fossilized in otherwise singular forms like *flores* 'flower' (line 03, < Sp. *flores*) or *kuentos* 'story' (line 06, < Sp. *cuentos*).

In sum, the impact of Spanish on Chamorro is significant. Hispanisms make up a considerable part of its lexicon and have also found their way into the language's structure. In a few cases even highly grammatical areas have been affected by the contact with Spanish. Nevertheless, the majority of the grammatical categories as well as the typological core of Chamorro language (including its predominantly agglutinative morphology, split ergative alignment, and VSO basic word order) have not been affected in a significant way (see Pagel 2010: 50–133 for more details).

On this basis the following section will focus on the genetic and contact–typological status of Modern Chamorro, with reference to previous classifications and arguments as well as the ecological frame of the Spanish–Chamorro contact. There is perhaps no other language in contact with Spanish that has received so many divergent contact–typological interpretations, which range from a rather superficial 'touch' of Spanish, to the pidginization of ancient Chamorro or the creolization of Spanish, up to, as is quoted in the title of this chapter, contact-induced changes that lead to the emergence of 'the opposite of an anti-creole'.

10.5   Assessing Modern Chamorro

One of the earliest hypotheses concerning a changing genetic relationship of Modern Chamorro must indeed be considered hypothetical in the first place. Studying Chamorro's core vocabulary, Fischer (1961) extracts about 20 per cent of items copied from Spanish – a high number in comparison to Swadesh's results from of a number of indigenous languages of Latin America, which for the most part were considered to have had a longer contact history with Spanish:

The number of borrowed words entering the basic vocabulary in 430 years (nineteen words) is considerably larger than the highest number reported by Swadesh in examining about 200 American Indian test vocabularies. The highest among these was six Spanish loans in a period of about 400 years in Mecayapan Nahuatl. (Fischer 1961: 261)

To underscore the consequences of his findings, Fischer sketches the following scenario:

Note . . . that if the introduction of Spanish words into Chamorro should continue at this rate for a total of two millennia, loan words would be in the majority in the basic vocabulary, and only 37% of the basic vocabulary would be 'native'. Since the basic vocabulary has been thought to be the most resistant part of the lexicon, perhaps *in this hypothetical case* the rest of the lexicon would consist even more predominantly of loan words. *If we further suppose* that historical records of this process of borrowing were not available, *we may speculate* whether future linguists would regard this future Chamorro as Austronesian or Indo-European. (1961: 261–262, emphasis mine)

It is important to take Fischer at his word here: he is setting out a 'hypothetical case', he 'suppose[s]' and 'speculate[s]' in order to confront his findings in Chamorro with Swadesh's glottochronological hypothesis. Chamorro seems to contradict Swadesh's finding of a relatively constant retention rate in a number of contact situations. Contact-induced change apparently occurred at a higher, faster rate in Chamorro. Nonetheless, Fischer does not provide a genetic or contact–typological evaluation of the language as an Austronesian–Indo-European mixed language. In order to do so it would have been imperative to include contact-induced change in the grammar of the language, which is explicitly beyond the scope of Fischer's study (the title being 'The retention rate of Chamorro basic vocabulary'). Nor does the author present a true prediction on the future status of Chamorro: the scenario set out by him was already obsolete at the time of his writing. Chamorro's contact situation with Spanish had declined radically in importance from 1898 until the 1950s, and at the beginning of the 1960s a community-wide language shift to English was on the horizon (and was documented for Guam by Odo 1972). There was hardly a chance that the scenario would become reality. We may conclude then that Fischer didn't seriously doubt the (synchronic) Austronesian character of Chamorro when writing his article.

Fischer's often quoted labelling of Modern Chamorro as 'a pidgin' (1961: 262) must be interpreted with similar caution. The author departs from the observation that his informants remarkably often disagreed about the 'correct' translations of the words from the Swadesh list into Chamorro: in 19 per cent of the cases (18 words) the speakers had given more than one possible translation. It was, however, hardly ever an Austronesian form competing with a Hispanic one but almost always more than one option with an Austronesian etymology. It is hence not the Spanish appearance of Chamorro but the apparent variability in the core vocabulary of the language that Fischer considers reminiscent of a pidgin situation in which bilinguals of different native language background may tend to favor words derived from their own language in speaking the pidgin. It may be suggestive to speak of Chamorro as something like a pidgin based on the language of the inferior group rather than on that of the superior group as is more common. (1961: 262)

Incidentally, the variability observed can often be attributed to methodological flaws. For instance, the three informants had submitted their translations in written form and were apparently never asked to explain why their lexical choices varied among them. Thus, the kinds of 'alternations' observed by Fischer are often the result of simple misunderstandings or ignorance of Chamorro's structure. A case in point is that of word number 3 in the list: the English pronoun 1PL *we*. It is underspecified from the point of view of Chamorro and is accordingly translated in three different ways by the informants: as *hit* (= pronoun 1PL.INCL), *hita* (= pronoun 1PL.INCL.EMPH), and *hame* (= pronoun 1PL.EXCL.EMPH) (Fischer 1961: 258). All three translations are acceptable in Chamorro, because this language makes a four-way distinction for the first person plural: inclusive/exclusive and non-emphatic/emphatic. In other words, the alternations noted by Fischer are grammatical and not lexical. Another interesting example is word number 17, Eng. *man*, which two of the informants translated as *taotao* 'human being, person, people' and the third as *lahe* 'man' (ibid.: 259). Here, of course, the polysemy of the English lexeme, not variability in the core vocabulary of Chamorro gives an explanation for the perceived alternation.

Seen in this context, it is hard to agree with Fischer's conclusion that Chamorro may be considered as a pidgin (though see Rodríguez-Ponga 1998: 514 or Munteanu 1997: 961), especially when *pidgin* is understood as a simplified but structured auxiliary language that lacks native speakers (e.g. Bakker 2008, Velupillai 2015). The absence of natural data in Fischer's study and an explicit focus on the core vocabulary preclude such a conclusion.

For Donald Topping (1973), author of a comprehensive grammar, dictionary and textbook of Chamorro, morphosyntax and phonology, not vocabulary are the levels on which a contact–typological classification must be based. Generally speaking, Topping considers these areas in Chamorro as untouched by Spanish. He applies the picture of a body with some flesh added but an unaltered skeleton:

There was wholesale borrowing of Spanish words and phrases into Chamorro, and there was even some borrowing from the sound system. But this borrowing was linguistically superficial. The bones of the Chamorro language remained intact: a little Spanish flesh was added through vocabulary borrowing, but Chamorro remained basically Chamorro. (Topping 1973: 6)

According to this perspective (and in a sense contrary to Fischer's assumption), the contact with Spanish has not had a more significant impact on

Chamorro than it had on other indigenous languages in Latin America or the Philippines. In his own words (same paragraph): 'While Spanish may have left a lasting mark on Chamorro as it did on many Philippine and South American languages, it had virtually no effect on Chamorro grammar' (1973: 7).[9]

Objections against this view are raised by Albalá and Rodríguez-Ponga (1986). In their extensive study of the linguistic and cultural contact with Spanish on the Marianas they conclude that the more systemic levels of Modern Chamorro, too, display remarkable influences of the former colonial language:

Como veremos a continuación, la influencia del español se encuentra tanto en el vocabulario como en la gramática y la fonología. (Albalá and Rodríguez-Ponga 1986: 66)

[As we will see in the following, the influence of Spanish can be observed in the vocabulary as well as in the grammar and the phonology (my translation)]

Con cierta frecuencia se lee que el chamorro sólo recibió influencia española en el vocabulario, dejando intacta la gramática. Sin embargo, cualquier estudio, por poco profundo que sea, puede descubrir enormes influencias gramaticales españolas en chamorro. (ibid.: 73)

[One often reads that Chamorro shows influence from the contact with Spanish exclusively at the level of vocabulary, leaving intact the grammar. Nevertheless, every study, even the least profound, can discover enormous grammatical influences from Spanish in Chamorro. (my translation)]

According to Albalá and Rodríguez-Ponga, the Spanish influence on Chamorro can be observed at all linguistic levels. Reapplying Topping's metaphor, Chamorro then would have been Hispanized 'down to the bones'. The consequences of such a statement for (contact–) typological and genetic classifications of the language are far-reaching, but seem to be underestimated by the authors. Albalá and Rodríguez-Ponga chose a term that allows for an interpretation of Chamorro as an Austronesian and an Indo-European language at the same time, but one that has also been traditionally delicate in linguistics:

Hoy el Chamorro aparece más como una lengua mixta, de base austronésica, con fuerte penetración española. Por eso su filiación debe considerarse en estas dos direcciones. (ibid.: 66)

[Today Chamorro is more like a mixed language with an Austronesian base and strong Spanish penetration. That's why its affiliation has to be spotted in these two directions. (my translation)]

---

[9] More than a decade earlier Solenberger (1962: 59) had put it in a similar way: 'Although during the 18th century Chamorro absorbed, usually in modified form, a great many Spanish loan words, it retains its Indonesian grammatical structure.'

What appears to be an elegant solution at first sight quickly becomes problematic. The authors do not discuss the term *lengua mixta* 'mixed language' in its historical context and, more importantly, fail to equip it with explanatory power in order to make it a productive category in contact linguistics. Two questions would have been crucial here:

1 How is the quantitative and qualitative relation between autochthonous Austronesian and contact-induced Indo-European elements in Modern Chamorro (on the different linguistic levels)?
2 What quantitative and qualitative criteria define a contact language as 'mixed' and thus sufficiently distinguish the languages classified in this category from other outcomes of language contact?

Regarding the first question, Albalá and Rodríguez-Ponga (1986) present an impressive catalogue of Hispanisms at the levels of vocabulary, phonology and morphosyntax in Chamorro, one that is being completed in later contributions in which also the term *mixed language* is maintained (Albalá 1997, 2000; Rodríguez-Ponga 1989, 1994, 1995, 1996, 1998, 1999, 2001, 2009). With the exception of the vocabulary, however, convincing statistics on the number and proportion of Hispanisms in Chamorro and general qualitative considerations are missing, as well as a functional definition of *mixed language*.

It is a few years later that Bakker and Mous (1994a, 1994b) assess the heuristic potential of this term. By *mixed language* they designate the results of a process called *language intertwining* in which subsystems of two languages A and B merge into a new language C. Contrary to other types of contact languages like creole or pidgin, where the precise origin of specific linguistic material is often diffuse, the languages involved in intertwining situations are known and their number is restricted to two. At least one of the speech communities in the contact was largely bilingual when the mixed language emerged.[10] Furthermore, the respective subsystems can be reconstructed and attributed for the most part to a specific language and there is no or little overall simplification (see Thomason 1997). An explanation of the unique 'mixture' claimed for mixed/intertwined languages (which, according to Greenberg 1999: 356, would be a result of an 'unnatural' process) has been sought in a distinctive bicultural identity of its speakers (Muysken 1981; Bakker and Mous 1994a; Bakker and Muysken 1995; Croft 2003; Matras and Bakker 2003; McWhorter 2005).

A prototypical mixed/intertwined language is Media Lengua, spoken in Ecuador. An etymological split has been observed here along a hypothetical

---

[10] The term *intertwined language* is preferred by some linguists, and is indeed a less ambiguous one. For the sake of clarity I will use *mixed/intertwined language* in the remainder of this chapter.

282

axis that separates lexicon from grammar. Media Lengua, mixed/intertwined language C, recruited its semantics and morphosyntax from Ecuadorian Quechua (or Quichua), language A, and its lexicon from Spanish, language B. According to Muysken (1997: 378), 'Media Lengua is [basically] Quechua with Spanish stems'. Here is an example, in which Hispanisms are underlined.

Example 2: *Media Lengua (Muysken 1997: 377, translation original)*

> *Media Lengua-ga así Ingichu-munda Castallanu-da abla-na kiri-xu-sha,*
> Media Lengua-TOP thus Quechua-from Spanish-ACC talk-NOM want-PROG-SUB
> *no abla-naku-ndu-mi asi, chaupi-ga Castellanu laya, i chaupi-ga Ingichu laya*
> not talk-pl-SUB-AFF thus, half-TOP Spanish like, and half-TOP Quechua like
> *abla-ri-na ga-n. Isi-ga asi nustru barrio-ga asi kostumbri-n abla-na.*
> talk-REFL-NOM be-3. This-TOP thus our community-TOP thus accustomed-3 talk-NOM.
> 'Media Lengua is thus if you want to talk Spanish from Quechua, but you can't, then you talk half like Spanish, and half like Quechua. In our community we are accustomed to talking this way'.

The agglutinating morphology of Quechua, realized almost exclusively by means of suffixes, is as clear here as is the Spanish etymology of most lexical items at the left edge of the phrases. Both languages indeed seem to intertwine and there is, at first glance, no indication of the structural simplification assumed for creole and pidgin languages (the exact meaning of *simplification* and its relation to *restructuring* remaining a theoretical problem: see e.g. DeGraff 2003; McWhorter 2011). In other words, Media Lengua's grammar is as complex as that of the model language of this subsystem, Quechua.[11]

With regard to the lexicon, Bakker and Mous (1994b) give rather precise statistics for the languages of the mixed/intertwined type. As it seems, they surpass in magnitudes the well-known cases of 'extreme borrowing' (Thomason and Kaufman 1988), or *massive copying* in our terminology:

> As for the proportion, one can see that extreme borrowing never exceeds roughly 45% of the lexicon, whereas in some of the mixed languages discussed the proportion of 'foreign' lexical elements is closer to or over 90%. (Bakker and Mous 1994b: 5)

With these figures as a starting point, Stolz (1998) takes up the mixed/intertwined language hypothesis for Chamorro once again. Relying, however, on the figure of 54.9 per cent Hispanisms calculated by Rodríguez-Ponga (1995), he is unable to avoid the conclusion that

---

[11] Following the argumentation in Greenberg (1999), of course, Media Lengua *is* still Quechua and has not become anything else. This opinion seems to be shared by Gómez Rendón (2005, 2007) and Shappeck (2011).

Von einer Mischsprache kann bezogen auf das Chamorro nur in einem eher unspezi-
fischen Sinn die Rede sein, der lediglich die nicht näher quantifizierte Kopräsenz
von Elementen aus genetisch unterschiedlichen Quellen als Kriterium setzt. (Stolz
1998: 19–20)

[One can speak of Chamorro as a mixed language only in a rather unspecific sense
one that has as its criteria merely the co-presence of elements from genetically different
sources which are not quantified any further. (my translation)]

It is likely that Albalá and Rodríguez-Ponga had this unspecific sense in mind
in characterizing Chamorro as a 'lengua mixta'. An indication is given by
Rodríguez-Ponga (2001) who both defends the labelling *mixed language* and,
at the same time, suggests a classification of Chamorro as a creole.[12]
According to his taxonomy, the latter seem to be only *one* possible manifestation of mixed languages:

No se trata, pues, de una lengua equiparable a otras lenguas austronésicas, porque no es
solamente esto: es una lengua mixta hispano-austronésica, como vengo defendiendo
desde hace años. Y una lengua nueva, que incorpora elementos de una lengua europea y
de una lengua indígena, que es el resultado del contacto en una situación de plurilin-
güismo en un determinado lugar, como efecto de un proceso de colonización, ¿no se
llama lengua criolla? (Rodríguez-Ponga 2001: 277)

[It is not a language comparable to other Austronesian languages because it's not only
that: it is a mixed Spanish–Austronesian language, as I've been writing for years. And a
new language, incorporating elements of a European and an indigenous language,
which is the result of contact in a situation of multilingualism in a certain place, as an
effect of a colonization process – is it not called a creole? (my translation)]

Other linguists, such as Thomason (1997, 2001b) or McWhorter (2005), have
made similar proposals. In particular, Thomason distinguishes between, on the
one hand, *bilingual mixed languages*, which correspond largely to the type laid
out by Bakker and Mous (1994a, 1994b), and, on the other, *mixed* or *contact
languages* as a general term covering *bilingual mixed languages, creoles*, and
pidgins. The term *mixed/contact languages* thus separates the three mentioned
types from other outcomes of contact-induced change such as *code
maintenance* or *code shift* and coincides in this sense with the *code creation*
mode in Figure 10.1. However, it is questionable what insights could be gained

---

[12] He is apparently referring to a classification of Alvar (1986) here which, in turn, is probably
based on the research by Albalá and Rodríguez-Ponga: 'Pero Filipinas no quedó sola en Oriente
y junto al chabacano, el español vio nacer otra lengua criolla, el *chamorro* de las islas de Guam,
Rota y Saipán, cuyo hispanismo es mucho mayor que el señalado por D. Topping, Pedro Ogo y
Bernadita Dungca en su Chamorro–English Dictionary.' ['But the Philippines did not remain a
singular case in the East, and, next to Chabacano, Spanish gave birth to another creole language,
Chamorro of the islands of Guam, Rota and Saipan, whose Hispanity is much greater than that
signalled by D. Topping, Pedro Ogo and Bernadita Dungca in their Chamorro–English Dictionary'] (Alvar 1986: 28, my translation).

from a classification of Chamorro as a 'mixed Hispano-Austronesian language' along the lines of this taxonomy. It has never been disputed that Chamorro is 'mixed' in the sense that it contains numerous copies from Spanish. On the contrary: Spanish influence on Chamorro has been acknowledged and also systemized to a certain extent in many earlier works such as Safford (1903a, 1903b, 1904a, 1904b, 1905), Preissig (1918), Costenoble (1940), and Topping (1973). Left open remain, however, the questions of how to characterize the Chamorro–Spanish 'mixture' and how to interpret it in genetic and contact–typological dimensions.

More helpful than the unspecific classification of Chamorro as 'lengua mixta' is therefore that as a 'lengua criolla': the term *creole* is bound to more specific criteria by which a possible candidate could be judged. Rodríguez-Ponga himself names three of them in the quoted paragraph; in a slightly adjusted form they read as follows:[13]

1 Creoles are 'new languages', i.e. they can be historically and linguistically distinguished from the languages involved in the circumstances of their coming into being.
2 Of the languages involved, in most cases one is a European language and the other(s) is (are) a non-European language(s).
3 The respective contact situation typically took place in a colonial context, at a certain place and within a multilingual setting.

Criteria 2 and 3 certainly match for the contact situation between Chamorro and Spanish on the Marianas. One could add that Modern Chamorro, as is also assumed by some linguists for creole languages, did not emerge gradually but rather 'abruptly' in line with an extensive Mesticization process that took place in the course of the eighteenth century (Rogers 1995; Rodríguez-Ponga 1999). But this is probably where the analogies end. Although Mesticization profoundly transformed Chamorro society (which motivates Rogers 1995: 104 to call the outcome of that process 'Neo-Chamorro'),[14] basic elements of Chamorro cultural identity such as matrifocality and the indigenous language remained intact. Chamorro language and people have existed on the Marianas prior to the arrival of Spanish-speaking people, and Chamorro

---

[13] In Rodríguez-Ponga (2009), where the same paper is published again, the author adds in a footnote: 'Dejo en el aire – como hice entonces – la respuesta a esta pregunta que formulé en la reunión de Bremen en la que presenté esta ponencia. Es aquí donde entraríamos a debatir si estamos ante un criollo, un semicriollo, un anticriollo, una lengua mixta, o simplemente una lengua con préstamo masivo.' ['As I did back then, I leave open the answer to the question that I asked at the meeting in Bremen where I presented this paper. It is here that we would enter the debate about whether we are dealing with a creole, a semi-creole, an anti-creole, a mixed language or simply a language with massive borrowing'] (2009: 196, my translation).

[14] See Pagel (2013a, 2013b) for an intercultural, intertextual, and linguistic analysis of a Chamorro fairy tale that reflects this transformation process.

continues to be the language spoken by at least a part of the Chamorro people today. Consequently, Chamorro language is a historically continuous phenomenon, with a history (known or not) beyond the colonial contact situation with Spanish.

Continuity is also given in the language's structure: contemporary varieties of Chamorro cannot be clearly distinguished from pre-contact varieties (or what has been handed down thereof) at any linguistic level except for that of cultural vocabulary. Despite massive Hispanic contributions, Modern Chamorro maintains the phonology and morphosyntax, and also large parts of the lexicon of pre-contact Chamorro. Appropriately, Rodríguez-Ponga (2013: 49) concludes in his analysis of Esteban Rodríguez's wordlist dating from 1565 that 'modern-day Chamorro anchors its roots in the language spoken in Guam in the sixteenth century, with absolute clarity and independence from later Philippine and Spanish influences'. Also from the perspective of typology Modern Chamorro shares significantly more features with other Malayo-Polynesian languages than it does with creoles (also those resulting from similar contact constellations such as the Philippine Chabacano, see Pagel 2010, 2015) or the Romance languages. It is evident, then, that in the case of Chamorro we are dealing with linguistic continuity and change, not with discontinuity and emergence, as are assumed for creolization. An application of the term *creole* in an underspecified fashion is not advisable since this will undermine the efforts made by contact linguistics to terminologically separate the more frequent and comparatively predictable cases of contact-induced change from the assumedly infrequent and unpredictable cases of creolization.

Whether the criteria articulated above capture the heart of the term *creole* as it has been used in contact linguistics is a different issue. A complete discussion is beyond the scope of this chapter (see Pagel 2010: 383–411, and 2018 for the history of term and concept as part of the contact linguistic paradigm), but two additional aspects with relevance for the Chamorro case shall be mentioned. A first one is the absence of a pidgin stage (although this is not considered as a necessary precondition for the emergence of creoles by all linguists – see below): there is no evidence whatsoever for the creation of a reduced auxiliary language that eventually became the first language of a new speaker generation (Rogers 1995; Rodríguez-Ponga 1999), nor is it likely that the ecology of the Spanish–Chamorro contact was conducive to the emergence of such a language. There was no rigorous ethnic segregation on the Spanish Marianas, and, because of the low numbers and relatively quick assimilation of the colonial personnel and other immigrants, enclavism as a whole and multilingualism probably remained limited. Colonial administration did not follow a pro-Spanish policy and never systematically discouraged the use of Chamorro. Spanish expanded into rather formal domains and was used in the colonial administration, in religion, in education, etc., while Chamorro remained the language of informal everyday life.

We would assume elaborated bilingualism and diglossia to have developed in such a contact ecology (as suggested by documents from the mid-eighteenth century onwards) but not a pidgin.

One has to bear in mind, however, that many criteria concerning the category *creole* are subject to critical discussion.[15] Among these criteria is also a pidgin stage preceding the creole language, which is considered to be a categorical precondition by some linguists (e.g. Holm 2000; Winford 2003) but only secondary by others (e.g. Bollée 1977, 2009; Siegel 2008). Yet, at least one more criterion is consensual in the creole discourse and must be added to the discussion on the 'creoleness' of Modern Chamorro: in the course of the creation of a creole language (be it out of a pidgin or not) the linguistic structure of the model language undergoes reduction and simplification processes (e.g. McWhorter 2007, 2011). As I have shown briefly in section 10.4 (and in detail in Pagel 2010), Modern Chamorro generally reproduces very few structures of Spanish and has in most cases formed something new on the basis of the copied elements, such as modal (irrealis) or tense (future) markers from Sp. *para* and *siempre*, or an indefinite article *un* 'which deviates vastly from the patterns of its Spanish etymological source' (Stolz 2012: 191). In those cases where we deal with true reproduction, there is little or no simplification but often an increase in context-embeddedness and/or optionality (as e.g. in copied grammatical gender). In its global appearance Modern Chamorro is neither a reduced and simplified variety of Spanish nor of pre-contact Chamorro. In complexity, Modern Chamorro does not diverge from other Malayo-Polynesian languages, but it clearly does from pidgins and creoles, even those with Malayo-Polynesian substrates (such as Philippine Chabacano, see Pagel 2010: 346–411). A classification of Chamorro as *creole* is therefore misguided and acceptable only under a highly unspecific meaning of the term, perhaps synonymous to a very general understanding of *mixed language* as discussed above.

Since *creole* is an a posteriori category and many deviations from the best known instances have been reported, modern contact linguistics has established various secondary, non-prototypical categories within the creole paradigm. There were also attempts to classify Chamorro in these secondary categories: in a later paper Rodríguez-Ponga considers a classification of Chamorro as a semi-creole, unfortunately without giving further explanations:

[E]l Chamorro actual es una lengua moderna nacida del contacto entre el español y la lengua prehispánica. Se trata, por tanto, de una lengua mixta hispano-austronésica. Más aún hay motivos suficientes para situarla (al menos en algún estado de su historia) en el grupo de lenguas criollas o – quizás mejor – semicriollas. (2009: 42)

---

[15] To catch a glimpse, see, for instance, Ansaldo, Matthews and Lim (2007), DeGraff (2003, 2005), Ennis and Pfänder (2010), Ludwig (2010), McWhorter (2000, 2005, 2007, 2011), Mufwene (2000, 2001, 2003, 2008), Siegel (2008), and Pagel (2018).

[Contemporary Chamorro is a modern language born out of the contact between Spanish and the pre-Hispanic language. Furthermore there are sufficient reasons to situate it (at least at a certain point of its history) into the group of creole or – perhaps better semi-creole languages. (my translation)]

The adjusted position struggles with the same problems discussed above: Modern Chamorro displays neither the reduction and simplification patterns found in creoles nor those found in semi-creoles like Afrikaans or Brazilian Portuguese – restructured languages in comparison with their ancestors Modern Dutch and European Portuguese, but with an unmistakable Germanic or Romance structure, respectively. To assume that Chamorro displayed these patterns at a certain point of its history raises the question when, why, and how this language has lost the structural properties of creole or semi-creole languages again. If we were to interpret present Chamorro's structure as the result of a recent 'decreolization', this restructuring would have been on the model of pre-contact Chamorro and not on that of Spanish (which would amount to a circular scenario).

Some linguists have chosen rather unconventional methods to test Modern Chamorro as a candidate for the creole type. Munteanu's (1997) analysis, for instance, is restricted to Chamorro's vocabulary and immediately raises the question as to whether a classification on this basis is practicable at all. Reading Munteanu's paper strengthens the suspicion that the author is paying for a positive classification with many compromises. According to him, Chamorro is a creole but an atypical one in two respects: first, it is not the result of an evolution *towards* a target language but *from* various source languages; and second, the dominant language (socially and in terms of the direction of the restructuring) was not European (Spanish) but Malayo-Polynesian (pre-contact Chamorro).[16] Especially the second restriction is so fundamental that it amounts to make the achieved classification absurd. One of the few commonly accepted extra-linguistic characteristics of creole languages is that these languages emerge out of attempts by ethnically and linguistically heterogeneous groups with low social prestige to acquire the language of a relatively homogeneous group with high social prestige (for example, in a community of plantation slaves shifting to the colonial language). Putting on stage the scenario outlined by Munteanu we would witness on the Marianas a

---

[16] 'En caso de definirse claramente el estatus "criollo" del chamorro, creemos que deberíamos contemplarlo como un criollo doblemente atípico. En primer lugar, no como resultado de una evolución hacia una lengua meta, sino desde varias lenguas fuente … igual que el papiamento … En segundo lugar, si aceptamos que en la génesis de tales criollos la correlación de fuerzas entre las lenguas de input no es igual y siempre existe una lengua dominante o base, que imprime su dirección de desarrollo a todo el proceso de criollización … en el caso del chamorro actual esta lengua no sería europea, concretamente el español, sino el chamorro antiguo, malayo-polinesio' (Munteanu 1997: 962).

prestigious and homogeneous group of Chamorro dominate a low-prestige and heterogeneous group comprising Spaniards, Mexicans, and Filipinos. The first would restrict the latter's access to the dominant language in this contact (pre-contact Chamorro), which would result in the emergence of a creolized variety of Chamorro among the Spanish speakers, and thus would eventually be adopted by the indigenous elite too.

Choosing yet another approach to the creole paradigm, Couto tests Modern Chamorro for a contact type he calls *anti-creole* (1996, 2002). A creole is usually claimed to recruit the majority of its vocabulary from the dominant language in the contact setting while its structure maintains patterns from the dominated languages, by a process identified by some creolists as *relexification*. Couto's anti-creole, on the other hand, is said to mix the vocabulary of the dominated language(s) with the structure of the language dominant in the contact setting, by a process called, analogously, *regrammaticalization*. From a socio-historical perspective, the genesis of an anti-creole is tied to the migration of a group A into the territory of a socially and demographically dominant indigenous group B and a certain enclavism of group A in that territory. An example given by Couto is Shelta, a language combining Irish-Gaelic vocabulary with English structure. An overlap with the mixed/inter-twined language type mentioned earlier is undeniable. Accordingly, Shelta has been described from that perspective too, for instance by Grant (1994). With regard to Chamorro, Couto (1996) observes correctly that, on the one hand, this language lacks the reduction and simplification patterns said to be typical of creoles, and, on the other hand, does not display enough regrammaticalization (on the Spanish model) to be regarded an anti-creole. Put differently, Chamor-ro's structure is considered too complex and too Austronesian to classify the language as a creole, but not Spanish enough to classify it as an anti-creole. The compromise proposed by Couto, however, appears to be a frank capitulation: although not being a creole, Chamorro is regarded 'basically the opposite of an anti-creole'.[17]

In order to understand such an interpretation, it is again critical to consider the context in which it is done. Couto's study focuses on anti-creoles, and in the case of Chamorro he relies on only a handful of words and on a comment made by Hall, according to which Chamorro derives 'between 90 to 95 per cent of its vocabulary from Spanish' (Hall 1966: 99) – utopian figures by any measure. In a sense it is the contact-theoretical focus and the methodology of

---

[17] '[E]le não apresenta os processos de simplificação e redução gramatical que caracterizam essas línguas [crioulas]. Em suma, embora não seja um crioulo, no fundo o chamorro é o oposto de anticrioulo.' ['It does not represent the simplification and grammatical reduction processes which characterize these [creole] languages. In sum, although Chamorro is not a creole, it is basically the opposite of an anti-creole'] (Couto 1996: 89, my translation).

Couto's and also Hall's studies that constitute ecological parameters for our discussion here. Both Couto and Hall are testing Chamorro as a possible candidate for the type of contact language they are studying: anti-creole for Couto and pidgin/creole for Hall. However, such an approach does not necessarily involve an in-depth analysis of the language, not to mention one based on 'natural' data (in the sense laid out in Chapter 2, this volume). Accordingly, the results obtained from it should be dealt with cautiously, measuring their scope against the context. Without further data, they cannot be objectified.

Based on a thorough linguistic analysis, Stolz's contribution to the lengthy volume on the mixed/intertwined language matter by Matras and Bakker (2003) is one of the latest attempts to determine a contact typological status for Modern Chamorro. Studying various sections of Chamorro morphosyntax, Stolz draws the following conclusion, which I see, on the whole, confirmed by my own analysis:

All in all, Hispanization of Chamorro grammar is overwhelmingly a superficial matter which mostly affects only the expression side of the linguistic sign. In addition, the Spanish-derived elements more often than not are optional. What is obligatory in Chamorro grammar has almost always an Austronesian past. Thus, it is legitimate to claim that except for a handful of cases Chamorro grammar has retained its inherited Austronesian structure despite the heavy pressure on the part of Spanish. (Stolz 2003: 282)

An evaluation of Chamorro's lexicon turns out to be more complicated. Again Stolz takes up the figure of 54.9 per cent Hispanisms calculated by Rodríguez-Ponga (1995), which is contradicted by an interesting observation made by Bakker and Mous for mixed/intertwined languages. In a preliminary comparative study these authors had found that

there do not seem to be languages with a proportion of borrowed items between 45% and 90%, so that there is no continuum between languages with heavy borrowing and mixed languages. (1994b: 6)

In other words, a language in a contact situation will copy either less than 45 per cent or more than 90 per cent of the vocabulary of the language(s) it is in contact with. In the first case we are dealing with a simple copying process that can be further qualified, and in the second we are dealing with language intertwining, a process out of which a mixed or intertwined language emerges. Chamorro, it seems, does not fit in either of the two categories. Stolz provides two explanations:

Given the reliability and the comparability of the above percentages, one is faced with the problem of finding a solution: either the borderlines between the categories have to be adjusted so that massive borrowing extends beyond the 50 per cent mark or Chamorro and Malti are neither an instance of massive borrowing nor of mixed languages but rather something else. (2003: 291)

Perhaps the most conclusive explanation is touched on in the introductory phrase: the figures taken up by Stolz may not be reliable because they were not obtained from Chamorro in actual use. Without denying in principle the gap stated by Bakker and Mous (the second language Stolz deals with in his paper is Malti and may indeed be a candidate to fill it), it seems more obvious to question the figure proposed by Rodríguez-Ponga, for the reasons touched in section 10.4. This figure was calculated essentially on the basis of a standard Chamorro–English dictionary compiled by Topping, Ogo, and Dungca (1975). It is clear that a dictionary is always arranged selectively in terms of quantity as well as quality and thus can hardly mirror the relevant language in text or interaction (see Topping, Ogo, and Dungca 1975: xii). In addition, one has to take into account the fact that regular diachronic change has happened in Chamorro since the 1960s and 1970s, when the dictionary was compiled. There are strong indications that this change even followed a certain direction: away from Hispanisms and towards Anglicisms as well as Austronesisms (see Salas Palomo and Stolz 2008). One major reason for this is that Spanish as a natively spoken language has ceased to exist on the Marianas. During the time the dictionary in question was being compiled there were still speakers of Spanish among the Chamorro, for whom this language (and, one must assume, elements copied into Chamorro) transported the high prestige it used to have in the colonial time. Today, however, there are no native speakers of Spanish left (Rodríguez-Ponga 1989: 294; Pagel 2010: 46, 148). Many of the less conventionalized Hispanisms are being replaced 'naturally' by autochthonous vocabulary, because the prestigious tone of Hispanic elements has disappeared (see Stolz 2003; Salas Palomo and Stolz 2008). Moreover, purist efforts regarding the language's structure are directed primarily against the Spanish influences too. In ecological terms, the foundation relations in the ecology of Modern Chamorro have shifted notably during the last decades: the last fragments of the colonial interaction with the Hispanic macro-ecology disappeared, Chamorro–Spanish bilingualism and diglossia, the relevant interactional norms and linguistic attitudes passed into memory and history. Linguistic elements from Spanish, formerly part of colonial bilingual interactions, either fossilized in Chamorro language or were being replaced by other material, especially from English. Contemporary Chamorro interactions are situated in the Malayo-Polynesian, the Anglo-American and the Asian macro-ecologies, but not anymore in the Hispanophony. In fact, ties to the latter are often being consciously suppressed, although they must be considered essentially covert ties already. Purist language policy, for instance, must make serious efforts to draw attention to Hispanisms in order to propose ways to avoid them. If avoided, the perceived 'Hispanity' of Chamorro is weakened and the foundation of this language in the Malayo-Polynesian and other non-Hispanic macro-ecologies is reaffirmed. In this regard, the Marianan case is considerably more absolute than that of the Philippines, where an aged but economically well-situated and influential group of mestizos still actively preserves the historical ties to the Hispanic macro-ecology (see Pagel 2010: 311ff.). In a certain way some considerations of linguists from the Spanish-speaking world regarding the status of Modern Chamorro could be interpreted as a parallel strategy: By overemphasizing and overstating, consciously or not, the 'Hispanity' of Modern Chamorro, its foundation in the Hispanic macro-ecology is being maintained.[18] As demonstrated in section 10.4, however, the percentage of Hispanisms in contemporary Chamorro texts and interaction is lower than suggested by those linguists and probably level off at around 30 per cent.[19] Calculating with this figure, then, Chamorro does not contradict Bakker and Mous's claim (but does not prove it either).

Combining Bakker and Mous's observations with his own, Stolz ultimately anticipates the only conclusive classification of Modern Chamorro: not a pidgin, not a creole, not an anti-creole or mixed/intertwined language, as these categories are not consistent with the synchronic and diachronic evidence from the ecology of the Chamorro–Spanish contact. Chamorro has evolved by adapting to new ecological conditions and can be said to have entered a novel language stage at which it displays a significant number of copies from Spanish, including a limited amount of 'Hispanity' in its structure. One way to picture the quantity and quality of Spanish copies in contemporary Chamorro in relation to the intensity of the respective contact process is provided by Thomason and Kaufman's (1988: 74–94) 'borrowing scale', as shown in Table 10.1.

There is firm evidence for copying from Spanish into Chamorro up to the third of the five levels of this scale. The copying of the Spanish comparative marker *más (que)*, the indefinite article *un*, and the preposition *para* are good candidates for the fourth level and involve little, perhaps even considerable structural change (see Pagel 2010: 81ff. for comparison; Stolz 2010, 2012 for *un*). The preposition *para* and its grammaticalization to either a modal (irrealis) or a tense (future) marker in Chamorro (see Pagel 2010: 98ff. and Chamorro 2012) also clearly indicate the limits of the concept and term *borrowing* (and others with similar metaphorical substance like *loan, transfer*, etc.): there is no element with an equivalent function to that of Ch. *para* in any of the varieties of Spanish, which begs the question what exactly the object of this 'borrowing process' was. The irrealis or future tense marker Ch. *para* is more accurately described as the result of selective copying (of phonetic substance and only some aspects of meaning, but no combinational and frequency

---

[18] See Mühlhäusler (Chapter 11 of this volume) for more reflections about the role of the linguist in the making of linguistic 'facts'.
[19] Bender (1971) and Stolz (1998) give similar figures.

Table 10.1 *Modern Chamorro on the 'Borrowing Scale'*

Contact level	What is being borrowed/copied?	Examples from Modern Chamorro
(1) Casual contact	Lexicon: content words, non-basic vocabulary before basic vocabulary	E.g. *mansana* 'apple', *iskuela* 'school', *baka* 'cow', *pali* 'priest', *bunitu/-a* 'beautiful', *bida* 'do'
(2) Slightly more intensive contact	Lexicon: function words: conjunctions and various adverbial particles Structure: minor phonological, syntactic and lexical semantic features	Subjunctions like *antes ki* 'before', *desde ki* 'since'; adverbials like *buenu* 'good', *esta* 'already', and others Diphthongs and consonant clusters in copied Hispanisms like *Bietnes* 'Friday', *Nobiembre* 'November' etc.; discourse markers like *pues, entonses*, comparative marker *mas (ke)*; *estaba* as past form of existentials *guaha* and *gaige*
(3) more intensive contact	Lexicon: function words: adpositions; derivational affixes on copied items; personal and demonstrative pronouns; low numerals	Prepositions like *para* and *asta* 'to, towards', *put* 'because of', *kon* 'with', *sin* 'without' and others; derivational suffixes *-itu/-ita, -eru/-era*, plural suffix *-es* and morphological gender distinction (with gender agreement optional and restricted) on copied items; personal pronoun 1Sg *yu'* (?), demonstrative pronoun *este* 'this'; all numerals (*uno* 'one', *dos* 'two', *tres* 'three' etc.)
(4) strong cultural pressure	Structure: slightly less minor structural features than in (2): in phonology phonemicization of previously allophonic alternations; in syntax indications of changing word order Structure: major structural features that cause relatively little typological change: in syntax extensive word order changes as well as other changes that will cause little categorical alternation; in morphology copied inflectional affixes and categories will be added to native words	Phonemicization of [e] and [i] (previously allophones of /i/ and /u/); *para* as syntactic alternative for dative shift (Pagel 2010: 107ff.) Comparison with *mas (ki/kinu)* and *itmas*, modal (irrealis) or tense (future) marker *para*, indefinite article *un*
(5) very strong cultural pressure	Structure: major structural features that cause significant typological disruption: changes in word structure rules (e.g. from flectional towards agglutinative morphology), categorial as well as more extensive ordering changes in morphosyntax (e.g. development of ergativity); added concord rules	None

properties)[20] on the model of the Spanish preposition *para* and subsequent, perhaps even simultaneous, grammaticalization.[21] There is no convincing evidence that the fifth level of the Thomason and Kaufman scale was achieved in the Chamorro-Spanish contact situation. There is even less evidence suggesting that Chamorro has 'bred' a 'new language' or mixed with Spanish to form a 'new language'. Modern Chamorro displays a considerable density of copies from Spanish and should therefore be considered as a high-copying language/code (in the sense of Johanson 2002a). But both from the genetic and the typological perspective Chamorro remains a Malayo-Polynesian language, lacking the core characteristics of the Romance, pidgin, creole, and mixed/intertwined languages.

10.6   Final Remarks

This chapter has had two aims: first, to demonstrate that Modern Chamorro is not a 'new language' in the historical–genetic or the contact linguistics sense of this term, contrary to many claims that have been too readily accepted in contact linguistics. An interpretation of Modern Chamorro as a 'new' or contact language would be possible only if this term were extracted from the taxonomical context of the relevant fields and understood in a maximally neutral (yet not sufficiently precise) way, for instance, as a code which, from the socio-historical perspective, has received its current shape in an ecology of substantial language contact within a reasonable time frame, and which displays considerable distance from what is perceived (by speakers and perhaps also linguists) as characteristic of the languages involved in the contact.

The second aim is deducible from the topic of this volume and can be described as the attempt to trace possible ecological explanations for some rather doubtful claims regarding the typological status of Modern Chamorro. Various studies involved in the debate have revealed, on closer inspection, one or more of the following problems: (1) absence of 'natural' empirical data, (2) an inadequate examination of Chamorro's structure, (3) unawareness of the ecological conditions and historical dynamics of the Chamorro–Spanish contact situation, (4) a loose interpretation of the defining parameters of the linguistic categories dealt with, and (5) failure to adequately factor in the results of other studies (for instance, quotations taken out of context and objectifying quantifications without considering the methodology).

By choosing an ecological approach to the Chamorro–Spanish contact, this chapter has demonstrated – for a specific case – some advantages of this

---

[20] See Johanson (2002a) on global vs. selective copying.
[21] See Heine and Kuteva (2003, 2005) for interesting thoughts on contact-induced grammaticalization.

approach over non-ecological ones. The framework laid out in the introductory chapter of this volume permits linguists to locate their specific case and object of investigation within a holistic, inclusive, and coherent theoretical space. This framework not only allows for but considers indispensable methodological pluralism as well as interdisciplinary exchange, accumulation, and comparison. Arguing within this framework of ecological linguistics, building on a sizeable corpus of 'natural' empirical data, referring to a maximum of ecological parameters relevant for its topic (including after all the role of the linguist individual and his/her unavoidably biased view) the present study arrived at conclusions sufficiently different from those of other studies discussed in this chapter.

Part V

The Multiplicity of Ecological Parameters:
Echoing the Theoretical Frame and Going
Beyond

11 Contact between Typologically Different Languages

Peter Mühlhäusler

11.1 Introduction

There is a saying: 'familiarity breeds similarity'. Translated to linguistics, it means languages spoken in the same linguistic ecology or communication community become more similar, no matter how dissimilar they were to start off with. The principle appears to be confirmed by the findings of the *World atlas of language structures* (*WALS* Online, http://wals.info). Typological similarity correlates very positively with geographic proximity. Areal features or Sprachbund phenomena result from contact over long periods of time and illustrate the outcome of prolonged and relatively stable development. How this development began and what processes led to the observed outcome have not been as well documented and understood. They call for an examination into incipient contact and the grammar of young languages.

Pidgins and creole languages lend themselves particularly well as sources of evidence of all kinds of language development, for the following reasons:

- they are young languages whose development can be more easily documented than languages with longer histories;
- they are less likely to have been subject to language planning and standardization;
- they are often small in terms of speaker numbers and geographic coverage; and
- for the purposes of this chapter, they can illustrate the results of an abrupt encounter between typologically different languages.

In this chapter I shall focus on two contact languages I have had extensive first-hand experience with: Tok Pisin (TP) and Pitkern-Norf'k (PN). Both languages have a very short history. The first traces of New Guinea Pidgin English, Tok Pisin's precursor, date back to the 1830s when whalers began to call on ports in the islands around New Guinea. Pitkern-Norf'k started its life when the British Mutineers of the Bounty and their Tahitian consorts settled on the uninhabited Pitcairn Island in 1789. The current name of the language reflects the fact that the entire population of Pitcairn Island relocated from Pitcairn to Norfolk Island in 1856.[1]

Both TP and PN emerged as a result of contacts between speakers of English and other, typologically dissimilar languages. In the New Guinea region, English was in contact with numerous Melanesian and Papuan languages. On Pitcairn Island, there was contact between speakers of different English dialects, Tahitian, Tubuaian, and St Kitts Creole English when the PN language first emerged. In both instances there were contacts with many other languages in their subsequent history.

I have opted to concentrate on pronouns and spatial deixis because English and the various contact languages involved exhibit clear typological differences in these two areas of grammar.[2] Both pronouns and spatial deixis are relatively self-contained sub-components of semantax and moderately well documented across languages. I shall also make some less detailed remarks on multifunctionality (conversion). Again, there are major typological differences between English and its Pacific contact languages in this area of grammar.

Let me add a very general observation: the way linguists conceive of language, language contact, and language typology is shaped by professional traditions, practices, and, perhaps more importantly, shared metaphors. These are our tools. Whether they are useful tools for the job at hand needs to be questioned as indeed has been done in the introduction to this volume. One of the reasons why the traditional approach to modern linguistics has been challenged in integrational linguistics (e.g. Harris 1981) and ecological (or eco-) linguistics (Mühlhäusler 2003) is the contention that traditional methods lack descriptive and explanatory power. The two principal metaphors that underpin modern linguistics have been the reification metaphor, which portrays languages as bounded objects with a set of fixed properties (the fixed linguistic code) and the conduit metaphor of communication (Reddy 1979) which sees communication as the transfer of messages from sender to receiver by means of a fixed code that transforms messages into signals and vice versa. The effect of these two metaphors combined arguably has been disastrous for the discipline because:

- they have long outlived their use-by date;
- linguists have tended to confuse these metaphors with descriptions of fact.

---

[1] A small number of families returned to Pitcairn Island in the 1860s and their descendants speak varieties of PN, which differ somewhat from those spoken on Norfolk Island.
[2] This chapter focuses on data analysis rather than theoretical issues, such as the general role of ecology in language evolution. Some of my views on these general matters can be found in my review of Mufwene's 'Ecology of language evolution' (Mühlhäusler 2005).

The problems that arise from such metaphors for the study of language contact are numerous; and I do not have the space to discuss them all in detail or propose solutions to all of them. It is important to keep in mind the metaphorical nature of many of our research tools and to be prepared to ditch them if they do not do the job. Applied to the concepts in the title of this chapter one should remember:

- that contact occurs in the mind of bilingual speakers or between people who use languages, not between languages;
- that languages are not fixed bounded objects with determinate properties;
- that a concept of *typologically similar* or *different languages* is difficult to sustain.

The first point of course, has been made by many others in contact linguistics from Weinreich (1953) onwards, but most linguists have felt that it was legitimate to abstract from the process of communication. However, the extent to which communicative practices impact on the outcomes of contact has tended to be underestimated. Factors such as differences in power relations, conceptions of identity, learner strategies and numerous other socio-historical contingencies can affect the outcome of language contact and it is dangerous to make generalizations. From an ecological perspective, contact phenomena are the outcome of an indefinitely large set of ecological factors that enable or impede inter-communication.

11.2   Tertia Comparationis

As regards the second point, languages (L) have traditionally been regarded by linguists as inventories of properties P1 to PX and the job of linguists has been seen as that of determining and comparing these properties. The individual properties can be used as *tertia comparationis* when comparing different stages in the history of a language or when establishing typological categories of languages. This is illustrated in Table 11.1, portraying typological properties (P) in three putative languages (L).

In this hypothetical example, languages L1 and L2 share four out of nine possible properties, L1 and L3 share 5 properties and L2 and L3 share

Table 11.1 *Typological Properties of Putative Languages*

L1			L2			L3		
P1	P2	P3	P1	P4	P7	P1	P4	P5
P4	P5	P6	P9	P11	P12	P7	P9	P11
P7	P8	P9	P13	P14	P15	P12	P13	P17

seven out of nine properties, which make them typologically more similar than any other pair.[3]

The properties used for comparison can be lexical, grammatical, pragmatic, and so on. Our first task is to establish an inventory of diagnostic properties. In the early stages of typological studies, this was regarded as a relatively unproblematic task and morphological properties such as inflectional, fusional, and isolating have been used widely and uncritically. The difficulties of establishing diagnostic typological properties have become evident in the various projects aiming to compare pidgin and creole languages (e.g. APICS, Michaelis et al. 2013) or the 'World atlas of varieties of English' (WAVE, Kortmann and Lunkenheimer 2013). For example, comparison across languages results in statements such as:

- Italian and Spanish are pro-drop languages;
- Tok Pisin and English are SVO languages;
- Latin and Pitjantjatjarra are free word order (non-configurational) languages.

Sometimes languages have conflicting properties: many Germanic languages have different word order in main clauses and subordinate clauses, and most Paama–Nyungan languages of Australia have a split accusative–nominative and ergative system. Some analysts would argue that a split system is a typological property in itself. Therefore, how many properties (and consequently language types) there are depends on the delicacy[4] of individual linguists' analyses as well as their interpretations of the phenomena observed. English has not been characterized as being a switch–reference language, though clearly, a change of third person referred to occurs in sentences such as:

> *He is a bastard and HE is a twit.*
> *She is beautiful and SHE is fickle.*

The change of referent is signalled by means of extra stress on the second pronoun. Arguably, English also has a split ergative system (see Mühlhäusler and Harré 1990: 207–210) as can be seen from sentences such as:

> *I did it.*
> **Me did it.*
> *The devil made me do it.*
> **The devil made I do it.*

However, this aspect of English grammar is conventionally not described in terms of ergativity.

---

[3] As pointed out by others, similarity can have several reasons, including derivation from a common ancestor, prolonged contacts, or being the outcome of recent creolization.
[4] To say that both Tahitian and Pitkern-Norf'k have a split relative–absolute orientation grammar says very little, as will become clear from the analysis in section 11.7.

11.3   Similarities and Differences

Unlike universalists who deem surface differences between languages as trivial and at times argue that all human languages are essentially the same, typologists are in the business of setting up different classes of languages, using either structural or social criteria or, in the case of pidgins and creoles, the combination of both. The history of linguistic typology is reminiscent of the history of biological classification systems, though the progress made in the transition from folk taxonomies to scientific taxonomies has not been as impressive in linguistics as it has in biology. This is due in part to the greater mismatch between genetics and typology in socially transmitted languages and to the smaller number of constraints on mixing linguistic species. This state of affairs that has made it possible for linguists to argue both that there are no mixed languages and that all languages are mixed, that some languages are more primitive than others or that there are no primitive languages, that languages can change in an indefinite number of ways, and that language change is determined by internally driven drift. There are numerous difficulties in operationalizing the notion of similarity when talking about languages.

On the face of it, the procedures seem straightforward. Typological similarity/difference is established based on shared properties, for instance, German shares more properties with Dutch than with English. But this is quite problematic to implement because:

- No language is mono-stylistic, and most languages have a baby talk or foreigner talk register. As observed by Ferguson (1971, 1975) all languages are typologically similar in their baby talk (BT) or foreigner talk (FT) registers; and we note that foreigner talk is the register that is most likely to function in language contact.
- Languages have a very large number of properties; pragmatically linguists can only select a few for typological purposes. Thus APICS selected 120, as opposed to 150 in WALS. Ideally one should only choose properties that are not universally implied by other properties, but in practice this is not done consistently. Depending on which properties are selected, languages will be more or less similar. Baker and Huber (2000), using one set of properties, conclude, for instance, that Pitkern-Norf'k is typologically closer to the Atlantic creoles; whereas Kortmann and Szmrecsanyi (2004), using a different set of properties, conclude that it is typologically closer to Melanesian Pidgin English.

There is the additional problem of what Silverstein (1971) has labelled 'multi-level generative systems', the situation where similar surface structures are the outcome of different rules applied to different deep structures, apparently a common phenomenon in pidgins. Thus, European and Melanesian speakers differ in the way they interpret the structure of the following Tok Pisin sentence:

Em	*I*	*haisim*	*ap*	*plak.*
PRONOUN	PREDICATEMARKER	verb	PARTICLE	NOUN

or

PRONOUN	PREDICATEMARKER	VERB	VERB	NOUN

'He hoisted up the flag.'

The problems go beyond similarity between languages, they also concern similarity within languages. I would like to address some of the worries I have about the notion of similarity in linguistics. Let me give you two examples:

- phonetic similarity; and
- semantic similarity.

Speech sounds are typically compared on the basis of features such as [consonantal], [voiced], [nasal], and so on. Let us ask: Which of the following pairs of sounds exhibits more similarity?

(i) [a] and [u]
(ii) [l] and [u]

Most people would opt for (i), ignoring that while these two sounds are similar from the perspective of their production they are quite dissimilar from the point of view of perception. By contrast, [l] and [u] are almost indistinguishable to some speakers when heard at the end of the word *bottle*.

Notwithstanding Jakobson, Fant, and Halle's (1969) attempt to posit features that are neutral with regard to production and perception, no one has resolved this discrepancy between the production and perception side. Linguists continue to privilege the former over the latter, as has been argued in detail by Hockett (1987).

Semanticists like phoneticians have also used decomposition or atomization and have come up with numerous proposals for universal semantic features. The problems of this approach were pointed out by Bolinger (1965). Consider the English items *bishop* and *to piss off* and ask: do these items have similar meanings? Do they share any semantic features? Linguists would agree that the answer is *no*. But let us now consider the multifunctional Tok Pisin word *pisop*, which means either 'Church dignitary' or 'to depart rapidly'.

When I carried out fieldwork in the East Sepik area I sometimes flew in the light airplane belonging to the *Pisop bilong Wewak* 'the Bishop of Wewak'. He was in the habit of dropping in for brief visits in outlying communities and departing about half an hour later for the next visit. Half an hour is long enough for blitzkrieg fieldwork or a brief sermon. Tok Pisin is an English-based pidgin and the English words *bishop* and *piss off* have become homophones in Tok Pisin. When words sound alike, there is a tendency for their meaning to become similar, and this is what happened with Tok Pisin '*pisop*'. After all, a bishop is someone who only visits briefly and leaves again. Or, to depart rapidly after a brief visit is what a Bishop does. This phenomenon has been commented on by a number of creolists (surveyed in Mühlhäusler 1982), where more examples can be found.

11.4   Linguistic Science

Linguistics has often been called a science. I hold a degree in linguistic science from the Science Faculty of the University of Reading (UK). To qualify as a science one needs to have falsifiable criteria for two things:

- whether two phenomena are the same or different;
- whether one is dealing with one or more than one phenomena.

Having observed the debates about synonymy, the discussion of whether one is dealing with the same phoneme within a language and the illegitimate debates about identity of phonemes across languages, among others, I have come to the conclusion that linguistics does not meet the requirements for being a science, a conclusion I share with Tony Crowley (1990). I note also the debates about geminate consonants, homophony and polysemy, the open junction, attempts to establish how many words there are in an utterance such as *go away* have not led to falsifiable statements about differences or number of analytic units. Thus, when analysing the sentence *go away!*, it remains undecided whether we are dealing with two words (surface form) or three (underlying deleted *you* is included) or, in some generative–transformational accounts, even eight (I TELL YOU FOR YOU TO GO AWAY). Identifying morphemes can raise similar issues. The word *footsies* in the expression *to play footsies under the table with someone* illustrates these. It is not clear, how many morphemes there are:

- *foot + s + ie + s,*
- *foot + sie + s,*
- *foot + sies*, or just
- *footsies*

If the first analysis is adopted, it is not clear whether the two instances of *s* are:

- separate morphemes with the same meaning,
- a single discontinuous morpheme, or
- two different morphemes.

Finally, there is the problem of assigning a meaning to the two instances of *s*. Among the solutions suggested to me are:

- they are both plural *s*;
- there is a plural and a diminutive;
- there are two diminutives.

I am not suggesting that there can be a determinate answer in either example. Rather I conclude that linguists cannot have scientific answers to many of their questions. And I could adduce additional examples. For a general discussion of the problems of segmentation in morphology the reader is referred to Palmer (1968).

11.5   The Role of the Linguist as Language Maker

Typology, as has been shown, has numerous problems. I have already identified:

- conceptual problems such as whether languages can be compared in principle – as yet there is no adequate metalanguage for comparison; and that includes semantics;
- the problems of establishing the right *tertia comparationis*; the significant dinosaur bones that tell us which other properties are implied.

An even more worrying problem is the quality of linguistic data. The American poet John Godfrey Saxe (in: *Daily Cleveland Herald*, 29 March 1869) once observed: 'Laws, like sausages, cease to inspire respect in proportion as we know how they are made.' I shall argue that very much the same applies to how grammars are written. Differences in descriptive practice are a major source of typological similarities and differences.

Let us consider the statement that the languages of Vanuatu exhibit significant typological similarities. We can verify this statement by looking at the 27 grammars written by a single linguist, the Revd. Dr Robert H. Codrington, during his stay on Norfolk Island. He was a leading scholar in Pacific philology at the time and, moreover, he systematically worked with first-hand data. But Codrington (1885: 252) in his famous *The Melanesian languages* points out that:

Mota, much better known than any other to the compiler, has been the medium through which generally speaking information concerning the Melanesian languages has been obtained. Mota has thus been a kind of standard to which the others have more or less been found or made to approximate.

Dr Codrington spent many years among the Melanesians; others carry out blitzkrieg fieldwork and are thus likely to be given unreliable information by their informants. The first missionary who worked on another Melanesian language, Motu (see Taylor 1976), recorded a high incidence of reduplication and the absence of a number of marked constructions. He was unaware that the language he described and used in bible translating was not true Motu but pidgin or Foreigner-Talk Motu, until his children, who had grown up among the locals, disabused him of this notion.

Also, linguistic data are not theory-neutral, and what is recorded and how is determined by the descriptive framework adopted. Missionaries tended to model their grammar on Greek and Latin; and languages thus described may appear more similar than they actually are. Likewise, descriptive similarity can be undermined by disagreements about the meaning of the descriptive terms used. We have yet to find out what Teichelmann and Schürmann (1840) meant in referring to 'aorist' in their Kaurna grammar. My colleague Susanne Hackmack (Bremen University), with whom I discussed this problem, informs me that the following definitions are found in R. L. Trask's *Dictionary of grammatical terms* (1993):

aorist:
1. A verb form marked for past tense but unmarked for aspect;
2. A verb form marked for both past tense and perfective aspect;
3. A verb form marked for perfective aspect;
4. A conventional label used in a highly variable manner among specialists in particular languages to denote some particular verb form or set of verb forms.

Crystal (1994: 22) hardly clarifies this matter when he characterizes aorist as:

a form of the verb in some inflecting languages, referring especially to an action, which lacks any particular completion, duration or repetition.

Even the basic metalinguistic terms of descriptive linguistics (N, V, NP) are anything but reliable. They are particularly problematic for the description of Polynesian languages that do not appear to distinguish between N and V (e.g. Tongan, see Broschart 1997). The reader can see why I am restricting myself to two languages that I know well and to a small part of their grammar.

11.6 Pronominal Grammar

11.6.1 *Description and Actual Use*

In what follows I shall briefly outline the grammatical properties of the pronouns found in the languages that were involved in the formation of Tok Pisin (English, Papuan and Austronesian languages) and Norf'k (English, Polynesian languages, St Kitts Creole). Before doing this, some problems with conventional descriptions of pronouns need to be commented on. The personal pronouns of English are conventionally given in Table 11.2.

Table 11.2 *Subject and Object Forms of English Personal Pronouns*

- *I* (first person singular)
- *you* (second person singular)
- *he* (third person singular masculine)
- *she* (third person singular feminine)
- *it* (third person singular neuter)
- *we* (first person plural)
- *you* (second person plural)
- *they* (third person plural)
- *me* (first person singular)
- *you* (second person singular)
- *him* (third person singular masculine)
- *her* (third person singular feminine)
- *it* (third person singular neuter)
- *us* (first person plural)
- *you* (second person plural)
- *them* (third person plural)

In our book *Pronouns and people* (1990) Rom Harré and I argued that the conventional description of English pronouns has little to do with how real speakers use them. For instance *we* can stand for any person and the early developmental meaning of *we* is probably DUAL – SECOND PERSON as in *we want to go to beddie byes*. The most common meaning in spoken everyday language again is probably SECOND PERSON, SINGULAR or PLURAL. If used as first person, the pronoun *we* tends to be paucal rather than plural, unlike *they*, which tends to refer to a larger group of people. Note the subtle difference in responsibility for what is said between *we say* and *they say*. Similar observations as to the discrepancy between an ideal pronoun chart and actual pronoun use in English have been made by Wales (1996).

We also noted that the personal pronouns serve the primary function of carving up people space creating distance and proximity, and that anaphoricity is a secondary phenomenon. In pidgins and L2 varieties the deictic function is dominant and anaphora rare and often absent in their early stages. As regards possessive pronouns it is noted that the distinction is made overtly in most Pacific languages, that between an alienable and inalienable possession is only present in the crypto-grammar of English, where one cannot coordinate:

> *I lost my trousers and son in the accident.
> *Her appearance and children are annoying.

It must be kept in mind that the description of the English pronoun system as well as those of Tok Pisin and Pitkern-Norf'k presented below and their contact

Table 11.3 *Tok Pisin Personal Pronouns (Thomason 2001a: 172)*

Person	Singular	Dual	Trial	Plural
First	mi	(excl.) *mitupela*	*mitripela*	*mipela*
		(incl.) *yumitupela*	*yumitripela*	*yumi*
Second	*yu*	*yutupela*	*yutripela*	*yupela*
Third	*em*	*(em)tupela*	*emtripela*	*ol*

languages are descriptive artefacts and hence of limited value to comparison. In the absence of any better tools I shall nevertheless make use of them.

11.6.2   Pronouns of Tok Pisin and other Melanesian Pidgins

The pronoun system of Tok Pisin, whose principal substratum languages were Austronesian, has been characterized by Thomason (2001a: 171) as follows:

In Tok Pisin, for instance, all the pronominal morphemes are ultimately derived from English, but the system certainly is not. It lacks the English gender and case distinctions (which are unknown in the languages of the original Pidgin's Austronesian-speaking creators) but has typical local categories of person and number. Tok Pisin pronouns differ from the pronouns of the main lexifier language (English) in a number of respects, as seen in a typical paradigm shown in [Table 11.3].

Thomason (2001a: 172) makes two claims about the Tok Pisin pronoun system:

• the system is essentially Austronesian;
• it was in place early in the development of Tok Pisin, a long time before its expansion in the 1920s.

Similar claims have been made for a range of Melanesian Pidgin Englishes by Terry Crowley (1990) and Keesing (1988). These claims do not take into account that the pronoun system of Tok Pisin used by Thomason represents the idealized end point of a long development. The fact that present day Tok Pisin system looks similar to that of Austronesian languages of New Guinea is no warranty that it looked like this in earlier stages. There are good developmental data for Tok Pisin's earlier developmental stages. For instance, Tok Pisin's predecessor, Samoan Plantation Pidgin, originally had a simple numberless system when it stabilized in the 1880s (Table 11.4).

The system was expanded when the indentured workers returned from Samoa to German New Guinea (Table 11.5).

The distinction INCLUSIVE vs. EXCLUSIVE precedes the distinction SINGULAR vs. DUAL vs. PLURAL, and as late as the 1920s second person

Table 11.4 *Early Samoan Plantation Pidgin Personal Pronouns*

Person	all numbers (SINGULAR, DUAL, PLURAL)
1	*mi*
2	*yu*
3	*him*

Table 11.5 *Later Samoan Plantation Pidgin Personal Pronouns*

1	*mi*
1	*yumi* (DUAL INCLUSIVE = the two of us, speaker and addressee)
2	*yu*
3	*him*

Table 11.6 *Pionnier's (Incomplete) Pidgin Pronominal Paradigm*

Number and person	Pronouns	Number and person	Pronouns
Singular		Trial	
1	*mi*	1 inclusive	*you mi tri fala*
2	*you*	1 inclusive	
3	*hème, i*[a]	2	
Dual		3	*tri fala*
1 inclusive	*you mi*	**Plural**	
1 exclusive		1	*you mi olguita*
2		1	
3	*tou fala*	2	
		3	*olguita, ol fala*

[a] *i* is not recorded by Pionnier in his pronominal paradigm, but is represented in dozens of occurrences in his texts.

dual inclusive or exclusive could not be found. Notwithstanding the absence of this pronoun in Pionnier's account of the language, Keesing (1988: 41) reconstructed it for the Solomons (Tables 11.6 and 11.7).

Keesing ignores that the absence of pronominal forms can inform us about the development of pidgin languages. We can interpret this development as a consequence of a number of processes:

- a language independent developmental hierarchy determines the order in which pronouns appear, whether there is a model or not;
- in the first stages both superstrate and substrate will be similar to the pidgin – the pidgin is a subset of those;

Table 11.7 *Supplementation of Pionnier's Paradigm*

Number and person	Pronouns	Number and person	Pronoun
Singular		**Plural**	
1	*mi*	1 inclusive	*yumi [olgeta]*
2	*you*	1 exclusive	*mifela*
3	*hem, i*	2	*yufela*
Dual		3	*olgeta*
1 inclusive	*yumi*		*(olgeta fela)*
1 exclusive	*mitufela*		*(ol fela)*
2	*yutufela*		*(hemfela)*
3	*tufela*		

- to what extent the additional categories are added from superstrate and substrate would appear dependent on their relative importance during the formation and, to a lesser extent, subsequent development of a contact language.

Tok Pisin over time approximates the distinctions made in its Austronesian substratum languages. As more and more speakers of Papuan (non-Melanesian) languages adopt Tok Pisin as a lingua franca, some influence from their languages is in evidence among non-fluent users, particularly the absence of an inclusive–exclusive distinction. However, as Papuan speakers of Tok Pisin gain fluency and are absorbed into the mainstream of Tok Pisin speakers they adopt the emergent norms of the language. Thus, the impact of the numerous pronoun systems of Papuan languages (documented in Laycock 1977) is negligible. Norf'k adds refinements from both English (gender) and Tahitian (dual) but no clear-cut INCLUSIVE–EXCLUSIVE distinction.[5]

11.6.3   Pronouns in Pitkern-Norf'k

Whereas Tok Pisin developed in the highly multilingual area of New Guinea and is spoken as a second language by speakers of over 600 Melanesian and Papuan languages, the number of languages involved in the formation and development of Pitkern-Norf'k is quite small, though not as small as Reinecke et al. (1975) suggests and has been repeated by numerous linguists since:

---

[5] Pronoun inventories are not a particularly reliable source for comparing languages. It is desirable to add a comparison of their deictic and anaphoric functions.

Pitcairn Island English with its offshoot on Norfolk Island is of extraordinary interest because it offers as near a laboratory case of Creole dialect formation as we are ever likely to have. The place, the time and sequence of events, and the provenience of each of the handful of original speakers are known as are most of the subsequent influences upon the Pitcairnese community and, to a lesser extent, upon the one on Norfolk. Only two languages, English and Tahitian, were in contact. (590)

The two other languages in use on Pitcairn Island were Tubuaian, a Polynesian language, which was not mutually intelligible with Tahitian and, more importantly, St Kitts Creole English (also known as Kittitian). There were thus three typologically distinct languages in contact, with English being the language of power.

The British mutineers did not necessarily speak Standard English and their pronouns may have been different from those used in this variety in a number of ways. One can get a number of indications of this when looking at PN pronoun forms. The second person singular pronoun is *yu*, as in Standard English, but for the first person dual *himii* (*hemii, hamii*) 'the two of us', the etymological source of which is 'thou and me'.

St Kitts Creole was used by only one of the mutineers, Edward Young. However, Young was the second last of the Bounty crew to die, he was very popular with both the women and the children and is said to have been the main storyteller and linguistic socializer of the children. His influence on Pitkern-Norf'k has been documented in Baker and Mühlhäusler (2013). Baker and Huber (2000: 835) made the following observations about St Kitts:

This was the first English colony in the Caribbean to be settled, starting with the arrival of 20 people from London in 1623. If the process that led to the formation of the Caribbean English Creoles began in the West Indies, its likeliest point of departure is thus St Kitts rather than anywhere else. Its subject and object personal pronouns can be arranged as follows: The dates given are those of the first documentation.

Person	Singular	Plural
1	*me* 'I' – 1785 –	*awwe* 'we, us' – 1785–, *we* 'us' 1996, *awe ye* 'we' (exclusive) – 1785 –
2	*you*	*aw you* – 1785–
3	(*him* SUBJ 1934), *he* OBJ – 1785–	*dem* 'they' – 1785–

St Kitts Creole's possessives take the same form as personal pronouns, but a few examples of the *for* + PERSONAL PRONOUN + NOUN structure are known, such as *you bin yerry foo mee mosser* '[if] you were to hear my Master'. There are several points of interest:

- St Kitts distinguishes between inclusive and exclusive first person non-singular;
- the form *awwe* 'we, us' is phonetically similar to Pitkern-Norf'k *auwa* 'we-PAUCAL', ingroup marker; and
- there is evidence for a periphrastic *fer* + PRON, though in St Kitts Creole it appears before the possessed, rather than after it as in Pitkern-Norf'k.

Tahitian was the principal language of the mutineers' entourage but by 1799, ten years after settlement, only eight women or 25 per cent of Pitcairn's population still spoke it. The British sailors knew some Tahitian, but the women were discouraged from using it or passing it on to the children. There are thus social reasons why the influence of Tahitian may have been much less than is suggested by population statistics. The personal pronoun system of Tahitian has been characterized by Ross and Moverley (1964: 163) as follows:

Tahitian has a rather elegant system of personal pronouns. They exist as singular, dual and plural, and, in the first person of the last two of these, a distinction is made between *exclusive* ('I and some person(s) other than you to whom I am talking') and *inclusive* ('I and you to whom I am talking'):

	I	II	III
sing.	*(v)au*, etc.	*'oe*	*'oia, ona*
dual	*maua* (excl.)	*'orua*	*raua*
	taua (incl.)		
pl.	*matou* (excl.)	*'outou*	*ratou*
	Tatou (incl.)		

Out of the encounter of English dialects, St Kitts Creole and Tahitian developed a complex pronoun system. That of the contemporary Norf'k variety of Pitkern-Norf'k has been characterized by Buffett and Laycock as shown in Table 11.8.

This set is at best tentative; it does not include the subject form *orl aklan* 'all of us Pitcairn descendants' and *orl auwa* 'all of us true blue Pitcairn descendants'. It also excludes an important variant of the possessive pronoun, which has prompted a number of subsequent researchers to draw incomplete conclusions on an important typological property of Pitkern-Norf'k. Thus, Heine and Kuteva (2001), in their paper on attributive possessives in creoles assign Pitkern-Norf'k to type C (POSSESSEE – INVARIABLE POSSESSIVE MARKER – POSSESSOR). This, however, is only one of several ways of signalling possession in Pitkern Norf'k. For pronouns, one finds *dems fence* 'their garden', *(ar) fence fer dem*, and *(ar) fence fer dems*, as well as *aklans said*

Table 11.8 *Pronouns of Norf'k (adapted from Buffett and Laycock 1989:11)*[6]

Subject	Object	Possessive	Predicate
ai	*mii*	*mais*	*main*
yu	*yuu*	*yus*	*yoen*
hi	*hem*	*his*	*his*
shi	*her*	*her*	*hers*
—	*et*	—	—
himii	*himii*	*himiis*	*himiis*
miienhem	*miienhem*	*auwas*	*milenhis*
miienher	*miienher*	*auwas*	*miienhers*
yutuu	*yutuu*	*yutuus*	*yutuus*
demtuu	*demtuu*	*demtuus*	*demtuus*
wi	*aklan*	*auwas*	*auwas*
yorlyi	*yorlyi*	*yorlyis*	*yorlyis*
dem	*dem*	*dems*	*dems*

'our place' and *(ar) said fer aklan*.[7] One might wish to refer to the presence of two or more typologically distinct ways of signalling the same grammatical relationship 'cumulative grammar'. Thus, both definite and indefinite, and specific and non specific determiners are used with two benefactive constructions, one involving a preposition, the other the verb 'give', elsewhere in grammar. Mixing need not lead to a levelled contact system but may simply increase the number of formal choices – constructions that are semantically equivalent and stylistically identical but may differ in regard to indexicality, as they may signify different family membership of the speaker.

In their discussion of the origin of 'Pitcairnese' pronouns, Ross and Moverley (1964: 163–164) argue that many elements are straightforward English or dialectal English, including the possessive *-s* form. They do not address the possibility that St Kitts Creole may be the source of *dem* and possibly *yorlyi*. They further argue that 'three pronouns which are undoubtedly of direct or indirect Tahitian provenance' are *hami, yorlye*, and *aklan*. *Hami* is calqued first person inclusive dual, *yorlye* is simply the Tahitian 2nd dual (though it does not have dual meaning), and *aklan* is said to be a translation of Tahitian *ta'ara ri'i* 'little people' (dialectal *arkels*).[8] I am quite uncertain that any of these are indeed of Tahitian origin.

---

[6] Detailed comments on the above chart can be found in Mühlhäusler (2012: 106-110).

[7] Nominal possession can be illustrated with place names where one will find a range of constructions *Miens Hied* as well as *Man Head* 'Man's Head'; *Ar Pine fe Robinsons* 'Robinson's Pine Tree', *Nellies Stoen* 'Nellie's Rock', *Stoen fe Georgie and Isaacs,* 'Georgie and Isaac's Rock'.

[8] They mistakenly equate the expression 'little people' with children, whereas in Tahitian it means 'people of a lower social rank'.

11.7   Spatial Orientation Systems

11.7.1   General Comments

Typologists distinguish between two types of spatial orientation systems: a relative one in which spatial deixis reflects location in relation to Ego or the speaker (i.e. right, left, front, back) and an absolute system in which location is expressed in terms of fixed reference points (e.g. North, South, East, West). Many languages in the Pacific area either combine both types or have an absolute system only (see contributions to Senft 1997). Recent research into the spatial description of islands (François 2004, 2010) and Oceanic atolls (Palmer 2009) reveals the complex way in which island populations adapt linguistically to land-sea boundaries and create intricate cognitive maps of their environment.

Although the relationship between spatial knowledge and talk about spatial knowledge is highly complex, linguists in the past have treated spatial terms as a system, which can be studied independent of context and use. This approach has come under attack from both anthropologically oriented linguists such as Senft (1997) and cognitive scientists such as Herskovits (1986). The latter points out that logical semantics cannot satisfactorily account for speakers' uses of spatial expressions. Both approaches conclude that a number of knowledges (world knowledge, pragmatic knowledge, contextual knowledge) interact with biological factors in ways that make any appeal to rules of grammar unworkable. This suggests that spatial terms are best approached from an ecological linguistic perspective (Mühlhäusler 2003), which focuses on the links between speakers and their social and natural environment in addition to their cognitive abilities.

The languages that were involved in the formation of both Tok Pisin and Pitkern-Norf'k represent both absolute and relative types of spatial deixis. I shall explore whether the grammar of the various contact languages is reflected in Tok Pisin and Pitkern-Norf'k or whether other factors shaped the spatial grammar of these languages. One of the problems is that the spatial grammars of the languages have not all been equally well documented and that there is little information about how such grammars were employed in actual talk about space, location, and movement.

11.7.2   Spatial Orientation in Tok Pisin

In the formation of Tok Pisin, the principal languages in contact were Melanesian (Austronesian) languages of the Gazelle-Peninsula of New Britain and the nearby Duke of York Islands. It is in its later development that Papuan languages of the New Guinea mainland were involved. Mosel (1982) provided a detailed analysis for Tok Pisin's principal substratum language: Tolai, an Austronesian language of Papua New Guinea. Mosel (1982: 112) emphasizes that 'the Tolai system of deictics is bound to the natural environment of the Tolai people'. Tolai local deictics do not only distinguish between 'here' and 'there', but are also marked for:

1 The level at which the indicated place is located relative to the speaker's position.
2 Whether the indicated place is:
 • a place at which an action takes place;
 • a place where something or somebody is found;
 • the goal of an action;
 • the source of an action.
3 Whether or not the place pointed at is known to the hearer.

In her analysis of local deixis in Tolai, Mosel (1982: 119–121) shows that there are two distinct classes of deictics:

• deictics indicating the speaker's position; and
• deictics indicating some place which is not the speaker's position.

The second class of deictics can be sub-classified into fifteen hierarchically ordered subclasses, which express concepts like +/−REMOTE (with respect to 1st, 2nd, and 3rd person), +/− ACTION, LOCATION, GOAL, SOURCE. Thus we find a rather sophisticated system of local deictics that 'consists of various hierarchically ordered subclasses which show different degrees of complexity' (Mosel 1982: 129 as paraphrased by Senft 1997: 19–20).

Regrettably, Mosel has practically nothing to say about spatial deixis in her comparison of Tok Pisin and Tolai grammars (Mosel 1980). It appears that only a small subset of the complex distinctions made in Tolai are found in Tok Pisin. One distinction that has been retained is that between:

> *bringim I kam* ' bring towards speaker'
> *bringim I go* 'take away from speaker'

In this example the main reference point is the recipient or goal rather than the speaking Ego. This construction causes problems to native English-speaking users of Tok Pisin as well as users from a Papuan language background whose interpretation is the opposite:

> *bringim I kam* 'take away from speaker'
> *bringim I go* 'bring towards speaker'

Tok Pisin has not really resolved the conflict and both interpretations continue to be encountered. This indeterminacy is also found with another construction: in an egocentric system, what is front and what is back depends on how speakers see themselves vis-à-vis the objects they are looking at. In English *in front of the house* implies that the house faces you and that the visible part is the front. In Tolai as well as in Tok Pisin the assumption is that the speaker and the object looked at are facing the same way. The front of a house cannot be seen if it faces away from the speaker.

We note that what is 'front' and what is 'back' in English is clear only when referring to non-moving objects. When referring to moving objects, for instance in the command to a cab driver *Pull up behind this car!*, native speakers often disagree on the meaning of this instruction. Without further negotiation, pointing or disambiguating by means of contextual clues, no determinate meaning is possible.

The use of Tok Pisin used by speakers of Papuan languages has added further problems, as they may have different spatial orientation systems in their first languages. An overview plus a number of detailed studies on their deictic systems can be found in Senft (1997). There is considerable variation in the way spatial deixis is grammaticalized and as yet considerable scope for miscommunication when spatial deixis is used. It appears that this area of grammar has remained underdeveloped and the typological conflicts may not be resolved by the time English replaces Tok Pisin as the principal lingua franca of Papua New Guinea, a development likely to occur if current census trends persist.

11.7.3   Spatial Orientation in Pitkern-Norf'k

Pitkern-Norf'k is the only creole/mixed language to my knowledge for which an absolute orientation system has been documented. The spatial orientation grammar of this language is unlike in English and any other English-based contact language. It is a mixed absolute and relative system which stabilized within a relatively short time (about fifty years) and, unlike other grammatical constructions in this language, remains unfixed. The principal languages that were involved in the formation of Pitkern-Norf'k were English, St Kitts Creole, and Tahitian. English is classified as having a relative (egocentric) system of spatial deixis. However, it seems plausible that the sailors of the *Bounty*, in order to find their way across the oceans, also had to talk in terms of absolute (celestial) orientation points. I have not been able to obtain reliable information about the grammar of spatial orientation in maritime English.

Little is known about the grammar of spatial deixis in St Kitts Creole. Spatial deixis has not been a topic in creole studies and typological information is not available. According to the texts I have perused, St Kitts Creole has an orientation system very much like that of English. Better data are available for Tahitian, though it must be kept in mind that the study of absolute spatial orientation systems is still in its beginnings for Tahitian and related Polynesian languages:

Tahitian
inia 'up'
Raro 'west'
ni'a 'east'
iraro 'down'

In related Marquesan, Ozanne-Rivierre (1997: 85–86) has identified the following:

iko 'across'
'itai 'seaward'
'uta 'to mountain'

Ozanne-Rivierre (ibid.) notes that in communication about land travel (a single valley) a different one, single west-east axis (corresponding to up and down) is employed. As regards Pitkern-Norf'k, both varieties employ an absolute spatial orientation system alongside a relative (egocentric) one. They share the up–down axis but there are a number of differences, suggesting that adaptation to local conditions rather than substratum influences shaped their spatial grammar.

Pitcairn Island is an isolated volcanic island mass 1,350 nautical miles southeast of Tahiti. It rises about 330 metres above sea level. The only settlement on the island is Adamstown located on the central north coast with a population fewer than fifty. The island is very rugged and was heavily vegetated when the mutineers arrived in 1790. Pitcairn place names were listed and annotated by Ross and Moverley (1964: 170–188) and a number of maps have been consulted. The data suggest that an absolute spatial orientation system developed on Pitcairn Island, with Adamstown (*in taun*) being the principal reference point. Movement towards Adamstown is also expressed by means of the preposition *in* as in *we gwen back in taun* 'we're going back into town' (from *Timiti's Crack* on the coast). Going from Adamstown to places higher up requires the preposition *up*:

Up a Goat House
Up a Hollow

Places on the coast require 'down':

Down the God
Down Freddie Fall

Out is extremely rarely used, for instance *Out Glenny*, as Glenny's Harbour is further away from Adamstown than the landing in Bounty Bay. Whereas the use of prepositions is compulsory in talking about movement, most place names do not have a locative preposition prefixed to them. Lexicalization of prepositions is in evidence, however, in:

Down Dorcas Coconut
Down Jack Cack on ha Rock
Down Side Lin-Fall
Up Side Nunk Fall
Up that Flagstaff
Up the Pit
Out Where Maria Fall

In 1856 the Pitcairners were relocated to Norfolk Island. Initially they found their new place of abode unfamiliar and frightening, and they rarely ventured into the interior of the island, for fear of getting lost. The different topography and the presence of a pre-existing settlement precluded the carryover of the Pitkern absolute spatial orientation system. Norfolk Island had at least two major settlements from the first two convict periods namely Kingston and Cascade, and the emergence of two other more recent settlements in Middlegate and Burnt Pine has meant that Norf'k has had to develop a much broader range of uses of spatial description.

Although there seems to be a great deal of agreement among speakers of Norf'k regarding the use of fixed lexicalized prepositions, some variation does occur in preposition usage depending on speakers' age and which part of the island they grew up in. The first group of data considered here are place names, which contain spatial prepositions that have become lexicalized, as shown in the following table, based on information in Edgecombe (1991: 102) and primary field data.

Table 11.10 below outlines location descriptors not lexicalized into place names per se.

The general preference when talking about movement is to employ the same prepositions as for location. The questions *Where are you?* and *Where are you going?* are both answered alike, for instance *up ar school* 'to the school' or 'at the school', *up ar stick* 'to the mountain forest' or 'in the mountain forest', *up bun pine* 'to Burnt Pine' or 'in Burnt Pine, and so on. More details can be found in Nash (2011).

Movement in Norf'k is talked about in terms of two axes, 'down–up' and 'out–away from the absolute reference point down'. This principal reference point is the administrative capital, Kingston: *Doun ar Toun*. The end point of the 'down–up' axis is *up Mt. Bates*. The other axis, *out*, denotes remoteness from Kingston (*out yenna* 'out yonder', *out Duncombe Bay* 'to or at Duncombe Bay', *out Anson* 'to or at Anson Bay', *out ar windmill* 'to or at the windmill just outside Kingston'). The use of *up down* and *out* is compulsory.

Table 11.9 *Norf'k Place Names with Lexicalized Prepositions*

Norf'k	English
Out Yenna	*Out yonder*
Out ar Station	*Out at the Cable Station*
Out ar Mission	*Out at the Melanesian Mission*
Out ar Windmill	*Out at the Windmill*
Down a Town	*Kingston*
Round Country	*The area around the airport*
Up in a stick	*Up in the mountainous wooded area*
Up Chats	*Up at Chat's house*
Cross ar Water	*Across the water*
Down side water run off rocks	*Cockpit*
Down Norf'k	*Cockpit*

Table 11.10 *Norf'k Place Names without Lexicalized Prepositions*

Norf'k	English
Out Steels Point	*Out at Steels Point*
Out Bucks Point	*Out at Bucks Point*
Out Duncombe	*Out at Duncombe Bay*
Out Headstone	*Out at Headstone*
Out Hundred Acres	*Out at the Old Hundred Acres reserve*
Out Dixies	*Out at Dixie Paddock*
Down Bumboras	*Down at Bumboras*
Up Town	*In Burnt Pine*
Roun(d) ar airport	*Around the airport*
Down Cascade	*At Cascades*

The preposition *te* 'to' is found when there is no reference to a specific location, such as when enquiring *Are your children going to school?*; but one cannot say **ai hufenet te skuul* 'I am going to school on foot'.

The spatial orientation grammar of Pitcairn-Norf'k, just like its pronominal grammar, illustrates the problem with tracing typological properties of contact languages exclusively to substratum, superstratum, and adstratum languages. In the present case, one might wish to argue that the general idea of an absolute orientation system was borrowed from Tahitian and that, moreover, the communicative practices of maritime English speaking sailors contributed to a mixed system. This, however, would ignore the typological differences between Pitcairn-Norf'k and its parent languages. It would also ignore the differences between Pitkern and Norf'k and the fact that historical contingencies can be shown to have influenced the spatial grammar of

Norf'k. Thus, an event that interfered with the direction of established routes was the construction of a military airport during the Second World War (1942). It involved the destruction of the famous straight Avenue of Pines and its replacement by two detours, which necessitate a round trip rather than travel in a straight line. This led to the emergence of the preposition *raun* to refer to localities situated either side of the former avenue. Examples are the place name *Round Country* and the expression *round ar plane* or *round ar drome* 'to the airport'. Just as the Pitkern-Norf'k pronoun system developed as an adaptation to the specific social ecology in which the language was used, the spatial orientation grammar can be characterized as an adaptation to the natural ecology (topology) of Pitcairn and Norfolk Islands.

11.8   Categorial Multifunctionality and Conversion

Let us consider briefly at a third area where contrasting languages contribute to a construction in a mixed language, one in which lexical roots can appear in more than one grammatical function. I presented a comparative account of this phenomenon in Pitkern-Norf'k and Tok Pisin in the *Journal of Pidgin Creole Linguistics* (2008). From the perspective of typology there are two very different ways of expressing this:

- All roots are inherently multifunctional, as they can be used as nouns, verbs, adjectives, or particles. Many Austronesian languages share this typological trait.
- Roots typically belong to only one grammatical category. New words can be derived from existing ones by means of zero derivation or conversion. This is what is generally found in English.[9] An example is the verb *to bottle*, which is derived from the noun *bottle* by a regular derivational process.

In the case of multifunctionality, there is no derivational direction, whereas in that of derivation there are rules constraining and permitting the process plus a fair bit of idiosyncrasy. Derivational morphology is a phenomenon located at the boundary between the lexicon and grammar.

I compared a comprehensive corpus of Papua New Guinea and Tok Pisin constructions with English and found that the outcomes are very different, in spite of the typological similarities of the two contact situations involving Austronesian Tolai and English. This has been confirmed by Mosel (1980). Ross and Moverley (1964) assert that the lack of distinction between the normal parts of speech in Tahitian has been carried over into Pitcairnese. My analysis of all multifunctional words of Norf'k shows otherwise:

---

[9] English incidentally has a few words that are neither inherently nouns nor verbs. They include *piss, fart, belch,* and *shit.*

- Norf'k, unlike Tahitian, has zero derivation except in the case of intransitive verbs, which behave formally and functionally like predicative adjectives;
- all patterns of derivation are also found in English but not vice versa. In this domain of grammar Norf'k is a subset of English. There is very little productivity, and such new words that appear in Norf'k follow English patterns; and
- somewhat surprisingly, the Tahitian vocabulary of Norf'k, in spite of Tahitian having an isolating morphosyntax, is less multifunctional than its English vocabulary.

To speak of Tahitian influences seems totally unwarranted.

Tok Pisin again has mostly zero derivation, unlike its Austronesian substratum. Its zero derivation has developed slowly, in response to community needs, and has eventually attained a great degree of productivity. The functional possibilities of lexical bases differ significantly from Tolai, its principal early lexifier language. Over time the language has begun to look more Austronesian, suggesting areal assimilation.

11.9   Conclusions

We have examined three typological properties (pronouns, spatial orientation grammar, and categorical multifunctionality) as they appear in two contact languages and in the grammars of the languages that were involved in their formation. The findings were as set out below.

Pronouns

Tok Pisin: the early development of pronominal distinctions was independent of substrate and superstrate languages. Over time the pronoun system has approximated that of Melanesian languages.

Pitkern-Norf'k: the pronominal distinctions are qualitatively and quantitatively different from those found in all three languages involved in its formation.

Spatial Deixis

Tok Pisin: in this respect Tok Pisin is simpler than its source languages. No single consistent system is used by all speakers of the language. Disambiguation requires pointing and other nonverbal means of communication.

Pitkern-Norf'k: the two varieties of the language each have their own absolute orientation system. Tahitian, St Kitts Creole, or English grammatical patterns did not appear to have been involved in this development.

Multifunctionality

Tok Pisin: while both Tolai and English have zero derivation, Tok Pisin derivational grammar is not a common denominator. Its system developed largely independently, from a very simple to a highly complex and very productive area of lexical grammar.

Pitkern-Norf'k: zero derivation as in English and St Kitts Creole, rather than inherent multifunctionality as in Tahitian, is in evidence. In this respect Pitkern-Norf'k is essentially a subset of English grammar. There is little productivity.

What one can conclude is that:

- each typological property appears to behave differently. Generalizations across grammars are not warranted;
- a typological comparison is much more difficult than commonly assumed;
- determining the provenance of forms and constructions in mixed languages is equally difficult;
- typological properties can change over time;
- constraints and possible mixed systems can be overruled by socio-economic factors, for example power distinctions or social indexicality.

The analysis and discussion of the data would also seem to demonstrate:

- the dangers of taking partial similarity as evidence of mixing and substratum influence;
- that the processes of contact and borrowing are not instantaneous and thus need to be studied longitudinally. Comparing endpoints cannot, in principle, provide an account of development;
- contact phenomena resulting from encounters between typologically dissimilar languages involve a very large number of parameters other than structural ones;
- observationally adequate description require many years of observation, not blitzkrieg fieldwork;
- perhaps, most importantly, the shape of contact languages is determined more by the cultural and natural ecology, in which they are spoken than by the grammars of the languages involved in their formation.

In conclusion, I would like to revisit an early observation: the job of a linguist is to search for truth, the method is to remove untruth, the instruments are theories, techniques and methods. Most of the instruments that linguists have employed in the past are either too blunt or too sharp to give us answers. The search for generalizations and general laws has prevented linguists from recognizing the importance of singularities or in the spirit of Edward Sapir: the search for a simple formula has been the downfall of many a linguist.

The case studies presented here do not exhaust the range of phenomena resulting from contact between typologically dissimilar languages. The much wider range of phenomena that remain to be considered include:

- Structural similarity may go hand in hand with pragmatic dissimilarity. While Pitkern-Norf'k and Tok Pisin may in many ways, particularly lexically, look like English, the way the speakers use these languages, e.g. the rules of interaction interpretation, are relatively different in some ways. The situation is similar to that described by Eades (1982) for South-East Queensland Aboriginal English or the Tahitian and New Caledonian French spoken by indigenous speakers. Conventional typological studies ignore this important dimension.

- There is no law that says that languages have to be integrated closed systems where 'tout se tient', as claimed by structuralists. On the contrary, effective communication is perfectly possible with non-focussed, messy languages. Tight systems have indexical rather than communicative functions. Many creoles remain highly variable throughout their life and yet others become variable during decreolization with no great loss to their expressive and communicative power. I am at a loss to say which Norf'k or which Tok Pisin should be the basis of typological studies.

- It is sometimes assumed, mainly because linguists need to put languages on a family tree, that mixed languages are more like one or another language, for example, Aïwo is variably classified with either Papuan or Austronesian. Linguists would seem to be unable to give valid criteria for either classification. However, I would like to argue that there is not real need why a mixed language should be genetically placeable. I do not think it makes great sense to regard speakers of Tayo to be speaking a Romance language, those of Tok Pisin as speaking a Germanic or Austronesian language, or Northern Territory Kriol speakers as speaking an Australian Aboriginal language. This also applies to the languages of Europe. To classify English and Bavarian (Mayerthaler and Mayerthaler 1990) as Germanic languages brings with it many problems.

There are strong ideological and political reasons to deny that a language is mixed, for instance, the claim that the Japanese language is totally unique (see Nickel 1990) or the doctrine that Afrikaans was a white language, a kind of advanced Dutch resulting from accelerating drift. I remember sneaking off from my Afrikaans class to the bookshop to acquire a book, which the students had been told not to read, *Studies in Portuguese and Creole* (Valkhoff 1966). In this book Valkhoff correctly argued that Afrikaans had a more non-white heritage but he used highly problematic typological arguments that convinced no one. Being right and being seen to be right in linguistics rarely coincide.

12 Theoretical and Practical Aspects of Ecological Language Planning

Peter Mühlhäusler

12.1 Introduction

The application of ecological linguistics remains an underdeveloped topic in ecological linguistic writings, though there are some authors who supplement their critique of ordinary languages with suggestions of how languages could be made more ecological, for instance by substituting *Mitwelt* for *Umwelt* in German, and *companion animal* for *pet* in English.

I have commented on this elsewhere (Mühlhäusler 2000b) and I shall not say much about micro and terminological language planning. I have tried to argue in my other chapter in this volume (Chapter 11) that an ecological linguistic approach can provide new insights into language contact phenomena, because it is concerned with far more parameters than structure-centred approaches to language. The same argument also goes for ecological language planning. Because ecological linguistics is parameter-rich, one can expect a wide range of applications.

Language planning has an impressive track record in the area of reducing the world's linguistic diversity and linguistic variation (Tollefson 1991; Mühlhäusler 1996d). Language planning aimed at stemming the loss of the world's linguistic diversity, on the other hand, thus far has shown to be largely ineffective. Positive general policies, school programmes, and sophisticated documentation in countries such as the USA, Canada, Australia, and France (including its overseas possessions) have done very little to arrest or reverse the decline of small languages. The reason for this is not necessarily lack of funding, goodwill, or linguistic expertise but failure to recognize what the problem is.

I shall begin by raising some general issues and then discuss some practical ones, in particular the question how the highly endangered languages on the West Coast of South Australia and the languages of Norfolk Island can be revived.

Kaplan and Baldauf's (1997) book on language planning bears the interesting subtitle *From practice to theory*. Unlike some linguists who believe that linguistic questions are essentially a logical matter, I feel that most linguistic questions are not and that it is impossible to do linguistics without getting your hands dirty. I have spent parts of every year since 1972 doing linguistic fieldwork and I have built up at Adelaide a department of active fieldworkers and a place where speakers of minority languages receive training in linguistics. By 2009 we had two Ph.D. dissertation submissions dealing with the ecology of minority languages of Northern Thailand and the Western Desert languages respectively, and others are in progress. We have just admitted our first Norfolk Islander to our doctoral programme and that put in place an interesting new initiative, a mobile language team comprising of two full positions plus funds equivalent to a half position for consultants to service the needs of the forty-two Aboriginal languages throughout South Australia. In cooperation with and with funding from the Australian government we have carried out about twenty projects concerned with strengthening linguistic diversity in South Australia and Norfolk Island and we run a regular course in language maintenance and planning. There is one consultancy project I have not tackled: the drafting of a languages policy for the indigenous languages of South Australia. The reason for not doing this is that written policies typically end up being substitutes for action. There already is a Draft Language Policy for South Australia, authored by Joe Lo Bianco in the 1990s, which is gathering dust in a bottom drawer of some governmental department, and there are national language policies, which are very supportive of Aboriginal languages but for which, as Fishman has observed in *Reversing language shift* (1991: 277–278), the connection between language policy and outcomes in Australia has been spurious.

The real question is: under what circumstances can policies become part of the ecological support system that strengthens endangered languages? I feel it is important to sketch some of the background to avoid the impression that ecological language planning is an armchair exercise. Importantly, being involved in the day-to-day practicalities of the exercise, one sees the many ideological positions and practices and can learn from their limitations.

The theoretical position I shall present to the reader is thus by and large an inductively constructed theory, and, like all theories, it lends itself to falsification and revision. The reader will find a more elaborate version of my views in the article in 'Current issues in language planning' (2000b) and a somewhat disappointing criticism by John Edwards (2001). The latter is disappointing, because it makes general observations from a very small empirical basis and ignores the basic principle of ecological planning, namely that the factors that sustain or threaten language ecologies differ from case to case. We also differ in our philosophical orientation, in particular in our assessment of modernization and enlightenment.

One of the fundamental problems is that while there are numerous ways of speaking, the notion of *a language* is a recent culture-specific notion associated with the rise of European nation states and the Enlightenment (see Mühlhäusler 2005: 13, where full arguments can be found, also in Mühlhäusler 1996d and Makoni and Pennycook 2007). They are invented by 'language makers' (Harris 1979) such as linguists, colonial administrators, politicians, and missionaries, who typically named, listed, and enumerated them. Such discursive artefacts can, through a range of processes and practices, become cultural artefacts, as Haugen (1972) argued with regard to the languages of Scandinavia. Language planners do not have to deal with pre-existing bounded entities that are recognized and named by their users. The Pacific linguist Biggs (1972: 144) has argued that 'everybody knows what languages they are speaking', a claim that can be disconfirmed easily.

Language users often have no idea what language they are speaking and their views about what constitutes a different language can differ widely from that of professional linguists, as I've tried to argue in my paper on the linguistic situation in Papua New Guinea (Mühlhäusler 2006). To plan languages in the sense that modern language planning did, the first step was to invent languages using a range of perfectly arbitrary criteria. That the object of discursive invention remains poorly defined can be seen from the difficulties arising when faced with questions such as: what is French? What is Bosnian? What is Norwegian? What is Fijian? What is Pitjantjatjara? What is Norf'k?

South Australia is said to have 42 Aboriginal languages distinguished by linguists but there are more than 400 language names, with many speakers unsure what their language might be. A couple of years ago, linguists of Adelaide were approached to help a group of Western Desert Aboriginal people produce a dictionary for the Antikirinya language; halfway through the project this group decided that they were Yankunytjatjara people, a language group that had been listed separately. Similarly, speakers who in earlier days claimed they spoke West Coast language were confused by being classified as speakers of Wirangu and Kokatha.

That there are real problems with the notion of *a language* has been typically ignored by linguists. After all, to do comparative linguistics, one needs languages to compare; to do descriptive linguistics, one needs languages to describe; and language planners need languages to be planned. Traditionally, linguists did not recognize their own complicity as language makers and their own questionable descriptive practices.

As regards descriptive practices, very narrowly focussed theories have determined what counts as legitimate data for linguists and in the process have excluded a vast number of phenomena that are involved in people's verbal behaviour: Excluded areas are indexical signs, and proper names, non-cognitive functions among numerous others. Evans (2009: 109, 182ff.) has deplored the patchy documentation of many highly endangered languages, in particular the limited wordlists we have had for many languages as well as the lack of documentation of verse and verbal art.

12.2   Language Planning: What is the Problem?

Linguists have had an uneasy relationship with language planning, having tended to see themselves as objective outsiders or as describers rather than as involved insiders or as makers of prescriptive rules. You will recall titles such as Hall's (1950) 'Leave your language alone!' and Max Müller's (1862: 34–35 [48]) dictum that humans cannot influence the direction in which languages change:

> The idea that language can be changed and improved by man is by no means a new one. We know that Protagoras, an ancient Greek philosopher, after laying down some laws on gender, actually began to find fault with the text of Homer, because it did not agree with his rules. But here, as in every other instance, the attempt proved unavailing. Try to alter the smallest rule of English, and you will find that it is physically impossible.

The views held by the leading linguists of their times did not prevent language planning from happening in many parts of the world, its main agents being governments, Christian missions, and teachers. It is interesting to note that many approaches to modern linguistics can trace their roots to very practical language planning issues.

Let me briefly comment on phonetics and phonology as an example. The development of a phonetic alphabet is the culmination of what was an important missionary problem: the need to have a consistent way to represent the sounds of the numerous unwritten languages spoken in the mission field. At the important missionary alphabet conference in London in 1854, two competing proposals by Karl Richard Lepsius and by Max Müller were discussed (Kemp 1981; Kneebone 2005). It is noted that Müller refined his proposal with the help of his friend, the Bishop of Melanesia, John Patteson, and it was subsequently implemented by the missionary philologist and Melanesian language specialist, Robert Henry Codrington, for the Mission Mota language constructed on Norfolk Island (Müller 1902). Phonemics in part developed and certainly was refined by Pike (1947) and Gudschinsky (1962) in response to another missionary problem, to have an emic system that is capable of representing the distinctive sounds of previously unwritten languages for the purpose of bible translation. Pike not only called phonemics a method for reducing unwritten languages to writings but also referred to phonemics as a weapon in the armoury of mission fighters. This brief account illustrates two issues:

1 The identification of language-planning problems.
2 The perception of the nature of the problems.

Regarding the first point, the ones who had a problem were the missionaries, not the speakers of the numerous unwritten languages they dealt with. The missionaries required a tool for effective conversion of heathens to Christianity. A phonetic writing system would simplify the recording and learning of exotic languages and allow its users to produce translations of the Bible and religious tracts.

As regards the second point, the missions saw the problem as a local technical one, requiring a technical solution. In language planning one distinguishes between corpus planning (comprising standardization, modernization, and graphization) and status planning. The development of mission languages typically involved: (a) the selection of a suitable language of the area for mission purposes and giving it status, and (b) the graphization of this variety. This is a typical example of non-ecological planning. There was little or no consideration for the totality of languages spoken in the mission field but a deliberate attempt to reduce its diversity by adopting a single variety as mission lingua franca: Mota for Melanesia, Kâte for Papuan speakers of New Guinea, Pitjantjatjara for Western Desert Aborigines. When examining the history of languages such as Kâte or Pitjantjatjara more closely, one will note that they are not just elaborations of pre-existing varieties but, in many instances, the result of deliberate language creation. There was no understanding of the social factors in implementing and sustaining literacy nor understanding of its effects on everyday social practices and the need to put in place an ecology of literacy to sustain it. Recent research such as Barton's (1994) 'An introduction to the ecology of written language' and Sebba's (2007) study on writing systems suggests that both the development and change of writing systems and the development of literate societies are not technical but ecological problems. Let me mention two cases from my own experience.

My late friend and former supervisor Don Laycock in collaboration with the Norfolk Islander Alice Buffett developed a writing system for the Norfolk writing language in 1988. Laycock did a very good technical job with his quasi-phonemic system, but twenty years later the system, now referred to as the Buffett system, experiences great resistance from members of the speech community. It ignores the social conventions that have emerged in representing the language in writing and it cannot represent the very considerable family-based variation in the pronunciation of the language. What was meant to strengthen an endangered language in fact has weakened the revival effort. The government has now convened a council of the elders representing the different family interests to develop a uniform writing system, something that should have been in place before any system had been developed.

My second very different example relates to a project named 'Desert Schools' (Clayton et al. 1996), which examined the irrelevance of literacy to Australian Western Desert societies. There was widespread truancy, a high

Figure 12.1 Western Desert Dreaming (Edwards 1983 : 8)

proportion of illiteracy in both English and Pitjantjatjara, no culture of reading and writing, and an emerging semi-lingualism among many young people who were competent neither in English or in an Aboriginal language. One of the questions the research team addressed was the connection between traditional culture and literacy. Western Desert cultures can be understood in terms of a closed system, which has been represented by William Edwards as shown in Figure 12.1.

People refuse to take responsibility for what is outside this system. Parents do not feel obliged to send their children to school or read to them at home. This does not mean that the system is static. New practices and objects can become integrated into Tjukurpa, the domestic cat or camel or Aussie footy for instance. We noted that an entry point for literacy was the traditional sand story, a story that involves the storyteller drawing lines and simple illustrations in the sand and that this could be an entry point for literacy. We also noted that literacy in Pitjantjatjara should happen first and that this literacy in turn would be an entry point for English literacy. It will probably be a while before such a programme can be implemented, as current wisdom is that so much time is needed to install English literacy that little time remains for teaching Aboriginal languages or in Aboriginal languages. Again, the problem is seen by administrators and educationists as one of imposing a high but narrow standard in the dominant English language, not that of creating a sustainable multilingual language ecology.

The central issue of ecological language revival is structural diversity. Past language planners tended to see diversity as a problem and developed strategies to replace complex linguistic ecologies with simpler streamlined preferable monocultural ones. This idea has its modern roots in the French Revolution and the French enlightenment where both the notion of one state – one language and that of the superiority of the French language, its clarity and suitability for expressing pure reason (Swiggers 1990) originates. In Mühlhäusler (1996d) I provided a detailed analysis of the French language policy in the Pacific area and its devastating effects on the linguistic diversity of the Region. Quite recent changes in French policies and their support for local languages thus far have done little to reverse the effect of earlier assimilation policies; and Tahitians, for instance, continue to lose their knowledge of traditional Tahitian. Language planning within European nation states has been a main cause of reducing their linguistic diversity and the same streamlining continues in the post-colonial states such as China, Indonesia, many African states, and India. It is noteworthy that the seemingly generous Indian language policies (allowing up to three languages to be official in each state) have not prevented the disappearance of India's numerous small languages which is accelerating.

What was a problem in the past, linguistic diversity, continues to be regarded as such in many parts of the world, though it is now beginning to be reframed as an asset or even as a solution. Increasingly, the aim of language planning is interpreted as that of protecting and reviving the world's linguistic diversity. The new discourses that have developed around the loss of linguistic diversity, the new perceived problem, on the one hand, provide reasons why this loss has to be prevented and, on the other, suggest how to prevent it. This new area of linguistics is complex and it is unlikely that agreed answers will emerge soon. One of the rarely mentioned but crucial issues is what we understand as a language. When we talk about language diversity, are languages closed systems comprising of a lexicon and a grammar, or are they inextricable components of a complex ecological network of interrelationships between speakers, ways of speaking, habitat, practices, and beliefs? If they are the former, the task is to document as many grammars and lexicons as possible and to preserve them for future use or for linguistic research. This indeed seems to be the practice of the endangered languages activities of the

Volkswagenstiftung and the Rausing Centre for Endangered languages at SOAS and other places. The view that language is somehow disconnected from all other parameters renders technological and cultural change and migration unproblematic but does not answer the question of the factors that underpin the continued use of languages. As already mentioned, it also under-documents all kinds of important phenomena such as bi-, dual- and multilingualism, language change, patterns of language use, metalinguistic use, acquisition and learning.

In Evans (2009), the narrow focus of most documentation programmes is criticized. Evans also argues for the need to document the verbal arts and ecological knowledge, without presenting a comprehensive programme for language documentation. Like the editors of another volume on language endangerment, the UNESCO *Atlas of endangered languages* (Moseley 2009), he is guided by the implicit assumption that some languages are more worthy of documentation than others. He does not consider pidgin languages and their important role in introducing, increasing, or maintaining linguistic diversity in some parts of the world. As discussed in Mühlhäusler et al. (1996), small intercommunity pidgins in traditional Papua New Guinea enabled inter-cultural communication while keeping a multitude of small local vernaculars distinct. They are an important component of complex multilingual ecologies in other parts of the world as well, for instance in North America (Drechsel 1997) (for more details see Chapter 11, this volume).

My own belief is that languages are not independent phenomena and cannot be reduced non-arbitrarily to a closed system and that most of modern linguistics has been the victim of what Roy Harris (1981) referred to as the 'language myth'. I shall not provide in this chapter a comprehensive argument for regarding languages as unbounded, ecological phenomena, as I have done this in a monograph (Mühlhäusler 2003) and in a small paper (Mühlhäusler 2002). Additional arguments can be found in the writings of my eco-linguistic colleagues. For our purposes here let me highlight two observations:

- Languages bring into being human perceptions of the world and conse-quently impact on the ways their speakers habitually interact with it. This is the neo-Whorfian argument which, unlike Whorf's original work, has been empirically tested in a number of instances (e.g., Gumperz and Levinson 1996);
- Languages are shaped by and ecologically adapted to the natural environ-ment in which they are spoken. Linguistic diversity reflects the need for different linguistic management tools for different natural and social ecologies.

This raises an interesting question. What happens if a language is transplanted to a different natural environment? For instance, English to Central Australia or Pitcairn Island. I have argued in a number of publications, beginning with Mühlhäusler (1996d), that such exotic languages contributed to the destruction of the natural environment and that it takes 300 years for language to develop the denotational resources for sustainable management. I can only briefly allude to my study of the relationship between plant naming and plant extinction on Pitcairn Island (Mühlhäusler 2000b) and to my student Jonathon Nichols's work on English and Pitjantjatjara water discourse in the Western Desert. That languages contain important TEK (Traditional Ecological Knowledge) is being increasingly acknowledged in the areas of weather knowledge, fire management, water use, horticulture, and so on, as is the relationship between linguistic loss and environmental degradation for example in the work of the members of Terra Lingua. If we accept the ecological characterization of languages, then we can make sense of the already alluded to new discourses that have emerged as arguments for preserving linguistic diversity. They are:

- scientific discourse
- economic discourse
- moral discourse
- aesthetic discourse

John Edwards (2001) takes a relatively dim view of the former two, though he accepts the value of diverse languages for the purposes of linguistic study such as typology or Greenbergian universals, and the recent *Word atlas of language structures* (WALS, Haspelmath et al. 2005). It is important to remember that very few languages are well documented and that most languages in all likelihood will disappear before they can be documented. To this should be added that linguistic documentation continues to have a very narrow focus with its findings being very limited and limiting.

A comprehensive survey of the different discourses can be found in Harré, Brockmeier, and Mühlhäusler (1998) and Mühlhäusler and Peace (2006); and I shall only briefly comment here.

12.3   Discourses on Language Planning

12.3.1   The Scientific Discourse

Whatever the shortcomings of linguists may have been, and ignoring the question of whether linguistics can be a science, no better linguistics will be possible without the preservation of the phenomena it studies. The loss of the bulk of the world's ways of speaking will result in an impoverished database from which generalizations about the nature of human language would be difficult to make.

As important as communalities and generalizations are, the world's linguistic heritage is full of differences and the rationale for keeping it that way was stated by Benjamin Lee Whorf as follows (1940/1956: 244):

> Western culture has made, through languages, a provisional analysis of reality and, without correctives, holds resolutely to that analysis as finding the only correctives lie in all those other tongues which by areas of independent evolution have arrived at different, but equally logical provisional analysis.

What this means for the discipline of linguistics has been outlined by Evans and Levinson (2009). Scientific discoveries do not happen through the application of mechanical discovery procedures but through the metaphors and discourses afforded by different languages. While languages do not differ so much in what they can express, they differ significantly in what they have to express (e. g. gender, aspect, distinctions, evidentiality, social relations and the pragmatics of implicit and explicit speech); they tend to privilege certain routine interpretations of the world. Importantly, through their lexicon they predispose their speakers to identify samenesses and differences. Konrad Lorenz's suggestion was for instance that our understanding of phylogenetic processes is metaphorically based on western concepts of ontogenesis and that it therefore limits possible understandings (1977: 47). There are many other examples given in 'Metaphors others live by' (Mühlhäusler 1995b) of how combining the metaphors and the words of different languages can lead to powerful insights in numerous domains of science. The results of a project at the University of Helsinki exploring the metaphors of others can be found in Idström and Piirainen (2012). Arguably, linguistics would have been very different had it been based on the metalinguistic categories of languages other than the western European ones. Brian Stross's comprehensive list of metalinguistic terms in Tzeltal (spoken in Chiapas, Mexico) provides an interesting example. Among its several hundred entries we find (Stross 1974: 236):

> *stek'leh k'op*/speech of an adolescent, adolescent speech
> *stenleh k'op*/talk or conversation occurring on plain or plateau
> *stenoh sba k'op*/conversation with several people talking at once so that the speech of any one individual can't be understood
> *stukel k'op*/talking alone with no response from listener(s) who may or may not be present
> *suhtem k'op*/broken promise, 'Indian-giver talk', word that has been gone back on
> *suht k'op*/broken promise, 'Indian-giver talk', word that has been gone back on (*suhtem k'op* is the preferred form)
> *suhtib k'op*/response, answer, reply
> *sukleh k'op*/talk or conversation coming from or occurring on a small hill

sutet k'op/the passing around of one word from person to person in a
   group (especially in a game that children play)
šʔahʔun k'op/moaning and groaning as when sick – saying *ʔah ʔah*
šaket k'op/talk from a distance to someone in house, coming from
   someone who doesn't want to come in
šʔawet k'op/speech that comes out very loud, that is shouted
šču̓il k'op/talk in which the topic is the sweethearts (i. e., lovers) of
   women not present
šhahun k'op/the laughing *brr-ing*, startled sound that we make if
   someone throws water on us when we are nude
šhururet k'op/speech or conversation the sound of which approximates a whirring sound

Tzeltal speakers virtually ignore arbitrary signs but employ a larger number of
tools for indexical signs. Many of their categories could be used to widen the
scope of western sociolinguistics, which remains focussed on a very restricted
range of social categories (Cameron 1990).

12.3.2   The Economic Discourse

The economic discourse of language diversity does not have either a long or a
distinguished history (Liddicoat and Bryant 2003). It would also be misguided
to see it as an opposition to an ecological one. Both concepts derive from
Greek *oikos* and both address the key question of how to make optimal use of
limited resources. A key difference has been the parameter-poor atemporal
language-free stance that most economists have taken. I notice however, that
this is changing and that through the internalization of numerous previously
disregarded externalities, economics thinking has become far more ecological.
I joined forces with a colleague of mine specializing in assigning economic
value to endangered fauna, flora and landscapes, and biological diversity in
general, to prepare a cost-benefit analysis of maintaining Australian Aboriginal
languages (Mühlhäusler and Damania 2004). One of the arguments has been
that linguistic diversity tends to coincide with environmental diversity, i.e.
that complex natural ecologies require more linguistic tools and languages for
their management than simpler more uniform ones. The diversity of languages
coincides roughly with the diversity of habitats. Rainforests with diverse
complex habitats tend to have more languages (e. g., 860 in Papua New
Guinea). This observation was also made earlier for Australia by Tindale
(1974: 133).

Drawing on the knowledge encoded in the world's languages, particularly
knowledge about water, fire management, and weather, a great deal could
be learned about better environmental management. A pilot project study of

weather discourse in a range of Aboriginal languages has already resulted in significant savings for both agriculture and tourism (see: www.bom.gov.au/ iwk/climate_culture/references.shtml).

The second economics argument was that language is closely connected to the identity and wellbeing of Aboriginal people. People with a strong feeling of identity and for their own language are less likely to become socially dysfunctional, criminal, or drug-takers; and the cost of strengthening language and identity is far less than that of keeping up a police force, prisons, and rehabilitation services. We already have applied the model and helped set up Aboriginal people's reintegration into society, thus demonstrating that the best use of the scarce commodity, money, is made by promoting languages and culture.

Finally, we argued for the potential of developing linguistic tourism as a source of employment and income. Linguistic and cultural tourism has become a source of income for Indigenous people in many parts of the world. If developed with sensitivity to the Indigenous population, it can be integrated into the lifestyle of speakers of small languages, as I shall demonstrate below with the examples of Norfolk Island and the West Coast of South Australia.

In an ecological approach, language is connected to the world; and one aspect is the utility of languages. In a world that is increasingly shaped by economic considerations, a world in which the speakers of many smaller languages wish to have model houses, cars, electronic articles, and travel, many are prepared to ditch their language for perceived socio-economic benefits. Internalizing languages into the economy and making them economic assets has become, for better or for worse, part of language revival. Without it, speakers will not have the instrumental motivation to continue speaking the language of their parents. Research into family language planning has shown that planning decisions are often made by the children rather than their parents and economic incentives are therefore crucial.

From a practical point of view, economic arguments are the most powerful ones when it comes to getting financial support. Once the above-mentioned Mühlhäusler and Damania (2004) paper had been accepted by Australian politicians (a process which took eighteen months), very significant sums of money followed, first about AU$500,000 per annum; and once positive feedback from the communities and government auditors reached Canberra, the sums increased. In 2009, my department was given AU$1,000,000 to set up an experimental Mobile Language Team that would operate out of Adelaide and would be able to respond to requests for language work throughout South Australia, work such as language awareness campaigns, language exhibitions, literacy development, writing systems etc. Following its initial success a larger amount was granted for the second triennium of operations. Information about its operations can be found on the Internet (see: www.mobilelanguageteam.org.au).

12.3.3   Moral Discourses

Moral discourses either take the shape of the growing body of literature deploring the destruction of the world's small languages by a few powerful languages (sometimes referred to as 'killer languages'), or they come in the form of well-formulated linguistic human rights. I must confess that I have used moral arguments in the past (Mühlhäusler 1996d, 2003) and I still strongly feel that the maintenance of the world's linguistic diversity is in part a moral issue. However, I have found the efficacy of moral argument very disappointing. I have been to quite a few talkfests where speaker after speaker deplored the loss of the world's languages, but at the same time nothing happened to strengthen the linguistic diversity in the speakers' home countries. Politicians of course love moral arguments because they can get by with repeating moral talk and token gestures.

The notion of linguistic human rights is central to moral arguments and there is a growing body of writing on this topic (Skutnabb-Kangas and Phillipson 1995; Phillipson 2000). To translate abstract moral rights into concrete activities is not a simple task and both the means and the will to implement language laws are often lacking, as the example of mother tongue education in the village school of Papua New Guinea has shown.

A particular problem with moral argument is that they typically focus on single named languages or a few languages. Ways of speaking that have no name do not feature, nor do language ecologies. For instance, in Germany, there is limited support for Sorbian, as it is recognized as a separate language, but far less for ways of speaking which are classified as dialects, such as my own language Alemannic, or Bavarian. To date, moral discourses that focus on endangered language ecologies rather than on a few charismatic languages are missing.

Again an authentic discourse about the loss of diversity is satisfying but achieves little, maybe some awareness-raising which is a good thing; but from awareness to action there is a long journey. Amery and Mühlhäusler (2005) have developed an approach, which distinguishes between language awareness, language appreciation, and language valuation. We have demonstrated this with the example of the Kaurna language of the Adelaide Plains (Amery 2000). When I set up the Linguistic Discipline at the University of Adelaide in 1992, virtually none of the first-year students had heard of the Kaurna language. Twenty years later, after numerous press reports and public events, the majority of new students have at least some knowledge of the name and role of the language. During the same period, public appreciation of the language reclamation efforts has grown, and people feel comfortable when they hear Kaurna songs, Kaurna welcomes to the land, and Kaurna language at public events. The world's first solar bus prominently features the Kaurna word *tindo* 'sun', which has been important in promoting the appreciation of the language and culture. From positive feelings to valuation (preparedness to contribute money or time to language work) there is a long journey, but in the case of Kaurna, there is a growing number of individuals who have volunteered their time, and cash donations for the cause are beginning to trickle in. This is a significant step forwards, as in the majority of Aboriginal revival programs, the speakers expect the work to be financed by the government and the schools to teach the language.

12.3.4   Aesthetic Discourses

Aesthetic arguments have been characterized by Harré, Brockmeier, and Mühlhäusler (1998: 186) as 'a doctrine of life as an art form. At its core is the idea of holistic rightness, the filling together in a dynamic equilibrium of the human race with all other things, organic and inorganic'. Valuing the diversity of languages and cultures independent of mundane human needs contributes to the quality of life. A related religious argument is that, whereas God created a perfect world, perfection is never in individual beings but manifests itself as structured totality of all beings.

12.4   Actual Perspectives of Ecological Language Planning

The remainder of this chapter addresses the question of how one can actually go about developing ecological language planning. We begin by looking at a quotation from Fishman's *Reversing language shift* (1991: 16):

> The real question for modern life and reversing language shift is . . . how one can build a home that one can still call one's own and, by cultivating it, find community, comfort, companionship and meaning in a world whose mainstreams are increasingly unable to provide the basic ingredients for their own members.

I am concerned both with the question of who can build a home for individual languages and language ecologies, and with a second question: will one policy fit all or should there be a different policy for different language ecologies? As regards the first question, the groups most commonly mentioned are the grassroots and the education system. Grassroots movements are important but tend to suffer from many limitations: small numbers (often single individuals) who are already involved in language maintenance or revival, unrealistic expectations about costs, outcomes, and time required, and internal conflicts. Sharing a common aim of keeping a language alive, does not prevent participants from fighting over the means: given that the education system in numerous instances has been one of the key instruments in destroying linguistic diversity, it is not easy to see how it can be transformed into an instrument for strengthening or reviving them. Even in those instances where the education system has embraced the cause of teaching small endangered languages, its ability to reverse language decline is constrained by many factors, particularly limited time for teaching languages other than main-stream ones (unless there is total immersion), lack of trained teachers, and lack of resources. Most education programs in language revival (sometimes also referred to as revitalization) moreover, are non-ecological. Languages are treated as systems with a grammar and a lexicon, links to life outside the classroom are limited, and the texts made available to learners are uninspiring. Even if these shortcomings were overcome, formal education can at best play a supplementary role in strengthening languages.

Support from politicians is much overestimated; negative policies at times are even the cause of people taking more interest in their language and develop it as an instrument of resistance, as in the case of Southern and Northern Ireland. In any case, politicians and their policies are very short-lived; and it is the support of permanent public servants, the mandarins, that ensures long-term consistent programmes. The success of Welsh language revival pro-grammes is said to have been helped greatly by the fact that a number of Whitehall officials supported the cause.

Home, as we have seen, is the English equivalent of Greek *oikos*, and our job is to either renovate a badly damaged home or, if too much damage has been done, to construct a new home. The central question of ecological language planning is: what is the support system that can sustain a language or language ecology over long periods of time? The problem is that there is no single solution, that each ecology requires a different support system.

Konrad Lorenz (1989) gave the metaphor of an aquarium, as the simplest exemplar of an ecology. He notes that there are a very large number of possible home aquariums having all sorts of different support systems. However, one can destroy an aquarium by having a single unsuitable factor: too much saltwater, too high or too low temperature, or the wrong species of fish in it.

What the support system for languages might require is a lot of consultation, extended participant observation and cooperation. It is, generally speaking, better to wait for a linguist to be asked to become involved than simply appearing as an ecological linguistic missionary.

Whatever solutions are required they are likely to take lots of time and money; and one of the practical tasks a linguist can do for a community speaking endangered languages is to help them obtain funding and develop a long-term economic plan for financing revitalization. One of my most time-consuming efforts during the last ten or so years has been to obtain funding from all kinds of agencies, and I fear I shall spend much of my remaining academic career writing grant applications. Let me give you a brief outline of what it costs to finance the revival of a small language, Wirangu, which I shall discuss in more detail shortly, for which we have spent the following amounts over the last six years:

1 AU$80,000 for linguistic expertise (two positions for field linguists);
2 AU$200,000 for a dedicated language display room;
3 AU$40.000 p. a. for Aboriginal workers;
4 about AU$50,000 each for production costs of three small books with video, CD, and TV production;
5 about AU$400,000 for running and upgrading the Far West Language Centre that grew out of the display room and now employs two part-time Aboriginal language workers.

That is, thus far we have spent in excess of AU$800.000 and more will be required to make this language viable again.

The cost of Norf'k language revival has been of a similar order of magnitude, but the activities sponsored were quite different. They included scholarships for two Norfolk Islanders to study linguistics, production of teaching materials, dual language signage, repatriation of language materials from Australia and the USA, among others.

Let me briefly outline some of the activities members of the University of Adelaide have been involved in on the West Coast of South Australia and on Norfolk Island. Before the arrival of white agriculturalists and missionaries in the late nineteenth century, the Far West Coast of South Australia was inhabited by three groups, the Mirning, whose territory stretched into Western Australia, the coastal Wirangu, and the Western Desert Kokotha (Gugada). These three groups, while linguistically and culturally distinct, nevertheless were economically interdependent and shared ceremonies and natural resources in frequent visits. Intermarriages between these groups were strictly regulated. The setting up of large sheep and cattle stations and grain farms cut them off from the previous sources of food and shelter and created dependency on white farmers and missionaries. The Lutheran Mission set up at Koonibba in the 1890s was possibly the key factor in the decline of the traditional language ecology, while at other Lutheran Missions, no indigenous languages were taught or used in evangelization: English was the language of the Koonibba Mission and the boarding school was the place where Aboriginal children learned it.

While set up in Wirangu country, the Lutheran Mission took in members of numerous groups. By the 1920s Wirangu had become a minority language at Koonibba and a mixed West Coast Mission koiné developed. The missionaries encouraged non-traditional intermarriages, though they discouraged marriages with white partners. As a result Mirning became extinct on the Far West Coast, Wirangu and Kokatha became severely endangered, as neither language was passed on to children in the early 1990s.

Because of numerous intermarriages, both within Aboriginal communities and with white people, there were very few Aboriginal people with a clear sense of Wirangu or Kokatha identity, so there was no clear sense of them being separate languages any longer. There was, however, a wish to restore the previous situation; and Adelaide University was approached by both Kokatha and Wirangu to help them accomplish this. We were able to produce dictionaries and grammars for both languages, with the help of historical sources, though the single most important publication has been a story book about hunting wombat for the Wirangu community. Because it featured one of the most important traditional events, because it was illustrated with pictures of an actual wombat hunt, and because it featured real members of the community in the illustrations, the story was memorized, retold, and re-enacted; and children are regularly taken to wombat country and told the story. Because it links language, people, culture and land, the story is also a clear example of an ecological approach to language revival. The first materials produced for Kokatha were a set of lexical flash cards; all illustrations were produced by children from Koonibba and featured the land and its inhabitants from an Aboriginal perspective.

As Wirangu and Kokatha are related languages, they share a large amount of grammar and maybe 40 per cent of lexical items, which reflect both common inheritance and a large tradition of prehistoric contacts. Instead of being a basis of commonalities, they have become a source of conflict, with members of one group accusing the other group of stealing their words and their knowledge. The situation is made worse by language having become a basis of native title land claims. What this illustrates is the non-ecological nature of the present language scene on the Far West Coast: competition has replaced mutually beneficial interrelations, with the result that the languages are in danger of becoming further weakened, while English is becoming even more dominant. To meet this challenge, we have produced three little language awareness brochures for the Far West Coast in which we attempt to explain the nature of language interrelationships and talk about prehistoric multilingualism. We have also helped to set up a language exhibition at the Far West Coast Language Centre. Meanwhile, Wirangu is making big steps forward, with elders and parents using the language with their children, but the long term gains of a stable language ecology for all languages is still remote.

The situation on Norfolk Island in the late 1980s was that the former stable diglossia comprising English and Norf'k (the mixed language spoken by the descendants of the Bounty mutineers from Pitcairn Island who had been resettled on Norfolk Island in 1856, see Chapter 11 in this volume for more details) had broken down. Norf'k was used in fewer and fewer domains and functions, with a concurrent loss in lexical and grammatical complexity. Once the language of the playground, it is now less used by children, who prefer English even outside school and in other non-formal settings. After many years of close cooperation between linguists at Adelaide, and the Norfolk Island Government, school, and Museum, one of the language teachers at school observed in 2010 that some children had begun to communicate in Norf'k with one another, a sign that the numerous activities have begun to bear fruit. Particularly important events have been the annual Norf'k language camp, a language and culture exhibit with resources for listening to the language, a jointly sponsored year of the Norf'k language, song competitions, and the emergence of a langscape in which Norf'k has become widely visible. The Government declared the language co-official with English in 2004 and UNESCO recognized it as an endangered language in 2008. This recognition drew worldwide attention, with 200+ newspaper and radio programmes about the language. Arguably, it was the single most important factor in raising awareness and appreciation of the language.

In 2010 the University of Adelaide began to research and develop family language policies for both Norf'k and the West Coast language, as it had been successfully argued that without family involvement, school programmes and public policies have little chance of success. There is now also a growing number of local people trained in linguistics and familiar with the ecological approach to language revival.

12.5   Conclusions

The ecological approach to language planning presented in this chapter has grown to one of practical work with a number of language communities over long periods of time. The aims of ecological planning include:

1 the maintenance of linguistic diversity;
2 the restoration of functional links between different languages;
3 the embedding of languages in a meaningful cultural, economic and ecological context; and
4 creating long-term sustainability of languages.

This approach is not one that lends itself to simple generalizations, since each language ecology is different and requires a different support system.

Engaging meaningfully in ecological language policy requires above all a long-term commitment, numerous visits to the language communities, and numerous contacts with their members, not just on language matters but on wider ecological issues. This approach differs significantly to non-ecological ones and, as I concluded in an earlier paper on this topic (Mühlhäusler 1996d: 211):

Ecological language planning differs from other types such as the neo-classical and similar streamlining approaches, in having as its principal objective structural diversity. It is acknowledged that the privileging of single languages may bring economic advantages in the short term, but there will be a long-term cost in dyseconomies which are likely to outweigh such benefits. Structural diversity should imply equitable relation between languages and their speakers. In my view, the well being of languages depends on such relationships with other languages rather than on their ability to outcompete others in the struggle for the fittest to survive.

The relevance of this observation has not changed since it was first made.

References

'Abd al-Wahhāb al-Nuwairī. 1924–1942. *Nihāyat al-'arab fi-funūn al-'adab*. Cairo: Dār al-Aktāb al-Miṣriyyah.

Abdulaziz, Mohamed and Ken Osinde. 1997. Sheng and Engsh: Development of mixed codes among the urban youth in Kenya. *International Journal of the Sociology of Language* 125: 43–63.

Aboh, Enoch. 2009. Clause structure and verb series. *Linguistic Inquiry* 40: 1–33.

Agnihotri, Rama Kant. 2007. *Hindi. An essential grammar*. London and New York: Routledge.

Ahulu, Samuel. 1995. Hybridized English in Ghana. *English Today* 11, 4: 31–36.

Aitchison, Jean. 1995. Tadpoles, cuckoos, and multiple births. Language contact and models of change. In Jacek Fisiak (ed.). *Linguistic change under contact conditions*. Berlin and New York: Mouton de Gruyter, pp. 1–13.

Albalá Hernández, Carmen P. 1997. El español de los chamorros de las islas Marianas. *Español Actual: Revista de Español Vivo* 68: 63–74.

2000. *Americanismos en las Indias del Poniente: Voces de origen indígena Americano en las lenguas del Pacífico*. Madrid and Frankfurt/M.: Iberoamericana and Vervuert.

Albalá Hernández, Carmen P. and Rafael Rodríguez-Ponga y Salamanca. 1986. *Relaciones de España con las Islas Marianas: La lengua chamorra*. Madrid: Fundación Juan March.

Alonso, José Luis. 1982. Onomástica y marginalidad en la Picaresca. *Imprévue* 1: 203–235.

Alvar, Manuel. 1986. Cuestiones de bilingüismo y diglosia en español. In Manuel Alvar, Echevarría Maitena, and García Constantino (eds.). *El castellano actual en las comunidades bilingües de España*. Salamanca: Consejería de Educación y Cultura, Junta de Castilla y León, pp. 11–48.

Álvarez, Manuel, Manuel Ariza, and Josefa Mendoza. 2000. La onomástica personal en Carmona (Sevilla) en el siglo XVI. In Dieter Kremer (ed.). Onomastik. Akten des 18. Internationalen Kongresses für Namenforschung. Trier, 12.-17. April 1993. Bd. 2: Namensysteme im interkulturellen Vergleich. Tübingen: Niemeyer, pp. 156–166.

Amery, Rob. 2000. *Warrabarna Kaurna! Reclaiming an Australian language*. Lisse: Swets and Zeitlinger.

Amery, Rob and Peter Mühlhäusler. 2005. *Cost benefit analysis of Kaurna language reclamation*. Adelaide: Adelaide University, Linguistics Department.

Andersen, Gisle. 2014. Pragmatic borrowing. *Journal of Pragmatics* 67: 17–33.

Anderson, Benedict. 1983. *Imagined communities: Reflections on the origin and spread of nationalism.* London: Verso.

Ansaldo, Umberto. 2009. *Contact languages: Ecology and evolution in Asia.* Cambridge: Cambridge University Press.

Ansaldo, Umberto, Stephen Matthews, and Lisa Lim (eds.). 2007. *Deconstructing creole.* Amsterdam and Philadelphia: Benjamins.

Ariza, Manuel, Antonio Salvador, and Antonio Viudas (eds.). 1988. *Actas del I Congreso Internacional de Historia de la Lengua Española: Cáceres, 30 de marzo - 4 de abril de 1987. Vol. 2.* Madrid: Arco Libros.

Arranz Márquez, Luis. 1991. *Repartimientos y encomiendas en la Isla Española: El repartimiento de Albuquerque de 1514.* Madrid: Ed. Fundación García Arévalo.

Aslanov, Cyril. 2000. Interpreting the language-mixing in terms of codeswitching: The case of the Franco-Italian interface in the Middle Ages. *Journal of Pragmatics* 32: 1273–1281.

2002. Quand les langues romanes se confondent . . . La Romania vue d'ailleurs. *Langage et société* 99: 9–52.

2006a. *Le français au Levant, jadis et naguère: À la recherche d'une langue perdue.* Paris: Champion.

2006b. *Evidence of francophony in mediaeval Levant: Decipherment and interpretation (MS. BnF. Copte 43).* Jerusalem: Hebrew University of Jerusalem Magnes Press.

2007. Linguistic hybridization in the Chronicle of Morea. In Deisis Paraskhou and Aristeas Spendzas (eds.). Η Πελοπόννησος μετά την Δ᾽ Σταυροφορία του 1204 (Πρακτικά διεθνους συνεδρίου – Μυστράς, 1–3 Οκτωβρίου 2004). Athens: Διεθνής Επιστημονική Εταιρεία Πληθωνικών και Βυζαντινών μελετών-Mystras: Κοινωφελές Ίδρυμα Βυζαντινών και Μεταβυζαντινών Σπουδών Μυστρά, pp. 37–48.

2008. L'ancien français, sociolecte d'une caste au pouvoir: Royaume de Jérusalem, Morée, Chypre. In Benjamin Fagard, Sophie Prévost, Bernard Combettes, and Olivier Bertrand (eds.). *Évolutions en français: Études de linguistique diachronique.* Bern: Lang, pp. 3–19.

Aslanov, Cyril and Benjamin Z. Kedar. 2010. Problems in the study of transcultural borrowing in the Frankish Levant. In Michael Borgolte and Bernd Schneidmüller (eds.). *Hybride Kulturen im mittelalterlichen Europa: Vorträge und Workshops einer internationalen Frühlingsschule.* Berlin: Akademie Verlag, pp. 278–279.

Auer, Peter. 1995. The pragmatics of code-switching: A sequential approach. In Lesley Milroy and Pieter Muysken (eds.). *One speaker, two languages. Cross-disciplinary perspectives on code-switching.* Cambridge: Cambridge University Press, pp. 115–135.

1999. From codeswitching via language mixing to fused lects: Toward a dynamic typology of bilingual speech. *International Journal of Bilingualism* 3, 4: 309–332.

2007a. The monolingual bias in bilingualism research, or: Why bilingual talk is (still) a challenge for linguistics. In Heller (ed.), pp. 319–339.

2007b. Mobility, contact and accommodation. In Carmen Llamas, Louise Mullany, and Peter Stockwell (eds). *The Routledge companion to sociolinguistics.* London and New York: Routledge.

Auer, Peter, Elizabeth Couper-Kuhlen, and Frank Müller. 1999. *Language in time. The rhythm and tempo of spoken interaction.* Oxford: Oxford University Press.

Auer, Peter and Frans Hinskens. 2005. The role of interpersonal accommodation in a theory of language change. In Auer, Hinskens, and Kerswill (eds.), pp. 335–357.

Auer, Peter, Frans Hinskens, and Paul Kerswill (eds.). 2005. *Dialect change. Convergence and divergence in European languages.* Cambridge: Cambridge University Press.

Augé, Marc. 2009. *Pour une anthropologie de la mobilité.* Paris: Payot.

Backus, Ad. 2003. Can a mixed language be conventionalized alternational codeswitching? In Matras and Bakker (eds.), pp. 237–270.

Baglioni, Daniele. 2006. *La scripta italoromanza del regno di Cipro: Edizione e commento di testi di scriventi ciprioti del Quattrocento.* Rome: Aracne Editrice.

Bailey, Charles-James N. 1979. Old and new views on language history and language relationships. In Helmut Lüdtke (ed.). *Kommunikationstheoretische Grundlagen des Sprachwandels.* Berlin and New York: Mouton de Gruyter, pp. 139–181.

Baker, Philip and Magnus Huber. 2000. Constructing new pronominal systems from the Atlantic to the Pacific. *Linguistics* 38, 5: 833–866.

Baker, Philip and Peter Mühlhäusler. 2013. The creole legacy of a bounteous mutineer: Edward Young's Caribbean contribution to the language of Pitcairn and Norfolk Islands. *Acta Linguistica Hafniensia: International Journal of Linguistics* 45, 2: 170–186.

Bakker, Peter. 1997. *A language of our own. The genesis of Michif, the mixed Cree-French language of the Canadian Metis.* New York: Oxford University Press.

2000a. Rapid language change: Creolisation, intertwining, convergence. In Colin Renfrew, April McMahon, and Larry Trask (eds.). *Time depth in historical linguistics.* Vol. 2. Cambridge: McDonald Institute for Archaeological Research, pp. 575–610.

2000b. Convergence intertwining: An alternative way towards the genesis of mixed languages. In Dicky Gilbers, John Nerbonn, and Jos Schaeken (eds.). *Languages in contact.* Amsterdam: Rodopi, pp. 29–35.

2003. Mixed languages as autonomous systems. In Matras and Bakker (eds.), pp. 107–150.

2008. Pidgins versus creoles and pidgincreoles. In Silvia Kouwenberg and Victor Singler (eds.). *The handbook of pidgin and creole studies.* Malden: Blackwell, pp. 130–157.

Bakker, Peter and Maarten Mous (eds.). 1994a. *Mixed languages: 15 case studies in language intertwining.* Amsterdam: IFOTT.

1994b. Introduction. In Bakker and Mous (eds.), pp. 1–11.

Bakker, Peter and Pieter Muysken. 1995. Mixed languages and language intertwining. In Jacques Arends, Pieter Muysken, and Norval Smith (eds.). *Pidgins and creoles: An introduction.* Amsterdam: Benjamins, pp. 41–52.

Bamgbose, Ayo. 1991. *Language and the nation. The language question in Sub-Saharan Africa.* Edinburgh: Edinburgh University Press.

Barton, David. 1994: *An introduction to the ecology of written language.* Oxford: Blackwell.

Bateson, Gregory. 1972. *Steps toward an ecology of mind.* New York: Ballantine.

Baudouin de Courtenay, Jan N. 1897. Statement of linguistic principles. In *Baudoin de Courtenay, Jan N. 1972. A Baudouin de Courtenay anthology. The beginnings of structural linguistics*. Ed. by Edward Stankiewicz. Bloomington and London: Indiana University Press, pp. 213–215.

Bechert, Heinz. 1993. *Einführung in die Indologie*. Darmstadt: Wissenschaftliche Buchgesellschaft.

Begon, Michael, Colin A. Townsend, and John L. Harper. 2006. *Ecology: From individuals to ecosystems*. 4th edn. Malden: Blackwell.

Bender, Byron W. 1971. Micronesian languages. In Thomas A. Sebeok (ed.). *Linguistics in Oceania. Current trends in linguistics vol. 8*. The Hague: Mouton, pp. 426–465.

Berman, Tzeporah. 1994. The rape of mother nature? Women in the language of environmental discourse. First published in *Trumpeter* 11, 4: 173–178. Quoted from the reprint in Fill and Mühlhäusler (eds.) 2001, pp. 258–269.

Berruto, Gaetano. 2003. Sul parlante nativo. In Hans-Ingo Radatz and Rainer Schlösser (eds.). *Donum Grammaticorum*. Festschrift für Harro Stammerjohann. Tübingen, Niemeyer, pp. 1–14.

Besters-Dilger, Juliane, Cynthia Dermarkar, Stefan Pfänder, and Achim Rabus (eds.). 2014. *Congruence in contact-induced language change. Language families, typological resemblance, and perceived similarity*. Berlin: de Gruyter.

Bickerton, Derek. 1973. The nature of a creole continuum. *Language* 49: 640–669.

Biggs, Bruce G. 1972. Implications of linguistic subgrouping with special reference to Polynesia. In Roger C. Green and Marion Kelly (eds.). *Studies in Oceanic culture history*. Vol. 3. Honolulu: Bishop Museum, pp. 143–152.

Bilger, Mireille (ed.). 1999. *Revue Française de Linguistique Appliquée* 4, 2. Special issue on L'oral spontané.

Biloa, Edmond. 1999. Structure phrastique du Camfranglais: état de la question. In George Echu and Allan W. Grunstrom (eds.). *Official bilingualism and linguistic communication in Cameroon*. New York: Lang, pp. 147–174.

Birch, Charles and John B. Cobb Jr. 1981. *The liberation of life: From the cell to the community*. Cambridge: Cambridge University Press.

Bissoonauth, Anu. 2011. Language shift and maintenance in multilingual Mauritius: The case of Indian ancestral languages. *Journal of Multilingual and Multicultural Development* 32, 5: 421–434.

Blanche-Benveniste, Claire. 2010. *Le français. Usages de la langue parlée*. Leuven and Paris: Peeters.

Blommaert, Jan. 1992. Codeswitching and the exclusivity of social identities: Some data from campus Kiswahili. *Journal of Multilingual and Multicultural Development* 13, 1–2: 57–70.

2010. *The Sociolinguistics of globalization*. Cambridge: Cambridge University Press.

Blommaert, Jan and Jie Dong. 2010: Language and movement in space. In Nikolas Coupland (ed.). *The Handbook of language and globalization*. Sussex: Wiley-Blackwell, pp. 366–385.

Blust, Robert. 1977. The Proto-Austronesian pronouns and Austronesian subgrouping: A preliminary report. *Working Papers in Linguistics* 9, 1: 1–15.

2000. Chamorro historical phonology. *Oceanic Linguistics* 39, 1: 83–122.

Bolinger, Dwight. 1965. The atomization of meaning. *Language* 41, 4: 555–573.

Bollée, Annegret. 1977. *Zur Entstehung der französischen Kreolendialekte im Indischen Ozean: Kreolisierung ohne Pidginisierung*. Geneva: Droz.

1982. Die Rolle der Konvergenz bei der Kreolisierung. In P. Sture Ureland (ed.). *Die Leistung der Strataforschung und der Kreolistik. Typologische Aspekte der Sprachkontaktforschung*. Tübingen: Niemeyer, pp. 391–405.

2009. Le créole mauricien: Un parler du deuxième génération? In Hookoomsing, Ludwig, and Schnepel (eds.), pp. 67–84.

Boretzky, Norbert, Wolfgang U. Dressler, Janez Orešnik, Karmen Teržan, and Wolfgang U. Wurzel (eds.). 1995. *Natürlichkeitstheorie und Sprachwandel. Beiträge zum internationalen Symposium über 'Natürlichkeitstheorie und Sprachwandel' an der Universität Maribor vom 13.5.–15.5.1993*. Bochum: Brockmeyer

Bourdieu, Pierre. 1979. *La distinction. Critique sociale du jugement*. Paris: Minuit.

Bowen, Donald J. 1971. Hispanic languages and influence in Oceania. In Thomas A. Sebeok (ed.). *Linguistics in Oceania. Current trends in linguistics vol. 8*. The Hague: Mouton, pp. 938–952.

Boyd-Bowman, Peter. 1970. Los nombres de pila en México desde 1540 hasta 1950. *Nueva Revista de Filología Hispánica* 19: 12–48.

1985. *Indice geobiográfico de más de 56 mil pobladores de la América Hispánica (1493–1519)*. México: Fondo de Cultura Económica.

Braudel, Fernand. 1981–1982. *The Mediterranean and the Mediterranean world in the age of Philip II (2 vols.)*. Ed. by Siân Reynolds, 4th edn. London: Fontana/Collins.

Britain, David. 2009. Language and space: The variationist approach. In Peter Auer and Jürgen Erich Schmidt (eds.). *Language and space: An international handbook of linguistic variation. Vol. 1: Theories and methods*. Berlin: Mouton de Gruyter, pp. 142–162.

Broschart, Jürgen. 1997. Why Tongan does it differently: Categorial distinctions in a language without nouns and verbs. *Linguistic Typology* 1: 123–165.

Buesa Oliver, Tomás. 1988. Recursos fónicos en la afectividad de los antropónimos. In Ariza, Salvador, and Viudas (eds.), pp. 1613–1640.

Buffett, Alice and Donald Laycock. 1989: *Speak Norfolk today*. Norfolk Island: Himii Publishing.

Bundgaard, Peer F. 2010. Husserl and language. In Daniel Schmicking and Shaun Gallagher (eds.). *Handbook of phenomenology and cognitive sciences*. Dordrecht: Springer Science + Business Media, pp. 369–400.

Burrus, Ernest J. 1954. Sanvitores' grammar and catechism in the Mariana (or Chamorro) language (1668). *Anthropos* 49: 934–960.

Button, Graham. 1987. Answers as interactional products: Two sequential practices used in interviews. *Social Psychology Quarterly* 50, 2: 160–171.

Calvet, Louis-Jean. 1994. *Les voix de la ville: Introduction à la sociolinguistique urbaine*. Paris: Payot.

1997. Vernaculaire. In Moreau (ed.), pp. 291–294.

2006. *Towards an ecology of world languages*. Cambridge: Polity Press.

Cameron, Deborah. 1990: Demythologizing sociolinguistics: Why language does not reflect society. In Joseph and Taylor (eds.), pp. 73–93.

Caravedo, Rocío. 1983. *Estudios sobre el español de Lima: Variación contextual de la sibilante*. Lima: Pontificia Universidad Católica del Perú.

1986. La variabilidad del segmento 'd' en el español de Lima. In José Moreno de Alba (ed.). *Actas del II Congreso Internacional sobre el Español de América*. México: Universidad Nacional Autónoma de México, pp. 281–287.

1987. Constricciones contextuales del español hablado en Lima. El caso de /s/. In Humberto López Morales and María Vaquero (eds.). *Actas del I Congreso Internacional sobre el Español de América*. San Juan: Academia Puertorriqueña de la Lengua Española, pp. 665–674.

Carayol, Michel and Robert Chaudenson. 1979. Essai d'analyse implicationnelle d'un continuum linguistique: français–créole. In Paul Wald and Gabriel Manessy (eds.). *Plurilinguism: Normes, situations, stratégies*. Paris: L'Harmattan, pp. 129–172.

Castells, Manuel. 1975. *La question urbaine*. Paris: Maspero.

Certeau, Michel de. 1980. *L'invention du quotidian*. Paris: Gallimard.

Chafe, Wallace. 1985. Linguistic differences produced by differences between speaking and writing. In David R. Olson, Nancy Torrance, and Angela Hildyard (eds.). *Literacy, language, and learning: The nature and consequences of reading and writing*. Cambridge: Cambridge University Press, pp. 105–123.

Chambers, Jack. 2001. Vernacular universals. In Josep M. Fontana, Louise McNally, Teresa Turell, and Enric Vallduvi (eds.). *ICLaVE 1: Proceedings of the First International Conference on Language Variation in Europe*. Barcelona: Universitat Pompeu Fabra, pp. 52–60.

2003. *Sociolinguistic theory: Linguistic variation and its social significance*. 2nd edn. Oxford: Blackwell.

2004. Dynamic typology and vernacular universals. In Kortmann (ed.), pp. 127–145.

2009. Cognition and the linguistic continuum: From vernacular to standard. In Filppula, Klemola, and Paulasto (eds.), pp. 19–32.

Chambers, John K. and Peter Trudgill. 1998. *Dialectology*. 2nd edn. Cambridge: Cambridge University Press.

Chambers, Jack, Peter Trudgill, and Natalie Schilling-Estes (eds.). 2002. *The handbook of language variation and change*. Malden: Blackwell.

Chamorro, Pilar. 2012. Future time reference and irrealis modality in Chamorro: A study of preverbal para. *Cahiers Chronos* 25: 91–113.

Chaudenson, Robert. 1992. *Des îles, des hommes, des langues: Essai sur la créolisation linguistique et culturelle*. Paris: L'Harmattan.

Chaudenson, Robert, Raymond Mougeon, and Edouard Beniak. 1993. *Vers une approche panlectale de la variation du français*. Paris: Didier Erudition.

Chawla, Saroj. 2001. Linguistic and philosophical roots of our environmental crisis. In Fill and Mühlhäusler (eds.), pp. 115–123.

Cheshire, Jenny, Paul Kerswill, and Ann Williams. 2005. Phonology, grammar, and discourse in dialect convergence. In Auer, Hinskens, and Kerswill (eds.), pp. 135–167.

Clayton, Jean, Jenny Barnett, Graeme Kemelfield, and Peter Mühlhäusler. 1996. *Desert schools: An investigation of English language and literacy among young Aboriginal people in seven communities*. Canberra: DEETYA. [www.iier.org.au/qjer/qjer15/clayton.html]

Clements, J. Clancy. 2009. *The linguistic legacy of Spanish and Portuguese: Colonial expansion and language change*. Cambridge: Cambridge University Press.

Clough, James C. 1876. *On the existence of mixed languages, being an examination of the fundamental axioms of the foreign school of modern philology, more especially as applied to the English*. London: Longmans, Green & Co.

Clyne, Michael. 2003. *Dynamics of language contact. English and immigrant languages*. Cambridge: Cambridge University Press.

Codrington, Robert H. 1885. *The Melanesian languages*. Oxford: Clarendon Press.

Comnena, Anna. 1928. *The Alexiad*. Trans. Elizabeth A. Dawes. London: Routledge & Kegan Paul.

Contini-Morava, Ellen. 1994. *Noun classification in Swahili*. Charlottesville: University of Virginia, Publications of the Institute for Advanced Technology in the Humanities. [http://jefferson.village.virginia.edu/swahili/swahili.html]

Costenoble, H. 1940. *Die Chamoro Sprache*. S'Gravenhage: M. Nijhoff.

Coulmas, Florian. 1981. Introduction: The concept of native speaker. In Florian Coulmas (ed.). *A Festschrift for native speaker*. The Hague: Mouton Publishers, pp. 1–25.

   2005. *Sociolinguistics. The study of speakers' choices*. Cambridge: Cambridge University Press.

Coupland, Nikolas. 2003. Sociolinguistic authenticities. *Journal of Sociolinguistics* 7: 416–31.

   2007. *Style: Language variation and identity*. Cambridge: Cambridge University Press.

   2010. Language, ideology, media and social change. In Karen Junod and Didier Maillat (eds.). *Performing the self*. SPELL: Swiss Papers in English Language and Literature 24. Tübingen: Narr, pp. 55–79.

Couto, Hildo H. do. 1996. *Introdução ao estudo das línguas crioulas e pidgins*. Brasilia: Editora da Universidade de Brasília.

   2002. *Anticrioulo: Manifestação lingüística de resistência cultural*. Brazil: Thesaurus.

Croft, William. 1990. *Typology and universals*. Cambridge: Cambridge University Press. [2nd edition, 2003]

   2000. *Explaining language change: An evolutionary approach*. Harlow: Longman.

   2003. Mixed languages and acts of identity: An evolutionary approach. In Matras and Bakker (eds.), pp. 41–72.

Crowley, Terry. 1990. *Beach-la-Mar to Bislama: The emergence of a national language in Vanuatu*. Oxford: Clarendon Press.

Crowley, Tony. 1990. That obscure object of desire: A science of language. In Joseph and Taylor (eds.), pp. 27–50.

Crystal, David 1994: *An encyclopedic dictionary of language and languages*. 2nd edn. Harmondsworth: Penguin.

Cunningham, Lawrence J. 1992. *Ancient Chamorro society*. Honolulu: Bess Press.

Darwin, Charles. 1901. *The descent of man, and Selection in relation to sex*. London: John Murray.

DeCamp, David. 1971. Toward a generative analysis of a post-creole speech continuum. In Hymes (ed.), pp. 349–370.

DeGraff, Michel. 2003. Against creole exceptionalism. *Language* 79, 2: 391–410.

   2005. Linguists' most dangerous myth: The fallacy of creole exceptionalism. *Language in Society* 34: 533–591.

Deleuze, Gilles and Félix Guattari. 1980. *Mille plateaux. Capitalisme et schizophrénie 2*. Paris: Éditions de Minuit.

Denoon, Donald (ed.). 1997. *The Cambridge history of the Pacific Islanders*. Cambridge: Cambridge University Press.

Dermarkar, Cynthia. 2014. French meets Arabic in Cairo: discourse markers as gestures. In Juliane Besters-Dilger, Cynthia Dermarkar, Stefan Pfänder, and Achim Rabus, (eds.). *Congruence in contact-induced language change. Language families, typological resemblance, and perceived similarity*. Berlin: De Gruyter, pp. 275–293.

Dermarkar, Cynthia, Françoise Gadet, Ralph Ludwig, and Stefan Pfänder. 2009. Vom Französischen in den Kolonien zum français global? Der Fall Ägypten als Spiegel für linguistische Arealtypologien. *Romanistisches Jahrbuch* 59/2008: 101–127.

Dermarkar, Cynthia and Stefan Pfänder. 2010. *Le français cosmopolite. Témoignages de la dynamique langagière dans l'espace urbain du Caire*. Berlin: Berliner Wissenschafts-Verlag.

Deumert, Ana. 2005. The unbearable lightness of being bilingual: English-Afrikaans language contact in South Africa. *Language Sciences* 27: 113–135.

Díaz, Norma, Ralph Ludwig, and Stefan Pfänder. 2002. Procesos lingüísticos en situaciones de contacto. Parámetros y perspectivas. In Norm Díaz, Ralph Ludwig, and Stefan Pfänder (eds.). *La Romania americana. Procesos lingüísticos en situaciones de contacto*. Frankfurt/M.: Vervuert, pp. 389–441.

Dixon, Robert M. W. 1999. *The rise and fall of languages*. Cambridge: Cambridge University Press.

Drechsel, Emanuel J. 1997. *Mobilian jargon*. Oxford: Clarendon Press.

Drescher, Martina and Ingrid Neumann-Holzschuh. 2010. Les variétés non-hexagonales du français et la syntaxe de l'oral. Première approche. In Martina Drescher and Ingrid Neumann-Holzschuh (eds.). *La syntaxe de l'oral dans les variétés non-hexagonales du français*. Tübingen: Stauffenburg, pp. 9–35.

Dressler, Wolfgang U. 1984. Explaining natural phonology. *Phonology Yearbook* Vol. 1, pp. 29–51.

Dressler, Wolfgang U., Willi Mayerthaler, Oswald Panagl, and Wolfgang U. Wurzel (eds.). 1987. *Leitmotifs in natural morphology*. Amsterdam: Benjamins.

Drew, Paul and John Heritage (eds.). 1992. *Talk at work: Interaction in institutional settings*. Cambridge: Cambridge University Press, pp. 3–65.

Dua, Hans R. 1992. Hindi-Urdu as pluricentric language. In Michael Clyne (ed.). *Pluricentric languages; Differing norms in different nations*. Berlin and New York: Mouton de Gruyter, pp. 381–400.

Dufour, Sophie, Sibylle Kriegel, Mushina Alleesaib, and Noël Nguyen. 2014. The perception of the French /s/-/ʃ/ contrast in early Creole-French bilinguals. *Frontiers in Psychology*, 5: 1200.

Durand, Guillaume and Kinvi Logossah. 2002. *Les noms de famille d'origine africaine de la population martiniquaise d'ascendence servile*. Paris: L'Harmattan.

Duranti, Alessandro. 2001. *Keyterms in language and culture*. Malden: Blackwell.

Duranti, Alessandro and Charles Goodwin (eds.). 1992. *Rethinking context: Language as an interactive phenomenon*. Cambridge: Cambridge University Press.

Dyen, Isidore. 1965. *A lexicostatistical classification of the Austronesian languages.* Baltimore: Waverly Press.

Eades, Diana. 1982. You gotta know how to talk: Information seeking in South-East Queensland Aboriginal Society. *Australian Journal of Linguistics* 2: 61–82.

Eckert, Penelope. 2004. Variation and a sense of place. In Fought (ed.), pp. 107–118.

Edgecombe, Jean. 1991. *Norfolk Island – South Pacific: Island of history and many delights.* Thornleigh: J. Edgecombe.

Edmondson, Jerold A., Crawford Feagin, and Peter Mühlhäusler (eds.). 1990. *Development and diversity – language variation across time and space.* Arlington: University of Texas and Summer Institute of Linguistics.

Edwards, John. 2001. The ecology of language revival. *Current Issues in Language Planning* 2, 2–3: 231–241.

Edwards, William H. 1983. Plants in Pitjantjatjara life and mythology. Unpublished paper presented at the Federal Conference of the Society for Growing Australian Plants, Adelaide.

Eichler, Ernst, Gerold Hilty, Heinrich Löffler, Hugo Steger, and Ladislav Zgusta (eds.). 1996. *Namenforschung/Name Studies/Les noms propres. Ein internationales Handbuch zur Onomastik/An International Handbook of Onomastics/Manuel international d'onomastique. Vol. 2.* Berlin and New York: Mouton de Gruyter.

Eldem, Edhem. 2006. Capitulations and Western trade. In Suraiya N. Faroqhi (ed.). *The Cambridge history of Turkey, Vol. 3: The later Ottoman Empire.* Cambridge: Cambridge University Press, pp. 283–335.

Eliasson, Stig. 2015. The birth of language ecology: Interdisciplinary influences in Einar Haugen's 'The ecology of language'. *Language Sciences* 50: 78–92.

Éloy, Jean-Michel. 2004. Des langues collatérales: problèmes et propositions. In Jean-Michel Éloy (ed.). *Des langues collatérales: Problèmes linguistiques, socio-linguistiques et glottopolitiques de la proximité linguistique.* Paris: L'Harmattan, pp. 5–25.

Ennis, Juan A. and Stefan Pfänder. 2010. Zur – fragwürdigen – Legitimation des Laboratoriums Kreol(istik). In Ludwig and Röseberg (eds.), pp. 257–282.

Erickson, Frederick. 2004. *Talk and social theory: Ecologies of speaking and listening in everyday life.* Cambridge: Polity Press.

Escobar, Anna María. 2007. Migración, contacto de lenguas encubierto y difusión de variantes lingüísticas. *Revista Internacional de Lingüística Iberoamericana* 10: 93–107.

Evans, Nicholas. 2009. *Dying words: Endangered languages and what they have to tell us.* Oxford: Blackwell.

Evans, Nicholas and Stephen C. Levinson. 2009. The myth of language universals: Language diversity and its importance for cognitive science. *Behavioral and Brain Sciences* 32: 429–492.

Everett, Daniel L. 2005. Cultural constraints on grammar and cognition in Pirahã: Another look at the design features of human languages. *Current Anthropology* 46, 4: 621–646.

    2008. *Don't sleep, there are snakes. Life and language in the Amazonian jungle.* London: Profile Books.

    2009. Pirahã culture and grammar: A response to some criticisms. *Language* 85, 2: 405–442.

Ferguson, Charles A. 1971. Absence of the copula and the notion of simplicity: A study of normal speech, baby talk, foreigner talk, and pidgins. In Hymes (ed.), pp. 141–150.

1975. Towards a characterisation of English foreigner talk. *Anthropological Linguistics* 17, 1: 1–14.

Ferguson, Charles A. and Charles E. DeBose. 1977. Simplified registers, broken languages and pidginization. In Albert Valdman (ed.). *Pidgin and creole linguistics*. Bloomington: Indiana University Press, pp. 99–125.

Fernández Rodríguez, Mauro. 2005. Leyenda e historia del término diglosia: Su invención y su primera expansion. In Luis Santos Ríos (ed.). *Palabras, norma, discurso: En memoria de Fernando Lázaro Carreter*. Salamanca: Universidad de Salamanca, pp. 447–464.

Feyerabend, Paul. 1993. *Against method*. 3rd edn. London and New York: Verso.

Feynman, Richard. 1967. *The character of physical law*. Cambridge, MA: MIT Press.

Fill, Alwin. 1998. Ecolinguistics: State of the art. First published in *Arbeiten aus Anglistik und Amerikanistik* 23, 1: 3–16. Quoted from the reprint in Fill and Mühlhäusler (eds.) 2001, pp. 43–53.

2000. Language and ecology: Ecolinguistic perspectives for 2000 and beyond. In *Selected Papers from AILA 99 Tokyo*. Tokyo, pp. 162–176.

Fill, Alwin and Peter Mühlhäusler (eds.). 2001. *The ecolinguistics reader. Language, ecology and environment*. London and New York: Continuum.

Fill, Alwin and Hermine Penz (eds.). 2007. *Sustaining language: Essays in applied ecolinguistics*. Wien: LIT.

Fill, Alwin, Hermine Penz, and Wilhelm Trampe (eds.). 2002. *Colorful green ideas: Papers from the conference 30 Years of Language and Ecology (Graz, 2000) and the symposium Sprache und Ökologie (Passau, 2001)*. Bern: Lang.

Filppula, Markku, Juhani Klemola, and Heli Paulasto (eds.). 2009a. *Vernacular universals and language contacts: Evidence from varieties of English and beyond*. New York and London: Routledge.

2009b. Vernacular universals and language contacts: An overview. In Filppula, Klemola, and Paulasto (eds.), pp. 1–16.

Fischer, John L. 1961. The retention rate of Chamorro basic vocabulary. *Lingua* 10: 255–266.

Fischer, Steven R. (ed.). 2013. *Oceanic voices – European quills. The early documents on and in Chamorro and Rapanui*. Berlin: Akademie Verlag.

Fishman, Joshua A. 1991. *Reversing language shift*. Clevedon: Multilingual Matters.

Flint, Elwyn H. 1964. Earlier work on the languages of Pitcairn and Norfolk Islands. In Ross and Moverley, pp. 102–104.

Fontanille, Jacques. 1998. *Sémiotique du discours*. Limoges: Presses Universitaires de Limoges.

Forlot, Guy and Jean-Michel Eloy. 2010. Le spontané et la réflexivité en (socio) linguistique. In Henri Boyer (ed.). *Pour une épistémologie de la sociolinguistique*. Limoges: Lambert-Lucas, pp. 163–170.

Fornel, Michel de and Louis Quéré (eds.). 1999. La logique des situations. *Nouveaux regards sur l'écologie des activités sociales. Numéro spécial de la revue Raisons Pratiques*, 10.

Fouchard, Jean. 1988. *Les marrons de la liberté*. Port-au-Prince: Éditions Henri Deschamps.

Fought, Carmen (ed.). 2004. *Sociolinguistic variation: Critical reflections*. Oxford: Oxford University Press.

Franceschini, Rita. 1998. Code-switching and the notion of code in linguistics: Proposals for a dual focus model. In Peter Auer (ed.). *Code-switching in conversation: Language, interaction and identity*. London: Routledge, pp. 51–74.

François, Alexandre. 2004. Reconstructing the geocentric system of Proto Oceanic. *Oceanic Linguistics* 43, 1: 1–32.

    2010. A comparison of geocentric directionals across Bank and Torres languages. Paper presented at the 8th Conference on Oceanic Linguistics, Auckland, New Zealand, 5 January 2010.

Frank, Michael C., Daniel L. Everett, Evelina Fedorenko, and Edward Gibson. 2008. Number as a cognitive technology: Evidence from Pirahã language and cognition. *Cognition* 108, 3: 819–824.

Gadet, Françoise. 2011. What can be learned about the grammar of French from corpora of French spoken outside France. In Marek Konopka, Jaqueline Kubczak, Christian Mair, František Štícha, and Ulrich H. Waßner (eds.). *Grammatik und Korpora 2009. Dritte Internationale Konferenz, Mannheim 22.-24.09.2009*. Tübingen: Narr, pp. 87–120.

Gadet, Françoise, Aidan Coveney, Jean-Philippe Dalbera, Dominique Fattier, and Ralph Ludwig. 2009. Sociolinguistique, écologie des langues, etc. *Langage & Société* 129: 121–135.

Gadet, Françoise and Emmanuelle Guerin. 2012. Des données pour étudier la variation: petits gestes méthodologiques, gros effets. *Cahiers de Linguistique* 38, 1: 41–65.

Gadet, Françoise, Ralph Ludwig, Lorenza Mondada, Stefan Pfänder, and Anne-Catherine Simon. 2012. Un grand corpus de français parlé: Le CIEL-F. Choix épistémologiques et réalisations empiriques. *Revue Française de Linguistique Appliquée* 17, 1: 39–54.

Gadet, Françoise, Ralph Ludwig, and Stefan Pfänder. 2009. Francophonie et typologie des situations. *Cahiers de Linguistique* 34, 1: 143–162.

García Cornejo, Rosalía. 1998. Sobre los nombres y apellidos en dos documentos andaluces del siglo XV. *Archivo Hispalense* 246: 171–198.

Gardner Chloros, Penelope. 2009. *Code-switching*, Cambridge: Cambridge University Press.

    2010. Language contact and code-mixing. In Hickey (ed.), pp. 188–207.

Garfinkel, Harold. 1967. *Studies in ethnomethodology*. Englewood Cliffs: Prentice-Hall.

Garfinkel, Harold and Harvey Sacks. 1970. On formal structures of practical actions. In John C. McKinney and Edward A. Tiryakian (eds.). *Theoretical sociology: Perspectives and developments*. New York: Meredith, pp. 337–366.

Garner, Mark. 2004. *Language: An ecological view*. Bern: Lang.

Gérard-Plasmans, Delphine. 2005. *La présence française en Égypte entre 1914 et 1936. De l'impérialisme à l'influence et de l'influence à la cooperation*. Darnétal: Éd. Darnétalaises.

Gibson, James J. 1979. *The ecological approach to visual perception*. Boston: Houghton Mifflin.

Glinert, Lewis. 1993. Language as a quasilect: Hebrew in contemporary Anglo-Jewry. In Lewis Glinert (ed.). *Hebrew in Ashkenaz: A language in exile*. Oxford: Oxford University Press, pp. 249–264.

Goatly, Andrew. 1996. Green grammar and grammatical metaphor, or language and myth of power, or metaphors we die by. First published in *Journal of Pragmatics* 25: 537–560. Quoted from the reprint in Fill and Mühlhäusler (eds.) 2001, pp. 203–225.

Goffman, Erving. 1961. *Encounters: Two studies in the sociology of interaction*, Indianapolis: Bobbs-Merrill.

 1963. *Behavior in public places: Notes on the social organization of gathering*. New York: Free Press.

 1964. The neglected situation. *American Anthropologist* 66, 6: 133–136.

 1981a. *Forms of talk*. Philadelphia: University of Pennsylvania Press.

 1981b. Footing. In Erving Goffman (ed.). *Forms of Talk*. Philadelphia: University of Pennsylvania Press, pp. 124–159.

Gómez Rendón, Jorge. 2005. La media lengua de Imbabura. In Hella Olbertz and Pieter Muysken (eds.). *Encuentros y conflictos: Bilingüismo y contacto de lenguas en el mundo andino*. Frankfurt/M. and Madrid: Vervuert and Iberoamericana, pp. 39–57.

 2007. Grammatical borrowing in Imbabura Quichua (Ecuador). In Matras and Sakel (eds.), pp. 481–522.

González Ollé, Fernando. 1962. *Los sufijos dimminutivos en castellano medieval*. Madrid: Gómez.

Goodwin, Charles. 1979. The interactive construction of a sentence in natural conversation. In George Psathas (ed.). *Everyday language: Studies in ethnomethodology*. New York: Irvington Publishers, pp. 97–121.

 1981. *Conversational organization: Interaction between speakers and hearers*. New York: Academic Press.

 2000. Action and embodiment within situated human interaction. *Journal of Pragmatics* 32: 1489–1522.

 2003. The semiotic body in its environment. In Justine Coupland and Richard Gwyn (eds.). *Discourse, the body and identity*. New York: Palgrave Macmillan, pp. 19–42.

 2007a. Environmentally coupled gestures. In Susan D. Duncan, Justine Cassell, and Elena T. Levy (eds.). *Gesture and the dynamic dimensions of language*. Amsterdam and Philadelphia: Benjamins, pp. 195–212.

 2007b. Participation, stance, and affect in the organization of activities. *Discourse and Society* 18, 1: 53–73.

Goodwin, Charles and Marjorie H. Goodwin. 2004. Participation. In Alessandro Duranti (ed.). *A companion to linguistic anthropology*. Oxford: Blackwell, pp. 222–244.

Gordon, Raymond G. Jr. (ed.). 2005. *Ethnologue: Languages of the world*. 15th edn. Dallas: SIL International. [Online version www.ethnologue.com]

Granberry, Julian and Gary S. Vescelius. 2004. *Languages of the pre-Columbian Antilles*. Tuscaloosa: University of Alabama Press.

Grant, Anthony P. 1994. Shelta: The secret language of Irish travelers viewed as a mixed language. In Bakker and Mous (eds.), pp. 123–150.

Greenberg, Joseph. 1966. *Language universals, with special reference to feature hierarchies*. The Hague: Mouton.

 1999. Are there mixed languages? In Joseph H. Greenberg, 2005. *Genetic linguistics: Essays on theory and method*. Oxford and New York: Oxford University Press, pp. 359–357.

Greenhill, Simon J., Robert Blust, and Russell D. Gray. 2008. The Austronesian basic vocabulary database: From bioinformatics to lexomics. *Evolutionary Bioinformatics Online* 4: 271–283.

Gudschinsky, Sarah C. 1962. *Handbook of literacy*. California: Summer Institute of Linguistics.

Gueunier, Nicole. 2000: Le français au Liban. In Gérald Antoine and Bernard Cerquiglini (eds.). *Histoire de la langue française*. Paris: CNRS Éditions, pp. 749–63.

Gumperz, John J. 1982. *Discourse strategies*. Cambridge: Cambridge University Press.

Gumperz, John J. and Stephen C. Levinson (eds.). 1996. *Rethinking linguistic relativity*. Cambridge: Cambridge University Press.

Haarmann, Harald. 1996. Ökolinguistik. In Hans Goebl, Peter H. Nelde, Zdenek Stary, and Wolfgang Woelck (eds.). *Kontaktlinguistik*/Handbücher zur Sprach- und Kommunikationswissenschaft (HSK), Vol. 12.1. Berlin: de Gruyter, pp. 842–852.

Haeckel, Ernst. 1866. *Generelle Morphologie der Organismen. Allgemeine Grundzüge der organischen Formen-Wissenschaft, mechanisch begründet durch die von Charles Darwin reformirte Descendenz-Theorie. Zweiter Band: Allgemeine Entwicklungsgeschichte der Organismen*. Berlin: Georg Reimer.

Hall, Robert A. Jr. 1950. *Leave your language alone!* New York: Doubleday Anchor. 1966. *Pidgin and creole languages*. Ithaca: Cornell University Press.

Halliday, Michael A. K. 1990. New ways of meaning: The challenge to applied linguistics. First published in *Journal of Applied Linguistics* 6: 7–36. Reprinted in Martin Pütz (ed.). 1992. *Thirty years of linguistic evolution*. Amsterdam: Benjamins, pp. 59–95. Quoted from the reprint in Fill and Mühlhäusler (eds.) 2001, pp. 175–202.

Hannerz, Ulf. 1980. *Exploring the city*. New York: Columbia University Press.

Harré, Rom. 1961. *Theories and things: A brief study in prescriptive metaphysics*. London: Sheed and Ward.

Harré, Rom, Jens Brockmeier, and Peter Mühlhäusler. 1998. *Greenspeak – A study of environmental discourse*. Thousand Oaks: Sage.

Harries, Lyndon. 1976. The nationalization of Swahili in Kenya. *Language in Society* 5: 153–164.

Harris, Roy. 1979. *The language makers*. London: Duckworth. 1981. *The language myth*. London: Duckworth.

Haspelmath, Martin. 2006. Against markedness (and what to replace it with). *Journal of Linguistics* 42, 1: 25–70.

Haspelmath, Martin, Matthew S. Dryer, David Gil, and Bernard Comrie. 2005. *The world atlas of language structures*. Oxford: Oxford University Press.

Haugen, Einar I. 1969. *The Norwegian language in America: A study in bilingual behavior*. Reprint vols. 1 and 2. Bloomington: Indiana University Press. 1972. The ecology of language. In Einar Haugen, *The ecology of language: Essays*. Selected and introduced by Anwar S. Dil. Stanford: Stanford University Press, pp. 325–339.

Have, Paul ten. 2002. Ontology or methodology? Comments on Speer's 'natural' and 'contrived' data: A sustainable distinction? *Discourse Studies* 4, 4: 527–530.

Haviland, John. 2005. Directional precision in Zinacantec deictic gestures: (Cognitive?) preconditions of talk about space. *Intellectica* 41–42: 25–54.

Heath, Christian. 1986. *Body movement and speech in medical interaction*. Cambridge: Cambridge University Press.

Heath, Christian and Jon Hindmarsh. 2000. Configuring action in objects: From mutual space to media space. *Mind, Culture and Activity* 7, 1–2: 81–104.

Heath, Christian and Paul Luff. 2000. *Technology in action*. Cambridge: Cambridge University Press.

Heine, Bernd and Tania Kuteva. 2001. Attributive possession in creoles. Manuscript, Universities of Cologne and Düsseldorf.

2003. On contact-induced grammaticalization. *Studies in Language* 27, 3: 529–572.

2005. *Language contact and grammatical change*. Cambridge: Cambridge University Press.

Heine, Bernd and Wilhelm J. G. Möhlig. 1980. *Language and dialect atlas of Kenya*. Berlin: Reimer.

Heller, Monica (ed.). 2007. *Bilingualism: A social approach*. Basingstoke: Palgrave Macmillan.

Herder, Johann Gottfried. 2002. *Philosophical writings*. Ed. by Michael N. Forster. Cambridge and New York: Cambridge University Press.

2005. *Sprachphilosophie: Ausgewählte Schriften*. Hamburg: Felix Meiner.

Heritage, John. 1984. *Garfinkel and ethnomethodology*. Cambridge: Polity Press.

Herskovits, Annette. 1986. *Language and spatial cognition: An interdisciplinary study of the prepositions in English*. Cambridge: Cambridge University Press.

Hickey, Raymond (ed.). 2010. *The handbook of language contact*. Oxford: Wiley-Blackwell.

Hinskens, Frans, Peter Auer, and Paul Kerswill. 2005. The study of dialect convergence and divergence: Conceptual and methodological considerations. In Auer, Hinskens, and Kerswill (eds.), pp. 1–48.

Hock, Hans Henrich. 1991. *Principles of historical linguistics*. Berlin: Mouton de Gruyter.

Hockett, Charles. 1987. *Refurbishing our foundations*. Amsterdam: Benjamins.

Holm, John A. 2000. *An introduction to pidgins and creoles*. Cambridge: Cambridge University Press.

Hookoomsing, Vinesh, Ralph Ludwig, and Burkhard Schnepel (eds.). 2009. *Multiple identities in action: Mauritius and some Antillean parallelisms*. Frankfurt/M.: Lang.

Hopper, Paul. 1988. Emergent grammar and the a priori grammar postulate. In Deborah Tannen (ed.). *Linguistics in context: Connecting observation and understanding*. Norwood: Ablex, pp. 103–120.

Horrocks, Geoffrey. 1997. *Greek: A history of the language and its speakers*. London and New York: Longman.

Humboldt, Wilhelm von. 1795. [Letter to Friedrich Schiller] XIX. Tegel, den 14 September 1795. In *Briefwechsel zwischen Schiller und Wilhelm v. Humboldt. Mit einer Vorerinnerung über Schiller und den Gang seiner Geistesentwicklung von W. von Humboldt*. 1830. Stuttgart and Tübingen: J. G. Cotta, pp. 196–202.

1820. On the comparative study of language and its relation to the different periods of language development. In Humboldt, Wilhelm von. 1997. *Essays on language*. Ed. by Theo Narden and Dan Farrelly. Frankfurt/M.: Lang, pp. 1–22.

1836. The diversity of human language-structure and its influence on the mental development of mankind. In Humboldt, Wilhelm von. 1999. *On language: On the diversity of human language construction and its influence on the mental development of the human species.* Ed. by Michael Losonsky. Cambridge: Cambridge University Press.

Husserl, Edmund. 1913. *Logische Untersuchungen II/1: Untersuchungen zur Phänomenologie und Theorie der Erkenntnis.* Revised 2nd edn, reprint 1980. Tübingen: Niemeyer.

1970. *The crisis of European sciences and transcendental phenomenology.* Translated by David Carr. Evanston: Northwestern University Press.

2001. *Logical investigations. Volume 2.* Translated by J. N. Findlay from the second German edition of Logische Untersuchungen. London and New York: Routledge.

Hutchins, Edwin. 2010. Cognitive ecology. *Topics in Cognitive Science* 2, 4: 705–715.

Hutton, Christopher. 2001. Cultural and conceptual relativism, universalism and the politics of linguistics: Dilemmas of a would-be progressive linguistics. In René Dirven, Bruce W. Hawkins, and Esra Sandikcioglu (eds.). *Language and ideology, vol. 1: Theoretical cognitive approaches.* Amsterdam: Benjamins, pp. 277–296.

Hübschmann, Heinrich. 1897. *Armenische Grammatik.* Leipzig: Breitkopf und Hartel. Reprint 1972. Hildesheim and New York: Olms.

Hymes, Dell (ed.). 1971. *Pidginization and creolization of languages. Proceedings of a conference held at the University of the West Indies, Mona, Jamaica April 1976.* Cambridge: Cambridge University Press.

1972. *Directions in sociolinguistics: The ethnography of communication.* New York: Holt, Rinehart, and Winston. [Reissued with corrections and additions 1986. Oxford: Blackwell.]

Idström, Ana and Elisabeth Piirainen (eds). 2012. *Endangered metaphors.* Amsterdam: Benjamins.

Iglesias Ovejero, Ángel. 2003. ¿A qué llamamos apellidos? In Dieter Kremer (ed.). *Miscelânia Patronimiana. Actos do V Colóquio (Lisboa) seguidas das Comunicações do VII Colóquio (Neuchâtel) e de duas Comunicações do VIII Colóquio (Bucureşti).* Tübingen: Niemeyer, pp. 105–115.

Irvine, Judith and Susan Gal. 2000. Language ideology and linguistic differentiation. In Paul V. Kroskrity (ed.). *Regimes of language ideologies, polities, and identities.* Santa Fe: School of American Research Press, pp. 35–84.

Jakobson, Roman. 1944. *Kindersprache, Aphasie und allgemeine Lautgesetze.* In Jakobson Roman. 1962. *Selected writings I: Phonological studies.* The Hague: Mouton, pp. 328–401. [English edition 1968: *Child language, aphasia and phonological universals.* The Hague: Mouton]

1963. Parts and wholes in language. In Jakobson, Roman. 1971. *Selected writings II: Word and language.* The Hague: Mouton, pp. 280–284.

Jakobson, Roman, C. Gunnar M. Fant, and Morris Halle. 1969. *Preliminaries to speech analysis. The distinctive features and their correlates.* Cambridge, MA: MIT Press.

Johanson, Lars. 2002a. Contact-induced change in a code-copying framework. In Mari C. Jones and Edith Esch (eds.). *Language change: The interplay of internal, external and extra-linguistic factors.* Berlin and New York: Mouton de Gruyter, pp. 285–313.

2002b. Do languages die of 'structuritis'? On the role of code-copying in language endangerment. *Rivista di Linguistica* 14, 2: 249–270.

2005. On copying grammatical meaning. *Sprachtypologie und Universallenforschung (STUF)* 58, 1: 75–83.

2008. Remodeling grammar. Copying, conventionalization, grammaticalization In Peter Siemund and Noemi Kintana (eds.). *Language contact and contact languages*. Amsterdam and Philadelphia: Benjamins, pp. 61–79.

Johnstone, Barbara. 2004. Place, globalization, and linguistic variation. In Fought (ed.), pp. 65–83.

Joseph, John E. and Talbot J. Taylor (eds). 1990. *Ideologies of language*. London and New York: Routledge.

Kager, René. 1999. *Optimality theory*. Cambridge: Cambridge University Press.

Kahane, Henry, Renée Kahane, and Andreas Tietze. 1958. *The Lingua Franca in the Levant: Turkish nautical terms of Italian and Greek origin*. Urbana: University of Illinois Press.

Kaplan, Robert B. and Richard B. Baldauf. 1997. *Language planning from practice to theory*. Clevedon: Multilingual Matters.

Kapoor, Kapil. 1994. *Language, linguistics, and literature: The Indian perspective*. New Delhi: Academic Foundation.

Karst, Josef. 1901. *Historische Grammatik des Kilikisch-Armenischen*. Strasbourg: Trübner. Reprint 1970. Berlin: de Gruyter.

Keesing, Roger M. 1988. *Melanesian Pidgin and the Oceanic substrate*. Stanford: Stanford University Press.

Kelkar-Stephan, Leena. 2005. *Bonjour maa: The French–Tamil language contact situation in India*. Aachen: Shaker.

Keller, Rudi. 1990. *Sprachwandel: Von der unsichtbaren Hand in der Sprache*. Tübingen: Francke.

Kemp, J. Alan (ed.). 1981. *Standard alphabet for reducing unwritten languages and foreign graphic systems to a uniform orthography in European letters*. Amsterdam: Benjamins.

Kendon, Adam. 1990. *Conducting interaction: Patterns of behaviour in focused encounters*. Cambridge: Cambridge University Press.

Kibbee, Douglas A. 2003. Language policy and linguistic theory. In Jacques Maurais and Michael A. Morris (eds.). *Languages in a globalizing world*. Cambridge: Cambridge University Press, pp. 47–57.

Kirsh, David. 1995. The intelligent use of space. *Artificial Intelligence* 73, 1–2: 31–68.

Klee, Carol and Rocío Caravedo. 2005. Contact-induced language change in Lima, Peru: The case of clitic pronouns. In David Eddington (ed.). *Selected proceedings of the 7th Hispanic Linguistic Symposium*. Sommerville: Cascadilla Proceedings Project, pp. 12–21.

Kneebone, Heidi-Marie. 2005. *The language of the chosen view: The first phase of graphization of Dieri by Hermannsburg missionaries, Lake Killalpaninna 1867–80*. Adelaide: Adelaide University.

Kortmann, Bernd (ed.). 2004a. *Dialectology meets typology: Dialect grammar from a cross-linguistic perspective*. Berlin and New York: Mouton de Gruyter.

2004b. Introduction. In Kortmann (ed.), pp. 1–10.

Kortmann, Bernd, Kate Burridge, Rajend Meshtrie, Edgar W. Schneider, and Clive Upton (eds.). 2004. *A handbook of varieties of English. Vol. 2: Morphology and syntax.* Berlin: Mouton de Gruyter.

Kortmann, Bernd and Kerstin Lunkenheimer. 2013. *The Mouton world atlas of variation in English.* Berlin: de Gruyter.

Kortmann, Bernd and Benedikt Szmrecsanyi. 2004. Global synopsis – morphological and syntactic variation in English. In Kortmann et al. (eds.), pp. 1142–1202.

Köhler, Wolfgang. 1947. *Gestalt Psychology: An introduction to new concepts in modern psychology.* New York: Liveright.

Kremer, Dieter. 1988a. Tradition und Namengebung. Statistische Anmerkungen zur mittelalterlichen Namengebung. In Ariza, Salvador, and Viudas (eds.), pp. 75–109.

1988b. Onomástica e historia de la lengua. In Ariza, Salvador, and Viudas (eds.), pp. 1583–1612.

1992. Spanisch: Anthroponomastik. Antroponimia. In Günter Holtus, Michael Metzeltin, and Christian Schmitt (eds.). *Lexikon der Romanistischen Linguistik Bd. VI, 1: Aragonesisch/Navarresisch, Spanisch, Asturianisch/Leonesisch.* Tübingen: Niemeyer, pp. 457–474.

Kriegel, Sibylle, Ralph Ludwig, and Fabiola Henri. 2008. Encoding path in Mauritian Creole and Bhojpuri: Problems of language contact. In Susanne Michaelis (ed.). *Roots of creole structures. Weighing the contribution of substrates and superstrates.* Amsterdam: Benjamins, pp. 169–196.

2009. Les rapports entre créole et bhojpouri à Maurice: Contact de langues et actes identitaires. In Hookoomsing, Ludwig, and Schnepel (eds.), pp. 203–252.

Kriegel, Sibylle, Ralph Ludwig, and Stefan Pfänder. In Press. Dialectes - créolisation - convergence. Quelques hypothèses à partir du berrichon et du poitevin-saintongeais. In Andreas Dufter, Klaus Grübel, and Thomas Scharinger (eds.). *Des parlers d'oïl à la francophonie.* Berlin: de Gruyter.

Kroch, Anthony S. 1978. Toward a theory of social dialect variation. *Language in Society* 7, 1: 17–36.

Kube, Sabine. 2005. *Gelebte Frankophonie in der Côte d'Ivoire. Dimensionen des Sprachphänomens Nouchi und die ivorische Sprachsituation aus der Sicht Abidjaner Schüler.* Münster: LIT.

Kuhn, Thomas S. 1970. *The structure of scientific revolution.* 2nd edn, enlarged. Chicago: Chicago University Press.

Kvaran, Guðrun. 2007. Das isländische Personennamensystem. In Andrea Brendler and Silvio Brendler (eds.). *Europäische Personennamensysteme.* Hamburg: Baar, pp. 310–321.

Labov, William. 1972. *Sociolinguistic patterns.* Philadelphia: University of Pennsylvania Press.

2001. *Principles of linguistic change. Vol. 2: Social factors.* Malden: Blackwell.

Laitin, David and Carol M. Eastman. 1989. Language conflict: Transactions and games in Kenya. *Cultural Anthropology* 4, 1: 51–72.

Lakoff, George and Mark Johnson. 1980. *Metaphors we live by.* Chicago: University of Chicago Press.

Las Casas, Bartolomé de. 1994. *Historia de las Indias. Edición de Miguel Angel Medina, Jesús Angel Barreda & Isacio Pérez Fernández.* 3 vols. Madrid: Alianza Editorial.

Latour, Bruno. 1997. *Nous n'avons jamais été modernes. Essai d'anthropologie symétrique*. Paris: La Découverte.

2009. Spheres and networks: Two ways to reinterpret globalization. *Harvard Design Magazine* 30: 138–44.

Laurier, Eric and Chris Philo. 2006. Natural problems of naturalistic video data. In Hubert Knoblauch, Jürgen Raab, Hans-Georg Soeffner, and Bernt Schnettler (eds.). *Video analysis: Methodology and methods. Qualitative audiovisual data in sociology*. Bern: Lang, pp. 183–192.

Laycock, Donald C. 1977. Me and you versus the rest. *IRIAN* 6, 3: 33–41.

LeBaron, Curtis D. and Jürgen Streeck. 1997. Built space and the interactional framing of experience during a murder interrogation. *Human Studies* 20: 1–25.

Lechevrel, Nadège. 2010. *Les approches écologiques en linguistique: Enquête critique*. Louvain-La-Neuve: Academia Bruylant.

Lepsius, C. Richard. 1880. *Nubische Grammatik: Mit einer Einleitung über die Völker und Sprachen Afrikas*. Berlin: Hertz.

Lévi-Strauss, Claude. 1962. *La pensée sauvage*. Paris: Librairie Plon.

Lévy, Jacques and Michel Lussault. 2003. *Dictionnaire de la géographie et de l'espace des sociétés*. Paris: Éditions Belin.

Liddicoat, Anthony J. and Pauline Bryant (eds.). 2003. *Language planning and economics*. Current Issues in Language Planning. Vol 4,1. Clevedon: Multilingual Matters.

Lobo Cabrera, Manuel. 2010. Indígenas canarios, moriscos y negros. In Salinero and Testón Núñez (eds.), pp. 209–219.

Lodge, Anthony. 2004. *A sociolinguistic history of Parisian French*. Cambridge: Cambridge University Press.

2010. Standardisation, koïnéisation, et l'historiographie du français. *Revue de Linguistique Romane* 74: 5–25.

Lorenz, Konrad. 1977. *Die Rückseite des Spiegels*. Munich: DTV.

1989. *Umweltgewissen*. LP Vienna: CBS Schallplattengesellschaft.

Löffler, Heinrich. 1996. Namen von Freien und Unfreien. In Eichler et al. (eds.), pp. 1296–1300.

Ludwig, Ralph. 1996. *Kreolsprachen zwischen Mündlichkeit und Schriftlichkeit. Zur Syntax und Pragmatik atlantischer Kreolsprachen auf französischer Basis*. Tübingen: Narr.

2001. Markiertheit. In Martin Haspelmath, Ekkehard König, Wulf Oesterreicher, and Wolfgang Raible (eds.). *Language typology and language universals. An international handbook*. Vol. 1. Berlin and New York: Mouton de Gruyter, pp. 400–419.

2002. Urbanidad, migración e hibridación de la lengua: Procesos de contacto en el español de Santiago de Chile. In Norma Díaz, Ralph Ludwig, and Stefan Pfänder (eds.). *La Romania americana. Procesos lingüísticos en situaciones de contacto*. Frankfurt/M.: Vervuert, pp. 357–386.

2003. Desde el contacto hacia el conflicto lingüístico: El purismo en el español. Concepto, desarrollo histórico y significación actual. *Boletín de Filología de la Universidad de Chile* 38: 167–196.

2010. Kreolisierung – ein entgrenzter Begriff? In Ludwig and Röseberg (eds.), pp. 93–127.

2014. Synonymie, analogie et métaphore: Rhétorique et cognition au 18e siècle. In Michèle Vallenthini, Charles Vincent, Rainer Godel (eds.). *Classer les mots, classer les choses. Synonymie, analogie et métaphore au XVIIIe siècle*. Paris: Garnier Classiques, pp. 19–44.

2018. Diachronies française et créole: rapports épistémiques. In Wendy Ayres-Bennett, Anne Carlier, Julie Glikman, Thomas M. Rainsford, Gilles Siouffi, and Carine Skupien Dekens (eds.). *Nouvelles voies d'accès au changement linguistique*. Paris: Classiques Garnier, pp. 143–177.

Ludwig, Ralph, Fabiola Henri, and Florence Bruneau-Ludwig. 2009. Hybridation linguistique et fonctions sociales: aspects des contacts entre créole, français et anglais à Maurice. In Hookoomsing, Ludwig, and Schnepel (eds.), pp. 165–202.

Ludwig, Ralph and Dorothee Röseberg (eds.). 2010. *Tout-Monde: Interkulturalität – Kreolisierung – Hybridisierung. Gesellschaftstheoretische Modelle zwischen alten und neuen Räumen*. Frankfurt/M.: Peter Lang.

Ludwig, Ralph and Sabine Schwarze. 2006. Die Vorstellung sprachlicher 'Reinheit' in der Romania. Von der stilistischen Pragmatik zur Symbolik einer nationalen und supranationalen Kultur. In Sabine Schwarze and Edeltraud Werner (eds.). *Identitätsbewahrung und Identitätsbegründung durch Sprache. Aktuelle Beiträge zum frankophonen Raum*. Hamburg: Kovač, pp. 3–34.

Luff, Paul, Christian Heath, Hideaki Kuzuoka, Jon Hindmarsh, Keiichi Yamazaki, and Shinya Oyama. 2003. Fractured ecologies: Creating environments for collaboration. *Human-Computer Interaction* 18, 1–2: 51–84.

Luff, Paul, Jon Hindmarsh, and Christian Heath (eds.). 2000. *Workplace studies. Recovering work practice and informing system design*. Cambridge: Cambridge University Press.

Lussault, Michel. 2007. *L'homme spatial. La construction sociale de l'espace humain*. Paris: Éditions du Seuil.

Lynch, Michael. 2002. From naturally occurring data to naturally organized ordinary activities: Comment on Speer. *Discourse Studies* 4: 531–537.

Lynch, Michael and David Bogen. 1994. Harvey Sacks's primitive natural science. *Theory, Culture and Society* 11 (4): 65–104.

Maalouf, Amin. 1983. *Les croisades vues par les Arabes*. Paris: Lattès.

Mackey, William F. 1979. Towards an ecology of language contact. In William F. Mackey and Jacob Ornstein (eds.). *Sociolinguistic studies in language contact: Methods and cases*. The Hague: Mouton de Gruyter, pp. 453–459.

1980. The ecology of language shift. First published in Nelde, H. Peter (ed.). *Sprachkontakt und Sprachkonflikt*. Wiesbaden: Steiner, pp. 35–41. Quoted from the reprint in Fill and Mühlhäusler (eds.) 2001, pp. 67–74.

McCormick, Kay. 2002. *Language in Cape Town's District Six*. Oxford: Oxford University Press.

McWhorter, John H. 2000. Defining 'creole' as a synchronic term. In Neumann-Holzschuh and Schneider (eds.), pp. 85–123.

2001. The world's simplest grammars are creole grammars. *Linguistic Typology* 5: 125–166.

2005. *Defining creole*. Oxford: Oxford University Press.

2007. *Language interrupted: Signs of non-native acquisition in standard language grammars*. Oxford and New York: Oxford University Press.

2008. *Our magnificent bastard tongue: The untold history of English*. New York: Gotham Books.

2011. Language simplicity and complexity. *Why do languages undress?* Boston: de Gruyter Mouton.

Maffi, Luisa (ed.). 2001. *On biocultural diversity: Linking language, knowledge, and the environment*. Washington, DC: Smithsonian Institution Press.

Makhairas, Leontios. 1932. *Recital concerning the sweet land of Cyprus, entitled 'chronicle'*. Ed. Richard M. Dawkins. Oxford: Clarendon Press.

Makoni, Sinfree and Alastair Pennycook. 2007. *Global Englishes and transcultural flows*. London: Routledge.

Matras, Yaron. 2000. Mixed languages: A functional–communicative approach. *Bilingualism: Language and Cognition* 3, 2: 79–99.

2010. Contact, convergence and typology. In Hickey (ed.), pp. 66–86.

Matras, Yaron and Peter Bakker (eds.). 2003. *The mixed language debate: Theoretical and empirical advances*. Berlin and New York: Mouton de Gruyter.

Matras, Yaron and Jeanette Sakel (eds.). 2007. *Grammatical borrowing in cross-linguistic perspective*. Berlin and New York: Mouton de Gruyter.

Mayerthaler, Willi. 1981. *Morphologische Natürlichkeit*. Wiesbaden: Athenaion.

Mayerthaler, Eva and Willi Mayerthaler. 1990. Aspects of Bavarian syntax or 'every language has at least two parents'. In Edmondson, Feagin, and Mühlhäusler (eds.), pp. 371–430.

Mazeland, Harrie. 2006. Conversation analysis. In *Encyclopedia of language and linguistics*. Vol. 3. 2nd edn. Oxford: Elsevier Science, pp. 153–162.

Mazrui, Alamin M. 1995. Slang and code-switching: The case of Sheng in Kenya. *Afrikanische Arbeitspapiere* 42: 168–179.

Mbaabu, Ireri. 1996. *Language policy in East Africa: A dependency theory perspective*. Nairobi: Educational Research and Publication (ERAP).

Meneses, Max. 2009. Las lenguas que cultivan los migrantes en Lima Metropolitana. In Julio Calvo and Luis Miranda (eds.). *Palabras fuera del nido. Vertientes sincrónica y diacrónica del español en contacto*. Lima: Fondo Editorial de la Universidad de San Martín de Porres, pp. 29–65.

Mesthrie, Rajend. 1991. *Language in indenture. A sociolinguistic history of Bhojpuri-Hindi in South Africa*. Johannesburg: Witwatersrand University Press.

Meyerhoff, Miriam. 2002. Community of practice. In Chambers, Trudgill, and Schilling-Estes (eds.), pp. 526–548.

2006. *Introducing sociolinguistics*. London and New York: Routledge.

Michaelis, Susanne M., Philippe Maurer, Martin Haspelmath, and Magnus Huber (eds.). 2013. *Atlas of pidgin and creole language structures online*. Leipzig: Max Planck Institute for Evolutionary Anthropology. [http://apics-online.info, accessed 03 06 2014]

Miller, Jim and Regina Weinert. 1998. *Spontaneous spoken language: Syntax and discourse*. Oxford: Clarendon Press.

Milroy, James and Lesley Milroy. 1993. *Real English. The grammar of English dialects in the British Isles*. London and New York: Longman.

Milroy, Lesley and Li Wei. 1995. A social network approach to code-switching: The example of a bilingual community in Britain. In Lesley Milroy and Pieter Muysken (eds.). *One speaker two languages. Cross-disciplinary perspectives on code-switching.* Cambridge: Cambridge University Press, pp. 136–157.

Minervini, Laura (ed.). 2000. *Cronaca del templare di Tiro (1243–1314). La caduta degli stati crociati nel racconto di un testimone oculare.* Naples: Liguori.

Mira Caballos, Esteban. 1997. *El indio antillano: Repartimiento, encomienda y esclavitud (1492–1542).* Sevilla and Bogotá: Muñoz Moya.

Mondada, Lorenza. 2005a. La constitution de l'origo déictique comme travail interactionnel des participants: Une approche praxéologique de la spatialité. *Intellectica* 41–42: 75–100.

  2005b. Espace, langage, interaction et cognition: Une introduction. *Intellectica* 41–42: 7–24.

  2005c. L'analyse de corpus en linguistique interactionnelle : De l'étude de cas singuliers à l'étude de collections. In Anne Condamine (ed.). *Sémantique et corpus.* Paris: Hermès, pp. 76–108.

  2006a. Video recording as the reflexive preservation of fundamental features for analysis. In Hubert Knoblauch, Jürgen Raab, Hans-Georg Soeffner, and Bernt Schnettler (eds.). *Video analysis: Methodology and methods. Qualitative audiovisual data in sociology.* Bern: Lang, pp. 51–68.

  2006b. La question du contexte en ethnométhodologie et en analyse conversationnelle. *Verbum* 28, 2–3: 111–151.

  2007. Multimodal resources for turn-taking: Pointing and the emergence of possible next speakers. *Discourse Studies* 9, 2: 195–226.

  2009. Emergent focused interactions in public places: A systematic analysis of the multimodal achievement of a common interactional space. *Journal of Pragmatics* 41: 1977–1997.

  2011. The interactional production of multiple spatialities within participatory democracy meetings. *Social Semiotics* 21, 2: 283–308.

  2013a. Interactional space and the study of embodied talk-in-interaction. In Peter Auer, Martin Hilpert, Anja Stukenbrock, and Benedikt Szmrecsanyi (eds). *Space in language and linguistics: Geographical, interactional and cognitive perspectives.* Berlin: de Gruyter, pp. 246–273.

  2013b. Embodied and spatial resources for turn-taking in institutional multi-party interactions: The example of participatory democracy debates. *Journal of Pragmatics,* 46: 39–68.

  2013c. The conversation analytic approach to data collection. In Jack Sidnell and Tanya Stivers (eds.). *The handbook of conversation analysis.* Malden: Blackwell, pp. 32–56.

Morales Pettorino, Félix, Oscar Quiroz Mejías, and Juan José Peña Alvarez. 1984–1987. *Diccionario ejemplificado de chilenismos y otros usos diferenciales del español de Chile.* Vols. I–IV. Valparaíso: Universidad de Playa Ancha de Ciencias de la Educación.

Moreau, Marie-Louise (ed.). 1997. *Sociolinguistique: Les concepts de base.* Sprimont: Mardaga.

Mosel, Ulrike. 1980. *Tolai and Tok Pisin: The influence of the substratum on the development of New Guinea Pidgin.* Canberra: Department of Linguistics, Research School of Pacific Studies, Australian National University for the Linguistic Circle of Canberra.

  1982. Local deixis in Tolai. In Jürgen Weissenborn and Wolfgang Klein (eds.). *Here and there: Cross-linguistic studies in deixis and demonstration.* Amsterdam: Benjamins, pp. 111–132.

Moseley, Christopher (ed.). 2009. *Atlas of the world's languages in danger*. Paris: UNESCO.

Mougeon, Raymond, Terry Nadasdi, and Katherine Rehner. 2005. Contact-induced linguistic innovations on the continuum of language use: The case of French in Ontario. *Bilingualism: Language and Cognition* 8, 2: 99–115.

Msimang, Christian Themba. 1987. Impact of Zulu on Tsotsitaal. *South African Journal of African Languages* 7:3, 82–86.

Mufwene, Salikoko S. 1994. On decreolization: The case of Gullah. In Marcyliena Morgan (ed.). *Language and the social construction of identity in creole situations*. Los Angeles: Center for Afro-American Studies, pp. 63–99.

1996. The founder principle in creole genesis. *Diachronica* XIII-1: 83–134.

2000. Creolization is a social, not a structural process. In Neumann-Holzschuh and Schneider (eds.), pp. 65–84.

2001. *The ecology of language evolution*. Cambridge: Cambridge University Press.

2003. Genetic linguistics and genetic creolistics: A response to Sarah G. Thomason's 'Creoles and genetic relationships'. *Journal of Pidgin and Creole Languages* 8, 2: 273–288.

2005. *Créoles, écologie sociale, évolution linguistique*. Paris: L'Harmattan.

2008. *Language evolution: Contact, competition and change*. London: Continuum.

2009. Some offspring of colonial English are creole. In Filppula, Klemola, and Paulasto (eds.), pp. 280–303.

2014. Language ecology, language evolution, and the actuation question. In Tor Afarli and Brit Maelhum (eds.). *Language contact and change: Grammatical structure encounters the fluidity of language*. Amsterdam: Benjamins, pp. 13–35.

Mufwene, Salikoko S. and Cécile B. Vigouroux. 2012. Individuals, populations, and timespace: Perspectives on the ecology of language. *Cahiers de Linguistique: Revue de Sociolinguistique et de Sociologie de la Langue Française* 38, 2: 111–137.

Municipalidad Distrital de Los Olivos. 2006. Webpage of the Los Olivos City Hall: www.munilosolivos.gob.pe/comentarios.htm (last access April 2013)

Munteanu, Dan. 1997. Notas sobre el léxico de orígen español en chamorro. *Anuario de Lingüística Hispánica* 12: 959–974.

Muysken, Pieter. 1981. Halfway between Quechua and Spanish: The case for relexification. In Arnold Highfield and Albert Valdman (eds.). *Historicity and variation in creole studies*. Ann Arbor: Karoma, pp. 52–78.

1994. Media Lengua. In Bakker and Mous (eds.), pp. 207–211.

1997. Media Lengua. In Sarah G. Thomason (ed.). *Contact languages: A wider perspective*. Amsterdam and Philadelphia: Benjamins, pp. 365–426.

2000. *Bilingual speech. A typology of code-mixing*. Cambridge: Cambridge University Press.

Mühlhäusler, Peter. 1982. Etymology and pidgin and creole languages. *Transactions of the Philological Society* 80, 1: 99–118.

1986. *Pidgin & creole linguistics*. Oxford: Basil Blackwell Ltd.

1995a. The interdependence of linguistic and biological diversity. In David Myers (ed.). *The politics of multiculturalism in Oceania and Polynesia*. Darwin: University of the Northern Territory Press, pp. 154–161.

1995b. Metaphors others live by. *Language and Communication* 15, 3: 281–288.

1996a. *Linguistic ecology: Language change and linguistic imperialism in the Pacific region*. London: Routledge.

1996b. Linguistic adaptation to changed environmental conditions: Some lessons from the past. In Alwin Fill (ed.). *Sprachökologie und Ökolinguistik*. Tübingen: Stauffenburg, pp. 105–130.

1996c. Introduction to: Charles-James N. Bailey. *Essays on time-based linguistic analysis*. Oxford: Clarendon Press, pp. 1–17.

1996d. Ecological and non-ecological approaches to language planning. In Marlis Hellinger and Ulrich Ammon (eds.). *Contrastive sociolinguistics*. Berlin: Mouton de Gruyter, pp. 205–212.

2000a. Humboldt, Whorf and the roots of ecolinguistics. In Martin Pütz and Marjolijn H. Versporr (eds.). *Explorations in linguistic relativity*. Amsterdam: Benjamins, pp. 89–100.

2000b. Language rights for the language of Norfolk Island. In Phillipson (ed.), pp. 79–82.

2002. Language as an ecological phenomenon. *The Linacre Journal: A Review of Research in the Humanities* 5: 61–68.

2003. *Language of environment, environment of language: A course in ecolinguistics*. London: Battlebridge.

2005. Review of Mufwene 'The ecology of language evolution' (2001). *Language* 81: 265–268.

2006. Naming languages, drawing language boundaries and maintaining languages, with special reference to the linguistic situation in Papua New Guinea. In Denis Cunningham, David E. Ingram, and Kenneth Sumbuk (eds.). *Language diversity in the Pacific: Endangerment and survival*. Clevedon: Multilingual Matters, pp. 24–39.

2008. Multifunctionality in Pitkern-Norf'k and Tok Pisin. *Journal of Pidgin and Creole Languages* 39: 75–113.

2012. The complexity of the personal and possessive pronoun system of Norfolk. In Bernd Kortmann and Benedikt Szmrecsanyi (eds.). *Linguistic complexity*. Berlin: de Gruyter, pp. 101–126.

Mühlhäusler, Peter and Richard Damania. 2004. Economic costs and benefits of Australian indigenous languages. Discussion Paper, Canberra, Department of Communication, Information Technology and the Arts (DCITA).

Mühlhäusler, Peter, Tom Dutton, Even Hovdhaugen, Jeff Williams, and Stephen A. Wurm. 1996. Pre-colonial patterns of intercultural communication in the Pacific Islands. In Stephen A. Wurm, Peter Mühlhäusler, and Darrell T. Tryon (eds.). *Atlas of languages of intercultural communication in the Pacific, Asia, and the Americas*. Berlin: Mouton de Gruyter, pp. 401–438.

Mühlhäusler, Peter and Rom Harré. 1990. *Pronouns and people: The linguistic construction of social and personal identity*. Oxford: Basil Blackwell.

Mühlhäusler, Peter and Adrian J. Peace. 2006. Environmental discourses. *Annual Review of Anthropology* 35: 457–479.

Müller, F. Max. 1862. *Lectures on the science of language*. From the 2nd London edn, revised. New York: Charles Scribner.

1902. *The life and letters of the Right Honourable Friedrich Max Müller*. Edited by his wife. Vol. 1. London: Longmans, Green and Co.

Myers-Scotton, Carol. 1993. *Social motivations for codeswitching: Evidence from Africa*. Oxford: Clarendon Press.

2002. *Contact linguistics: Bilingual encounters and grammatical outcomes*. New York: Oxford University Press.

2003. What lies beneath: Split (mixed) languages as contact phenomena. In Matras and Bakker (eds.), pp. 73–106.

2006a. *Multiple voices. An introduction to bilingualism*. Malden: Blackwell.

2006b. How code-switching as an available option empowers bilinguals. In Martin Pütz, Joshua A. Fishman, and JoAnne Neff-van Aertselaer (eds.). *'Along the routes to power'. Explorations of empowerment through language*. Berlin and New York: Mouton de Gruyter, pp. 73–84.

Náñez Fernández, Emilio. 1973. *El diminutivo. Historia y funciones en el español clásico y moderno*. Madrid: Gredos.

Nash, Joshua. 2011. Insular toponymies: Pristine place naming on Norfolk Island, South Pacific and Dudley Peninsula, Kangaroo Island, South Australia. Ph.D. thesis, University of Adelaide.

Neumann-Holzschuh, Ingrid and Edgar W. Schneider (eds.). 2000. *Degrees of restructuring in creole languages*. Amsterdam and Philadelphia: Benjamins.

Nevins, Andrew, David Pesetsky, and Cilene Rodrigues. 2009a. Pirahã exceptionality: A reassessment. *Language* 85, 2: 355–404.

2009b. Evidence and argumentation: A reply to Everett. *Language* 85, 3: 671–681.

Nickel, Gerhard. 1990. Some problems of teaching English in Japan. In Edmondson, Feagin and Mühlhäusler (eds.), pp. 647–662.

Noonan, Michael. 2010. Genetic classification and language contact. In Hickey (ed.), pp. 48–65.

Nurse, Derek and Hinnebusch, Thomas J. 1993. *Swahili and Sabaki: A linguistic history*. Berkeley: University of California Press.

Oberlies, Thomas. 2005. *A historical grammar of Hindi*. Graz: Leykam.

Ochs, Elinor. 1979. Planned and unplanned discourse. In Givon, Talmy (ed.). *Discourse and syntax*. New York: Academic Press, pp. 51–80.

Odo, Carol. 1972. *A survey of language use and attitudes on Guam*. Agaña: Guam Department of Education.

Onedera, Peter R. 2011a. Chamoru kontra Chamorro. *Guam Pacific Daily News* 02/01/2011.

2011b. Bula kinalamten gi i mes Chamorro. *Guam Pacific Daily News* 02/15/2011.

Operstein, Natalie. 2015. Contact-genetic linguistics: Toward a contact-based theory of language change. *Language Sciences* 48: 1–15.

Organisation Internationale de la Francophonie (OIF), Conseil Consultatif. 2007. *La Francophonie dans le monde 2006–2007*. Paris: Nathan.

2010. *La langue française dans le monde*. Paris: Nathan.

Orlove, Benjamin. 1993. Putting race in its place: Order in colonial and postcolonial Peruvian geography. *Social Research* 60, 2: 301–36.

Ortaylı, Ilber. 1999. Greeks in the Ottoman administration during the Tanzimat period. In Dimitri Gondicas and Charles P. Issawi (eds.), *Ottoman Greeks in the age of nationalism: Politics, economy, and society in the nineteenth century*. Princeton: Darwin Press, pp. 161–167.

Ortony, Andrew (ed.). 1979. *Metaphor and thought*. New York: Cambridge University Press.

Ozanne-Rivierre, Francoise. 1997. Spatial reference in New Caledonian languages. In Senft (ed.), pp. 83–100.

Pagel, Steve. 2008. The old, the new and the in-between: Comparative aspects of Hispanisation on the Marianas and Easter Island (Rapa Nui). In Stolz, Bakker and Salas Palomo (eds.), pp. 167–201.

2010. *Spanisch in Asien und Ozeanien*. Frankfurt/M.: Lang.

2013a. The Chaifi. A fairytale from the Marianas, narrated by Georg Fritz: A commented re-edition, part 1: Background, intercultural, and intertextual aspects. In Fischer (ed.), pp. 123–151.

2013b. The Chaifi. A fairytale from the Marianas, narrated by Georg Fritz: A commented re-edition, part 2: Linguistic aspects. In Fischer (ed.), pp. 153–176.

2015. Beyond the category: Towards a continuous model of contact-induced change. *Journal of Language Contact* 8, 1: 146–179.

2018. *Die Wurzeln der Kontaktlinguistik. Zur Entstehung des Sprachkontaktparadigmas in der Sprachwissenschaft unter besonderer Berücksichtigung der Rolle der Romanistik*. Postdoctoral thesis, University Halle-Wittenberg.

Paprotte, Wolf and René Dirven. 1985. *The ubiquity of metaphor*. Amsterdam: Benjamins.

Palmer, Frank R. 1968. Review of Sydney M. Lamb 'Outline of Stratificational Grammar'. *Journal of Linguistics* 4: 287–295.

Palmer, Bill. 2009. Route description tasks in Kiribati. Paper presented at the 8th Conference on Oceanic Linguistics, Auckland, New Zealand, 5 January 2010.

Parker, Simon. 2004. *Urban theory and the urban experience: Encountering the city*. New York: Routledge.

Parkin, David. 1977. Emergent and stabilized multilingualism: Polyethnic peer groups in urban Kenya. In Howard Giles (ed.). *Language, ethnicity and intergroup relations*. London and New York: Academic Press, pp. 185–210.

Patterson, Orlando. 1982. *Slavery and social death: A comparative study*. Cambridge, MA: Harvard University Press.

Pérez Díaz, Aisnara and María de los Ángeles Meriño Fuentes. 2006. *Nombrar las cosas. Aproximación a la onomástica de la familia negra en Cuba*. Guantánamo: Ed. El Mar y la Montaña.

Perrott, Daisy Valerie. 1951. *Teach yourself Swahili*. London: English Universities Press.

Pfänder, Stefan. 2010. *Gramática mestiza. Con referencia al castellano de Cochabamba*. La Paz: Inst. Boliviano de Lexicografía y Otros Estudios Lingüísticos.

Phillipson, Robert (ed.). 2000. *Rights to language: Equity, power, and education*. New Jersey: Lawrence Erlbaum Assoc.

Pike, Kenneth L. 1947. *Phonemics: A technique for reducing languages to writing*. Ann Arbor: University of Michigan.

Pilares, Guido. 1995. Pragmática del quechua: Nuevos enfoques. *Revista Andina* 26: 431–42.

Polomé, Edgar C. 1967. *Swahili language handbook*. Washington, DC: Center for Applied Linguistics.

Pope, Kathrin M. 1952. *From Latin to Modern French with special consideration of Anglo-Norman: Phonology and morphology*. Manchester: Manchester University Press.

Poplack, Shana and David Sankoff. 1988. Code switching. In Ulrich Ammon, Norbert Dittmar, and Klaus J. Mattheier (eds.). *Sociolinguistics – Soziolinguistik*.

An international handbook of the science of language and society. Vol. 2. Berlin and New York: Mouton de Gruyter, pp. 1174–1180.

Popper, Karl. 1935. *Logik der Forschung: Zur Erkenntnistheorie der modernen Naturwissenschaft.* Wien: Springer.

Potter, Jonathan. 2002. Two kinds of natural. *Discourse Studies* 4, 4. 539 542.

Preissig, Edward R. von. 1918. *Dictionary and grammar of the Chamorro language of the island of Guam.* Washington, DC: Government Printing Office.

Prince, Alan and Paul Smolensky. 1993. *Optimality theory: Constraint interaction in generative grammar.* New Brunswick: Rutgers Center for Cognitive Science.

Quintana Rodríguez, Aldina. 2006. *Geografía lingüística del Judeoespañol: Estudio sincrónico y diacrónico.* Bern: Lang.

Raible, Wolfgang. 1980. Edmund Husserl, die Universalienforschung und die Regularität des Irregulären. In Gunter Brettschneider and Christian Lehmann (eds.). *Wege zur Universalienforschung. Sprachwissenschaftliche Beiträge zum 60. Geburtstag von Hansjakob Seiler.* Tübingen: Narr, pp. 42–50.

Rapadas, Juan, Mamie Balajadia, and Donald Rubinstein. 2005. Guam: Caught amidst change and tradition. In Anthony J. Marsella, Ayda A. Austin, and Bruce Grant (eds.). *Social change and psychosocial adaptation in the Pacific islands: Cultures in transition.* New York: Springer, pp. 145–170.

Reddy, Michael J. 1979. The conduit metaphor: A case of frame conflict in our language about language. In Ortony (ed.), pp. 284–324.

Reinecke, John E., Stanley M. Tsuzaki, David DeCamp, Ian F. Hancock, and Richard E. Wood. 1975. *A bibliography of pidgin and creole languages.* Honolulu: University Press of Hawaii.

Rheeden, Hadewych van. 1994. Petjo: The mixed language of the Indos in Batavia. In Bakker and Mous (eds.), pp. 223–237.

Richard, Jean. 1962. *Documents chypriotes des Archives du Vatican.* Paris: Librairie Orientaliste Paul Geuthner.

Robins, Robert H. 1997. *A short history of linguistics.* 4th edn. London: Longman.

Rodríguez Álvarez, Angel. 2008. *Ramón Pané y la relación sobre las antigüedades de los indios: El primer tratado etnográfico hecho en América.* San Juan: Ed. Nuevo Mundo.

Rodríguez-Ponga y Salamanca, Rafael. 1989. Huellas de la lengua española en Micronesia. In Florentino Rodao García (ed.). *España y el Pacífico.* Madrid: Agencia Española de Cooperación Internacional, Asociación Española de Estudios del Pacífico, pp. 293–297.

1994. Antropónimos hispánicos en las islas Marianas. *Revista Española del Pacífico* 4: 75–84.

1995. El elemento español en la lengua chamorra (Islas Marianas). Ph.D. thesis, Universidad Complutense de Madrid, Facultad de Filología.

1996. Formas de 'ser' y 'estar' en Chamorro. Actas del Cuarto Congreso de Hispanistas de Asia, *Seúl, 21–23 de junio de 1996.* Seoul: Asociacíon Asiática de Hispanistas, pp. 49–55.

1998. Las preposiciones hispano-chamorras. *La Torre: Revista de la Universidad de Puerto Rico* 3, 7–8: 511–522.

1999. ¿Qué se hablaba en las Islas Marianas a finales del siglo XIX? In Miguel Luque Talaván, Juan J. Pacheco Onrubia, and Fernando Palanco Aguado (eds.). *España y el Pacifico. Interpretación del pasado, realidad del presente*. Madrid: Asociacíon Española de Estudios del Pacífico, pp. 521–527.

2001. Los numerales hispano-chamorros. In Klaus Zimmermann and Thomas Stolz (eds.). *Lo propio y lo ajeno en las lenguas austronésicas y amerindias: Procesos interculturales en el contacto de lenguas indígenas con el español en el Pacífico e Hispanoamérica*. Frankfurt/M. and Madrid: Vervuert and Iberoamericana, pp. 253–278.

2009. *Del español al chamorro: Lenguas en contacto en el Pacífico*. Madrid: Ed. Gondo.

2013. Esteban Rodríguez' vocabulary of the language of Guam (1565). In Fischer (ed.), pp. 25–52.

Rogers, Robert F. 1995. *Destiny's landfall: A history of Guam*. Honolulu: University of Hawaii Press.

Roggenbuck, Simone. 1999. Bäume der Erkenntnis: Zum Baum als Topos und Leitbild in der Linguistik. *Vox Romanica* 58: 1–25.

2005. *Die Wiederkehr der Bilder: Arboreszenz und Raster in der interdisziplinären Geschichte der Sprachwissenschaft*. Tübingen: Narr.

Rorty, Richard. 1989. *Contingency, irony, and solidarity*. Cambridge: Cambridge University Press.

Ross, Alan S. C. and Albert W. Moverley. 1964. *The Pitcairnese language*. London: Deutsch.

Rudd, Philip W. 2008. Sheng: The mixed language of Nairobi. Ph.D. thesis, Ball State University, Muncie, Indiana.

2010. Filling the gap: The place of urban vernaculars in Africa. Paper presented at the OSD/AFRICOM Roundtable on African Languages and Cultures. Kelley Barracks, Stuttgart, Germany, 22–23 June, co-sponsored by the Center for Advanced Study of Languages (CASL) at University of Maryland. [www.casl.umd.edu/africom_panel2]

Sacks, Harvey. 1992. *Lectures on conversation*. 2 vols. Oxford: Blackwell.

Sacks, Harvey, Emanuel A. Schegloff, and Gail Jefferson. 1974. A simplest systematics for the organization of turn-taking for conversation. *Language* 50: 696–735.

Safford, William E. 1903a. The Chamorro language of Guam. *American Anthropologist* 5, 2: 289–311.

1903b. The Chamorro language of Guam – II. *American Anthropologist* 5, 3: 508–529.

1904a. The Chamorro language of Guam – III. *American Anthropologist* 6, 1: 95–117.

1904b. The Chamorro language of Guam – IV. *American Anthropologist* 6, 4: 501–534.

1905. The Chamorro language of Guam – V. *American Anthropologist* 7, 2: 305–319.

Sailaja, Pingali. 2009. *Indian English*. Edinburgh: Edinburgh University Press.

Sakel, Jeanette. 2007. Types of loan: Matter and pattern. In Matras and Sakel (eds.), pp. 15–29.

Salas Palomo, Rosa and Thomas Stolz. 2008. Pro or contra Hispanisms: Attitudes of native speakers of modern Chamorro. In Stolz, Bakker, and Salas Palomo (eds.), pp. 237–267.

Salinero, Gregorio and Isabel Testón Núñez (eds.). 2010. *Un juego de engaños. Movilidad, nombres y apellidos en los siglos XV a XVIII*. Madrid: Casa de Velázquez.

Salzmann, Tabea. 2014. *Language, identity and urban space: The language use of Latin American migrants*. Frankfurt/Main: Peter Lang.

Sankoff, David and Gillian Sankoff. 1973. Sample survey methods and computer-assisted analysis in the study of grammatical variation. In Regna Darnell (ed.). *Canadian languages in their social context*. Edmonton: Linguistic Research, pp. 7–64.

Sapir, Edward. 1907. Herder's 'Ursprung der Sprache'. *Modern Philology* 5, 1: 109–142.

1929. The status of linguistics as a science. First published in *Language* 5, 4: 207–214. Reprinted in Edward Sapir, 2008. *The collected works I: General linguistics*. Berlin and New York: Mouton de Gruyter, pp. 219–226.

Saussure, Ferdinand de. 1915/1986. *Cours de linguistique générale (Publié par Charles Bally et Albert Sechehaye)*. Édition critique préparée par Tullio de Mauro. Paris: Payot.

Scheflen, Albert E. 1972. *Body language and social order: Communication as behavioral control*. Englewood Cliffs: Prentice Hall.

Schegloff, Emanuel A. 1968. Sequencing in conversational openings. *American Anthropologist* 70: 1075–1095.

1991. Reflections on talk and social structure. In Deidre Boden and Donald H. Zimmerman (eds.). *Talk and social structure: Studies in ethnomethodology and conversation analysis*. Cambridge: Polity Press, pp. 44–70.

1992. On talk and its institutional occasions. In Drew and Heritage (eds.), pp. 101–134.

1996. Turn organization: One intersection of grammar and interaction. In Elinor Ochs, Emanuel A. Schegloff, and Sandra A. Thompson (eds.). *Interaction and grammar*. Cambridge: Cambridge University Press, pp. 52–133.

1998. Body torque. *Social Research* 65, 3: 535–596.

2002. On 'opening sequencing': A framing statement. In James E. Katz and Mark A. Aakhus (eds.). *Perpetual contact: Mobile communication, private talk, public performance*. Cambridge: Cambridge University Press, pp. 321–385.

2006a. On possibles. *Discourse Studies* 8: 141–157.

2006b. Interaction: The infrastructure for social institutions, the natural ecological niche for language, and the arena in which culture is enacted. In Stephen C. Levinson and Nicholas J. Enfield (eds.). *Roots of human sociality*. Oxford: Berg, pp. 70–96.

Schleiermacher, Friedrich D. E. 1813. From 'On the different methods of translating'. Translated by W. Bartscht. In Rainer Schulte and John Biguenet (eds.). 1992. *Theories of translation: An anthology of essays from Dryden to Derrida*. Chicago: University of Chicago Press, pp. 36–54.

Schneider, Edgar W., Kate Burridge, Bernd Kortmann, Rajend Mesthrie, and Clive Upton (eds.). 2004. *A handbook of varieties of English. Vol. 1: Phonology*. Berlin: Mouton de Gruyter.

Schröder, Anne. 2003a. *Status, functions, and prospects of Pidgin English. An empirical approach to language dynamics in Cameroon*. Tübingen: Narr.

2003b. Aspect in Cameroon Pidgin English. In Peter Lucko and Peter Lothar, and Hans-Georg Wolf (eds.). *Studies in African varieties of English*. Frankfurt/M.: Lang, pp. 83–100.

2007. Camfranglais: A language with several (sur)faces and important sociolinguistic functions. In Anke Bartels and Dirk Wiemann (eds.). *Global fragments. (Dis) orientation in the new world order*. Amsterdam and New York: Rodopi, pp. 281–298.

2012. Tense and aspect in Cameroon Pidgin English. In Eric A. Anchimbe (ed.). *Language contact in a postcolonial setting. The linguistic and social context of English in Cameroon*. Berlin: de Gruyter Mouton, pp. 165–190.

Schuchardt, Hugo. 1884. *Dem Herrn Franz von Miklosich zum 20. November 1883: Slawo-Deutsches und Slawo-Italienisches*. Graz: Leuschner und Lubensky.

1914. Zur methodischen Erforschung der Sprachverwandtschaft II. *Revue Basque* 8, 2/3: pp. 389–396.

Schütz, Alfred. 1953. Common-sense and scientific interpretation of human action. *Philosophy and Phenomenological Research* 14, 1: 1–38.

1962. *Collected papers I: The problem of social reality*. The Hague: Martinus Nijhoff.

Sebba, Mark. 2007. *Spelling and society*. Cambridge: Cambridge University Press.

Sedlatschek, Andreas. 2009. *Contemporary Indian English: Variation and change*. Amsterdam: Benjamins.

Senft, Gunter (ed.). 1997. *Referring to space: Studies in Austronesian and Papuan languages*. Oxford: Clarendon Press.

Sewtohul, Goswami K. 1990. *Diksyoner Kreol Bhojpuri*. Port Louis: Ledikasyon.

Shappeck, Marco. 2011. Quichua–Spanish language contact in Salcedo, Ecuador: Revisiting Media Lengua syncretic language practices. Ph.D. thesis, University of Illinois at Urbana-Champaign.

Siegel, Jeff. 2008. *The emergence of pidgin and creole languages*. Oxford and New York: Oxford University Press.

Silverstein, Michael. 1971. Language contact and the problem of convergent generative systems: Chinook Jargon. In Hymes (ed.), pp. 191–193.

Simmel, Georg. 1908. Sociology of the senses: Visual interaction. In Robert E. Park and Ernest W. Burgess (eds.). 1969. *Introduction to the science of sociology*. Chicago: University of Chicago Press, pp. 146–151.

Sinha, R. Mahesh K. and Anil Thakur. 2005. Divergence patterns in machine translation between Hindi and English. MT Summit X Phuket, Thailand Sept. 2005, pp. 346–353.

Skutnabb-Kangas, Tove and Robert Phillipson (eds.). 1995. *Linguistic human rights*. Berlin: Mouton de Gruyter.

Slabbert, Sarah. 1994. A re-evaluation of the sociology of Tsotsitaal. *South African Journal of Linguistics* 12:1, 31–41.

Sloterdijk, Peter. 2005. *Écumes. Sphères III*. Paris: Maren Sell Éditeurs.

Smith, Barry. 1994. Topological foundations of cognitive science. In Carola Eschenbach, Christopher Habel, and Barry Smith (eds.). *Topological foundations of cognitive science: Papers from the workshop at the FISI-CS, Buffalo, New York, July 1994*. Hamburg: Graduiertenkolleg Kognitionswissenschaft, pp. 3–22.

Smith, Norval. 2000. Symbiotic mixed languages: A question of terminology. *Bilingualism: Language and Cognition* 3:2, 122–123.

Snell, Rupert and Simon Weightman. 2003. *Teach yourself Hindi*, Maidenhead: McGraw-Hill, Teach Yourself Language Complete Courses.

Sokolowski, Robert. 2000. *Introduction to Phenomenology*. Cambridge: Cambridge University Press.

Solé, Robert. 2006. *Dictionnaire amoureux de l'Égypte*. Paris: Plon.

Solenberger, Robert R. 1962. The social meaning of language choice in the Marianas. *Anthropological Linguistics* 4, 1: 59–64.

Speer, Susan. 2002: 'Natural' and 'contrived' data: A sustainable distinction? *Discourse Studies* 4: 511–525.

Speer, Susan and Ian Hutchby. 2003. From ethics to analytics: Aspects of participants' orientations to the presence relevance of recording devices. *Sociology* 37, 2: 315–337.

Stafford, Roy Lawrence. 1967. *An elementary Luo grammar with vocabularies*. Nairobi: Oxford University Press.

Stauffer, Robert C. 1957. Haeckel, Darwin, and ecology. *Quarterly Review of Biology* 32: 138–144.

Stewart, William Alexander. 1965. Urban negro speech: Sociolinguistic factors affecting English teaching. In Roger W. Shuy (ed.). *Social dialects and language learning*, National Council of Teachers of English, pp. 10–18.

Stolz, Christel and Thomas Stolz. 1996. Funktionswortentlehnung in Mesoamerika: Spanisch–Amerindischer Sprachkontakt (Hispanoindiana II). *Sprachtypologie und Universalienforschung (STUF)* 49, 1: 86–123.

Stolz, Thomas. 1998. Die Hispanität des Chamorro als sprachwissenschaftliches Problem. *Iberoamericana* 70, 2: 5–38.

   2003. Not quite the right mixture: Chamorro and Malti as candidates for the status of mixed languages. In Matras and Bakker (eds.), pp. 271–315.

   2010. Don't mess with ergatives! How the borrowing of the Spanish indefinite article affects the split-ergative system of Chamorro. *Sprachtypologie und Universalienforschung (STUF)* 63, 1: 79–95.

   2012. The attraction of indefinite articles: On the borrowing of Spanish un in Chamorro. In Claudine Chamoreau and Isabelle Léglise (eds.). *Dynamics of contact-induced language change*. Berlin and Boston: de Gruyter, pp. 167–194.

Stolz, Thomas, Dik Bakker, and Rosa Salas Palomo (eds.). 2008. *Hispanisation: The impact of Spanish on the lexicon and grammar of the indigenous languages of Austronesia and the Americas*. Berlin and New York: Mouton de Gruyter.

Stross, Brian. 1974. Speaking of speaking: Tenejapa Tzeltal metalinguistics. In Richard Bauman and Joel Sherzer (eds.). *Explorations in the ethnography of speaking*. Cambridge: Cambridge University Press, pp. 213–239.

Suchman, Lucy. 1987. *Plans and situated actions: The problem of human-machine communication*. Cambridge: Cambridge University Press.

Suchman, Lucy and Brigitte Jordan. 1990. Interactional troubles in face-to-face survey interviews. *Journal of the American Statistical Association* 85: 232–241.

Swiggers, Pierre. 1990. Ideology and the 'clarity' of French. In Joseph and Taylor (eds.), pp. 112–131.

Szmrecsanyi, Benedikt and Bernd Kortmann. 2009. Vernacular universals and angloversals in a typological perspective. In Filppula, Klemola, and Paulasto (eds.), pp. 33–53.

Tabouret-Keller, Andrée. 1997. Language and identity. In Florian Coulmas (ed.). *The handbook of sociolinguistics.* Oxford: Blackwell, pp. 315–326.

Tagliavini, Carlo. 1982. *Le origini delle lingue neolatine: Introduzione alla filologia romanza.* 6. ed. interamente rielaborata ed aggiornata, 16. rist. 2004. Bologna: Pàtron.

Taylor, Andrew J. 1976. History of research in Austronesian languages: Western part of South-eastern mainland Papua. In Stephen A. Wurm (ed.). *New Guinea area languages and language study, Vol. 2: Austronesian Languages.* Canberra: Australian National University, Research School of Pacific Studies, Department of Linguistics, pp. 141–155.

Teichelmann, Christian G. and Clamor W. Schürmann. 1840. *Outlines of a grammar, vocabulary, and phraseology, of the Aboriginal language of South Australia, spoken by the Natives in and for some distance around Adelaide.* Adelaide: Libraries Board of South Australia.

Thom, René. 1980. *Modèles mathématiques de la morphogénèse.* Paris: Christian Bourgois Éditeur.

Thomason, Sarah G. 1997. A typology of contact languages. In Arthur Spears and Donald Winford (eds.). *The structure and status of pidgins and creoles.* Amsterdam and Philadelphia: Benjamins, pp. 71–88.

  2001a. *Language contact: An introduction.* Edinburgh: Edinburgh University Press.

  2001b. Contact-induced typological change. In Martin Haspelmath, Ekkehard König, Wulf Oesterreicher, and Wolfgang Raible (eds.). *Sprachtypologie und sprachliche Universalien.* Handbücher zur Sprach- und Kommunikationswissenschaft, Vol. 20.2. Berlin and New York: de Gruyter, pp. 1640–1648.

  2002. Creoles and genetic relationship. *Journal of Pidgin and Creole Languages* 17, 1: 101–109.

  2009. Why universals VERSUS contact-induced change? In Filppula, Klemola and Paulasto (eds.), pp. 349–364.

  2014. Contact-induced language change and typological congruence. In Besters-Dilger et al. (eds.), pp. 201–216.

Thomason, Sarah G. and Terrence Kaufman. 1988. *Language contact, creolization, and genetic linguistics.* Berkeley: University of California Press.

Thurston, William R. 1987. *Processes of change in the languages of North-Western New Britain.* Canberra: Dept. of Linguistics, Research School of Pacific Studies, Australian National University.

Tiayon-Lekobou, Charles-Borromé. 1985. Camspeak: A speech reality in Cameroon. MA dissertation, Department of English, University of Yaoundé, Cameroon.

Tindale, Norman B. 1974. *Aboriginal tribes of Australia.* Berkeley: University of California Press.

Tollefson, James. W. 1991. *Planning language, planning inequality.* London: Longman.

Tomasello, Michael. 1999. *The cultural origins of human cognition.* Cambridge and London: Harvard University Press.

Topping, Donald M. (with the assistance of Bernadita C. Dungca). 1973. *Chamorro reference grammar.* Honolulu: University of Hawaii Press.

Topping, Donald M., Pedro M. Ogo, and Bernadita C. Dungca. 1975. *Chamorro–English dictionary*. Honolulu: University of Hawaii Press.

Toulmin, Stephen E. 1972. *Human understanding*. Princeton: Princeton University Press.

1978. *Kritik der kollektiven Vernunft*. Frankfurt/M.: Suhrkamp.

Trampe, Wilhelm. 1990. *Ökologische Linguistik. Grundlagen einer ökologischen Wissenschafts- und Sprachtheorie*. Opladen: Westdeutscher Verlag.

1991. Sprache und ökologische Krise: Aus dem Wörterbuch der industriellen Landwirtschaft. In Elisabeth Feldbusch, Rainer Pogarell, and Cornelia Weiß (eds.). *Neue Fragen der Linguistik. Vol. 2*. Tübingen: Niemeyer. Reprinted and translated into English in Fill and Mühlhäusler (eds.) 2001, pp. 232–240.

Trask, Robert L. 1993. *A dictionary of grammatical terms in linguistics*. London: Routledge.

1996. *Historical linguistics*. New York: Oxford University Press.

Trudgill, Peter. 2009. Vernacular universals and the sociolinguistic typology of English dialects. In Filppula, Klemola and Paulasto (eds.), pp. 304–322.

Underwood, Robert A. 1984. Language survival, the ideology of English and education in Guam. *Educational Research Quarterly* 8, 4: 72–81.

1987. American education and the acculturation of the Chamorros of Guam. Ph.D. thesis, University of Southern California.

United States Census Bureau. 2003. *2000 census of population and housing: The Commonwealth of the Northern Mariana Islands*. Revised: www.census.gov/prod/cen2000/island/CNMIprofile.pdf (last access July 2014)

2004. *2000 census of population and housing: Guam*. Revised: www.census.gov/prod/cen2000/island/GUAMprofile.pdf (last access July 2014)

2013. *2010 census data*. www.census.gov/2010census/data/ (last access July 2014)

Usāmah ibn Munqidh. 1999. *Kitāb al-I'tibār*. Beirut: Dār al-Kutūb al-'Ilmiyyah.

Valenciennes, Henri de. 1948. *Histoire de l'empereur Henri de Constantinople*. Ed. J. Longnon. Paris: Librairie Orientaliste Paul Geuthner.

Valkhoff, Marius F. 1966. *Studies in Portuguese and creole*. Johannesburg: Witwatersrand University Press.

Van Coetsem, Frans. 1988. *Loan phonology and the two transfer types in language contact*. Dordrecht: Foris.

2000. *A general and unified theory of the transmission process in language contact*. Heidelberg: C. Winter.

2003. Topics in contact linguistics. *Leuvense Bijdragen* 92: 27–99.

Vandenbussche, Wim, Ernst H. Jahr, and Peter Trudgill (eds.). 2013. *Language ecology for the 21st century: Linguistic conflicts and social environments*. Oslo: Novus Press.

Van Langendonck, Willy. 1996. Bynames. In Eichler et al. (eds.), pp. 1228–1232.

Van Name, Addison. 1869–1870. Contributions to creole grammar. *Transactions of the American Philological Association (1869–1896)* 1: 123–167.

Varol Bornes, Marie-Christine. 2008. *Le judéo-espagnol vernaculaire d'Istanbul*. Bern: Lang.

2009. Morphosyntactical calques in Judeo-Spanish. In David M. Bunis (ed.). *Languages and literatures of Sephardic and Oriental Jews*, Jerusalem: Bialik Institute – Misgav Yerushalayim, pp. 260–273.

Velupillai, Viveka. 2015. *Pidgins, creoles, and mixed languages. An introduction.* Amsterdam: Benjamins.

Voegelin, Charles F., Florence M. Voegelin, and Noel W. Schutz. 1967. The language situation in Arizona as part of the southwest culture area. In Dell H. Hymes and William E. Bittle (eds.). *Studies in southwestern ethnolinguistics: Meaning and history in the languages of the American Southwest.* The Hague: Mouton de Gruyter, pp. 403–451.

Wagner, Max L. 1914. *Beiträge zur Kenntnis des Judenspanischen von Konstantinopel.* Vienna: A. Hoelder.

Wales, Katie. 1996. *Personal pronouns in present-day English.* Cambridge: Cambridge University Press.

Wartburg, Walther von. 1946/1971. *Évolution et structure de la langue française.* 10th edition. Bern: Francke.

Weinreich, Uriel. 1953. *Languages in contact: Findings and problems.* New York: Linguistic Circle.

Weinrich, Harald. 1990. Ökonomie und Ökologie in der Sprache. *Zeitschrift für französische Sprache und Literatur* 100: 213–223.

Whinnom, Keith. 1971. Linguistic hybridization and the special case of pidgins and creoles. In Hymes (ed.), pp. 91–115.

Whitney, William D. 1881. On mixture in language. *Transactions of the American Philological Association (1869–1896)* 12: 5–26.

    1867. *Language and the study of language. Twelve lectures on the principles of linguistic science.* New York: Charles Scribner & Co.

    1875. *The life and growth of language. An outline of linguistic science.* New York: D. Appleton & Co.

Whorf, Benjamin L. 1940. Science and linguistics. In Whorf, 1956, pp. 207–219.

    1945. Grammatical categories. *Language* 21: 1–11.

    1956. *Language, thought, and reality: Selected writings of Benjamin Lee Whorf.* Ed. by John B. Carroll. Cambridge, MA: Technology Press of MIT.

Wilhelm, Raymund. 2001. Diskurstraditionen. In Martin Haspelmath, Ekkehard König, Wulf Oesterreicher, and Wolfgang Raible (eds.). *Language typology and language universals. An international handbook. Vol. 1.* Berlin and New York: Mouton de Gruyter, pp. 467–477.

Winford, Donald. 2003. *An introduction to contact linguistics.* Malden: Blackwell.

    2008. Atlantic Creole syntax. In Silvia Kouwenberg and John Victor Singler (eds.). *The handbook of pidgin and creole studies.* New York: Wiley-Blackwell, pp. 19–47.

    2009. The interplay of 'universals' and contact-induced change in the emergence of New Englishes. In Filppula, Klemola, and Paulasto (eds.), pp. 206–230.

Winkler, Pierre. 2013. Translating Father Sanvitores' Lingua Mariana. In Fischer (ed.), pp. 53–82.

Woidich, Manfred. 2006. *Das Kairenisch–Arabische: Eine Grammatik.* Wiesbaden, Harrassowitz.

Wray, Alison and George W. Grace. 2007. The consequences of talking to strangers: Evolutionary corollaries of socio-cultural influences on linguistic form. *Lingua* 117: 543–578.

Wunderlich, Dieter. 1976. Skizze zu einer integrierten Theorie der grammatischen und pragmatischen Bedeutung. In Dieter Wunderlich (ed.). *Studien zur Sprechakttheorie.* Frankfurt/M.: Suhrkamp, pp. 51–118.

Wurzel, Wolfgang U. 1984. *Flexionsmorphologie und Natürlichkeit*. Berlin: Akademie Verlag.

Zentella, Ana Celia, 1997. *Growing up bilingual: Puerto Rican children in New York*. Malden: Blackwell.

Zobel, Erik. 2002. The position of Chamorro and Palauan in the Austronesian family tree: Evidence from verb morphosyntax. In Fay Wouk and Malcolm Ross (eds.): *The history and typology of western Austronesian voice systems*. Canberra: Pacific Linguistics, Research School of Pacific and Asian Studies, Australian National University, pp. 405–434.

Zuckermann, Ghil'ad. 2009. Hybridity versus revivability: Multiple causation, forms and patterns. *Journal of Language Contact* (Varia 2): 20–47.

Zúñiga, Jean Paul. 2010. Les esclaves africains et leurs descendants à Santiago du Chili (XVIIe siècle). In Salinero and Testón Núñez (eds.), pp. 187–207.

Index

ablative, 207
accommodation, 13, 188, 216, 245, 251, 259
accusative–nominative, 300
acrolect, 142, 184
adjective, 49, 53, 172, 221, 225–226, 319–320
adstrate, 318
adverb, adverbial, 198, 228, 257, 276, 292
affiliation, 148, 165, 169, 175–176, 236, 266, 269, 280
affix, 225–228, 292
Afrikaans, 287, 322
age, 3, 50, 63, 112, 119–120, 159, 167, 169, 236, 262, 265, 317
agreement, 225–227, 230, 277, 292
Aïwo, 322
allative, 207
allophone, 292
American English, 210, 264–265
analogy, analogical, 13–14, 17, 20, 26–27, 57–58, 62, 269, 271
Anglo-Norman, 137, 140
Anglo-Romani, 216, 230–231
anthroponymy, anthroponym, anthroponymic, 39, 136, 147, 149, 151, 155–157, 159, 163, 166, 171, 174–176
anti-creole language, 63, 264, 277, 284, 288, 291
Antikirinya, 325
apellido, 151–154, 171, 175
Arabic, 36, 39, 131–134, 136–138, 144, 189, 203, 237–239, 241, 243, 245, 247, 249–252, 255, 257–261
Arawak, Arawakan, 154–155, 161
areal features, 297
Armenian, 39, 131, 136–137, 142–143, 237, 241
article, 118, 136, 190, 208, 219, 250, 258, 275–276, 286, 291
Ashaninka, 111
aspect, 182
aspect, aspectual, 219, 225, 305, 332
Atlantic Creoles, 301

Atlas of Pidgin and Creole Structures (APICS), 300–301
augmentative, 277
Australian Aboriginal languages, 322, 324–325, 329, 333
Austronesian languages, 41, 269, 283–284, 305, 307, 314, 319, 322
Awajun, 111
Aymara, 122

baby talk, 301
Bantu languages, 223, 227–228
Basilect, basilectal, 184, 200
Bassa, 218
Bavarian, 322, 335
Bhojpuri, 179, 191–193, 197–199, 201
bilingual mixed language, *see* intertwined language
bilingualism, bilingual, xiii, 7, 30, 113, 115, 126, 138–139, 188, 201, 216, 229–231, 264, 281, 286, 290, 299, 330
borrowing, xvi, 7, 28–29, 57, 59, 134, 138, 144, 179, 181, 184, 188, 191, 212, 216, 230, 260, 272–273, 278–279, 282, 284, 289, 291, 321
Bosnian, 325
Brazilian Portuguese, 30, 287
British English, 201–202, 207–208, 211
Burgundian, 132

calque, calquing, xvi, 28–29, 179, 181–182, 212, 273, 312
Cameroon Pidgin English, 217–221
Camfranglais, 40, 214–215, 217–221, 223, 230, 232
Campus Swahili, 231
Carib languages, 154
case, 225, 307
Castilian, *see* Spanish
castolect, 139
Catalan, 237
categorical multifunctionality, 41, 320